XML Programming Using the Microsoft XML Parser

SOO MEE FOO AND WEI MENG LEE

XML Programming Using the Microsoft XML Parser
Copyright ©2002 by Soo Mee Foo and Wei Meng Lee

ISBN (pbk): 1-893115-42-9

Printed and bound in the United States of America 12345678910

Editorial Directors: Dan Appleman, Peter Blackburn, Gary Cornell, Jason Gilmore, Karen Watterson
Technical Reviewer: Ronald Landers
Managing Editor: Grace Wong
Project Managers: Alexa Stuart, Erin Mulligan
Development Editor: Kenyon Brown
Copy Editors: Kit Cooley
Production Editor: Kari Brooks
Compositor: Impressions Book and Journal Services, Inc.
Artist: Kurt Krames
Indexer: Rebecca Plunkett
Cover Designer: Tom Debolski
Marketing Manager: Stephanie Rodriguez

Distributed to the book trade in the United States by Springer-Verlag New York, Inc.,175 Fifth Avenue, New York, NY, 10010 and outside the United States by Springer-Verlag GmbH & Co. KG, Tiergartenstr. 17, 69112 Heidelberg, Germany.
In the United States, phone 1-800-SPRINGER, email orders@springer-ny.com, or visit http://www.springer-ny.com.
Outside the United States, fax +49 6221 345229, email orders@springer.de, or visit http://www.springer.de.

For information on translations, please contact Apress directly at 901 Grayson Street, Suite 204, Berkeley, CA 94710.
Phone 510-549-5930, fax: 510-549-5939, email info@apress.com, or visit http://www.apress.com.

The source code for this book is available to readers at http://www.apress.com in the Downloads section. You will need to answer questions pertaining to this book in order to successfully download the code.

Contents at a Glance

About the Authors .... *xi*

About the Technical Reviewer .... *xi*

Acknowledgments .... *xiii*

Introduction .... *xiv*

Chapter 1: Introduction to the Extensible
　　　　　　Markup Language (XML) *1*

Chapter 2: Addressing XML Parts Using XPath *41*

Chapter 3: The Extensible Stylesheet Language
　　　　　　Transformation (XSLT) *69*

Chapter 4: The Document Object Model (DOM) *107*

Chapter 5: Support of XML in ActiveX Data
　　　　　　Objects (ADO) 2.1 and Above *151*

Chapter 6: XML Support in SQL Server 2000 .... *197*

Chapter 7: Simple API for XML (SAX) *269*

Chapter 8: XML Schemas *291*

Chapter 9: The Wireless Markup Language (WML) *319*

Chapter 10: Simple Object Access Protocol (SOAP)
　　　　　　 and Web Services *347*

Appendix A: Installing Microsoft XML Tools *393*

Appendix B: Document Object Model (DOM)
　　　　　　 Level 1 Core Interfaces *399*

Appendix C: XML-Data Reduced (XDR) Schema *417*

Index *429*

Contents

About the Authors ....*xi*
About the Technical Reviewer ....*xi*
Acknowledgments ....*xiii*
Introduction ....*xiv*

Chapter 1: Introduction to the Extensible
                 Markup Language (XML) *1*

W3C and XML *2*
Basic XML Terminology *6*
Rules of XML *6*
Document Type Definition (DTD) *11*
CDATA and PCDATA *18*
Elements or Attributes *19*
XML Schemas *22*
XML Encoding and Unicode *23*
Namespaces *27*
XML Parsers *29*
Microsoft XML Parser (MSXML) *31*
Uses and Benefits of XML *31*
XML and Web Browser Support *32*
Using the Microsoft XML Parser Release 3.0 SP1 .....*36*
XML Editors *39*
Useful Web Links *39*
Summary *40*

Chapter 2: Addressing XML Parts Using XPath *41*

XPath Expression *42*
XPath Data Model *44*
Location Path *50*
Functions *58*
Abbreviated Syntax *65*
Useful Web Links *67*
Summary *67*

Chapter 3: The Extensible Stylesheet Language Transformation (XSLT) *69*

Motivation for XSLT *70*
Support of XSLT in MSXML3 ....*72*
A First Look at XSLT *73*
XSLT Fundamentals *79*
Client-Side versus Server-Side XSLT Transformation *102*
Useful Web Links *105*
Summary *105*

Chapter 4: The Document Object Model (DOM) *107*

Introduction to DOM *107*
XML DOM Parsers *108*
Support of DOM in MSXML3 ....*108*
Representing XML Document as a Tree *111*
Creating a DOM Tree of an XML Document in Memory *114*
Saving a DOM Tree *118*
Fundamental APIs for Processing a DOM Tree *119*
Client-Side DOM Programming–Shopping Cart *131*
Server-Side DOM Programming–Shopping Cart *145*
Useful Web Links *148*
Summary *149*

Chapter 5: Support of XML in ActiveX Data Objects (ADO) 2.1 and Above *151*

Universal Data Access *151*
The ADO Object Model *154*
Connection Object *155*
Recordset Object *161*
Command Object *170*
Record Object *175*
Stream Object *175*
Error Handling *179*
Case Study: Updating Book Prices
   Using Three-Tier Architecture *183*
Useful Web Links *195*
Summary *195*

Chapter 6: XML Support in SQL Server 2000 ....*197*

Additional Software Installation and Configuration *197*
Retrieving and Transforming Rowset Data
    into XML Data *203*
Providing Rowset Data from XML Data Using
    the OPENXML Provider *228*
Accessing SQL Server Using HTTP *235*
Persisting Changes Using Updategram *257*
Useful Web Links *268*
Summary *268*

Chapter 7: Simple API for XML (SAX) *269*

An Alternative to DOM *269*
SAX in MSXML3 ....*278*
Error Handling in SAX *281*
Using SAX *284*
When Do You Use SAX? *288*
Useful Web Links *290*
Summary *290*

Chapter 8: XML Schemas *291*

XML Schema and XDR Schema *293*
First Look at XML Schema *293*
XML Schema Data Types *300*
Groupings *310*
Linking Schemas and Redefining Definitions *312*
Documenting the Schema Using <annotation> *313*
Tools for Validating XML Schemas *314*
Useful Web Links *318*
Summary *318*

Chapter 9: The Wireless Markup Language (WML) *319*

Architecture of WAP *319*
Understanding the Wireless Markup Language (WML) *322*
Testing WML Applications *329*
Tailoring WAP Content with XML and XSLT *330*
Using the Microsoft XSL ISAPI *337*
Useful Web Links *345*
Summary *345*

Chapter 10: Simple Object Access Protocol (SOAP) and Web Services *347*

Introduction to SOAP *347*
Web Services *350*
Creating a Web Service *357*
Consuming a Web Service *358*
Developing Web Services Using the Microsoft SOAP Toolkit
    Version 2.0 ....*358*
Providing Web Services Using the SOAP Toolkit:
    A Case Study *359*
Web Services Security *388*
Useful Web Links *390*
Summary *391*

Appendix A: Installing Microsoft XML Tools *393*

Installing IE Tools for Validating XML Documents *393*
Checking the Version of the Installed XML Parser *395*

Appendix B: Document Object Model (DOM) Level 1 Core Interfaces *399*

Understanding Basic Terms in the DOM *399*
Fundamental Interfaces *400*
Extended Interfaces *413*

Appendix C: XML-Data Reduced (XDR) Schema *417*

Basic Elements in XDR Schema *417*
General Layout *418*
Specification of the Content Model *419*
Data Types *424*
Annotations *427*

Index *429*

About the Authors

Wei Meng Lee currently holds a full-time job as a lecturer at the School of Information and Communications Technology, Ngee Ann Polytechnic (Singapore). Besides teaching, he offers consultant services to the industry and conducts in-house training in the areas of Web development. He is also a contributing author to magazines like *XML Journal*, *XML Magazine*, and *.NET Magazine*, and he is the co-author of *Beginning WAP, WML and WMLScript* (Wrox) and *Dynamic WAP Application Development* (Manning).

A frequent speaker at developer conferences and seminars, Wei Meng spoke at the Wrox Professional Wireless Developer Conference (July 2000, Amsterdam) and Wireless Developer Conference (December 2000, San Jose). Contact Wei Meng at wei_meng_lee@hotmail.com.

Soo Mee Foo is currently lecturing at Ngee Ann Polytechnic (Singapore) in Web technologies and security. She also conducts workshops for IT professionals and is involved in designing Web-based courseware and industrial projects. She is a co-author of *Beginning WAP, WML and WMLScript* and *Dynamic WAP Application Development*. Soo Mee can be contacted at soomee_foo@hotmail.com.

About the Technical Reviewer

Ronald Landers is the owner of Right-Click Consulting, LLC, a Los Angeles–based consulting, development, and training firm. The company specializes in Microsoft-based technologies including Active Server Pages, SQL Server, Visual Basic, Internet Explorer, and XML. Mr. Landers is a faculty member and instructor at UCLA Extension and has been teaching and consulting for the past 12 years.

Acknowledgments

FIRST AND FOREMOST I want to thank Gary Cornell for giving us this opportunity to write this book. I actually met Gary at the Wireless Developer Conference in San Jose in December 2000. After a few e-mail exchanges, Gary took the bold step and said, "Let's go into contract." The rest, they say, is history. Thank you, Gary!

The folks at Apress have been very helpful and encouraging, especially our editorial director, Jason Gilmore. Jason has been very patient with us throughout the writing stage, offering many suggestions to improve our writing early in the project. I also want to express my heartfelt thanks to folks like Kenyon Brown, Erin Mulligan, Kit Cooley, Kari Brooks, Grace Wong, and the many unnamed heroes who have worked tirelessly to turn our raw manuscript into one that we are proud of.

I also wish to express my gratitude to our technical editor, Ron Landers, who has definitely made this book a better read by his many suggestions.

Special thanks to *XML Journal* and *XML Magazine* for permission to use some of the articles of mine that they have published. A big thanks to Altova for supplying me with their superb XMLSpy software suite for evaluation and testing during the writing of this book. You guys have solid technical support!

Last, but not least, I want to thank my co-author Soo Mee for making this book a reality. And of course, my family has always been my strongest support.

—Wei Meng Lee

I would like to take this opportunity to thank Gary Cornell for his trust in us to write this book. I would also like to thank the great team of people that helped bring this book into reality. Specifically, I express thanks to Jason Gilmore for his encouragement and help in getting the book started, which is always a hurdle at the beginning. Also, my utmost thanks go to Alexa Stuart, Erin Mulligan, Kenyon Brown, Kit Cooley, Kari Brooks, Stephanie Rodriguez, and Grace Wong, who certainly need tremendous patience to work with me, and who have undoubtedly worked very hard to keep the schedule especially during the festive season.

My sincere thanks here to Wei Meng, who has never forgotten to institute fun into this writing project.

Last, but not least, thanks to my family for being understanding at all times.

—Soo Mee Foo

Introduction

MOST XML BOOKS in the market today fall into two main categories: They either focus just on the theoretical aspects of the language, or they contain everything related to XML and weigh more than five kilograms! When we first taught XML to beginners, we wanted to find a book that covered just enough of XML without overwhelming them. We looked for a book that covered not just the fundamentals of XML, but one that also contained the most important XML-related technologies. Not only that, the book had to illustrate some of the practical uses of XML in the real world.

We realized that we had to produce a book that targeted beginning to intermediate XML programmers. As trainers, we know the importance of a book that explains concepts clearly and contains concrete code examples illustrating the theory just explained. We carefully reviewed the various XML technologies and specifications that are available today, and in the end, we decided on the most common XML technologies in use today: XPath, XSLT, DOM, SAX, XML in SQL Server, WML, SOAP and XML Schema.

During the writing of this book, a couple of new Microsoft products were launched. Most notably, Microsoft released the .NET Framework and Visual Studio .NET for public beta testing. In addition, the Microsoft XML parser has since matured to version 4 as this book goes into print. The release of these products was important to this book. First, we have based our concepts and code on Microsoft XML Parser 3.0. However, the release of version 4 does not alter the concepts we have covered in this book; version 4 offers better performance and adds some new features. Second, Visual Studio .NET has made developing and consuming Web services very simple. It takes care of generating WSDL files and class proxies automatically. Contrast this to using the SOAP Toolkit for developing and consuming Web services (which is covered in this book), developing Web services using VS .NET seems a trivial task. However, our approach in this book is to show how all the building blocks of Web services are built and assembled. Readers who have used the SOAP Toolkit would then be well positioned to build Web services using any tools and platform.

Writing a book on XML is like shooting a moving target. The XML standards are always changing, and new specifications come and go. We hope you will enjoy this book as much as we have enjoyed writing it!

Introduction to the Extensible Markup Language (XML)

XML IS A MARKUP LANGUAGE that is designed to describe data. It attaches meaning to data in a document by using a meaningful tag name.

One of the greatest misunderstandings of the Extensible Markup Language is that it is an extension of HTML. While XML and HTML share similar characteristics, such as the use of tags to markup data, it is important to know that XML has a much broader purpose than just for the Web. By itself, XML does *not* do anything. It simply uses tags to describe the data in a document and allows the document author to use meaningful tags to describe the data that is stored (so that by looking at the document, the meanings of the data represented become apparent). In addition, the document author has the freedom to use whatever tag name he deems fit, hence the name extensible. The only time where XML really gets useful is when it is used in conjunction with applications that can understand XML.

Roots of XML and HTML

Both XML and HTML are based on the Standard Generalized Markup Language (SGML). SGML was developed in the early '80s, and was widely used for large documentation projects. HTML was developed in 1990, and its primary use is in creating Web pages. XML was developed in 1996 and gained W3C's endorsement in 1998. The aim of XML is to produce a markup language that is simpler to use than SGML (but by no means less powerful).

In this chapter, we describe the syntax of XML and the terminology that comes with it. While it is tempting for us to describe the usefulness and the specific uses of XML at this juncture, our opinion is that beginners who are learning XML are often not able to visualize the use of XML at this stage. As such, we take a progressive approach, concentrating on the fundamentals in this chapter and explaining the various uses of XML in the remaining chapters.

Chapter 1

W3C and XML

XML is a universal format for describing data. The XML 1.0 specification has been adopted by the World Wide Web Consortium (W3C) as a Recommendation on February 10, 1998. This means that vendors can develop products that are based on the XML 1.0 specification and that products built by different vendors can expect to interoperate as long as they adhere to the specification recommended by W3C.

Since 1998, we have witnessed a flooding of XML standards. Many names come and go. In the next section, we look at various XML jargon and how to make sense out of it.

Making Sense out of Chaos

You might have heard of terms like SOAP, XSLT, XML Namespace, DTD, XML Schema, and XPath. All these terms add to the already chaotic XML marketplace. In fact, one of the reasons for the relatively slow adoption of XML has been due to poor education of the developers that use it. XML strikes fear in the developer by seeming to be unnecessarily difficult to learn and complicated. Add to it the confusion caused by the various XML technologies, and it is not too difficult to see why XML has not been widely received until recent years.

In order to better make sense of all the various terms that together comprise a cohesive definition of XML, we can divide the XML technologies into three layers: Grammars, Protocols, and Standards (see Figure 1-1).

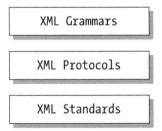

Figure 1-1. Dividing XML technologies into the three layers of Grammars, Protocols, and Standards

XML Standards

There are currently six components of the XML standards family, which comprise the following:

- XML specification

- Extensible Stylesheet Language Transformation (XSLT)

- XML Path (XPath)

- Document Type Definition (DTD)

- XML Namespace

- XML Schema

The W3C defines the core XML technologies in which other technologies can be built on top. We look at the standards in more detail throughout the rest of this book.

XML Protocols

The XML protocols define how protocols can be designed and built using XML technologies. Some of the XML protocols include:

- Simple Object Access Protocol (SOAP): A lightweight XML-based wire transmission protocol for exchanging information in a distributed environment.

- XML RPC: A Remote Procedure Calling Protocol that works over the Internet. Requests and Responses are transmitted between client and server using messages coded in XML.

- ebXML: ebXML is a set of specifications that together enable a modular electronic business framework through the exchange of XML messages.

- BizTalk: The Microsoft® BizTalk Framework is an XML framework for application integration and electronic commerce. It is an industry initiative started by Microsoft and supported by a wide range of organizations, from technology vendors like SAP and CommerceOne to technology users like Boeing and BP/Amoco.

XML Grammars

The XML grammars define the use of XML for specific applications. Some of the grammars of XML are as follows:

- Wireless Markup Language (WML)

- Extensible HTML (XHTML)

- Voice Extensible Markup Language (VoiceXML)

WML is a specification defined by the WAP Forum and is used for developing wireless applications that typically run on mobile phones. The XHTML is fast becoming a standard on the World Wide Web as the replacement language for HTML. XHTML, in a way, is a "stricter" version of HTML that conforms to the rules in XML. It is also touted as the future language for developing mobile applications in WAP version 2.0. Finally, the VoiceXML is a Web-based markup language based on XML for representing human-computer dialogues. It is used to create voice applications.

 NOTE *WML is discussed in further detail in Chapter 9.*

Comparing HTML and XML: A Quick Overview

Newcomers to XML always have a hard time visualizing the usefulness of XML and how it differs from HTML. To demonstrate this difference, consider the following example:

```
<html>
    <title>A HTML page</title>
    <b>A Programmer's Introduction to C#</b><br>
    <i>Eric Gunnerson</i><br>
    <b><i>1893115860</i></b><br>
</html>
```

Figure 1-2 illustrates how the preceding HTML code would be rendered within the Internet Explorer browser.

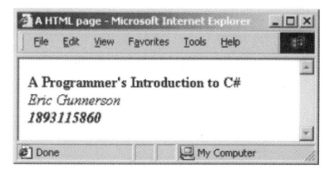

Figure 1-2. Displaying HTML in a Web browser

The document itself says nothing about the *content* (which is about books). HTML describes the *layout* of the data, not the content. Contrast this to an XML document that contains the same information:

```
<book>
    <title>A HTML page</title>
    <book_title>A Programmer's Introduction to C#</book_title>
    <author>Eric Gunnerson</author>
    <isbn>1893115860</isbn>
</book>
```

The preceding XML document does not contain any information about the formatting of the various pieces of information. What it does contain is a description of the data, namely the book title, author, and ISBN number. Thus XML describes the content of the data.

The usefulness of XML is that it provides a context to the data stored in a document. The main problem with HTML is that it does not attach meaning to the data stored in it. Referring to the previous example, given an HTML document, it is difficult to make sense of which element is referring to the book title and which is referring to the author. If this limitation is lifted, better search engines could be built to improve the search accuracy, since it is now able to search intelligently based on the tag name (as in the case of the XML document).

Basic XML Terminology

An XML document is essentially a plain text file containing markups and text. As you learned in the previous example, if you know HTML, you already have an idea of what an XML document looks like. Before we dive straight into the rules of XML, consider Figure 1-3, which graphically illustrates typical XML syntax, defining each component of that syntax.

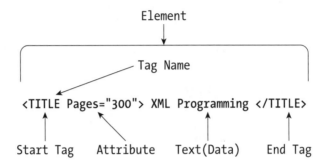

Figure 1-3. Components of an XML element

An element that does not contain any text is known as an *empty element*. For example,

```
<NewLine></NewLine>
```

does not contain any text. It can be rewritten as

```
<NewLine/>
```

Rules of XML

Let's now use an XML document to illustrate the various rules in XML. Since the case study in this book revolves around book publishers, we shall use books as an example.

An XML document that conforms to the syntactical rules described next is known as *well-formed*.

Consider the XML document shown in Listing 1-1.

Listing 1-1. Books.xml

```xml
<?xml version="1.0"?>
<BOOKS>
   <BOOK Pages="357" Type="SOFTCOVER">
      <TITLE>A Programmer's Introduction to C#</TITLE>
      <AUTHOR>Eric Gunnerson</AUTHOR>
      <ISBN>1893115860 </ISBN>
      <SYNOPSIS>Eric Gunnerson, the test lead for and member of Microsoft's
C# design team, has written a comprehensive C# tutorial for programmers to help
them get up to speed</SYNOPSIS>
      <PRICE>$34.95 </PRICE>
   </BOOK>
   <BOOK Pages="380" Type="SOFTCOVER">
      <TITLE>Cryptography in C &amp; C++</TITLE>
      <AUTHOR>Michael Welschenbach</AUTHOR>
      <ISBN>189311595X </ISBN>
      <SYNOPSIS>Detailed treatment of public key cryptography with detailed
coverage of the RSA algorithm that is now in the public domain </SYNOPSIS>
      <PRICE>$49.95 </PRICE>
   </BOOK>
   <BOOK Pages="400" Type="SOFTCOVER">
      <TITLE>C++ for VB Programmers</TITLE>
      <AUTHOR>Jonathan Morrison</AUTHOR>
      <ISBN>1893115763 </ISBN>
      <SYNOPSIS>Morrison teaches VB programmers how to use C++ while addressing
their Visual Basic knowledge—making the transition as easy as possible.
      </SYNOPSIS>
      <PRICE>$49.95</PRICE>
   </BOOK>
</BOOKS>
```

The preceding XML document contains several components.

Rule 1: Processing Instruction (PI)

Every XML document starts with a PI, which are basically the instructions that inform the parser in how to process the document. We talk more about parsers and PI in subsequent chapters. For now, our XML document has a PI that indicates the version of the XML document:

```xml
<?xml version="1.0"?>
```

Rule 2: Root Element

Every XML document needs to have a unique outermost element. In our case, the <BOOKS> element is known as the root element. Consider the following XML document:

```
<?xml version="1.0"?>
    <Book>
        <Title>A Programmer's Introduction to C#</Title>
    </Book>
    <Book>
        <Title>C++ for VB Programmers</Title>
    </Book>
```

In this case, since <BOOK> is not the unique outermost element, it thus does not conform to the rules of XML. To work around this constraint, you need to enclose the two <BOOK> elements with a unique element, like this:

```
<?xml version="1.0"?>
<Books>
    <Book>
        <Title>A Programmer's Introduction to C#</Title>
    </Book>
    <Book>
        <Title>C++ for VB Programmers</Title>
    </Book>
</Books>
```

Now that there is a unique outermost element, the XML document is well-formed.

Rule 3: Attribute Values Must Be Enclosed in Quotation Marks

In XML, all attribute values must be enclosed in either a pair of single quotes (') or a pair of double quotes ("). No quote mixing is allowed. This rule is particularly important to HTML designers who often leave out the quotes for HTML attributes.

Rule 4: Case Sensitivity

Unlike HTML, XML is case-sensitive. <BOOKS> and <Books> are two different elements, and the start tag and end tag must match exactly.

Rule 5: All Elements Must Be Closed

All elements must be closed by specifying a / character in front of the tag name. For example, the </BOOKS> tag closes the <BOOKS> tag. For empty elements, the / character would appear after the tag name. For example,

```
<PUBDATE></PUBDATE>
```

is equivalent to:

```
<PUBDATE/>
```

Rule 6: Elements Must Be Nested Properly

Another bad habit of HTML designers is the improper nesting of elements. For example:

```
<B><I>HTML is loose!</B></I>
```

In this case, the <B> element overlaps the <I> element. This is not allowed in XML. In XML, elements must be nested properly because the XML document represents a top-down hierarchy of data, and improper nesting would not be valid in such a structure. Rewriting the preceding example to conform to valid XML syntax, it should appear as:

```
<B><I>HTML is loose!</I></B>
```

Rule 7: Special Characters Are Represented By Entities

Special characters in XML are represented by their respective entities. An entity is a representation of a special character in XML. For example, our earlier example contains a book titled *Cryptography in C & C++*:

```
<TITLE>Cryptography in C &amp; C++</TITLE>
```

However, the character & has special meaning in XML and thus it could not be represented as it is in the XML document. It must be represented by its entity. In XML, the following characters have special meaning as listed in Table 1-1.

Table 1-1. XML Special Characters

CHARACTER	ENTITY REFERENCE
&	&amp;
<	&lt;
>	&gt;
'	&apos;
"	&quot;

As is shown in Table 1-1, an entity reference has the following syntax:

```
&Name;
```

The reason for having an entity reference is to ensure that the parser is able to differentiate between the tags and the actual content of the XML document. For example, we may want to represent a code snippet:

```
<Code>if income<5000 then </Code>
```

Since the < character is used in XML as an indicator for the start of a tag, the parser would actually mistake "5000" as a tag name, which is clearly incorrect. In this case, the < must be replaced by its entity:

```
<Code>if income&lt;5000 then </Code>
```

Since an entity reference starts with the & character, now you know why the & character is itself special in XML!

Defining Your Own Entities

Using entities is like using constants in programming. For example, in Visual Basic, you may have the following snippets of code:

```
Dim Area as Single
Dim Radius as Single
Const PI = 3.14
Radius = 5
Area = PI * Radius * Radius
```

Defining PI as a constant allows you to use the constant "PI" to represent the value 3.14. There is no need to type "3.14" every time you do a calculation involving it. And who knows, if there ever is a need to change the value of PI (God forbid!), you only need to modify the constant definition.

The same concept can be applied to XML. In XML, you are able to define your own entities. Consider the following example:

```
<?xml version="1.0"?>
<!DOCTYPE Statement [
    <!ENTITY PI "3.14">
]>
<Statement>
   The value of PI is &PI;
</Statement>
```

Figure 1-4 displays how this example would be rendered using Internet Explorer 5.0.

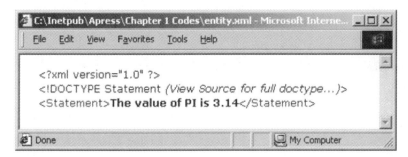

Figure 1-4. Displaying an entity using Internet Explorer 5.0

The value of PI is automatically substituted by the entity PI defined in the <!ENTITY> element. We discuss the <!DOCTYPE> element in more detail in the next section.

Document Type Definition (DTD)

A key advantage of XML is its extensibility (hence its name). This means that anyone is free to use whatever tag name he/she prefers. If you are the only one using the XML documents that you have created, this is fine. However, once there is a need to exchange XML documents with another party, problems arise.

To understand this problem, consider the following situation. A publisher stores information of its newly published books in XML format so that it can be distributed to its distributors for updating. Listing 1-2 shows the XML document as created by the publisher:

Listing 1-2. XML document (1) containing book information

```xml
<?xml version="1.0"?>
<BOOKS>
  <BOOK Pages="" Type="">
     <TITLE></TITLE>
     <AUTHOR></AUTHOR>
     <AUTHOR></AUTHOR>
       <ISBN></ISBN>
     <SYNOPSIS></SYNOPSIS>
     <PRICE></PRICE>
  </BOOK>
  <BOOK Pages="" Type="">
     <TITLE></TITLE>
     <AUTHOR></AUTHOR>
     <AUTHOR></AUTHOR>
     <ISBN></ISBN>
     <SYNOPSIS></SYNOPSIS>
     <PRICE></PRICE>
  </BOOK>
</BOOKS>
```

However, the distributor is not aware of the publisher's format and may design its application software to assume the XML structure displayed in Listing 1-3.

Listing 1-3. XML document (2) containing book information

```xml
<?xml version="1.0"?>
<BOOKS>
  <BOOK Price="" ISBN="" Pages="" Type="" >
     <TITLE></TITLE>
     <AUTHORS>
         <AUTHOR></AUTHOR>
         <AUTHOR></AUTHOR>
     </AUTHORS>
     <SYNOPSIS></SYNOPSIS>
  </BOOK>
  <BOOK Price="" ISBN="" Pages="" Type="" >
     <TITLE></TITLE>
     <AUTHORS>
         <AUTHOR></AUTHOR>
```

```
        <AUTHOR></AUTHOR>
      </AUTHORS>
      <SYNOPSIS></SYNOPSIS>
    </BOOK>
</BOOKS>
```

There is clearly a misunderstanding. In this situation, one party will have to give way (which in the real world is rarely the case!) and format its XML document to suit the other party. An alternative is to define a common structure that both parties can adhere to. The *Document Type Definition* (DTD) provides the rules for defining the structure of an XML document. Such rules are used as contracts to bind multiple parties when they exchange XML documents.

Let's now take a look at a sample DTD and see how it defines the structure of an XML document:

```
<!DOCTYPE BOOKS [
   <!ELEMENT BOOKS (BOOK)*>
   <!ELEMENT BOOK (TITLE, PRICE, PUBLISHER, EDITIONS?, AUTHORS, SYNOPSIS)>
      <!ATTLIST BOOK ISBN  CDATA  #REQUIRED>
      <!ATTLIST BOOK Pages CDATA  #REQUIRED>
      <!ATTLIST BOOK Type  CDATA  #REQUIRED>
      <!ELEMENT TITLE              (#PCDATA)>
      <!ELEMENT PRICE                 EMPTY>
         <!ATTLIST PRICE US CDATA #REQUIRED>
         <!ATTLIST PRICE CN CDATA #REQUIRED>
      <!ELEMENT PUBLISHER         (#PCDATA)>
      <!ELEMENT EDITIONS          (#PCDATA)>
      <!ELEMENT AUTHORS           (AUTHOR)+>
         <!ELEMENT AUTHOR         (#PCDATA)>
      <!ELEMENT SYNOPSIS          (#PCDATA)>
]>
```

The preceding DTD defines an XML document with the following structure:

The DOCTYPE declaration identifies the root element of an XML document.

The root element is <BOOKS>. The syntax for declaring an element is:

<!ELEMENT ElementName (Composition)>

The root element <BOOKS> can contain multiple <BOOK> elements. The * indicates zero or more occurrences.

The <BOOK> element contains child elements—<TITLE>, <PRICE>, <PUBLISHER>, <EDITIONS>, <AUTHORS>, and <SYNOPSIS>. All these elements must appear within the <BOOK> element except the <EDITIONS> element. The ? indicates the element can appear either once or not at all.

The <BOOK> element contains three attributes—**ISBN**, **Pages**, and **Type**. The syntax for declaring an attribute is:

<!ATTLIST *ElementName AttributeName* CDATA #REQUIRED>

The <TITLE>, <PUBLISHER>, <EDITIONS>, and <SYNOPSIS> elements contain character data, while the <PRICE> is an empty element. The <PRICE> element itself would contain two attributes—**US** and **CN**.

The <AUTHORS> element would contain one or more <AUTHOR> element. The + indicates one or more occurrences.

The following sample XML document conforms to the DTD that was discussed in the preceding section:

```
<?xml version="1.0"?>
<BOOKS>
  <BOOK ISBN="1893115860" Pages="357" Type="SOFTCOVER">
     <TITLE>A Programmer's Introduction to C#</TITLE>
     <PRICE US="$34.95" CN="$49.95" />
     <PUBLISHER>Apress</PUBLISHER>
     <EDITIONS>2</EDITIONS>
     <AUTHORS>
         <AUTHOR>Eric Gunnerson</AUTHOR>
     </AUTHORS>
     <SYNOPSIS>Eric Gunnerson, the test lead for and member of Microsoft's
C# design team, has written a comprehensive C# tutorial for programmers to help
them get up to speed</SYNOPSIS>
  </BOOK>
  <BOOK ISBN="0596000111" Pages="558" Type="SOFTCOVER">
     <TITLE>SSH, The Secure Shell: The Definitive Guide</TITLE>
     <PRICE US="$39.95" CN="$50.95" />
     <PUBLISHER>OReilly</PUBLISHER>
     <AUTHORS>
         <AUTHOR>Daniel J. Barrett</AUTHOR>
         <AUTHOR>Richard Silverman</AUTHOR>
     </AUTHORS>
```

```
    <SYNOPSIS>SSH (Secure Shell) is a popular, robust, TCP/IP-based product for
network security and privacy, supporting strong encryption and authentication.
    </SYNOPSIS>
  </BOOK>
</BOOKS>
```

Internal DTD

To associate a given DTD with an XML document, you can include the DTD within the XML document. Listing 1-4 demonstrates how this is accomplished.

Listing 1-4. Template.xml

```
<?xml version="1.0"?>
<!DOCTYPE BOOKS [
   <!ELEMENT BOOKS (BOOK)*>
   <!ELEMENT BOOK (TITLE, PRICE, PUBLISHER, EDITIONS?, AUTHORS, SYNOPSIS)>
      <!ATTLIST BOOK ISBN  CDATA  #REQUIRED>
      <!ATTLIST BOOK Pages CDATA  #REQUIRED>
      <!ATTLIST BOOK Type  CDATA  #REQUIRED>
      <!ELEMENT TITLE             (#PCDATA)>
      <!ELEMENT PRICE                EMPTY>
         <!ATTLIST PRICE US CDATA #REQUIRED>
         <!ATTLIST PRICE CN CDATA #REQUIRED>
      <!ELEMENT PUBLISHER         (#PCDATA)>
      <!ELEMENT EDITIONS          (#PCDATA)>
      <!ELEMENT AUTHORS           (AUTHOR)+>
         <!ELEMENT AUTHOR         (#PCDATA)>
      <!ELEMENT SYNOPSIS          (#PCDATA)>
]>
<BOOKS>
  <BOOK ISBN="1893115860" Pages="357" Type="SOFTCOVER">
    <TITLE>A Programmer's Introduction to C#</TITLE>
    <PRICE US="$34.95" CN="$49.95" />
    <PUBLISHER>Apress</PUBLISHER>
    <EDITIONS>2</EDITIONS>
    <AUTHORS>
        <AUTHOR>Eric Gunnerson</AUTHOR>
    </AUTHORS>
    <SYNOPSIS>Eric Gunnerson, the test lead for and member of Microsoft's
C# design team, has written a comprehensive C# tutorial for programmers to help
them get up to speed</SYNOPSIS>
  </BOOK>
```

```
<BOOK ISBN="0596000111" Pages="558" Type="SOFTCOVER">
    <TITLE>SSH, The Secure Shell: The Definitive Guide</TITLE>
    <PRICE US="$39.95" CN="$50.95" />
    <PUBLISHER>OReilly</PUBLISHER>
    <AUTHORS>
        <AUTHOR>Daniel J. Barrett</AUTHOR>
        <AUTHOR>Richard Silverman</AUTHOR>
    </AUTHORS>
    <SYNOPSIS>SSH (Secure Shell) is a popular, robust, TCP/IP-based product for
network security and privacy, supporting strong encryption and authentication.
    </SYNOPSIS>
  </BOOK>
</BOOKS>
```

The DTD is embedded within the XML document, and hence it is known as an internal DTD.

External DTD

DTD provides a good way for "standardizing" the structure of an XML document. The true benefit of a DTD comes when the DTD can be shared and communicated between different people working on creating XML documents of similar structure. Instead of embedding a DTD within an XML document, a DTD can be linked externally. Listing 1-5 shows the DTD saved as an external file.

Listing 1-5. An external DTD file (Books.dtd)

```
<!ELEMENT BOOKS (BOOK)*>
    <!ELEMENT BOOK (TITLE, PRICE, PUBLISHER, EDITIONS?, AUTHORS, SYNOPSIS)>
        <!ATTLIST BOOK ISBN  CDATA  #REQUIRED>
        <!ATTLIST BOOK Pages CDATA  #REQUIRED>
        <!ATTLIST BOOK Type  CDATA  #REQUIRED>
        <!ELEMENT TITLE            (#PCDATA)>
        <!ELEMENT PRICE                EMPTY>
            <!ATTLIST PRICE US CDATA #REQUIRED>
            <!ATTLIST PRICE CN CDATA #REQUIRED>
        <!ELEMENT PUBLISHER        (#PCDATA)>
        <!ELEMENT EDITIONS         (#PCDATA)>
        <!ELEMENT AUTHORS          (AUTHOR)+>
            <!ELEMENT AUTHOR       (#PCDATA)>
        <!ELEMENT SYNOPSIS         (#PCDATA)>
```

The external DTD, Books.dtd, can then be used within an XML file, as is demonstrated in Listing 1-6.

Listing 1-6. Template.xml makes use of an external DTD file

```
<?xml version="1.0"?>
<!DOCTYPE BOOKS SYSTEM "Books.dtd" >
<BOOKS>
   <BOOK ISBN="1893115860" Pages="357" Type="SOFTCOVER">
      <TITLE>A Programmer's Introduction to C#</TITLE>
      <PRICE US="$34.95" CN="$49.95" />
      <PUBLISHER>Apress</PUBLISHER>
      <EDITIONS>2</EDITIONS>
      <AUTHORS>
         <AUTHOR>Eric Gunnerson</AUTHOR>
      </AUTHORS>
      <SYNOPSIS>Eric Gunnerson, the test lead for and member of Microsoft's
C# design team, has written a comprehensive C# tutorial for programmers to help
them get up to speed</SYNOPSIS>
   </BOOK>
   <BOOK ISBN="0596000111" Pages="558" Type="SOFTCOVER">
      <TITLE>SSH, The Secure Shell: The Definitive Guide</TITLE>
      <PRICE US="$39.95" CN="$50.95" />
      <PUBLISHER>OReilly</PUBLISHER>
      <AUTHORS>
         <AUTHOR>Daniel J. Barrett</AUTHOR>
         <AUTHOR>Richard Silverman</AUTHOR>
      </AUTHORS>
      <SYNOPSIS>SSH (Secure Shell) is a popular, robust, TCP/IP-based product for
network security and privacy, supporting strong encryption and authentication.
      </SYNOPSIS>
   </BOOK>
</BOOKS>
```

The DTD is referenced by the Document Type Declaration:

```
<!DOCTYPE BOOKS SYSTEM "Books.dtd" >
```

Notice the keyword **SYSTEM**. The SYSTEM keyword indicates that the location of the DTD is specified in the Uniform Resource Identifier (URI) that follows. In our case, the URI is "Books.dtd." The parser would expect to find it in the same path as that of the source XML document. You can substitute the URI with any other URL that contains the DTD.

Alternatively, instead of using the SYSTEM keyword, you may sometimes encounter the **PUBLIC** keyword. For example, the Wireless Markup Language (WML) uses the following document type declaration:

```
<!DOCTYPE wml PUBLIC "-//WAPFORUM//DTD WML 1-1//EN"
                     "http://www.wapforum.org/DTD/wml_1-1-xml">
```

Notice that following the PUBLIC keyword, there are two addresses. The first address indicates a "well-known" DTD that the parsers processing the document should understand. The second address indicates the location to fetch this well-known DTD in the event that the parser does not understand the first address identifier. We discuss the WML DTD in more detail in Chapter 9.

Valid XML Documents

An XML document that conforms to the rules specified in the DTD is known as a *valid XML document*. Recall that earlier on we mentioned the well-formed XML document?

A well-formed XML document may or may not be valid, but a valid XML document is surely well-formed.

A valid XML document is one that has been validated against a DTD or schema and hence is definitely well-formed; in contrast, a well-formed document may or may not be validated against a DTD or schema and hence could be invalid.

CDATA and PCDATA

Earlier we saw that special characters in XML can be represented using entities. However, entities make the XML document look messy, especially if a document contains multiple special characters. Consider the following situation where you want to represent a statement like the following:

```
A Processing Instruction : <?xml version="1.0"?>
```

Using entities, we can use the following:

```
<Statement> A Processing Instruction : &lt;?xml version=&quot;1.0&quot;?>
</Statement>
```

Using entities provides more opportunity for introducing errors. It would be nice if a block of text can be designated as pure text so that it would not be mistaken as XML tags or elements.

XML provides the CDATA section for doing just that. Rewriting our statement using a CDATA section, we have:

```
<![CDATA[ A Processing Instruction : <?xml version="1.0"?> ]]>
```

The syntax for a CDATA section is:

```
<![CDATA[ cdata ]]>
```

The *cdata* would be treated as character data and will not be recognized as markup. Hence there is no need to explicitly escape special characters like < and > using entities.

PCDATA

Another term that appears similar to CDATA is *PCDATA*. PCDATA stands for Parsed Character Data. You have seen the use of PCDATA in DTD, like the following:

```
<!ELEMENT PUBLISHER          (#PCDATA)>
```

The preceding element declaration simply means that the parser will parse the text contained within the <Publisher> element and treat it as normal text. For example:

```
<Publisher><Apress/></Publisher>
```

Even though the text contains the string <Apress/> (which is a valid empty element) it will cause the DTD to signal an error.

You may be wondering why then do we declare an element as PCDATA? Well, in the previous example, we really want the <Publisher> element to contain the text "Apress", rather than a subelement called <Apress>. By declaring the <Publisher> element as PCDATA, we are signaling to the parser to expect a text within the element, rather than some other information like subelements.

Elements or Attributes

Beginners to XML often face the dilemma of choosing between attributes or elements to represent a piece of information. For example, is it better to represent the information of a product using attributes or elements? Imagine you have the following product information:

- Price

- Weight

- Dimension—Length, Breadth, Height

- Colors

- Description

- Product ID

By using elements, we can represent information in this way:

```
<?xml version="1.0"?>
<Product>
    <ProductID>EX-76-9213</ProductID>
    <Description>Cabinet</Description>
    <Dimension>
        <Length>1</Length>
        <Breadth>0.5</Breadth>
        <Height>1-9</Height>
    </Dimension>
    <Weight>7</Weight>
    <Colors>
        <Color>Green</Color>
        <Color>Black</Color>
    </Colors>
</Product>
```

By using all attributes, we can represent information in this way:

```
<?xml version="1.0"?>
<Product ProductID="EX-76-9213" Description="Cabinet"
         Length="1" Breadth="0.5" Height="1-9" Weight="7"
         Color1="Green" Color2="Black" />
```

Both methods have their own disadvantages, notably:

- Using all elements makes the document unnecessarily large. This is due to the use of the start and end tags to denote every piece of information.

- Using attributes forces us to drop some meaningful elements like <Colors> and <Dimension>, which aptly describes the information that we are representing. Instead, we are forced to use a unique attribute name for items like color1 and color2.

- Readability becomes an issue, as the first example seems long-winded whereas the second one seems cryptic.

A better solution would be to use a combination of elements and attributes, as in the following example:

```
<?xml version="1.0"?>
<Product ProductID="EX-76-9213" Weight="7">
    <Description>Cabinet</Description>
    <Dimension>
        <Length>1</Length>
        <Breadth>0.5</Breadth>
        <Height>1-9</Height>
    </Dimension>
    <Colors>
        <Color>Green</Color>
        <Color>Black</Color>
    </Colors>
</Product>
```

In reality, there isn't much difference between the two methods. You are free to use either one or a combination of both. In fact, this topic has been fiercely debated in the programming community. Our position, however, is that you should use the method that improves the readability of your document.

We do have some observations on the use of elements and attributes, however:

- The order of attributes is not important, at least from a technical standpoint. You can arrange them in any way you want. Contrast this to using elements, whose order is governed by the DTD.

- Duplicate attribute names are not allowed. Duplicate element names are allowed.

- Elements take up too much space but aid readability, whereas attributes reduce space but decrease readability.

XML Schemas

While DTD can be used to validate an XML document, it possesses the following problems:

- The DTD itself is not an XML document. This would prevent XML parsers from reading the DTD and manipulating it. A better way is for the DTD to be expressed in XML so that it can be manipulated programmatically, just like the XML document itself.

- DTD is not extensible.

- No support of data type. This is a major disadvantage of using a DTD.

Consider the following element:

```
<Age>4x</Age>
```

It is clear that the content of the <Age> element should strictly contain numeric data. A DTD would not be able to enforce the data type.

To overcome the limitation of DTD, the W3C is working on *XML Schema*. XML Schema is a description language (much like DTD) that is structured in XML. However, before the XML Schema was recommended as a specification in May of 2001, Microsoft had already implemented a subset of the W3C XML Schema known as *XML-Data Reduced* (XDR). The current version of MSXML3 supports the XDR.

Besides XDR, there are a couple of different schemas available in the market. They are:

- Document Content Description (DCD): The DCD incorporates a subset of the XDR and expresses it in a way that is consistent with the ongoing W3C RDF (Resource Description Framework) effort; in particular, DCD is an RDF vocabulary. See `http://www.w3.org/TR/NOTE-dcd` for more information.

- Schema for Object Oriented XML (SOX): SOX was developed by Veo Systems and provides functionality like inheritance to XML structures. See `http://www13.w3.org/TR/NOTE-SOX/` for more information.

- Document Description Markup Language (DDML): A schema language for XML documents. DDML encodes the logical (as opposed to physical) content of DTDs in an XML document. This allows schema information to be explored and used with widely available XML tools. DDML is deliberately simple, providing an initial base for implementations. While introducing as few complicating factors as possible, DDML has been designed with future extensions, such as data typing and schema reuse, in mind. (See `http://www.w3.org/TR/NOTE-ddml` for more information.)

 NOTE *We discuss XML Schema in greater depth in Chapter 8, XML Schemas.*

XML Encoding and Unicode

XML uses the ISO10646 standard (Unicode) for encoding characters. Two popular character-encoding schemes are UTF-8 and UTF-16, which uses 8 bits and 16 bits per character respectively. However, do note that if you create an XML document using Notepad in Microsoft Windows 95/98, the file is saved as an 8-bit file. Notepad in Windows 95/98 does not support Unicode. To save your XML document as Unicode, use Notepad under Windows 2000 (remember to choose the "Unicode" Encoding method).

Consider the example shown in Listing 1-7.

Listing 1-7. XML document using GB2312 encoding (Ansi.xml)

```
<?xml version="1.0" encoding="gb2312"?>
<!--Saved as ANSI but with GB2312 encoding-->
<Encoding>
    <CharRef>&#x9F8D;</CharRef>
    <Chinese>¿Æ ¹/₄¹/₄</Chinese>
    <Special>å</Special>
</Encoding>
```

The above XML document is saved in the UTF-8 file format. Note that the PI has an additional attribute "encoding" with a value of "gb2312." This indicates that all the special characters in the document are interpreted using the gb2312 encoding scheme. Within this XML document, we have three elements worth our attention.

The first,

```
<CharRef>&#x9F8D;</CharRef>
```

indicates a character reference. There are times when it is impossible for you to enter special characters via the keyboard or other input devices. But all these special characters are defined in Unicode. To embed all these special characters in the XML document, we can refer to them using a *character reference*. The syntax for using a character reference is:

```
&#xnumber;
```

In our example, we have the character represented by 龍, which is the Chinese character for "dragon"(see Figure 1-5).

Figure 1-5. The Chinese character for "dragon"

NOTE The full list of Unicode characters can be found in the book *The Unicode Standard 3.0* published by Addison-Wesley Publishing Company, ISBN: 0201616335.

Some sample characters can also be found at the Unicode Web site: `http://www.unicode.org`.

The second element of interest is the gb2312 encoding of two characters:

```
<Chinese>¿Æ ¹/₄ ¹/₄ </Chinese>
```

When an XML parser loads the XML document, it checks to see the value of the encoding attribute. It will then interpret special characters according to the encoding scheme. In our case, it will interpret the two characters that mean "technology"(see Figure 1-6).

Figure 1-6. The Chinese characters for "technology"

The third element contains a special character (å) defined in Unicode. However, since the file is saved in the UTF-8 format, it will cause a problem when the document is loaded using Internet Explorer 5.0 (see Figure 1-7).

Figure 1-7. Attempting to load a file saved in UTF-8 containing the character å

Removing the third element, Internet Explorer 5.0 should display the Chinese characters correctly, as shown in Figure 1-8.

Figure 1-8. Displaying the Chinese characters correctly in Internet Explorer 5.0

We will talk more about Microsoft Internet Explorer's support of XML in the section on "XML and Web Browser Support" in this chapter.

Let's now consider another XML document by looking at Listing 1-8.

Listing 1-8. Unicode.xml

```
<?xml version="1.0" ?>
<!--Saved as UNICODE but with no encoding-->
<Encoding>
    <CharRef>&#x9F8D;</CharRef>
    <Chinese>¿Æ¹/ ¹/ </Chinese>
              4  4
    <Special>å</Special>
</Encoding>
```

This time, we save the file as Unicode file format. Using Internet Explorer 5.0, we will see an output similar to that shown in Figure 1-9.

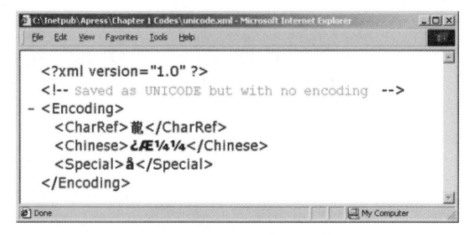

Figure 1-9. Displaying an XML document saved as a Unicode file with no encoding

Note that the character specified by the <Chinese> element is not displayed as a Chinese character; it is displayed as a literal string. Also, the character enclosed by the <Special> element is displayed without problem, unlike the previous example.

You might be tempted to add an encoding attribute to the above document, such as this:

```
<?xml version="1.0"  encoding="gb2312"?>
<!--Saved as UNICODE but with encoding-->
<Encoding>
    <CharRef>&#x9F8D;</CharRef>
    <Chinese>¿Æ¹/ ¹/ </Chinese>
              4  4
    <Special>å</Special>
</Encoding>
```

Unfortunately, it won't work, as the error message in Figure 1-10 states.

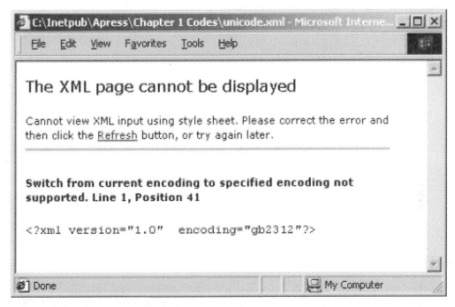

Figure 1-10. Attempting to display an XML document that is saved as Unicode with encoding in Internet Explorer 5.0 results in an error message.

CAUTION   *In general, it is advisable to save your XML document in the Unicode format if you need to embed special characters. If you have special characters that are unable to be input using input devices, use character references.*

Namespaces

One of the more confusing topics in XML is undoubtedly the concept of *namespaces*. A good way to explain namespaces is to consider an example. Continuing with the publisher example, consider Listing 1-9.

Listing 1-9. NamespaceApressBooks.xml

```xml
<?xml version="1.0"?>
<BOOKS>
  <BOOK Pages="357" Type="SOFTCOVER">
    <TITLE>A Programmer's Introduction to C#</TITLE>
    <AUTHOR>
        <TITLE>Mr.</TITLE>
        <NAME>Eric Gunnerson</NAME>
    </AUTHOR>
    <ISBN>1893115860 </ISBN>
    <SYNOPSIS>Eric Gunnerson, the test lead for and member of Microsoft's
C# design team, has written a comprehensive C# tutorial for programmers to help
them get up to speed</SYNOPSIS>
    <PRICE>$34.95 </PRICE>
  </BOOK>
</BOOKS>
```

Notice that there are two instances where the <TITLE> element appears. One is used to describe the title of a book while the other is used for salutation. While it is obvious to the reader the different contexts in which the <TITLE> element is used, it is not obvious to the parser processing this document. For example, if you write a program to print out all the titles of all the books in the element, how would the parser know the correct title to print?

To solve this problem, there must be a way to add "contextual" information to the XML document. XML Namespace accomplishes this. Rewriting our XML document, we have:

```xml
<?xml version="1.0"?>
<BOOKS xmlns="http://www.apress.com"
       xmlns:People="http://www.apress.com/people">
  <BOOK Pages="357" Type="SOFTCOVER">
    <TITLE>A Programmer's Introduction to C#</TITLE>
    <AUTHOR>
        <People:TITLE>Mr.</People:TITLE>
        <NAME>Eric Gunnerson</NAME>
    </AUTHOR>
    <ISBN>1893115860 </ISBN>
    <SYNOPSIS>Eric Gunnerson, the test lead for and member of Microsoft's
C# design team, has written a comprehensive C# tutorial for programmers to help
them get up to speed</SYNOPSIS>
    <PRICE>$34.95 </PRICE>
  </BOOK>
</BOOKS>
```

In this rewrite of the original XML document, we have declared two namespaces with the *xmlns* attribute:

```
xmlns="http://www.apress.com"
xmlns:People="http://www.apress.com/people"
```

The first namespace is the *default namespace* while the second one is the *People* namespace. Both namespaces refer to a URL. Also note that the <TITLE> element used for salutation has been rewritten with the "People:" prefix:

```
<People:TITLE>Mr.</People:TITLE>
```

Elements that do not have the "People:" prefix belong to the default namespace.

So, what is the use of the namespaces? It is for parsers to differentiate elements with the same name but with different meanings. For instance, you may write an application that parses the above XML document to print out all the titles of books. Using the namespace, you know that the <People:TITLE> element refers to a salutation, rather than the title of a book.

Notice that the namespaces used in this example uses URLs. In fact, you can use any identifier you want. The use of the URL in this case is simply a case of reducing the possibility of namespace collision—it is unlikely someone else will use the same URL. It is perfectly possible that someone else will use the same URL as you, but it's not likely.

CAUTION *The use of the URL does **not** mean that Internet connectivity is required when this XML document is parsed. In fact, you can use any string as a namespace.*

The importance of the namespace will be much clearer when we discuss XSLT in Chapter 3. For now, it is useful to think of a namespace as similar to two different people having the same name but different social security number.

XML Parsers

Until this point we have been talking about the various features of XML, and along the way we have mentioned the term "XML parsers" several times. Just what is an XML parser?

Suppose you are now given an XML document. And this document contains information about titles of books from a publisher. Your task is to selectively filter out all the titles that have been published in the last two years and list them in a report. What you may do is you may write an application that reads the XML document from the beginning to the end (since an XML document is just a plain text file) and along the way look out for the element that contains the publication date. You detect the start of an element by looking for the start tag <> and the end tag </>.

Hmmm . . . not too difficult a task. Right?

Wrong! If the XML document is not well-formed (for example, missing /), your application may then not work correctly. Furthermore, if the XML document's format were changed, your application would fail. In other words, your application is closely coupled to the document format.

Rather than reinvent the wheel, all these functionalities mentioned above can be achieved using XML parsers. An XML parser is simply an application that reads an XML document and processes it based on the instructions given and returns the desired result. It will take care of checking the well-formedness of a document as well as its validity (if a DTD or XML Schema is specified). Any structural change to an XML document would not affect the parser.

A number of parsers are available at the moment. They are:

- Oracle XML parser for Java: An XML parser/XSL processor with error recovery, support for namespaces, DOM 1.0, SAX 1.0, and a large number of encoding sets. Implements the XSLT 1.0 Recommendation.

- Xerces-C++: A validating XML parser for C++. Supports DOM 1 and 2, SAX 1 and 2, and namespaces.

- JAXP: Standard extension for XML parsing in Java 1.1 and later. Provides a standard way to seamlessly integrate any XML-compliant parser with a Java application. Supports the XML 1.0 Specification, SAX 1.0, DOM Level 1 Core and XML namespaces.

NOTE *This book focuses on the Microsoft XML parser release 3.0. For a partial listing of XML parsers available, go to* `http://www.xmlsoftware.com/parsers/`.

Microsoft XML Parser (MSXML)

The MSXML has come a long way, first released as version 2.0 (IE5) and currently available as version 4.0. Depending on the software and operating system installed, you would most likely have the MSXML 2.0 (Internet Explorer 5.0) or MSXML 2.5 (Windows 2000) on your system.

Starting January 2000, Microsoft has shown its commitment to XML by releasing a new XML Parser every other month. The January preview release was version 2.6 and Microsoft has since renamed it to version 3.0 starting from the March release. The current release is 4.0. Each preview release contains improvement in performance as well as support for the W3C XML 1.0 Specifications.

The long-awaited production release of MSXML 3.0 finally occurred in November 2000. It includes support for the following:

- XSL Transformation (XSLT) version 1.0. It also supports the XML Path language (XPath) Recommendation specification version 1.0.

- SAX. MSXML3 supports the Simple API for XML (SAX) event-based parsing. The SAX is an interface that allows developers to write applications that process XML documents. MSXML3 supports the current implementation of SAX2.

We discuss the MSXML3 in more detail in the rest of this book.

Uses and Benefits of XML

So what are the uses and benefits of XML? XML is platform agnostic. Since an XML document is a text file, it can be read by any platform. This characteristic allows XML document to be exchanged between two machines running on different platforms.

An XML document can be transformed from one format into another. The rules of XML facilitate the transformation of a document from one format into another using the XSL Transformation (XSLT) language. The benefit of this is that documents can be described in a singular markup language (XML) and be transformed into different formats for use on different mediums.

XML allows meaning to be attached to a document. As XML allows the document author to invent his own tags (using meaningful names), it provides contextual meaning to the data represented in a document. For example, search engines (or Web spiders) could be enhanced with the ability to look for meaningful tags in documents, thereby improving the reliability and accuracy of the search.

XML and Web Browser Support

So far we have been busy creating XML documents and discussing the various rules in XML. It would be nice if we could have an application that views an XML document and validates it against a DTD. Well, if you have Microsoft Internet Explorer 5.0 or Netscape Navigator 6.0, you already have that application!

Beginning with Internet Explorer 4.0, Microsoft has provided XML supported on its Web browser. Let's take a look at how Internet Explorer 5.0 can be used to view our XML document.

Internet Explorer

Microsoft Internet Explorer includes a built-in XML parser that loads an XML document and displays it in a hierarchical fashion. Using our earlier XML document (template.xml), we load the XML document into Internet Explorer 5.0 by selecting File ➤ Open [specify the location of the XML document].

Figure 1-11 shows the output that Internet Explorer displays.

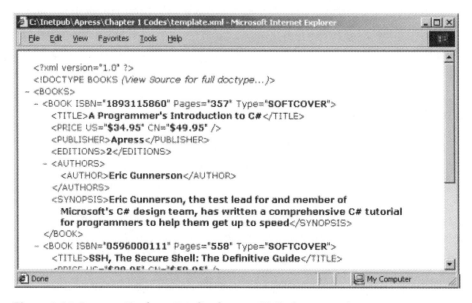

Figure 1-11. Internet Explorer 5.0 displays an XML document in a hierarchical fashion.

Notice the – and + characters. Clicking on the – will collapse the structure, as shown in Figure 1-12.

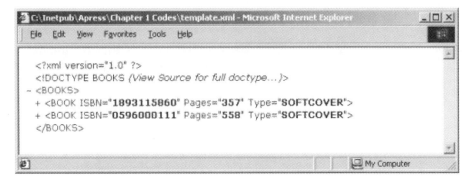

Figure 1-12. Displaying an XML document in Internet Explorer 5.0

Similarly, clicking on the + will expand the structure. An interesting thing is that when you do a View Source on the page displayed, you will see XML content instead of HTML. However, in actual fact, Internet Explorer has actually transformed the XML document into Dynamic HTML (DHTML). In a later section we'll show you how you can view the DHTML codes.

If the XML document loaded is not well-formed, Internet Explorer 5.0 will display an error message, such as the one that appears in Figure 1-13.

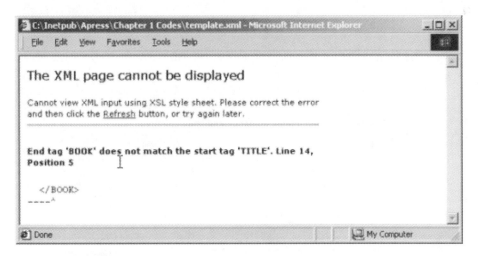

Figure 1-13. Internet Explorer 5.0 displays an error message if the XML document is not well-formed.

XML Validation Tools

Microsoft makes available the Internet Explorer Tools for Validating XML and Viewing XSLT Output. You can download the Internet Explorer Tool from http://msdn.microsoft.com/downloads.

Appendix A covers the download and installation of the Internet Explorer Tool.

Once the Internet Explorer Tool is installed correctly on your system, restart your Web browser. You can test it by first loading an XML document (as in the previous section).

Next, right-click the page and you should see two additional items on the context-sensitive menu:

- Validate XML

- View XSL Output

To validate an XML document against its DTD (see Figure 1-14), select Validate XML.

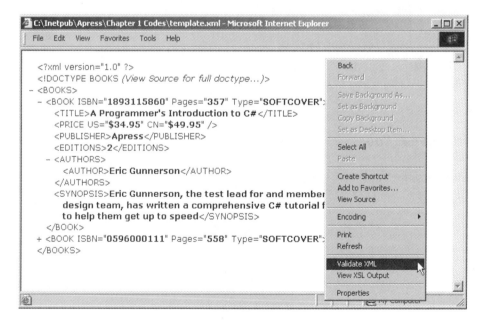

Figure 1-14. Validating an XML document against a DTD

If the document is valid, you should see the dialog box that appears in Figure 1-15, informing you that the validation was successful.

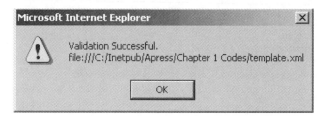

Figure 1-15. Validation succeeded

If the document does not conform to the DTD, you will see an error message. Figure 1-16 displays the error message that appears when the XML document is not valid.

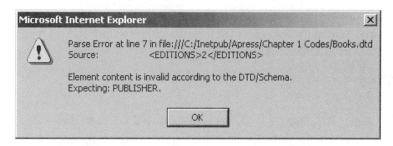

Figure 1-16. Reporting the line in error when validation fails

Netscape Navigator

With Netscape Navigator version 6.0, it is also possible to view XML documents. Viewing the same XML document using Netscape Navigator 6.0 yields the following results, as shown in Figure 1-17.

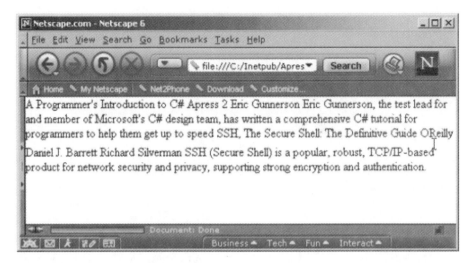

Figure 1-17. Displaying an XML document using Netscape Navigator version 6.0

A key difference in the treatment of XML documents between Internet Explorer and Netscape Navigator is that Netscape Navigator will display all the text content in the XML document without any hierarchical structure. The end result is that the output seems messy.

Using the Microsoft XML Parser Release 3.0 SP1

In this book, we focus our attention on the MSXML 3.

Obtaining and Installing the MSXML3

To download the MSXML 3.0 parser, point your Web browser to
`http://msdn.microsoft.com/downloads/default.asp?URL=/downloads`
`/sample.asp?url=/msdn-files/027/001/591/msdncompositedoc.xml`.

Once the MSXML 3.0 is downloaded, simply double-click the installation file and follow the instructions on screen. The MSXML 3.0 will be installed side-by-side with your existing XML parser, which means you now have two different versions of the MSXML parser. Your existing XML parser is contained in either MSXML.dll or MSXML2.dll. Do a search and you should see the file(s) installed in your Windows System directory.

The MSXML 3.0 will install the following DLL libraries:

- MSXML3.dll

- MSXML3a.dll

- MSXML3r.dll

If you encounter problems in installing the MSXML 3.0, you can manually install the parser by using the regsvr32.exe (available on your machine) tool:

```
C:\WINDOWS\SYSTEM>regsvr32 msxml3.dll
```

If the parser is installed correctly, you should see the dialog box that appears in Figure 1-18.

Figure 1-18. Manually registering the MSXML3 parser

If you want to remove the existing MSXML parser, you can use the xmlinst.exe utility provided by Microsoft or remove the dynamic link library manually:

```
C:\WINDOWS\SYSTEM>regsvr32 -u msxml.dll
```

If the old parser is uninstalled correctly, you should see a dialog box similar to the one shown previously.

CAUTION   *Internet Explorer 5.0 will use the older MSXML parser even if the MSXML3 is installed. To ensure that Internet Explorer uses the MSXML3, use the* **xmlinst.exe** *utility.*

Using the Help Files

Before the MSXML 3.0 reached production status, a lot of developers were experimenting with it and needed a reference containing the objects and properties supported by the MSXML 3.0. Unfortunately, the documentation available from Microsoft's Web site pertained to the MSXML 2.5 release. The actual documentation for MSXML 3.0 comes with the MSXML 3.0 SDK release (which can be downloaded from the same URL). The MSXML 3.0 SDK includes header and .lib files, as well as documentation for the MSXML 3.0 Release. Once the SDK is downloaded, proceed to install it. The MSXML 3.0 documentation can then be located from the following directory:

```
C:\Program Files\Microsoft XML Parser SDK\Docs
```

The name of the documentation is xmlsdk30.chm, which appears in Figure 1-19.

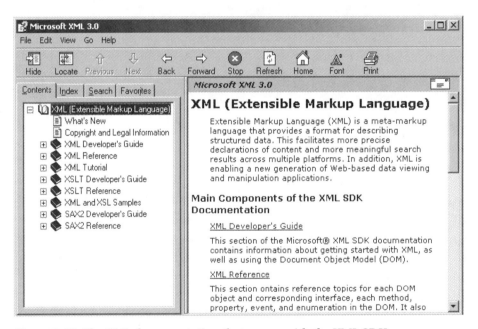

Figure 1-19. The XML documentation that comes with the XML SDK

XML Editors

As XML documents are plain text files (saved either as ANSI or Unicode format), any text editor that is capable of saving files in the above two formats can be used to create XML documents.

NotePad

NotePad comes free with your Microsoft Windows 95/98/ME/NT/2000/XP operating system. It is good for beginners as a tool to really understand the rules in XML. Notepad under Windows 2000 has the ability to save files in the Unicode format and that is a bonus to developers creating XML documents with multiple-language support.

A minor irritation of Notepad is that it will append an extension of ".txt" to the filename of a document. To prevent Notepad from adding a .txt extension, simply enclose your file name within a pair of double quotes when saving your file, as shown in Figure 1-20.

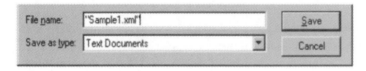

Figure 1-20. Tips for saving XML files correctly in Notepad

Some other XML editors are available at:

- XMLSpy: `http://www.xmlspy.com/`

- XML Pro: `http://www.vervet.com/`

- Xmetal 2.0: `http://www.softquad.com/`

Useful Web Links

You can find other useful information on the Web at the following addresses:

- Internet Explorer Tools for Validating XML and Viewing XSLT Output at
  `http://msdn.microsoft.com/code/sample.asp?url=`
  `/msdn-files/027/000/543/msdncompositedoc.xml`

- The Unicode Consortium at `http://www.unicode.org`

- World Wide Web Consortium at `http://www.w3.org/`

- Extensible Markup Language (XML) 1.0 Specification (Second Edition) at `http://www.w3.org/TR/2000/REC-xml-2000 1006`

- Document Content Description (DCD) at `http://www.w3.org/TR/NOTE-dcd`

- Schema for Object Oriented XML (SOX) at `http://www13.w3.org/TR/NOTE-SOX/`

- Document Description Markup Language (DDML) at `http://www.w3.org/TR/NOTE-ddml`

- XML Protocol Comparisons at `http://www.w3.org/2000/03/29-XML-protocol-matrix`

Summary

In this chapter, we took a good look at XML and its accompanying technologies. It is important to note that XML technologies are continually evolving, and we can expect to see the introduction of more jargon and new terminology. However, you need to understand the fundamentals of XML in order to make use of it. In addition, we have discussed the basic rules of XML, DTD, and XML Schema.

The rest of this book is devoted to the discussion of the various pieces of the XML puzzle and how you as a developer can make use of them in your daily development work using the Microsoft XML Parser.

CHAPTER 2

Addressing XML Parts Using XPath

XPATH, THE XML *PATH LANGUAGE*, is a language for addressing parts of an XML document. The language does not conform to the XML syntax. It can be used to formulate an expression that can be evaluated to some literal value, such as a number or string. It is also used to express an absolute or relative location path with respect to a current node, also called *context node*, in a conceptual tree structure of an XML document.

XPath is designed to be a compact language that is used by XSLT (Extensible Stylesheet Language Transformation) and in the XML queries to the SQL Server 2000, which will be discussed later in this book.

NOTE *XSLT is discussed in Chapter 3, and XPath queries to the SQL Server 2000 are discussed in Chapter 6.*

In this chapter, we first look at the form that an XPath expression can take on. Then we present the data model that is used in XPath in order to see how an XML document can be converted into a tree that is based on this model. We also describe the terminology and syntax of XPath, and explain how an XPath expression is formulated to extract the desired part of an XML document.

XPath Expression

An XPath expression can be evaluated to return one of the following types of results:

- Boolean

- Numeric

- String

- Node-set as defined in the XPath data model

Boolean

An XPath expression may be evaluated as either `true` or `false`. Such expressions are normally used in a predicate for testing if a condition is satisfied. We will discuss more about the use of predicates for specifying matching criteria when we discuss a special type of expression, namely the *location path*, used to select certain parts of an XML document.

Numeric

An XPath expression may simply return a numeric value. Such XPath expressions may include one or more arithmetic operator.

There are five arithmetic operators:

- addition   +

- negation or subtraction   -

- multiplication   *

- division   **div**

- modulus   **mod**

Some valid examples of this category of numeric expression are:

- 1.23 is a numeric literal that has the value 1.23

- 5 + 3 - 1 is evaluated to the numeric value 7

- 5 * 7 div 2 is evaluated to the numeric value 17.5

- 10 mod 3 is evaluated to the numeric value 1

String

An XPath expression may simply be a string literal, which is a sequence of Unicode characters enclosed within single or double quotes such as 'technology' and "¿Æ $\frac{1}{4}\frac{1}{4}$." String expressions are commonly used together with some XPath functions or comparative operators such as the equality (=) or less-than (<) operators.

For example, an XPath expression used as predicate may involve testing if two string values are equal. We will see some examples when we discuss predicates in greater detail.

 NOTE *XPath functions are also discussed in a later section.*

Node-Set

An XPath expression may be evaluated to return a set of zero or more nodes. The term *node* is defined in the data model used by XPath and will be discussed next. Basically it can be mapped into XML components such as an element, attribute, character data, comment, namespace, and procession instruction.

An XPath expression that is used to extract parts of an XML document is also called a location path, which will be elaborated further after we have considered the XPath data model.

XPath Data Model

XPath treats an XML document as a tree consisting of a single root node, and possibly with other descendant nodes. Each node in the tree represents a node of any of the valid component types in an XML document described in Chapter 1. This tree structure forms the basic data model of XPath, which may consist of the following types of nodes:

- Root node (present in every data model)

- Element node

- Attribute node

- Text node

- Namespace node

- Processing instruction node

- Comment node

Representing an XML Document as a Tree

Consider the following XML document, BooksCatalog.xml:

```xml
<?xml version="1.0"?>
<BOOKS>
  <BOOK ISBN="1893115860" Pages="357" Type="SOFT">
     <!--This is the first book-->
     <TITLE>A Programmer's Introduction to C#</TITLE>
     <AUTHOR>Eric Gunnerson</AUTHOR>
     <PRICE>34.95</PRICE>
  </BOOK>
  <BOOK ISBN="189311595X" Pages="380" Type="HARD">
     <TITLE>Cryptography in C &amp; C++</TITLE>
     <AUTHOR>Michael Welschenbach</AUTHOR>
     <PRICE>49.95</PRICE>
  </BOOK>
```

```
<BOOK ISBN="1893115763" Pages="400" Type="SOFT">
    <TITLE>C++ for VB Programmers</TITLE>
    <AUTHOR>Jonathan Morrison</AUTHOR>
    <PRICE>49.95</PRICE>
  </BOOK>
</BOOKS>
```

The preceding document can be depicted as a tree, as shown in Figure 2-1, which for the sake of simplicity, shows only the first two <BOOK> elements due to space. The attribute nodes are represented as ellipses with dotted lines and the text nodes are represented as rectangles.

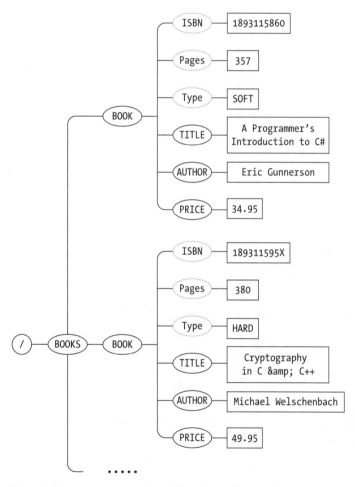

Figure 2-1. Partial tree representation of BooksCatalog.xml

The traversing order of the nodes in a tree representing an XML document is known as *document order*. The order is rather straightforward, namely from top (parent) to bottom (child) and from left to right. It is a preorder traversal of the document tree.

When evaluating an XPath expression, it is with respect to a *context node*. If the context node (or current node) is the node representing the <BOOKS> element, then according to the document order defined for XPath, the node representing the third child element is the node indicated by the number 3 in Figure 2-2. To locate child nodes, we need to traverse one level down the tree from the context node (indicated by the number 0). To locate the third child, count the third node from the left of all the nodes at this level.

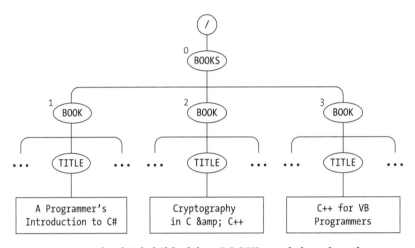

Figure 2-2. Locating the third child of the <BOOKS> node based on the document order

Understanding the Properties of Nodes

Each of the nodes is associated with a *string-value*. Depending on the node type, the node may also have an *expanded-name*, which comprises a local component and a namespace URI. The URI used in the expanded-name may be null, or otherwise an absolute URI specification.

We shall next discuss each type of node as well as their string-value and expanded-name properties whenever applicable to the node type concerned.

Root Node

This is the root of the tree. Do not confuse this with the root element of an XML document. The latter is a child of the root node. In our example shown in Figure 2-1, the root of the tree is the first node in the topmost level, whereas the root element of the represented XML document is <BOOKS>.

The string-value of the root node is the concatenation of string-values of all the text nodes that are children of element nodes in the document, where the order of concatenation is according to the document order defined earlier. Going to the same example depicted in Figure 2-1, the string-value of the root node is the following string:

```
A Programmer's Introduction to C# Eric Gunnerson $34.95 Cryptography in C &
C++ Michael Welschenbach $49.95 C++ for VB Programmers Jonathan Morrison
$49.95
```

The root node is addressed as the first slash / symbol in an XPath expression that represents a location path. It does not have an expanded-name.

Element Node

There is an element node for each element in an XML document.
    Consider the following <SYNOPSIS> element:

```
<SYNOPSIS xmlns:myNS="http://wwww.apress.com">
   <!--About the author-->
   Eric Gunnerson is a member of Microsoft's C# design team.
   <myNS:RATING>Excellent</myNS:RATING>
</SYNOPSIS>
```

The <SYNOPSIS> element consists of three child nodes; the first is a comment node, followed by a text node and finally another element node. The string-value of an element node is the concatenation of string-values of all its descendant text nodes traversed according to the document order. The <SYNOPSIS> element has two descendant text nodes; one is its child while the other is its grandchild. Hence, the string-value of the <SYNOPSIS> element node is evaluated to:

```
Eric Gunnerson is a member of Microsoft's C# design team. Excellent
```

Besides the three types of child node, an element can also take on children that are processing instruction nodes.

The expanded-name of an element node is the result of expanding the qualified name (of the format *prefix:local_name*) into the namespace URI (if any) referenced by the prefix and the local name. Hence, an XPath expression for addressing a node-set, such as rate:Rating, will be equal to the expression for the <myNS:RATING> element if their expanded-names resolve to the same namespace URI (`http://www.apress.com` in our example) and local name (RATING in this case).

Attribute Node

An attribute node represents an attribute in a document. The element that is associated with an attribute is also the parent of the attribute. However, the reverse is not true—i.e., the attribute node concerned is not a child of the element node. Consider the following start-tag of a <BOOK> element in an XML document:

```
<BOOK Pages="357" Type="&#x20;SOFT&#x20;&#x20;COVER">
```

The string-value of an attribute node is the normalized value of an attribute as would be handled in an XML document. Specifically, all character and entity references are resolved and whitespaces are processed accordingly. In our example, the string-value of the attribute of name Type is "SOFT COVER."

The expanded-name of an attribute node is computed by expanding the qualified name into the namespace URI and local name as in the case for an element node.

An exception needs to be brought up here. Consider the following start-tag of the <BOOKS> element:

```
<BOOKS xmlns="http://www.apress.com"
       xmlns:People="http://www.apress.com/people">
```

The xmlns and xmlns:People attributes are not represented as attribute nodes. Rather, they are represented as namespace nodes.

Text Node

A continuous block of character data in an XML document without intervening tags, processing instructions, and comments constitutes a text node. The string-value of a text node is the character data.

For example, the PCDATA string of the following <TITLE> element in Bookscatalog.xml is represented as a text node in Figure 2-1, which contains the string-value, "A Programmer's Introduction to C#":

```
<TITLE>A Programmer's Introduction to C#</TITLE>
```

A text node does not have an expanded-name.

Namespace Node

There is a namespace node for each distinct namespace prefix and a maximum of one default namespace in the scope of an element within an XML document. Note that there is one implicitly declared namespace prefix, xml, which is bound to the URI, http://www.w3.org/XML/1998/namespace.

Each namespace node has an expanded-name in which the local part is the namespace prefix (which is empty for the default namespace) and the namespace URI is always null. The string-value of a namespace node is the absolute URI specification that is bound to the namespace.

Consider the start-tag of the <BOOKS> element that we have seen earlier:

```
<BOOKS xmlns="http://www.apress.com"
       xmlns:People="http://www.apress.com/people">
```

The preceding <BOOKS> element is associated with the following namespace nodes:

- A default namespace node with no prefix and is bound to the URI http://www.apress.com

- A namespace node with the prefix People and is bound to the URI http://www.apress.com/people

- The implicitly declared namespace node with the prefix xml

Each of the child element nodes of the <BOOKS> element will have a namespace node for every attribute of the <BOOKS> element whose name starts with xmlns: unless the child element redeclares the prefix.

Processing Instruction Node

A processing instruction node is used to represent each of the processing instructions in an XML document. Each of these PI nodes has an expanded-name, where the local part is the PI's target name and the namespace URI is null. The string-value of a PI node is the instruction string that follows the target name and any whitespace.

For example, the following processing instruction in an XML document is represented as a processing instruction node where its string-value is the string "x1 x2 x3":

```
<?myprocess x1 x2 x3?>
```

Comment Node

This node is used to represent a comment in a document, as long as the comment does not occur within the document type declaration. This type of node does not have an expanded-name and its string-value is the content enclosed within <!-- and -->.

The following example is a comment in an XML document that is represented as a comment node in the XPath data model with the string-value "This is the first book":

```
<!--This is the first book-->
```

Context

The evaluation of an XPath expression is with respect to a context consisting of the following:

- Context node—node of reference when evaluating an XPath expression

- Context size—size of node-set containing all nodes that need to be iterated through in evaluating an XPath expression

- Context position—position of the current context node in a node-set

- Set of variable bindings

- Function library

- Set of namespace declarations in scope for the expression

Location Path

The location path is the most important form of an XPath expression. It consists of one or more location steps. A path leads to the result of locating a node or set of nodes in a tree structure of an XML document.

A location path may be relative or absolute. The latter would start with the / symbol, indicating the root node of the tree containing the context node. A relative path will use the context node as the first node of reference to evaluate the path.

We shall start with a few examples to make the use of location path clearer.

Table 2-1 shows some examples of location path expression, their definitions and results with respect to a given context node using the tree that was shown in Figure 2-1 previously.

Table 2-1. Examples of Location Path

LOCATION PATH	DESCRIPTION
/	Returns the root node of the document. This is an absolute location path.
	Using the BooksCatalog.xml, the string-value of the root node is "A Programmer's Introduction to C# Eric Gunnerson 34.95 Cryptography in C & C++ Michael Welschenbach 49.95 C++ for VB Programmers Jonathan Morrison 49.95."
/BOOKS	Returns all <BOOKS> elements, which are children of the root node of the document. This is an absolute location path.
BOOK	Returns all <BOOK> elements, which are children of the context node. This is a relative location path, with reference to the context node.
	If the context node is the <BOOKS> element node, the result would be the set of all the three <BOOK> element nodes. Otherwise, the result set is empty.
BOOK/TITLE	Returns all child <TITLE> elements of <BOOK> elements, which are children of the context node. This is a relative location path, with reference to the context node.
	If the context node is the <BOOKS> element node, the result would be the set of all the three <TITLE> element nodes. Otherwise, the result set is empty.
//AUTHOR	Returns all <AUTHOR> elements in the document that contains the context node. The double-slash // implies descendants of the root node. This is an absolute location path. The result set would be the same for a given XML document regardless of the context node.
//@Type	Returns all <Type> attributes of the document that contain the context node. Attribute node type is specified by the @ symbol. This expression will result in the same node-set for a given XML document regardless of the context node.

Different location steps in a path are delimited by the / character. The order of evaluation of the multiple steps in a location path is from left to right. Note that as evaluation proceeds from left to right, the context node may change at each step.

Location Steps

A location step has the following syntax, consisting of three components:

*Axis::Node-Test Predicate**

The *Axis* and *Node-Test* components are delimited by the symbol :: without any space between them. The asterisk * that follows the *Predicate* component indicates that there could be 0 or more predicates following the space after Node-Test.

As we have already been using the Node-Test portion, even though you may not have realized it yet, we will take a look at it first followed by the use of predicates and finally the axis component.

Node-Test

In all the previous examples, we see only the *Node-Test* portion in action. The examples we used express this component as the name of the node to be selected by the location step. However, this can only address the requirements for selecting nodes that have a name. These nodes include the element, attribute, and namespace nodes.

To refer to comment nodes, which do not have a name, we can use the function comment(). Other provisions include text() that returns all text node children of the context node and processing-instruction() that returns all PI nodes of the context node. The third function may take on an argument such as processing-instruction("myproc"), in which case, it will return the processing instruction that has the process name (i.e., target) "myproc."

Another node-test function is node(), which can refer to any node type. The function simply returns the context node itself.

Predicates

Besides merely specifying the tag name of the node to be located in a location step, a predicate can be specified to include conditions or filters within [and] in order to locate the desired node or set of nodes. An XPath expression used as a filter will evaluate to a Boolean value, true or false. Table 2-2 lists descriptions of locations.

Table 2-2. Examples of Location Paths Using Predicates

LOCATION PATH	DESCRIPTION
BOOK[@ISBN]	Returns all <BOOK> elements, which are children of the context node and which have an ISBN attribute.
//BOOK[@Type='SOFT']/TITLE	Returns all <TITLE> elements that are children of BOOK elements in the document containing the context node and which have a Type attribute with value, "SOFT."
BOOK[AUTHOR='Eric Gunnerson']	Returns all <BOOK> elements that are children of the context node and which have an <AUTHOR> child element with the string-value, "Eric Gunnerson."
//AUTHOR[.='Eric Gunnerson']	Returns all <AUTHOR> elements with the value, "Eric Gunnerson," and which are in the document that contains the context node.
	The . symbol in the predicate expression is an abbreviation that refers to the node being evaluated in the current location step. In this case, as we step through all the <AUTHOR> elements, we will substitute . with the value of each of the <AUTHOR> elements.
//PRICE[. < 40]	Returns all <PRICE> elements whose values are less than 40, and which are in the document that contains the context node.

Operators

Some of the filters that we include in the previous examples make use of operators such as the equality (=) and less than (<, expressed as <) operators.

Table 2-3, Table 2-4, and Table 2-5 list the different types of operators, namely comparative, arithmetic, and logical operators, respectively, which can be used in an XPath expression.

Table 2-3. List of Comparative Operators Defined in XPath 1.0

COMPARATIVE OPERATOR	FUNCTION
=	Equality
!=	Inequality
< or <	Less than
<= or <=	Less than or equal to
> or >	More than
>= or >=	More than or equal to

Table 2-4. List of Arithmetic Operators Defined in XPath 1.0

ARITHMETIC OPERATOR	FUNCTION
+	Addition
-	Negation or Subtraction
*	Multiplication
div	Division
mod	Remainder from a truncating division

Table 2-5. List of Logical Operators Defined in XPath 1.0

LOGICAL OPERATOR	FUNCTION
and	And
or	Or

In Table 2-6, we list some examples of predicate expressions that make use of some of the operators that we have discussed in this section.

Table 2-6. Examples with More Complex Predicate Expressions

EXAMPLE	DESCRIPTION
BOOK[PRICE <= 40*1.03]	Returns all child <BOOK> elements of the context node that have a PRICE value less than or equal to 41.2. Note that we are not allowed to use the symbol <= in the predicate. We need to escape it using the character reference for < or resort to the use of the CDATA section as discussed in Chapter 1.
//BOOK[@ISBN and TITLE]	Returns all <BOOK> elements in the document containing the context node and which have an ISBN attribute and a child <TITLE> element.

Axes

We shall now look at the final component in an expression that specifies a location step. An axis specifies a relationship, such as child and parent, of the node-test component with respect to the context node to be used to evaluate the current location step.

For example, the location path, /BOOKS, can be expressed more explicitly as /child::BOOKS, where child is an axis delimited from the node-test, BOOKS, via the :: symbol. Table 2-7 lists the possible types of values for the axis component. The examples given are with respect to the BooksCatalog.xml document.

Table 2-7. List of Axes Defined in XPath 1.0

AXIS	DESCRIPTION AND EXAMPLES
self	This indicates the context node. Its abbreviated form is the . symbol. To refer to the context node, use the expression self::node().
	The following two expressions are equivalent:
	• //PRICE[. < 40]
	• //PRICE[self::node() < 40]
child	This indicates that the node-test is a child of the context node. It is the default axis value when no axis is explicitly specified for a node-test. Note that this axis cannot be used to return attribute or namespace nodes of the context node. Attributes and namespace nodes are not children of any node though they can have parent nodes.
	The following two expressions, where the node-test is the <PRICE> element node, are equivalent:
	• //PRICE
	• //child::PRICE
parent	This indicates that the node-test is a parent of the context node.
	The following will return the first <BOOK> element node if the context node is the <AUTHOR> element node with the value, "Eric Gunnerson:"
	• parent::BOOK[@ISBN]
descendant	A descendant of the context node can be any of its child elements or child of its child, etc. Note that this axis cannot be used to return attribute or namespace nodes of the context node.
	If the context node is the <BOOKS> element node, the following will return all the <TITLE> elements:
	• descendant::TITLE
descendant-or-self	This is similar to the descendant axis except that it may include the context node itself.
	If the context node is the <BOOKS> element node, the following first expression will return an empty node-set while the second expression will return the <BOOKS> element that is the context node itself:
	• descendant::BOOKS
	• descendant-or-self::BOOKS

(continued)

Table 2-7. List of Axes Defined in XPath 1.0 (continued)

AXIS	DESCRIPTION AND EXAMPLES
ancestor	An ancestor of the context node can be its parent or any node higher up in the tree hierarchy.
	The following expressions are examples of location step and the node-sets they return, assuming that the context node is the <PRICE> element node with value 34.95:
	• parent::BOOKS returns an empty node-set
	• ancestor::BOOKS returns the <BOOKS> element
	• ancestor::BOOK returns the first <BOOK> element shown in the tree structure in Figure 2-1
ancestor-or-self	This is similar to the ancestor axis except that it may include the context node itself.
	If the context node is the first <BOOK> element node (with ISBN value 1893115860), the following first expression will return an empty node-set while the second expression will return the <BOOK> element itself:
	• ancestor::BOOK
	• ancestor-or-self::BOOK
preceding-sibling	This axis includes all the sibling element nodes of the context node that precede it according to the document order. If the context node is an attribute or namespace node, it results in an empty node-set.
	The following expressions are examples of location step and the node-sets they return, assuming that the context node is the <BOOK> element node with the author, Michael Welschenbach:
	• preceding-sibling::BOOK returns the first <BOOK> element shown in the tree structure in Figure 2-1 with the string-value "A Programmer's Introduction to C# Eric Gunnerson 34.95"
	• preceding-sibling::TITLE returns an empty node-set
	• preceding-sibling::BOOKS returns an empty node-set
following-sibling	This axis includes all the sibling element nodes of the context node that follow it according to the document order. If the context node is an attribute or namespace node, it results in an empty node-set.

(continued)

Table 2-7. List of Axes Defined in XPath 1.0 (continued)

AXIS	DESCRIPTION AND EXAMPLES
	If the context node is the \<BOOK\> element node with the author Eric Gunnerson, the expression following-sibling::* will return the last \<BOOK\> element of BooksCatalog.xml with the string-value "Cryptography in C & C++ Michael Welschenbach 49.95 C++ for VB Programmers Jonathan Morrison 49.95."
	If the context node is the comment node within the first \<BOOK\> element of the tree structure shown in Figure 2.1, the expression following-sibling::AUTHOR will return the \<AUTHOR\> element with the string-value "Eric Gunnerson."
preceding	This is similar to preceding-sibling except that the preceding axis also includes all the descendant element nodes of the preceding siblings of the context node.
	The following expressions are examples of location step and the node-sets they return, assuming that the context node is the \<BOOK\> element node with the author Michael Welschenbach:
	• preceding::* returns the first \<BOOK\> element shown in the tree structure in Figure 2-1, as well as the \<TITLE\>, \<AUTHOR\> and \<PRICE\> elements of the first \<BOOK\> element
	• preceding::TITLE returns the \<TITLE\> element with the string-value A Programmer's Introduction to C#
following	This is similar to following-sibling except that the following axis also includes all the descendant element nodes of the following siblings of the context node.
	For example, if the context node is the \<BOOK\> element node with the author Michael Welschenbach, the expression following::* will return the third \<BOOK\> element of BooksCatalog.xml, as well as the \<TITLE\>, \<AUTHOR\> and \<PRICE\> elements of this third \<BOOK\> element.
attribute	This indicates that the node-test is an attribute of the context node.
	The following two expressions are equivalent:
	• @ISBN
	• attribute::ISBN

(continued)

Table 2-7. List of Axes Defined in XPath 1.0 (continued)

AXIS	DESCRIPTION AND EXAMPLES
namespace	This indicates that the node-test is a namespace of the context node.

- //child::BOOK[namespace::apress] returns all the <BOOK> elements in the document containing the context node, and which are from the namespace declared with the prefix name, *apress*. A possible namespace declaration for *apress* might be:

  `<BOOKS xmlns:apress="http://www.apress.com">`

- //child::BOOK[@ISBN='1893115860']/namespace::* returns all the namespaces of the <BOOK> elements in the document containing the context node, and which have an ISBN value as specified in the predicate.

An axis is described as a forward axis if it causes a traversal of the tree in accordance to the document order. Otherwise, it is called a reverse axis. Some examples of forward axes are child, descendant, and following. Examples of reverse axes include parent, ancestor, and preceding.

Functions

The XPath function library has a rich set of functions that you may use in an XPath expression.

As with the XPath expression, an XPath function returns a result that can be of any of the following valid types:

- Boolean

- Numeric

- String

- Node-set

Table 2-8 to Table 2-11 list, respectively, the functions defined in XPath 1.0 according to the return types, as well as alphabetical order of the function names within each table. The *object* type is used for any argument that can be of more than one of the basic types, namely Boolean, number, string, and node-set. Also, examples are given in cases where the definitions are less straightforward.

Table 2-8. Functions of the Boolean Type

FUNCTION	DESCRIPTION AND EXAMPLES
boolean(object obj)	The argument, obj, may be the Not-a-Number (NaN) constant, number, string, or node-set.
	This function converts its argument, obj, to the appropriate Boolean value based on the value of obj:
	• Number: If obj is zero or NaN, it is converted to false. If obj is any other number, it is converted to true. Hence, both the functions boolean(0) and boolean(NaN) return false while boolean(1.23) will return true.
	• String: If obj is a string of zero length, it is converted to false. Otherwise, it is converted to true.
	• Node-set: If obj is an empty node-set, it is converted to false. Otherwise, it is converted to true. If the context node is pointing to a <BOOK> element of BooksCatalog.xml, then boolean(child::TITLE) will return true while boolean(child::ISBN) will return false.
contains(string s1, string s2)	The function returns true if and only if s1 contains s2.
	If the context node is the second <BOOK> element of BooksCatalog.xml, then the function contains(child::TITLE, 'Crypto') will return true.
false()	This function simply returns the value false.
lang(string s)	The function returns true if s matches the value of the xml:lang attribute of either the context node or, in the case where the context does not have the attribute, the nearest ancestor node of the context node that has the xml:lang attribute.
	Consider the following XML document fragment:

	``xml
	<BOOKS>
	    <BOOK ISBN="1893115860" xml:lang="en">
	       <AUTHOR>Eric Gunnerson</AUTHOR>
	    </BOOK>
	    <BOOK ISBN="1893115763">
	       <AUTHOR>Jonathan Morrison</AUTHOR>
	    </BOOK>
	</BOOKS>
	``

	• If the context node points to the first <AUTHOR> element, lang('en') will return true but lang('fr') will return false.

(continued)

Table 2-8. Functions of the Boolean Type (continued)

FUNCTION	DESCRIPTION AND EXAMPLES
	• If the context node points to the second <AUTHOR> element, then both lang('en') and lang('fr') will return false.
not(boolean b)	This function is a negation of its argument. Hence, it returns true if b is false, and false if b is true.
starts-with(string s1, string s2)	The function returns true if and only if s1 starts with s2.
true()	This function simply returns the value true.

Table 2-9. Functions of the Node-Set Type

FUNCTION	DESCRIPTION AND EXAMPLES
id(object obj)	The argument obj may be a string or node-set. Otherwise, it is first converted into a string as if using the string() function.
	If obj is a string, the function returns the element with the unique ID specified as obj. If obj is a node-set, the function returns a node-set, which is the union of the result of applying the function with the argument that is the string-value of each node in obj.
	Assuming that the ISBN attribute for the <BOOK> element in BooksCatalog.xml has been declared in a DTD or Schema for validating the document to be an attribute that has unique ID value. And suppose the ISBN values used in the document follow the proper rules for a unique ID, then the function id(//@ISBN) will return all the books that have a proper ISBN value. Note that in this case, //@ISBN is evaluated to a node-set of all the three ISBN attribute nodes in the document.

Table 2-10. Functions of the Number Type

FUNCTION	DESCRIPTION AND EXAMPLES
ceiling(number n)	If n is not numeric, it is first converted into a number as if using the number() function.
	This function returns the smallest possible integer that is not less than n.
	For example, ceiling(1.23) returns the value 2.
count(node-set ns)	This function returns the number of nodes in ns.
	Consider the document BooksCatalog.xml:
	• count(//comment()) returns 1
	• count(//BOOK) returns 3

(continued)

Table 2-10. Functions of the Number Type (continued)

FUNCTION	DESCRIPTION AND EXAMPLES
floor(number n)	If n is not numeric, it is first converted into a number as if using the number() function.
	This function returns the largest possible integer that is not greater than n.
	For example, floor(1.99) returns the value 1.
last()	This function returns the context size, i.e., size of the node-set for the expression under evaluation.
	For example, //BOOK[last()] and //BOOK[3] are equivalent when used on BooksCatalog.xml since the size of the node-set indicated by //BOOK is 3.
number(object obj)	The argument, obj, is optional. If obj is supplied when the function is called, it can be a Boolean, string or node-set. If obj is not supplied, it defaults to a node-set that contains only the context node.
	If obj exists, it is converted based on the following rules:
	• String obj that consists of optional whitespace followed by an optional negation sign (-), followed by a number and optional whitespace is converted to the IEEE 754 number that is nearest to the mathematical value represented by the string. Any other string is converted to NaN.
	For example, number('-5.12') returns the numeric value -5.12 and number('abc') returns NaN.
	• Boolean true is converted to 1 and Boolean false is converted to 0. For example, number(true()) returns 1 and number(false()) returns 0.
	• Node-set obj is first converted to a string as if using the string() function and thereafter the first rule just specified for String obj is used.
position()	This function returns the context position from the context of the expression under evaluation. That is, it returns the position of the context node under evaluation.
	Positioning is labeled starting from 1 and it is in the order of traversal of the tree. Hence, the labeling order for a forward axis is the reverse of that for a reverse axis.
	Following are two examples that will make the definition clearer:
	• /BOOKS/BOOK[position()=last()] will return the <BOOK> element whose author is Jonathan Morrison

(continued)

Table 2-10. Functions of the Number Type (continued)

FUNCTION	DESCRIPTION AND EXAMPLES
	• If the context node is the <BOOK> element whose author is Jonathan Morrison, the location path preceding-sibling::BOOK[position()=last()] will return the <BOOK> element whose author is Eric Gunnerson since preceding-sibling is a reverse axis.
	• There is also an abbreviated format for specifying the desired position of a node we are looking for. Both //BOOK[position()=2] and //BOOK[2] are equivalent.
round(number n)	If n is not numeric, it is first converted into a number as if using the number() function.
	This function returns the integer that is closest to n. If n has a fractional value of 0.5, there are two integers that satisfy the first condition just specified. In this case, the integer closer to the positive infinity is returned.
	For example, round(1.12) returns the value 1, round(-1.5) returns -1, round('1.5') returns 2 and round('a') returns NaN.
string-length(string s)	The argument s is optional.
	If s is not supplied when the function is called, it defaults to the string-value of the context node.
	This function returns the number of characters in s. Consider the document BooksCatalog.xml. The function string-length(//AUTHOR[1]) will return the value 14, since //AUTHOR[1] points to the <AUTHOR> element with the string-value "Eric Gunnerson."
sum(node-set ns)	The function returns the sum of the result of converting the string-value of each node in ns to a number as if using the number() function.
	For example, sum(//attribute::Pages) will return the value 1137 using BooksCatalog.xml.

Table 2-11. Functions of the String Type

FUNCTION	DESCRIPTION AND EXAMPLES
concat(string s1, string s2, string s3)	There can be any number of arguments. Any non-string argument is first converted into a string as if using the string() function.
	This function returns the concatenation of all its string arguments from left to right.
local-name(node-set ns)	The argument ns is optional.
	If no argument is supplied, the default is a node-set that contains only the context node. The function returns the local name portion of the expanded-name of the first node in ns according to the document order. If ns is empty or if the first node of ns has no expanded-name, the function returns an empty string.
	Let's assume that we change the start-tag and end-tag of the first <BOOK> element of BooksCatalog.xml to <ap:Magz> and </ap:Magz> respectively, where ap is a properly declared namespace prefix. Then the function local-name(/BOOKS/child::*) will return the string "Magz".
	The function local-name(/BOOKS//comment()), on the other hand, will return an empty string since the comment node does not have an expanded-name.
name(node-set ns)	The argument ns is optional.
	If no argument is supplied, the default is a node-set that contains only the context node.
	The function returns the qualified name as used in the XML document to represent the expanded-name of the node in question. If ns is empty or if the first node of ns has no expanded-name, the function returns an empty string.
	Let's assume that we change the start-tag and end-tag of the first <BOOK> element of BooksCatalog.xml to <ap:Magz> and </ap:Magz> respectively, where ap is a properly declared namespace prefix. The function name(/BOOKS/child::*) will return the string "ap:Magz."
namespace-uri(node-set ns)	The argument ns is optional.
	If ns is not supplied when the function is called, it defaults to a node-set containing only the context node.
	This function returns the namespace URI of the first node (in the document order) of ns. The function will return an empty string if the nodes are not element or attribute nodes.

(continued)

Table 2-11. Functions of the String Type (continued)

FUNCTION	DESCRIPTION AND EXAMPLES
	For example, namespace-uri(//attribute::*) will return the namespace URI of the first attribute node of the document containing the context node, i.e., if indeed the first attribute node has a namespace.
normalize-space(string s)	The argument s is optional.
	If s is not supplied when the function is called, it defaults to the string-value of the context node.
	The function returns the result of stripping leading and trailing whitespace characters from s, and replacing sequences of whitespace characters in s by a single space.
	For example, normalize-space(' Eric Gunnerson') will return the string value "Eric Gunnerson."
string(object obj)	The argument obj is optional.
	If no argument is supplied, the default of obj is a node-set that contains only the context node.
	If obj exists, it is converted based on the following rules:
	• Boolean true is converted to the string "true" and Boolean false is converted to the string "false."
	• Node-set obj is converted to the string-value of the first node in obj. If the node-set is empty, an empty string is returned.
	• If obj has the value NaN, it is converted to the string "NaN."
	• If obj is positive 0 or negative 0, it is converted to the string "0."
	• If obj is positive infinity, it is converted to the string "Infinity." If obj is negative infinity, it is converted to the string "-Infinity."
	• If obj is an integer, it is converted to a string containing characters corresponding to the digits in the integer and in the same order as they appear in the original integer value. The resultant string must not have any leading zero and decimal point. Furthermore, it is preceded by a minus sign (-) if obj is a negative.
	• If obj is a real number, it is converted to a string containing characters corresponding to the digits and decimal point in the number and in the same order as they appear in the original real number. The

(continued)

Table 2-11. Functions of the String Type (continued)

FUNCTION	DESCRIPTION AND EXAMPLES
	resultant string must have one decimal point, at least one digit before and one digit after the decimal point. Other than being used as the one digit required to precede the decimal point, the resultant string should not have any other leading zeros. Also, it is preceded by a minus sign (-) if obj is negative. For example, if obj is 23.7, it is converted into the string "23.7."
substring(string s, number n1, number n2)	This function returns the substring of s starting at the position n1 of s, and the length of the substring is n2. The position of the first character of s is 1.
	For example, substring('Eric Gunnerson', 2, 8) will return the string "ric Gunn."
	n2 is optional. If it does not exist, the function returns the substring starting from position n1 till the end of the string s. The function substring('Eric Gunnerson', 2) will return the string "ric Gunnerson."
substring-after(string s1, string s2)	This function returns the substring of s1 that follows the first occurrence of s2 in s1. It returns an empty string if s1 does not contain s2.
	For example, substring-after('34.95', '.') will return "95," and substring-after('34.95', '34') will return ."95."
substring-before(string s1, string s2)	This function returns a substring of s1 that precedes the first occurrence of s2 in s1. It returns an empty string if s1 does not contain s2.
	For example, substring-before('34.95', '.') will return "34."
translate(string s1, string s2, string s3)	This function returns s1 with occurrences of characters in s2 replaced by the character at the corresponding position in s3.
	For example, translate('Eric', 'CDE', 'cde') will return "eric."
	The function translate('Eric', 'CDE', 'cd') will return "ric." i.e., any character in s2 that has no character in the corresponding position in s3 is dropped out of s1.

Abbreviated Syntax

Abbreviations may be used in an XPath expression to keep it shorter and more readable in certain situations. Table 2-12 lists the abbreviations that may be used in an XPath Expression.

Table 2-12. Abbreviations Used in an XPath Expression

ABBREVIATION	DESCRIPTION AND EXAMPLES
Default axis	A node-test without a preceding axis implies that the child axis should be used.
	The cumbersome full expression /child::BOOKS/child::BOOK[child::TITLE] can be simplified to /BOOKS/BOOK[TITLE].
.	This indicates the context node itself. It is an abbreviation for self::node().
..	This indicates the parent of the context node and is an abbreviation for parent::node().
	For example, the function name(..) returns the name of the parent element node of the context node.
@	This indicates the attribute of the context node and is an abbreviation of the attribute axis.
*	This is a wild-card character used to indicate all the child elements of the context node.
	For example, */child::BOOK returns all the <BOOK> elements who are grandchildren of the context node.
	The location path child::BOOK[child::TITLE]/@* returns all the attributes of the child <BOOK> elements of the context node that have one or more <TITLE> elements.
[position]	This indicates the position of a node in a node list and is an abbreviation of a predicate of the following format: [position()=x] where x is an expression that is evaluated to a numeric value.
	For example, child::BOOK[position()=2] can be simplified to child::BOOK[2].
/ - when not used it as root and delimiter	When the slash / symbol is used neither as a root nor a delimiter between location steps, it acts as an abbreviation for the descendant axis. Following are some examples using this abbreviation:
	• //BOOK indicates all <BOOK> descendants of the document root (indicated by the first /) containing the context node.
	• BOOKS//TITLE indicates all <TITLE> descendants (indicated by the second /) of all the <BOOKS> elements that are children of the context node.

Useful Web Links

For more information, we recommend you read:

- XML Path Language (XPath) Version 1.0 Specification on the Web at
  `http://www.w3.org/TR/1999/REC-xpath-19991116`

- XML 1.0 Specification (Second Edition) at
  `http://www.w3.org/TR/2000/REC-xml-20001006`

- IEEE Standard 754 Floating Point Numbers at the Microsoft Web site at
  `http://research.microsoft.com/~hollasch/cgindex/coding`
  `/ieeefloat.html`

- IEEE Standard 754 Floating Point Numbers at the IEEE Web site
  (Registration is required) at
  `http://standards.ieee.org/reading/ieee/std/busarch/754-1985.pdf`

Summary

In this chapter, we discussed XPath as a language to access parts of an XML document. We use XPath in the next chapter when we discuss another piece of the XML puzzle, namely transforming an XML document into another desired form.

CHAPTER 3

The Extensible Stylesheet Language Transformation (XSLT)

ONE OF THE DIFFERENCES between XML and HTML is that XML does not contain markup information. While XML concentrates on the content of the data it is describing, it lacks the necessary information for it to be displayed in a viewable format like HTML. As such, the Extensible Stylesheet Language (XSL) was developed to convert XML documents to a browser-friendly format like HTML.

> **NOTE**   *Note that using XSL to convert XML documents to HTML is just one of its uses. XSL is generally used to transform XML documents from one format to another as well as for formatting XML documents.*

The XSL is a language for describing a stylesheet. Because the original XSL was used for specifying formatting semantics as well as transforming XML formats, it was later decided to further split the XSL into three subcomponents:

- Extensible Stylesheet Language Transformation (XSLT). XSLT concentrates on transforming XML document formats.

- XML Path (XPath). XPath is an expression language used for referencing elements in an XML document. XPath was covered in Chapter 2.

- XSL Formatting Objects (XSL-FO). XSL-FO is used for specifying formatting semantics.

You have seen the XPath language in Chapter 2. In this chapter, we will focus on transforming XML documents using XSLT.

Motivation for XSLT

The current version of XSLT stands at version 1.0. It became a Recommendation by the World Wide Web Consortium (W3C) on November 16, 1999.

 NOTE *At the time of writing, XSLT 1.1 is being proposed. The working draft can be found on the Web at* `http://www.w3.org/TR/xslt11/`.

The primary motivation for XSLT is to transform the structure of an XML document from one format to another using an XSLT Processor, as shown in Figure 3-1.

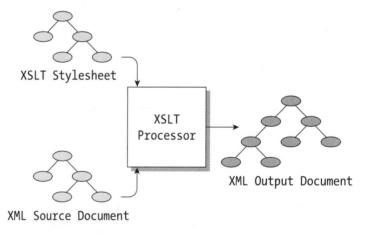

Figure 3-1. Transforming XML using XSLT

There are several popular XSLT processors available, which include:

- SAXON, developed by Michael Kay. Information is available on the Web at `http://users.iclway.co.uk/mhkay/saxon/`.

- XALAN, developed under the Apache XML project. Information is available on the Web at `http://xml.apache.org/xalan/index.html`.

- MSXML versions 2 and 3. Information is available on the Web at `http://msdn.microsoft.com/xml`.

In this chapter, we will use the MSXML3 for performing XSL Transformation.

An XSLT stylesheet is itself an XML document. As such, it follows the rules of XML, i.e., it must be well-formed. A typical XSLT stylesheet (Listing 3-1) has the following format.

Listing 3-1. A sample XSLT stylesheet

```
<?xml version="1.0"?>
<xsl:stylesheet xmlns:xsl="http://www.w3.org/1999/XSL/Transform" version="1.0">
    <xsl:template match="/">
        <!--Target markups-->
        <!--XSLT Elements-->
    </xsl:template>
</xsl:stylesheet>
```

Each component in Listing 3-1 is discussed in further detail in the following sections. We will discuss how to attach a stylesheet to an XML document in the section "Attaching the Stylesheet to the XML Document."

Processing Instructions

The processing instruction (PI) indicates that the stylesheet is an XML document:

```
<?xml version="1.0"?>
```

As mentioned previously, an XSLT stylesheet is an XML document; therefore, the PI is necessary.

Root Element of a Stylesheet

The <xsl:stylesheet> element is the root element of a stylesheet. This root element is a container for all other XSLT elements (described later in this chapter).

```
<xsl:stylesheet xmlns:xsl="http://www.w3.org/1999/XSL/Transform"  version="1.0">
```

The <xsl:stylesheet> element also defines the namespace for the "xsl" prefix. The current namespace for XSLT 1.0 is http://www.w3.org/1999/XSL/Transform.

It is important to key in the previous URI exactly as it is shown. If any character is missing or capitalized wrongly, the XSLT processor will not perform the transformation correctly. The use of this namespace is to inform the XSLT processor that this stylesheet adheres to the XSLT 1.0 specification and that the transformation process should behave as defined in the specification.

NOTE   *Users of Internet Explorer might encounter the name-space URL* `http://www.w3.org/TR/WD-xsl` *that is used in the older XSL stylesheets. Be aware that the MSXML3 parser supports this outdated namespace URI, which refers to the older XSL specification. All the examples used in this chapter use the newer namespace URI. Microsoft provides the xsl-xslt-converter.xslt stylesheet, which updates Microsoft Internet Explorer 5.0 XSL stylesheets to XSLT-compliant stylesheets. For more information, please refer to* `http://msdn.Microsoft.com/downloads/`.

Start of Transformation

The <xsl:template> element specifies a template and begins the transformation by looking for a node to start with.

```
<xsl:template match="/">
```

Within the template, you can embed target markups that you want to generate. For example, if you are generating HTML, you can insert HTML tags within the template. You can also use other XSLT elements to perform more complex transformation.

In the latter part of this chapter (XSLT Elements), we talk about XSLT elements in more detail.

Support of XSLT in MSXML3

The MSXML3 fully supports the XSLT and XPath version 1.0 of the World Wide Web Consortium (W3C) recommendations. In addition, MSXML3 maintains backward compatibility with the implementations of Section 2 of the December 1998 XSL Working Draft of Extensible Stylesheet Language (XSL). There is no support for XSL formatting objects though. Table 3.1 shows the namespace to use for each version of XSL(T).

Table 3-1. Namespaces Used in XSL(T)

VERSION	NAMESPACE
XSLT 1.0 Namespace URI	`http://www.w3.org/1999/XSL/Transform`
XSL WD Namespace URI	`http://www.w3.org/TR/WD-xsl`

A First Look at XSLT

Let's look at a simple XSLT stylesheet in action. In this example, we have two documents, an XML document whose format you want to transform and a stylesheet that performs the actual transformation.

The XML Document

Consider the following XML document that is displayed in Listing 3-2.

Listing 3-2. Books.xml

```
<?xml version="1.0"?>
<BOOKS>
  <BOOK Pages="357" Type="SOFTCOVER">
     <TITLE>A Programmer's Introduction to C#</TITLE>
     <AUTHOR>Eric Gunnerson</AUTHOR>
     <ISBN>1893115860</ISBN>
     <SYNOPSIS>Eric Gunnerson, the test lead for and member of Microsoft's
C# design team, has written a comprehensive C# tutorial for programmers to help
them get up to speed</SYNOPSIS>
     <PRICE>$34.95 </PRICE>
  </BOOK>
</BOOKS>
```

Instead of displaying the XML document in the default hierarchical structure in Internet Explorer 5.0, we want to display it in HTML. To do so, we have to transform the XML document into HTML using an XSLT stylesheet.

The XSLT Stylesheet

The XSLT stylesheet that is used to transform Books.xml into an HTML format is displayed in Listing 3-3.

Listing 3-3. HTML.xsl

```
<?xml version="1.0"?>
<xsl:stylesheet xmlns:xsl="http://www.w3.org/1999/XSL/Transform" version="1.0">
<xsl:template match="/">
<html>
```

```
<body>
   <table cellspacing="0" border="1">
      <font face="Arial,Helvetica,Univers,Zurich BT" color="#69002f" size="-1">
         <b><xsl:value-of select="BOOKS/BOOK/TITLE"/></b>
      </font><br/>
         <tr><td width="175" bgColor="#f4f4ef">
         <font face="Arial,Helvetica,Univers,Zurich BT" size="-2">
         by <xsl:value-of select="BOOKS/BOOK/AUTHOR"/>
         </font><BR/></td></tr>
         <tr><td width="175" bgColor="#e5e5d8">
         <font face="Arial,Helvetica,Univers,Zurich BT" size="-2">
         <xsl:value-of select="BOOKS/BOOK/@Type"/>,
         <xsl:value-of select="BOOKS/BOOK/@Pages"/> PAGES
         </font><BR/></td></tr>
         <tr><td width="175" bgColor="#f4f4ef">
         <font face="Arial,Helvetica,Univers,Zurich BT" size="-1">
         <b>ISBN:</b> <xsl:value-of select="BOOKS/BOOK/ISBN"/>
         </font><BR/></td></tr>
         <tr><td width="175" bgColor="#e5e5d8">
         <font face="Arial,Helvetica,Univers,Zurich BT" size="-1">
         <b>PRICE: </b><xsl:value-of select="BOOKS/BOOK/PRICE"/>
         </font><BR/></td></tr>
   </table>
</body>
</html>
</xsl:template>
</xsl:stylesheet>
```

Within the stylesheet, there is a namespace declared with the prefix "xsl." The stylesheet itself contains two types of tags:

Tags belonging to the target output: HTML in this case, e.g., <html>, <b>, etc.

Tags specific to XSLT: Indicated by tag names with the "xsl" prefix. These are called *XSLT elements*, e.g., <xsl:stylesheet>, <xsl:template>, etc.

The XSLT elements are the instructions that manipulate the XML document while the rest of the tags in the stylesheet are simply copied into the target output.

Attaching the Stylesheet to the XML Document

Once you create the stylesheet, you need to attach it to the XML document using the <?xml:stylesheet?> PI:

```
<?xml version="1.0"?>
<?xml:stylesheet type="text/xsl" href="HTML.xsl"?>
<BOOKS>
```

That's it! We can now see the XSLT transformation in action!

Transformation by Internet Explorer

Using Internet Explorer 5.0, you can load the XML document through the File ➤ Open method. Internet Explorer performs the XSL transformation and loads the document, as shown in Figure 3-2.

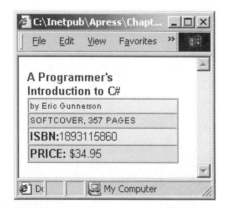

Figure 3-2. Internet Explorer performs the XSL transformation

The XSLT stylesheet has transformed the XML document into HTML. To confirm that the Web browser is really seeing HTML, right-click on the Web page and select View XSL Output, as shown in Figure 3-3. (You need to have the Internet Explorer Tool installed. See Appendix A for installation information.)

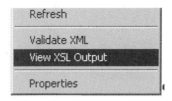

Figure 3-3. Confirming the XSL output

The HTML that is generated by Internet Explorer is shown in Figure 3-4.

```
XSL Transformation Ouput - Microsoft Internet Explorer                                    _ |□| x|
<html>
<body>
<table cellspacing="0" border="1">
<font face="Arial,Helvetica,Univers,Zurich BT" color="#69002f" size="-1"><b>A Programmer's Introdu
        by Eric Gunnerson</font><BR></td></tr>
<tr><td width="175" bgColor="#e5e5d8"><font face="Arial,Helvetica,Univers,Zurich BT" size="-2">S
<tr><td width="175" bgColor="#f4f4ef"><font face="Arial,Helvetica,Univers,Zurich BT" size="-1"><b:
<tr><td width="175" bgColor="#e5e5d8"><font face="Arial,Helvetica,Univers,Zurich BT" size="-1"><d
</table>
</body>
</html>
```

Figure 3-4. HTML generated by Internet Explorer

Behind the Scenes

It is time to take a closer look at what goes on behind the scenes to understand how XSLT works (Figure 3-5).

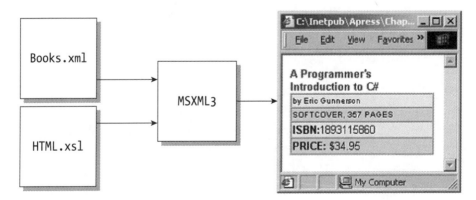

Figure 3-5. MSXML3 uses the XML document and the XSL stylesheet to produce HTML.

The MSXML3 (Internet Explorer 5.0 in this case) uses two documents:

- Books.xml

- HTML.xsl

It then churns out the HTML output based on the instructions in the stylesheet. Let's dissect the stylesheet to see how it transforms the XML document into HTML.

```
<?xml version="1.0"?>
<xsl:stylesheet xmlns:xsl="http://www.w3.org/1999/XSL/Transform" version="1.0">
<xsl:template match="/">
<html>
<body>
    <table cellspacing="0" border="1">
        <font face="Arial,Helvetica,Univers,Zurich BT" color="#69002f" size="-1">
            <b><xsl:value-of select="BOOKS/BOOK/TITLE"/></b>
        </font><br/>
        <tr><td width="175" bgColor="#f4f4ef">
        <font face="Arial,Helvetica,Univers,Zurich BT" size="-2">
        by <xsl:value-of select="BOOKS/BOOK/AUTHOR"/>
        </font><BR/></td></tr>
        <tr><td width="175" bgColor="#e5e5d8">
        <font face="Arial,Helvetica,Univers,Zurich BT" size="-2">
            <xsl:value-of select="BOOKS/BOOK/@Type"/>,
            <xsl:value-of select="BOOKS/BOOK/@Pages"/> PAGES
        </font><BR/></td></tr>
        <tr><td width="175" bgColor="#f4f4ef">
        <font face="Arial,Helvetica,Univers,Zurich BT" size="-1">
            <b>ISBN:</b> <xsl:value-of select="BOOKS/BOOK/ISBN"/>
        </font><BR/></td></tr>
        <tr><td width="175" bgColor="#e5e5d8">
        <font face="Arial,Helvetica,Univers,Zurich BT" size="-1">
            <b>PRICE: </b><xsl:value-of select="BOOKS/BOOK/PRICE"/>
        </font><BR/></td></tr>
    </table>
</body>
</html>
</xsl:template>
</xsl:stylesheet>
```

The stylesheet starts with the <xsl:stylesheet> element. The <xsl:stylesheet> element is the topmost element in a stylesheet and it defines the XSLT namespace. In our example we use "xsl" as the prefix for XSLT elements but it is perfectly all right to use another name. For example, you can declare the XSLT namespace as "xslt." In doing so, all subsequent references to XSLT elements must then start with the "xslt" prefix. Therefore, since we've used "xsl" as the prefix, all subsequent elements must be prefixed with "xsl."

```
<xsl:stylesheet xmlns:xsl="http://www.w3.org/1999/XSL/Transform" version="1.0">
```

The next element in the stylesheet is <xsl:template>. This element contains an attribute named match. The value of / indicates to match the stylesheet against the root node of the XML document (which is the start of the XML document; not the root element). We will talk more about the <xsl:template> element later on.

```
<xsl:template match="/">
```

The next few lines of the stylesheet are HTML codes that are simply copied to the output. Note that as the stylesheet is based on XML, all the non-XSLT elements tags inserted must adhere to the XML rules—that is, rules of well-formedness. This is evident by the <br/> elements in the stylesheet.

The next XSLT element: <xsl:value-of> retrieves the book title.

```
<xsl:value-of select="BOOKS/BOOK/TITLE"/>
```

The selection is based on the XPath value of the select attribute. The value of "BOOKS/BOOK/TITLE" looks for the <TITLE> element, which is a child of <BOOK>. The <BOOK> element, in turn, is a child of <BOOKS>.

Retrieving Attributes

To retrieve the value of an attribute, simply precede the attribute name with the @ character, as can be seen in the following line:

```
<xsl:value-of select="BOOKS/BOOK/@Type"/>
```

The end result of the transformation is that HTML codes are produced. The HTML codes are then displayed on the Web browser as shown previously.

XSLT Fundamentals

In this section, we discuss XSLT elements and XSLT functions in more details and see how they can be useful to your developmental work.

XSLT Elements

Now that you have looked at XSLT in action, let's look at XSLT progressively in more detail by using shorter examples. Consider the XML document that is provided in Listing 3-4.

Listing 3-4. TourGuides.xml

```xml
<?xml version="1.0"?>
<TourGuides>
    <TourOperator contact="(08)93222006">
        <OperatorName>Perth Trams</OperatorName>
        <Type>City Tram Tour</Type>
    </TourOperator>
    <TourOperator contact="(08)94217223">
        <OperatorName>The Perth Mint</OperatorName>
        <Type>Historical Walk and Gold Pour</Type>
    </TourOperator>
</TourGuides>
```

For purposes of understanding the transformation, we represent this XML document as a tree, as shown in Figure 3-6.

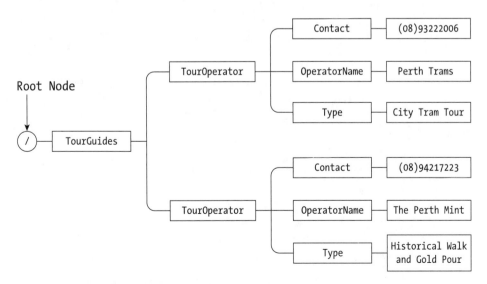

Figure 3-6. Representing the XML document as a tree

<xsl:template> and <xsl:value-of>

Let's first look at the <xsl:template> element. Consider the template:

```
<xsl:template match="/">
    <xsl:value-of select="TourGuides/TourOperator/Type"/>
</xsl:template>
```

The <xsl:template> element first matches the root node of the XML tree. After the matching, the root node is the context node, as explained in Chapter 2. The <xsl:value-of> element retrieves the value of the node as indicated by the select attribute. In this case, it looks for the pattern "TourGuides/TourOperator/Type." It will retrieve the first instance of such pattern. The preceding template will return:

```
City Tram Tour
```

If we want to display the contact number of this particular tour operator, we can modify our template to retrieve the value of the contact attribute:

```
<xsl:template match="/">
    <xsl:value-of select="TourGuides/TourOperator/@contact"/>
</xsl:template>
```

The @ character preceding the attribute name contact indicates that contact is an attribute.

<xsl:for-each>

While the previous example displays information about the first tour operator, we might want to display all the tour operators in the XML document. In such cases, we can use the <xsl:for-each> element to display information about all tour operators, as shown in Listing 3-5.

Listing 3-5. Using the <xsl:for-each> element for locating repeating patterns

```
<xsl:template match="/">
    <xsl:for-each select="TourGuides/TourOperator">
        <xsl:value-of select="OperatorName"/> -
        <xsl:value-of select="@contact"/>
    </xsl:for-each>
</xsl:template>
```

The <xsl:template> element first matches with the root node of the XML document and sets it as the context node. Next the <xsl:for-each> element matches all nodes in the XML document, which has the following pattern:

```
<TourGuides>
    <TourOperator>
```

In our XML document, we have two such patterns. The <xsl:for-each> element acts like a conventional looping construct in programming languages. In the first iteration, the context node would be changed to point to the first tour operator (as indicated in bold):

```
<TourGuides>
    <TourOperator contact="(08)93222006">
        <OperatorName>Perth Trams</OperatorName>
        <Type>City Tram Tour</Type>
    </TourOperator>
    <TourOperator contact="(08)94217223">
        <OperatorName>The Perth Mint</OperatorName>
        <Type>Historical Walk and Gold Pour</Type>
    </TourOperator>
</TourGuides>
```

The second iteration would set the context node to point to the second tour operator:

```
<TourGuides>
    <TourOperator contact="(08)93222006">
        <OperatorName>Perth Trams</OperatorName>
        <Type>City Tram Tour</Type>
    </TourOperator>
    <TourOperator contact="(08)94217223">
        <OperatorName>The Perth Mint</OperatorName>
        <Type>Historical Walk and Gold Pour</Type>
    </TourOperator>
</TourGuides>
```

Therefore, the XSL template shown in Listing 3-5 will produce the following output:

```
Perth Trams - (08)93222006
The Perth Mint - (08)94217223
```

Using the Recursive Descent Operation (//)

The preceding template can also be rewritten using the *recursive descent operator (//)*. The recursive descent operator looks for all occurrences of a particular element or attribute, regardless of their locations in the XML document. Consider the following example:

```
<xsl:template match="//TourOperator">
    <xsl:value-of select="OperatorName"/> -
    <xsl:value-of select="@contact"/>
</xsl:template>
```

In the preceding template, all <TourOperator> elements in the XML document would be matched (regardless of their relative location). However, this method forces the XSLT processor to search through the whole XML document to find the required element and hence is not a very efficient way of retrieving elements. The advantage of using this method is that it provides you with a quick and easy way to retrieve text without needing to know the structure of a document.

<xsl:apply-templates>

It is also possible to list all the tour operator names followed by all the tour types available. In this case, we can use the <xsl:apply-templates> element to accomplish that. Listing 3-6 provides an example of using this feature.

Listing 3-6. Using the <xsl:apply-templates> element to match other templates

```
<xsl:template match="/">
    <xsl:apply-templates select="TourGuides/TourOperator/OperatorName"/>
    <xsl:apply-templates select="TourGuides/TourOperator/Type"/>
</xsl:template>

<xsl:template match="OperatorName">
    <xsl:value-of select="."/>
</xsl:template>

<xsl:template match="TourOperator">
    <xsl:value-of select="."/>
</xsl:template>
```

Three <xsl:template> elements are present in Listing 3-6. The first <xsl:template> element provides the starting point for the root node to be matched. Within it contains two <xsl:apply-templates> elements. The first such element will look for the template that matches "TourGuides/ TourOperator/OperatorName." The second <xsl:template> element matches the pattern "TourGuides/TourOperator/Type." Here is the match for the first pattern:

```
<xsl:template match="OperatorName">
   <xsl:value-of select="."/>
</xsl:template>

<xsl:template match="TourOperator">
   <xsl:value-of select="."/>
</xsl:template>
```

The <xsl:value-of> element will retrieve the value of the <OperatorName> element. Since there are two such patterns ("TourGuides/TourOperator/ OperatorName") in the XML document, the two operator names are retrieved.

The second <xsl:apply-templates> element performs a similar function as the first one, except that it is now looking for the <Type> element:

```
<xsl:apply-templates select="TourGuides/TourOperator/Type"/>
```

The third <xsl:template> element is matched as follows:

```
<xsl:template match="OperatorName">
   <xsl:value-of select="."/>
</xsl:template>

<xsl:template match="TourOperator">
   <xsl:value-of select="."/>
</xsl:template>
```

This is the output generated:

```
Perth Trams
The Perth Mint
City Tram Tour
Historical Walk and Gold Pour
```

A good way to visualize the <xsl:apply-templates> element is to imagine that you are calling a function. And all the <xsl:template> elements are functions waiting to be called.

<xsl:if>

As in all programming languages, XSLT includes decision-making elements that allow conditional processing. The decision-making element in XSLT is the <xsl:if> element, as shown in Listing 3-7.

Listing 3-7. Using the <xsl:if> element for decision making

```
<?xml version="1.0"?>
<Magazines>
    <Magazine Price="5.95">
        <Title>SQL Server magazine</Title>
        <Publisher>Penton</Publisher>
    </Magazine>
    <Magazine Price="4.95">
        <Title>Web Techniques</Title>
        <Publisher>CMP</Publisher>
    </Magazine>
    <Magazine Price="4.99">
        <Title>Wireless Business and Technology</Title>
        <Publisher>Sys-con media</Publisher>
    </Magazine>
    <Magazine Price="5.95">
        <Title>MSDN</Title>
        <Publisher>CMP</Publisher>
    </Magazine>
</Magazines>
```

Suppose you want to display the title of all magazines that cost more than $5. Here is the template that accomplishes that:

```
<xsl:template match="/">
    <xsl:for-each select="Magazines/Magazine">
        <xsl:if test="@Price &gt; 5">
            <xsl:value-of select="Title"/>
        </xsl:if>
    </xsl:for-each>
</xsl:template>
```

You will get the following:

```
SQL Server magazine
MSDN
```

The selection is performed by the <xsl:if> element. The <xsl:if> element contains an attribute called test. The <xsl:if> element is a conditional statement and the condition is specified in the test attribute.

> **NOTE** *You can actually use XPath predicates (filtering) to accomplish the preceding example. But the use of the <xsl:if> element in this example is only for illustration purposes. XPath is discussed in Chapter 2.*

<xsl:choose> and *<xsl:when>*

Multiple <xsl:if> elements make the codes unnecessarily complex. XSLT provides a SELECT-like element pair known as <xsl:choose> and <xsl:when>.

Now suppose we want to categorize the magazines into three categories with the following price range:

Category A: Less than $5

Category B: From $5 to less than $5.50

Category C: $5.50 or more

You can write the template using multiple <xsl:if> elements like this:

```
<xsl:template match="/">
    <xsl:for-each select="Magazines/Magazine">
        <xsl:value-of select="Title"/> -
        <xsl:if test="@Price &lt; 5">
            Category A
        </xsl:if>
        <xsl:if test="@Price &gt;= 5 and @Price &lt; 5.5">
            Category B
        </xsl:if>
        <xsl:if test="@Price &gt;= 5.5">
```

```
            Category C
        </xsl:if>
    </xsl:for-each>
</xsl:template>
```

You will get the following output:

```
SQL Server magazine - Category C
Web Techniques - Category A
Wireless Business and Technology - Category B
MSDN - Category C
```

Well, this is really unwieldy. Fortunately, XSLT provides a select-equivalent kind of element known as <xsl:choose>. Another element, <xsl:when> is used in conjunction with the <xsl:choose> element. The following template illustrates the use of these two elements:

```
<xsl:template match="/">
    <xsl:for-each select="Magazines/Magazine">
        <xsl:value-of select="Title"/> -
        <xsl:choose>
            <xsl:when test="@Price &lt; 5">Category A</xsl:when>
            <xsl:when test="@Price &gt;= 5 and @Price &lt; 5.5">Category B</xsl:when>
            <xsl:when test="@Price &gt;= 5.5">Category C</xsl:when>
        </xsl:choose>
    </xsl:for-each>
</xsl:template>
```

This will produce the exact same output as the previous one, but it sure looks much neater using the <xsl:choose> and <xsl:when> elements. In fact, this works much like the Select/Case construct does in Visual Basic.

<xsl:variable>

Like all programming languages, XSLT allows you to create variables. Consider the following example:

```
<xsl:variable name="GST" select="3"/>
<xsl:template match="/">
    The Good and Services Tax rate is <xsl:value-of select="$GST"/> %
</xsl:template>
```

We use the <xsl:variable> element to declare a variable called GST and sets it to a value of 3 using the select attribute:

```
<xsl:variable name="GST" select="3"/>
```

In fact, we can rewrite this line without using the select attribute:

```
<xsl:variable name="GST">3</xsl:variable>
```

To retrieve the value of the variable, simply precede the variable name with the $ character:

```
The Good and Services Tax rate is <xsl:value-of select="$GST"/> %
```

Variables allow more complicated and involved operations to be performed in a stylesheet.

XSLT Functions

Besides supporting the functions defined in XPath (refer to chapter 2 for more information about XPath functions), XSLT also provides some useful functions. Table 3-2 lists the XSLT functions provided by MSXML3.

Table 3-2. XSLT Functions

XSLT FUNCTION	DESCRIPTION
current	Returns a node set that has the current node as its only member.
element-available	Returns True if and only if the expanded-name is the name of an instruction.
format-number	Converts the first argument to a string using the format pattern string specified by the second argument.
function-available	Returns True if the function is available in the function library.
generate-id	Returns a string that uniquely identifies the node in the *node-set* argument that is first in document order.
node-set	Converts a tree into a node set. The resulting node always contains a single node and the root node of the tree.
system-property	Returns an object representing the value of the system property identified by the name.
unparsed-entity-uri	Returns declarations of unparsed entities in the document type definition (DTD) of the source document

Let's first look at an example involving XPath functions.

NOTE   *XPath functions are discussed in Chapter 2.*

The following stylesheet in Listing 3-8 shows how XPath functions can be used to perform simple arithmetic operations.

Listing 3-8. Using XPath functions

```
<?xml version="1.0"?>
<xsl:stylesheet xmlns:xsl="http://www.w3.org/1999/XSL/Transform" version="1.0">
<xsl:variable name="amt">5</xsl:variable>
<xsl:template match="/">
   There are <xsl:value-of select="count(Magazines/Magazine/Title)"/>
   magazines in this document costing a total of $
   <xsl:value-of select="sum(Magazines/Magazine/@Price)"/>.
   There are <xsl:value-of select="count(Magazines/Magazine[@Price&lt;=5])"/>
```

```
    magazines costing $<xsl:value-of select="$amt"/> or less.
    The rest cost more than $<xsl:value-of select="$amt"/>, they are:
    <xsl:for-each select="Magazines/Magazine[@Price&lt;=5$amt]">
        <xsl:value-of select="Title"/>
    </xsl:for-each>
</xsl:template>
</xsl:stylesheet>
```

In Listing 3-8, we want to find out the total cost of all the magazines in the document as well as print out all the magazines that cost more than $5. We first count the total number of magazines using the count() function:

```
There are <xsl:value-of select="count(Magazines/Magazine/Title)"/>
magazines in this document costing a total of $
<xsl:value-of select="sum(Magazines/Magazine/@Price)"/>.
```

The count() function takes in an XPath expression and returns an integer value containing the number of such occurrences. To sum up the total prices of all the magazines, use the sum() function:

```
There are <xsl:value-of select="count(Magazines/Magazine/Title)"/>
magazines in this document costing a total of
$<xsl:value-of select="sum(Magazines/Magazine/@Price)"/>.
```

Next, we use the <xsl:for-each> element to iteratively display all magazines that are priced more than $5:

```
    <xsl:for-each select="Magazines/Magazine[@Price&gt;$amt]">
        <xsl:value-of select="Title"/>
    </xsl:for-each>
```

The preceding template will produce the following output:

```
There are 4 magazines in this document costing a total of $21.85.
There are 2 magazines costing $5 or less.
The rest cost more than $5, they are:
SQL Server magazine
MSDN
```

If we need to selectively print out the magazine titles based on their positioning in the XML document, we can use the position() function. For example, if we want to print out the third magazine in the XML document, we have:

```
<xsl:value-of select="Magazines/Magazine[position()=3]/Title"/>
```

Alternatively, we can rewrite this line as:

```
<xsl:value-of select="Magazines/Magazine[3]/Title"/>
```

To format the display of the total price, you can use the XSLT function format-number(). The following line of code will display the total price as "21.9" using the format pattern string "0.0" :

```
<xsl:value-of select="format-number(sum(Magazines/Magazine/@Price), '0.0')"/>
```

Table 3-3 shows the different output controlled by the format pattern string.

Table 3-3. Examples Using the XSLT Function—format-number()

NUMBER	FORMAT PATTERN STRING	RESULT
21.85	0.0	21.9
21.85	0.00	21.85
21.85	000.00	021.85
1985.90	#,###.00	1,985.90
1985.90	###.00	1,985.90
1985.90	#,###.##	1,985.9

Transforming XML Document Structure with XSLT

We have looked at the fundamentals of XSLT in the last section. In this section, we focus on how we can use XSLT to transform an XML document structure from one format to another. In the real world, business entities might use XML for information interchange and it is rarely the case where the XML document structure is uniform among all communicating parties. In such cases, it is necessary to transform an XML document from one structure to another.

Copying XML Elements Using <xsl:copy> and <xsl:copy-of>

Often, we only want to transform a certain portion of an XML document and simply copy the rest of the document to the output. In this case, we can use the <xsl:copy> and <xsl:copy-of> elements for this purpose.

Let's examine the following XML document:

```
<?xml version="1.0"?>
<html>
    <body>
        <p>It is the rule in war, if our forces are ten to the enemy's one, to
<b>surround</b> him; if five to one, to <b>attack him</b>; if twice as
numerous, to divide our army into two.</p>
    </body>
</html>
```

After applying a stylesheet, we might want to retain certain markups in the source document, for example the <p> elements. To do so, we can use the <xsl:copy> and <xsl:copy-of> elements. Let's see how it is done:

```
<xsl:template match="/">
    <xsl:for-each select="html/body/p">
        <xsl:copy/>
    </xsl:for-each>
</xsl:template>
```

The template will produce the result:

```
<p />
```

What it does is simply copy the context node into the output. In this case the context node is <p>. Actually, this is not what we want, as we want to copy out the content of the element. We should change it to:

```
<xsl:template match="/">
    <xsl:for-each select="html/body/p">
        <xsl:copy>
            <xsl:value-of select="."/>
        </xsl:copy>
    </xsl:for-each>
</xsl:template>
```

You should then get the output:

```
<p>It is the rule in war, if our forces are ten to the enemy's one, to surround
him; if five to one, to attack him; if twice as numerous, to divide our army
into two.</p>
```

The preceding template can be interpreted as "copy the <p> element and all its content into the output." Recall that the <xsl:value-of> element retrieves the value of the node, including its child nodes.

While the preceding template copies the <p> element and its content, we have lost the formatting elements <b> within the <p> element. To copy the content of <p>, including its child nodes tags, we can use the <xsl:copy-of> element:

```
<xsl:template match="/">
    <xsl:for-each select="html/body/p">
        <xsl:copy-of select="."/>
    </xsl:for-each>
</xsl:template>
```

The preceding template will copy the following:

```
<p>It is the rule in war, if our forces are ten to the enemy's one, to
<b>surround</b> him; if five to one, to <b>attack him</b>; if twice
as numerous, to divide our army into two.</p>
```

To summarize, the <xsl:copy-of> element will perform a "deep copy," including child elements.

Creating Attributes Using <xsl:attribute>

There are many times when you want to reformat the layout of an XML document. For example, an XML document might only contain elements and you might want to reformat them using a mixture of elements and attributes. To see how this can be done, let's use the previous example on magazines:

```
<?xml version="1.0"?>
<Magazines>
    <Magazine Price="5.95">
        <Title>SQL Server magazine</Title>
        <Publisher>Penton</Publisher>
    </Magazine>
    <Magazine Price="4.95">
        <Title>Web Techniques</Title>
        <Publisher>CMP</Publisher>
    </Magazine>
    <Magazine Price="4.99">
        <Title>Wireless Business and Technology</Title>
        <Publisher>Sys-con media</Publisher>
    </Magazine>
    <Magazine Price="5.95">
        <Title>MSDN</Title>
        <Publisher>CMP</Publisher>
    </Magazine>
</Magazines>
```

We want to represent Publisher as an attribute; therefore, the template appears like this:

```
<xsl:template match="/Magazines">
  <xsl:for-each select="Magazine">
     <xsl:copy>
        <xsl:attribute name="Publisher">
           <xsl:value-of select="Publisher/." />
        </xsl:attribute>
        <xsl:attribute name="Price">
           <xsl:value-of select="@Price"/>
        </xsl:attribute>
        <xsl:copy-of select="Title"/>
     </xsl:copy>
  </xsl:for-each>
</xsl:template>
```

We first look for all the <Magazine> elements and then copy the element itself and add all the necessary attributes to it using the <xsl:attribute> element. We also copy the <Title> element to the output.

The preceding template will produce the following output:

```
<Magazine Publisher="Penton" Price="5.95">
    <Title>SQL Server magazine</Title>
</Magazine>
<Magazine Publisher="CMP" Price="4.95">
    <Title>Web Techniques</Title>
</Magazine>
<Magazine Publisher="Sys-con media" Price="5.00">
    <Title>Wireless Business and Technology</Title>
</Magazine>
<Magazine Publisher="CMP" Price="5.95">
    <Title>MSDN</Title>
</Magazine>
```

The publisher is now represented as an attribute.

Creating Elements Using <xsl:element>

Besides creating attributes, we can also create new elements using the <xsl:element> element. For example, the following template shows how new elements are created:

```
<xsl:template match="/Magazines/Magazine">
    <xsl:element name="{name()}">
       <xsl:value-of select="Title"/>
    </xsl:element>
</xsl:template>
```

The new elements in the template create the following output:

```
<Magazine>SQL Server magazine</Magazine>
<Magazine>Web Techniques</Magazine>
<Magazine>Wireless Business and Technology</Magazine>
<Magazine>MSDN</Magazine>
```

 NOTE *The braces {} convert the result of name() to a string.*

The <xsl:value-of> element within the <xsl:element> element specifies the name of the element to create.

Controlling Output with <xsl:output>

The default output of an XML transformation is an XML document. Consider the XSLT document shown in Listing 3-9.

Listing 3-9. Using the <xsl:output> element to control output of the transformation

```
<?xml version="1.0"?>
<xsl:stylesheet xmlns:xsl="http://www.w3.org/1999/XSL/Transform" version="1.0">
    <xsl:template match="/Magazines">
        <xsl:for-each select="Magazine">
            <b><xsl:value-of select="Title"/></b><br/>
            <i><xsl:value-of select="Publisher"/></i><br/>
            <i><xsl:value-of select="@Price"/></i><br/>
        </xsl:for-each>
    </xsl:template>
</xsl:stylesheet>
```

The preceding template will produce the following output:

```
<?xml version="1.0" encoding="UTF-16"?><b>SQL Server magazine</b><br />
<i>Penton</i><br /><i>5.95</i><br /><b>Web Techniques</b><br /><i>CMP</i>
<br /><i>4.95</i><br /><b>Wireless Business and Technology</b><br />
<i>Sys-con media</i><br /><i>5.00</i><br /><b>MSDN</b><br /><i>CMP</i>
<br /><i>5.95</i><br />
```

The XML Processing Instruction (PI) at the top of the output document indicates that this is an XML document. What happens if we want to format this as HTML? We just need to insert the <html> tags, like this:

```
<?xml version="1.0"?>
<xsl:stylesheet xmlns:xsl="http://www.w3.org/1999/XSL/Transform" version="1.0">
    <xsl:template match="/Magazines">
        <html>
        <xsl:for-each select="Magazine">
            <b><xsl:value-of select="Title"/></b><br/>
            <i><xsl:value-of select="Publisher"/></i><br/>
            <i><xsl:value-of select="@Price"/></i><br/>
```

```
        </xsl:for-each>
        </html>
    </xsl:template>
</xsl:stylesheet>
```

These modified templates will then produce the following output:

```
<html><b>SQL Server magazine</b><br><i>Penton</i><br><i>5.95</i><br>
<b>Web Techniques</b><br><i>CMP</i><br><i>4.95</i><br><b>Wireless
Business and Technology</b><br><i>Sys-con media</i><br><i>5.00</i><br>
<b>MSDN</b><br><i>CMP</i><br><i>5.95</i><br></html>
```

As you can see, the XML PI is no longer there! This is because of the presence of the <html> tag in the template. Either the <html> or <HTML> tag will cause the XML PI to be omitted. When the XSLT Processor (MSXML3 in this case) sees the <html> tag, it presumes that you are generating HTML output and omits the XML PI. Also note that the <br/> element has been modified to <br>, since HTML browsers do not expect to see
 (although they will still work when they see one).

However, there are times when you want to transform an XML document into a format other than HTML, and yet you want to omit the PI. For example, you might want to format an XML document into the Wireless Markup Language (WML), covered in Chapter 9. In this case, you do not want the output to contain a PI as the WML deck has its own set of prologue (more on that in the chapter on WML). To do so, you can use the <xsl:output> element to explicitly control the output format, as shown in Listing 3-10.

Listing 3-10. Using the `<xsl:output>` element to suppress the XML PI

```
<?xml version="1.0"?>
<xsl:stylesheet xmlns:xsl="http://www.w3.org/1999/XSL/Transform" version="1.0">
<xsl:output method="xml" indent="yes" omit-xml-declaration="yes" />
    <xsl:template match="/Magazines">
        <xsl:for-each select="Magazine">
            <b><xsl:value-of select="Title"/></b><br/>
            <i><xsl:value-of select="Publisher"/></i><br/>
            <i><xsl:value-of select="@Price"/></i><br/>
        </xsl:for-each>
    </xsl:template>
</xsl:stylesheet>
```

The template contains the <xsl:output> element. Table 3-4 lists the three attributes.

Table 3-4. Attributes for the <xsl:output> Element

ATTRIBUTES	PURPOSE(S)
method	Specifies the output generated by the template. Types include XML, HTML, Text, etc.
indent	Specifies if the output should contain white spaces to aid readability.
omit-xml-declaration	Indicates if the output should omit the PI.

The template in Listing 3-10 produces the following output:

```
<b>SQL Server magazine</b><br />
<i>Penton</i><br />
<i>5.95</i><br />
<b>Web Techniques</b><br />
<i>CMP</i><br />
<i>4.95</i><br />
<b>Wireless Business and Technology</b><br />
<i>Sys-con media</i><br />
<i>5.00</i><br />
<b>MSDN</b><br />
<i>CMP</i><br />
<i>5.95</i><br />
```

Note that the PI is omitted (as indicated in the attribute) and the output is formatted with white spaces. If we change the <xsl:output> element to

```
<xsl:output method="html" indent="yes" omit-xml-declaration="yes" />
```

the <br/> element would be modified to become <br> as shown here:

```
<b>SQL Server magazine</b><br><i>Penton</i><br><i>5.95</i><br>
<b>Web Techniques</b><br><i>CMP</i><br><i>4.95</i><br><b>Wireless
Business and Technology</b><br><i>Sys-con media</i><br><i>5.00</i><br>
<b>MSDN</b><br><i>CMP</i><br><i>5.95</i><br>
```

The resultant output is then HTML.

Inserting Text Using <xsl:text>

There may be times when you merely want to insert a long string of text into the output. For instance, Listing 3-11 transforms an XML document into WML.

Listing 3-11. Using the <xsl:text> element to insert string literals

```
<?xml version='1.0'?>
<xsl:stylesheet xmlns:xsl="http://www.w3.org/1999/XSL/Transform" version="1.0">
<xsl:template match="/Magazines">
<!DOCTYPE wml PUBLIC "-//WAPFORUM//DTD WML 1.1//EN"
"http://www.wapforum.org/DTD/wml_1.1.xml">
  <wml>
     <card id="card1" title="Magazines">
        <p>
           <xsl:for-each select="Magazine">
             <b><xsl:value-of select="Title"/></b><br/>
             <i><xsl:value-of select="Publisher"/></i><br/>
             <i><xsl:value-of select="@Price"/></i><br/>
           </xsl:for-each>
        </p>
     </card>
  </wml>
</xsl:template>
</xsl:stylesheet>
```

We want to copy the Document Type Declaration (the line in bold) to the output, as it is mandatory in WAP. However, it will cause a problem with the transformation. To insert a string into the output, you should use the <xsl:text> element:

```
<xsl:text disable-output-escaping="yes">
    &lt;!DOCTYPE wml PUBLIC "-//WAPFORUM//DTD WML 1.1//EN"
       "http://www.wapforum.org/DTD/wml_1.1.xml"&gt;
</xsl:text>
```

The <xsl:text> element contains the disable-output-escaping attribute. If you set the value to "yes," the preceding string will result in:

```
<!DOCTYPE wml PUBLIC "-//WAPFORUM//DTD WML 1.1//EN"
  "http://www.wapforum.org/DTD/wml_1.1.xml">
```

Note that the < and > entities have been converted to < and > respectively. If we set the attribute value to "no," the entities would not be converted, like this:

```
&lt;!DOCTYPE wml PUBLIC "-//WAPFORUM//DTD WML 1.1//EN"
            "http://www.wapforum.org/DTD/wml_1.1.xml"&gt;
```

Transforming with Namespaces

A very interesting aspect of XSL transformation is the use of namespaces. Let's review the following XML document from Chapter 1.

```
<?xml version="1.0"?>
<?xml-stylesheet type="text/xsl" href="6.xsl"?>
<BOOKS xmlns="http://www.apress.com"
       xmlns:People="http://www.apress.com/people">
  <BOOK Pages="357" Type="SOFTCOVER">
    <TITLE>A Programmer's Introduction to C#</TITLE>
    <AUTHOR>
        <People:TITLE>Mr.</People:TITLE>
        <NAME>Eric Gunnerson</NAME>
    </AUTHOR>
    <ISBN>1893115860 </ISBN>
    <SYNOPSIS>
        Eric Gunnerson, the test lead for and member of Microsoft's C#
        design team, has written a comprehensive C# tutorial for programmers
        to help them get up to speed</SYNOPSIS>
    <PRICE>$34.95 </PRICE>
  </BOOK>
</BOOKS>
```

The preceding XML document defines two namespaces:

Default namespace: http://www.apress.com

People namespace: http://www.apress.com/people

To transform the XML document into HTML (for simplicity, we just want to display the title and author information in this example), we might be tempted to use the following template:

```
<?xml version="1.0"?>
<xsl:stylesheet xmlns:xsl="http://www.w3.org/1999/XSL/Transform" version="1.0">
   <xsl:template match="/BOOKS">
   <html>
          <b><xsl:value-of select="BOOK/TITLE"/></b><br/> by
          <i><xsl:value-of select="BOOK/AUTHOR/TITLE"/></i>
          <i><xsl:value-of select="BOOK/AUTHOR/NAME"/></i><br/>
   </html>
   </xsl:template>
</xsl:stylesheet>
```

However, the output does not seem to contain what we want:

```
<?xml version="1.0" encoding="UTF-16"?>A Programmer's Introduction to C#Mr.Eric
Gunnerson1893115860 Eric Gunnerson, the test lead for and member of Microsoft's
C# design team, has written a comprehensive C# tutorial for programmers to help
them get up to speed$34.95
```

The problem arises because of the namespace declaration in the XML source. To enable the XSLT template to transform correctly, we need to modify our templates using the same namespace as those defined in the XML source, like this:

```
<?xml version="1.0"?>
<xsl:stylesheet xmlns:xsl="http://www.w3.org/1999/XSL/Transform" version="1.0"
                xmlns:t="http://www.apress.com"
                xmlns:p="http://www.apress.com/people" >
   <xsl:template match="/t:BOOKS">
   <html>
          <b><xsl:value-of select="t:BOOK/t:TITLE"/></b><br/> by
          <i><xsl:value-of select="t:BOOK/t:AUTHOR/p:TITLE"/></i>
          <i><xsl:value-of select="t:BOOK/t:AUTHOR/t:NAME"/></i><br/>
   </html>
   </xsl:template>
</xsl:stylesheet>
```

Note the prefixes "t" and "p" preceding the element's name. Table 3-5 summarizes the prefixes used in the XML source and XSLT template:

Table 3-5. Prefixes Used in the XML Source and XSLT Template

PREFIX–NAMESPACE IN XML SOURCE	PREFIX–NAMESPACE IN XSLT TEMPLATE
Default—http://www.apress.com	t—http://www.apress.com
People—http://www.apress.com/people	p—http://www.apress.com/people

To properly identify the elements to transform, the element names used in the XPath expression in the template must be prefixed:

```
<b><xsl:value-of select="t:BOOK/t:TITLE"/></b><br/> by
<i><xsl:value-of select="t:BOOK/t:AUTHOR/p:TITLE"/></i>
<i><xsl:value-of select="t:BOOK/t:AUTHOR/t:NAME"/></i><br/>
```

NOTE *It does not matter that the prefix used in the template differs from the prefix used in the XML source as long as they are using the same namespace.*

The previous template will produce the output correctly:

```
<html xmlns:t="http://www.apress.com" xmlns:p="http://www.apress.com/people">
   <b>A Programmer's Introduction to C#</b><br/> by
   <i>Mr.</i><i>Eric Gunnerson</i><br/>
</html>
```

Hence it is important to realize that when transforming XML documents with namespaces, the corresponding stylesheet must also point to the same namespace.

Generating Comments Using the <xsl:comment> Element

So far the discussion has not touched on including comments in the output. To insert comments into the output, you can use the <xsl:comment> element.

By modifying our template in the previous section, we now have:

```
<html>

        <xsl:comment>Title and author information</xsl:comment>
        <b><xsl:value-of select="t:BOOK/t:TITLE"/></b><br/> by
        <i><xsl:value-of select="t:BOOK/t:AUTHOR/p:TITLE"/></i>
        <i><xsl:value-of select="t:BOOK/t:AUTHOR/t:NAME"/></i><br/>
</html>
```

The output becomes:

```
<html xmlns:t="http://www.apress.com" xmlns:p="http://www.apress.com/people">
  <!--Title and author information-->
  <b>A Programmer's Introduction to C#</b><br> by
  <i>Mr.</i><i>Eric Gunnerson</i><br>
</html>
```

Client-Side versus Server-Side XSLT Transformation

So far we have only been using the Web browser to perform XSL Transformation. This is evident from the XML stylesheet PI attached to the XML document:

```
<?xml version="1.0"?>
<?xml:stylesheet type="text/xsl" href="HTML.xsl"?>
<BOOKS>
```

What this means is that the Web browser (Internet Explorer in this case) is expected to perform the transformation. While this method (when deployed in a Web environment) relieves the Web server from the task of transformation, it is client-dependent. A Web browser that does not understand XSLT would not be able to process an XML document with a stylesheet attached. As a result, most of the transformation should be done on the server side. That is, the Web server performs the transformation and sends the results back to the client. The client is totally ignorant of the transformation and thus this method is client-independent.

 NOTE *We will illustrate server-side transformation using Microsoft Active Server Pages (ASP). We assume that readers are already familiar with ASP. For those technically curious, ASP is a server-side technology that utilizes scripting languages, like VBScript and JScript to create dynamic Web pages.*

Let's take a look now on how we can use ASP to perform server-side transformation in Listing 3-12.

Listing 3-12. Books.asp

```
<%
    '--Create an instance of the DOM object--
    Set xml = Server.CreateObject("MSXML2.DOMDocument")
    '--Let it run synchronously--
    xml.async = false
    '--Load the XML document--
    xml.load (Server.MapPath("Books.xml"))
    Set xsl = Server.CreateObject("MSXML2.DOMDocument")
    xsl.async = false
    '--Load the XSLT stylesheet--
    xsl.load (Server.MapPath("HTML.xsl"))
    Response.write (xml.transformNode(xsl))
%>
```

To load the ASP document (Figure 3-7), simply use a Web browser.

Figure 3-7. Loading an ASP document using a Web browser

Let's now take a closer look at the code:

```
Set xml = Server.CreateObject("MSXML2.DOMDocument")
xml.async = false
xml.load (Server.MapPath("Books.xml"))
```

An instance of the DOM object using the Server.CreateObject() method is first created. Next, the *async* property is set to *false* so that our codes can be executed sequentially. Finally the XML document is loaded using the load() method.

Likewise, we load the XSLT stylesheet:

```
Set xsl = Server.CreateObject("MSXML2.DOMDocument")
xsl.async = false
xsl.load (Server.MapPath("HTML.xsl"))
```

The final step in performing server-side transformation is:

```
Response.write (xml.transformNode(xsl))
```

The transformNode() method takes in a stylesheet and applies it to the XML document. The method returns the result of the transformation, which is written back to the browser in our case using the Response.Write() method.

Finally, the Web browser receives the output listed in Listing 3-13.

Listing 3-13. HTML generated by Book.asp
```
<html>
<body>
<table cellspacing="0" border="1">
<font face="Arial,Helvetica,Univers,Zurich BT" color="#69002f" size="-1">
<b>A Programmer's Introduction to C#</b></font><br><tr>
<td width="175" bgColor="#f4f4ef">
<font face="Arial,Helvetica,Univers,Zurich BT" size="-2">
        by Eric Gunnerson</font>
<BR></td></tr>
<tr><td width="175" bgColor="#e5e5d8">
<font face="Arial,Helvetica,Univers,Zurich BT" size="-2">SOFTCOVER,
357 PAGES</font>
<BR></td></tr>
<tr><td width="175" bgColor="#f4f4ef">
<font face="Arial,Helvetica,Univers,Zurich BT" size="-1"><b>ISBN:</b>
1893115860</font>
<BR></td></tr>
<tr><td width="175" bgColor="#e5e5d8">
<font face="Arial,Helvetica,Univers,Zurich BT" size="-1">
<b>PRICE: </b>$34.95 </font>
<BR></td></tr>
</table>
</body>
</html>
```

You can also use browsers other than Internet Explorer as server-side transformation is independent of the browser that you use.

Useful Web Links

- W3C's XSLT version 1.0 Specification Recommendation at
  `http://www.w3.org/TR/xslt.html`

- W3C's XSLT version 1.1 Specification Working Draft at
  `http://www.w3.org/TR/xslt11/`

- W3C's XSL version 1.0 Candidate Recommendation at
  `http://www.w3.org/TR/xsl/`

- Microsoft XSL to XSLT Converter 1.1 at
  `http://msdn.Microsoft.com/downloads/`

Summary

In this chapter, we have taken a quick look at the transforming capability of XSLT stylesheets. While XSLT can sometimes be daunting to the beginners, it is a powerful and flexible tool to perform XML transformation. In particular, we have shown how XSLT can help transform XML documents into another markup language like HTML. At the same time, we have also shown how XML can be transformed from one format into another. Readers familiar with procedural programming languages may not get used to the declarative syntax of XSLT. Nevertheless the best way to learn XSLT is through experimentation.

The concepts that are covered in this chapter are enough to get you started experimenting with XSLT. In later chapters, you will see how XSLT can be combined with XML to create compelling cross-platform applications!

CHAPTER 4

The Document Object Model (DOM)

WE HAVE SEEN HOW AN XML document can be transformed into an HTML document for presentation and into another XML document. What else can we do with an XML document? The next natural thing we would like to do is to manipulate the data and structure in an XML document. The basic functions would include insertion of new information, modification or deletion of existing data in the document. In this chapter, we introduce DOM programming as a technique for achieving this objective.

Introduction to DOM

The Document Object Model (DOM) provides an application programming interface (API) that is platform- and language-neutral. Application developers can access and manipulate the data in an XML document through these interfaces using their favorite scripting or programming languages and without having to worry about the platform on which the scripts will run.

 NOTE *The freedom in choosing the platform and language is, however, dependent on the parser to be used to expose the XML DOM implementation of an XML document. We will look at DOM parsers in a moment.*

The World Wide Web Consortium (W3C) releases the DOM specifications according to levels:

- The DOM Level 1 specification was released as W3C Recommendation in October 1998. The working draft of the second edition is submitted in September 2000 to incorporate errata changes of the earlier version.

- The DOM Level 2 modules were released as W3C Recommendations in November 2000.

• The DOM Level 3 working drafts were submitted in the first half of 2001. The latest working draft available at the point of this writing is dated September 13, 2001.

DOM-based APIs are being developed in the specifications for the Mathematical Markup Language (MathML), Scalable Vector Graphics (SVG), and Synchronized Multimedia Integration Language (SMIL).

DOM is a tree-based API to documents that requires the entire XML document to be represented in memory while processing it. An alternative to DOM is the event-based Simple API for XML (SAX), which can be used to process large XML documents with limited memory available for processing.

 NOTE *SAX is discussed in Chapter 7.*

XML DOM Parsers

XML DOM parsers are software that are able to interpret an XML document as a DOM instance, typically representing it as a tree of nodes in memory. We shall call this tree the document tree as used in the DOM specifications or simply DOM tree.

Note that the DOM specifications do not specify the data structure for implementation, but typically a tree structure is most natural for representing a DOM implementation of an XML document. A tree structure enables ease of access to its various types of nodes by their relative position. The tree traversal order is typically top-down and left-to-right.

XML DOM parsers include the MSXML that is in the Microsoft's Internet Explorer, Oracle's XML Parser for Java v2, and Xerces of the Apache Software Foundation.

All conforming implementations of DOM must fully implement the fundamental interfaces of the DOM specification.

Support of DOM in MSXML3

MSXML3 implements the fundamental and extended interfaces of DOM Level 1 specification.

The DOM Level 1 specification consists of two parts, namely Core and HTML. The Core DOM provides fundamental interfaces for representing any structured document and also extended interfaces for representing an XML document. The HTML DOM provides high-level interfaces that are used with the fundamental Core DOM to provide a representation of an HTML document.

All conforming implementations of DOM Level 1 must fully implement the fundamental interfaces and exception listed in Table 4-1.

Table 4-1. DOM Level 1 Fundamental Interfaces and Exception

FUNDAMENTAL INTERFACE/EXCEPTION	DESCRIPTION
Interface DOMImplementation	Provides methods for performing operations that are independent of any specific instance of the document object model.
Interface DocumentFragment	A lightweight Document that is used to represent a portion of a document tree or a new fragment of a document.
Interface Document	Represents an entire XML document. An entry point for accessing the entire document is provided as the root of the document tree. Note that this root is not the root element of the represented XML document. This root is above the latter in the tree hierarchy.
Interface Node	Represents a node in the document tree. A node in a tree can represent different valid components in an XML document such as element, attribute, text, comment and processing instruction, document type, as well as DOM-specific components such as a document instance and document fragment.
Interface NodeList	An ordered (based on the document tree) collection of nodes, where the individual nodes may be addressed by an index, starting from 0 for the first node in the collection.

(continued)

Table 4-1. DOM Level 1 Fundamental Interfaces and Exceptions (continued)

FUNDAMENTAL INTERFACE/EXCEPTION	DESCRIPTION
Interface NamedNodeMap	As in NodeList, NamedNodeMap refers to a collection of nodes. However, in this case, the nodes may be addressed by an index as well as by name. It is typically used for attribute nodes.
Interface CharacterData	This is an extension of the Node interface, specifically for handling any character data.
Interface Attr	This is another extension of the Node interface, specifically for handling an attribute.
Interface Element	This is an extension of the Node interface, specifically for handling an element.
Interface Text	This is an extension of the CharacterData interface, specifically for handling a text node.
Interface Comment	This is an extension of the CharacterData interface, specifically for handling a comment node.
Exception DOMException	An instance of DOMException is used to raise an exception when an undesirable or exceptional circumstance occurs. An example of such exceptional circumstance is an unsuccessful attempt to access a nonexistent node in a given context.

In addition, MSXML3 also implements extended interfaces, which are shown in Table 4-2.

Table 4-2. DOM Level 1 Extended Interfaces

EXTENDED INTERFACE	DESCRIPTION
Interface CDATASection	This is an extension of the Text interface, specifically for handling a CDATA section.
Interface DocumentType	This is an extension of the Node interface, specifically for handling the document type (through the <!DOCTYPE> element) of an XML document.
Interface Entity	This is for representing a parsed or unparsed entity.
Interface EntityReference	This is for representing an XML entity reference such as and ".
Interface Notation	This is an extension of the Node interface, specifically for handling a notation.
Interface ProcessingInstruction	This is an extension of the Node interface, specifically for handling a processing instruction.

Each interface and exception may consist of one or more of the following types of components:

- Predefined constants

- Properties, also called attributes (which should not be confused with the attributes used in an XML document that are associated with elements)

- Methods, also called functions

Refer to Appendix B for a complete list of properties and methods that are associated with each interface and exception in Table 4-1 and Table 4-2.

Representing XML Document as a Tree

As mentioned earlier, the MSXML parser represents an XML document as a tree of nodes in memory when the document is loaded. The DOM library provides programmers with APIs to manipulate the tree that is built in the memory.

Figure 4-1 depicts the role of the parser in facilitating the programming that can be incorporated into an application to access and edit data in an XML document.

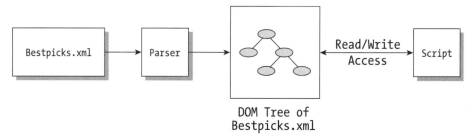

Figure 4-1. *Transforming an XML document into a DOM tree for read/write access by an application*

Each of the components in an XML document can be mapped onto a *node*. Hence we would find different types of nodes such as element node, attribute node, comment node, and processing-instruction node. On top of that, there is an additional node, which alludes to the entire document and is called the Document node of the tree structure.

Consider the following XML document, Bestpicks.xml:

```
<?xml version="1.0"?>
<BOOKS xmlns:apress="http://www.apress.com">
   <apress:BOOK ISBN="1893115860" Pages="357" Type="SOFT">
      <!--This is the first book-->
      <TITLE>A Programmer's Introduction to C#</TITLE>
      <AUTHOR>Eric Gunnerson</AUTHOR>
      <PRICE>34.95</PRICE>
   </apress:BOOK>
   <BOOK ISBN="189311595X" Pages="380" Type="HARD">
      <TITLE>Cryptography in C &amp; C++</TITLE>
      <AUTHOR>Michael Welschenbach</AUTHOR>
      <PRICE>49.95</PRICE>
   </BOOK>
   <BOOK ISBN="1893115763" Pages="400" Type="SOFT">
      <TITLE>C++ for VB Programmers</TITLE>
      <AUTHOR>Jonathan Morrison</AUTHOR>
      <PRICE>49.95</PRICE>
   </BOOK>
</BOOKS>
```

The Bestpicks.xml document can be depicted as a tree as shown in Figure 4-2, which for the sake of simplicity, shows only the first two <BOOK> elements due to space. The attribute nodes are represented as ellipses with dotted lines and the text nodes are represented as rectangles.

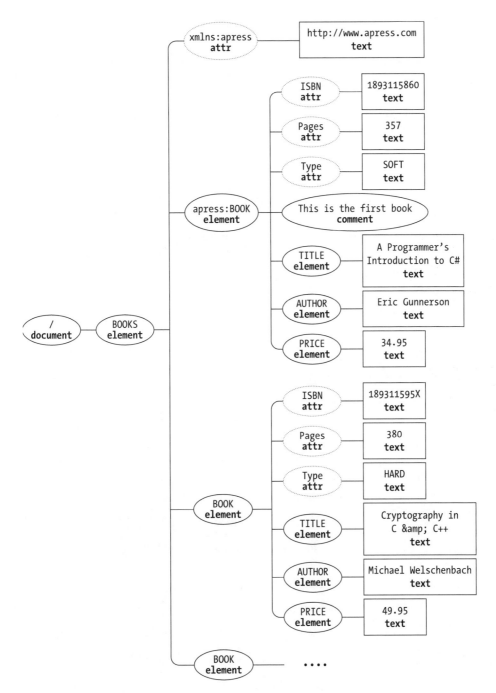

Figure 4-2. Partial tree representation of Bestpicks.xml

Creating a DOM Tree of an XML Document in Memory

The creation of a DOM representation of an XML document in the memory before further manipulating it through the DOM API involves three basic steps:

1. Create an instance of the Document interface, i.e., a DOM instance or DOM object

2. Specify the asynchronization requirement

3. Load content into the instance of DOM created in the first step

As shown in the following example, the basic steps can be coded in VBScript where data is loaded from the document, Bestpicks.xml, using the MSXML parser at the client:

```
<script language="VBScript">
<!--
    Dim docObj
    Set docObj = CreateObject (MSXML2.DOMDocument)
    docObj.async = false
    docObj.load ("Bestpicks.xml")
//-->
</script>
```

To load data from the same XML document at the server using ASP and VBScript, do the following:

```
<%
    Dim docObj
    Set docObj = Server.CreateObject (MSXML2.DOMDocument)
    docObj.async = false
    docObj.load (Server.MapPath("Bestpicks.xml"))
%>
```

The client-side script allows us to easily add a display statement after the loading statement to check the loaded contents of the DOM instance:
```
    msgbox docObj.xml
```

The content of the document, to which docObj points, appears as shown in Figure 4-3.

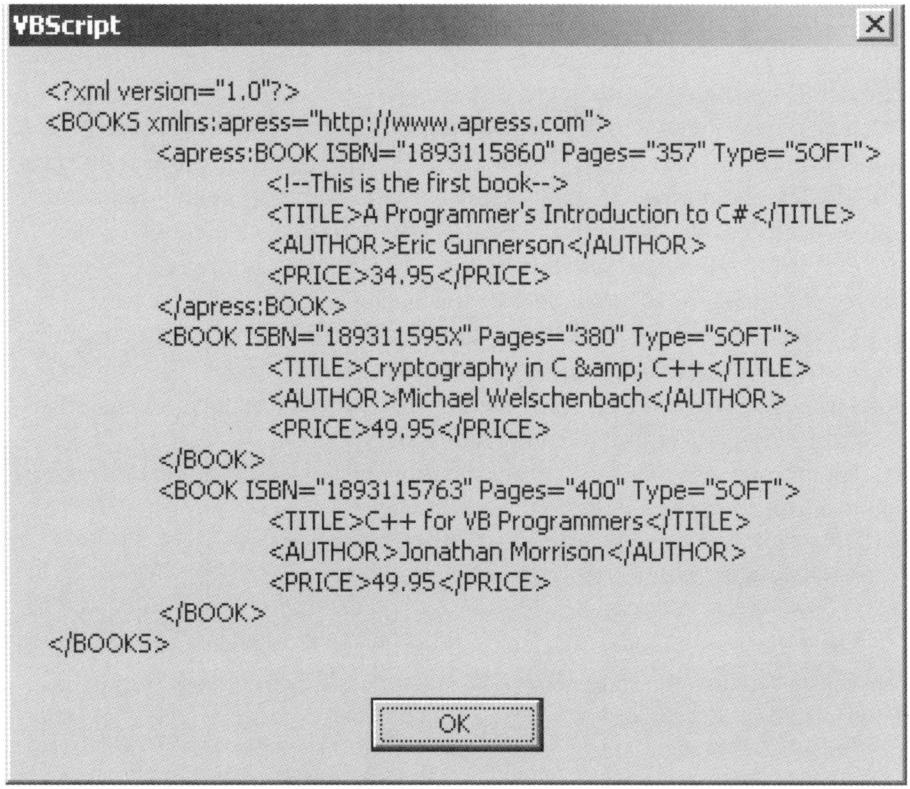

```
VBScript                                                        ×

<?xml version="1.0"?>
<BOOKS xmlns:apress="http://www.apress.com">
        <apress:BOOK ISBN="1893115860" Pages="357" Type="SOFT">
                <!--This is the first book-->
                <TITLE>A Programmer's Introduction to C#</TITLE>
                <AUTHOR>Eric Gunnerson</AUTHOR>
                <PRICE>34.95</PRICE>
        </apress:BOOK>
        <BOOK ISBN="189311595X" Pages="380" Type="SOFT">
                <TITLE>Cryptography in C &amp; C++</TITLE>
                <AUTHOR>Michael Welschenbach</AUTHOR>
                <PRICE>49.95</PRICE>
        </BOOK>
        <BOOK ISBN="1893115763" Pages="400" Type="SOFT">
                <TITLE>C++ for VB Programmers</TITLE>
                <AUTHOR>Jonathan Morrison</AUTHOR>
                <PRICE>49.95</PRICE>
        </BOOK>
</BOOKS>


                        [        OK        ]
```

Figure 4-3. Display of the DOM object for Bestpicks.xml using a message box

We next look at each of the three steps in greater detail.

Creating an Instance of DOM

The DOM Level 1 does not provide a way to create a Document instance. That is, the creation of a Document instance is an implementation-specific operation. The Microsoft-specific APIs that are used for creating Document instances are shown in the following code snippet; the first is used in client-side script while the second is used in server-side script:

```
Set docObj = CreateObject (MSXML2.DOMDocument)
```

and

```
Set docObj = Server.CreateObject (MSXML2.DOMDocument)
```

Setting Asynchronization Flag

The asynchronization requirement is specified either as true (default value) or false before the document object just created is populated with content. A false value indicates that the next call for loading content into the document object is a blocked operation. That is, loading must be completed before the script that follows is processed.

On the other hand, a true value to the async property allows processing of the script that follows to continue after the load operation is set to action.

For the latter case, MSXML3 provides properties for use with a document object to check its loading state before processing the DOM tree. This can be done using the event handler onDataAvailable or through explicitly testing the readyState property of the Document instance.

For example, the following causes the function processData() to be executed when data becomes available:

```
docObj.onDataAvailable = processData()
```

There are several constant values defined for the readyState property to indicate the current loading state of the XML document (DOM) object. They are as listed in Table 4-3.

Table 4-3. Possible Values of readyState

VALUE OF *READYSTATE*	DESCRIPTION
1	Loading of data is in progress.
2	Data has been loaded. Reading and parsing of data are in progress.
3	Some data has been read and parsed, which is available for read-only access.
4	The entire loading of the document is completed. The result may be a success or failure. Further check is needed to ensure successful loading.

The parseError object holds error information regarding a DOM object (e.g., docObj) and checks if the error code is 0, which indicates successful loading, or otherwise:

```
if docObj.readystate = 4 then
    set loadingErr = docObj.parseError
    if  loadingErr.errorCode = 0 then
```

```
        msgbox "successful loading"
    else
        msgbox "loading failed"
    end if
end if
```

Loading XML Data into a DOM Instance

In our example, the load() method is used to load the XML data or content into the DOM instance, docObj. Specifically, the XML content is loaded from an XML document named Bestpicks.xml. A DOM instance loaded from an XML document would have a non-null URL name that can be accessed using the URL property of the DOM instance. The following code:

```
msgbox (docObj.url)
```

will display a message box that is similar to the one that appears in Figure 4-4.

Figure 4-4. Displaying URL of data source for a DOM object

If the source of XML data is a string, the loadXML() method is used for both client- and server-side scripts, as illustrated in the following example:

```
docObj.loadXML ("<?xml version='1.0'?>" &_
               "<BOOKS><BOOK>" &_
               "<TITLE>A Programmer's Introduction to C#</TITLE>" &_
               "</BOOK></BOOKS>")
```

If the source of XML data for loading is passed to an ASP script through a request, we should load the data from the Request object as defined in the ASP programming model:

```
docObj.load Request
```

NOTE *We look at an example on loading from the Request object later in this chapter.*

Saving a DOM Tree

You can save a DOM representation residing in the memory into an XML document as a text file with extension *.xml,* which is in turn stored in some permanent storage. This is appropriate only in server-side processing for obvious security reasons; no client would freely let a script create a file locally.

The following server-side ASP script fragment shows how a DOM tree that is referred to as docObj is saved as a text stream into a file named mysample.xml through the save() method:

```
docObj.save (Server.MapPath("mysample.xml"))
```

After this line is executed, check the server directory and you should see the file, mysample.xml, created in the same folder as the current ASP script. If you want to save the data into a subdirectory, named *samples,* of the folder containing the current ASP script, simply modify the path as shown here:

```
docObj.save (Server.MapPath("samples/mysample.xml"))
```

Alternatively, you may retrieve and save the DOM tree into a temporary string variable in an application using the xml property of the document object. To accomplish this either on the client or server side, simply incorporate the following VBScript statement:

```
tempString = docObj.xml
```

In addition, we may want to display the string in a message box by incorporating the following VBScript statement into a client-side script:

```
msgbox docObj.xml
```

We have seen how a DOM object defined in the DOM Level 1 specification, also known as a DOMDocument object as used in MSXML3, is created and loaded with data. We are now ready to manipulate the DOM tree that is built by the MSXML3 parser. The rest of the chapter demonstrates the use of some of the DOM Level 1 interfaces to access and manipulate the DOM tree.

Fundamental APIs for Processing a DOM Tree

In this section, we introduce the properties and methods of some of the core interfaces implemented by the MSXML parser. The interfaces discussed include the Document, Node, NodeList, Element, and Attr interfaces.

Reference to the DOM Tree

When the DOM tree is first created, the reference to the DOM tree is the root node of the tree, which is a Document node, or sometimes also called a DOM node. In the previous section, we saw how a DOM tree is created to represent the document Bestpicks.xml through the loading method:

```
docObj.load ("Bestpicks.xml")
```

In this example, the reference to the DOM tree is the Document node named docObj.

Reference to the Document Root Element

To start traversing to the next level after the root of the DOM tree for Bestpicks.xml, we need to reference the node representing the document root element, <BOOKS>, which can easily be accomplished by using the documentElement property of the Document node, docObj:

```
Set BOOKSnode = docObj.documentElement
```

The variable BOOKSnode now references the <BOOKS> element of the DOM tree that is shown in Figure 4-5.

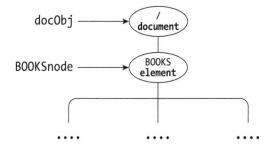

Figure 4-5. References to root node and document element

Fundamentals of a Node

Every node in the DOM tree is an instance of the Node interface. Each node has properties and methods as defined in DOM Level 1.

In addition, each specific type of node, such as an element node, may further extend the Node interface with additional properties and methods that pertain to that node type.

What Do We Know about a Node?

Each node of the DOM tree has a name, type, and value. We can find out the name, type, and value of a node, such as BOOKSnode, using the following properties:

```
BOOKSnode.nodeName
BOOKSnode.nodeType
BOOKSnode.nodeValue
```

The values of the properties nodeName, nodeType, and nodeValue of a node depend on the type of the node as described in Table 4-4.

Table 4-4. Name, Type, and Value of a Node

TYPE OF NODE	VALUE OF *NODENAME*	CONSTANT AND NUMERIC VALUES OF *NODETYPE*	VALUE OF *NODEVALUE*
Element	Name of the element tag	ELEMENT_NODE(1)	null
Attr	Name of the attribute	ATTRIBUTE_NODE (2)	Value of the attribute
Text	#text	TEXT_NODE (3)	Text value of the node
CDATA Section	#cdata-section	CDATA_SECTION_NODE (4)	CDATA content
Entity-Reference	Name of the referenced entity	ENTITY_REFERENCE_NODE (5)	null
Entity	Entity name	ENTITY_NODE (6)	null
Processing-Instruction	target	PROCESSING_INSTRUCTION_NODE (7)	Value of the instruction portion
Comment	#comment	COMMENT_NODE (8)	Value of the comment node
Document	#document	DOCUMENT_NODE (9)	null
Document Type	Name of document type	DOCUMENT_TYPE_NODE (10)	null
Document Fragment	#document-fragment	DOCUMENT_FRAGMENT_NODE (11)	null
Notation	Notation name	NOTATION_NODE (12)	null

The following is a list of other properties of a Node object as defined by DOM Level 1. More detailed descriptions of the properties are given in Appendix B.

- parentNode

- childNodes

- firstChild

- lastChild

- previousSibling

- nextSibling

- attributes

- ownerDocument

MSXML extends the property set defined in DOM Level 1 with several other useful properties such as the nodeTypeString and xml properties. In fact, we have seen the latter earlier in this chapter when we discussed the saving of a DOM tree. The nodeTypeString property refers to the type of node by character string, e.g., "element" instead of the value 1.

Consider Listing 4.1 (NodeProperties.html), which contains a script to access some of the properties of some nodes in the DOM tree representing the XML document Bestpicks.xml:

Listing 4-1. NodeProperties.html

```
<html>
<script language="vbscript">
<!--
    'Initializing and loading a DOM object
    Dim docObj
    Set docObj = CreateObject("Msxml2.DOMDocument")
    docObj.async = false
    docObj.load "Bestpicks.xml"

    'Initializing 2 Node objects
    Set BOOKSnode = docObj.documentElement
    Set firstBOOK = BOOKSnode.firstChild

    'Displaying name, type and value properties of docObj
    document.write "<h2>Name, type and value of <em>docObj</em></h2>"
    document.write "<p>nodeName: <b>" & docObj.nodeName & "</b>"
    document.write "<br>nodeType: <b>" & docObj.nodeType &_
                    " (" & docObj.nodeTypeString & ")</b>"
    document.write "<br>nodeValue: <b>" & docObj.nodeValue & "</b>"

    'Displaying name, type and value properties of BOOKSnode
    document.write "<h2>Name, type and value of <em>BOOKSnode</em></h2>"
    document.write "<p>nodeName: <b>" & BOOKSnode.nodeName & "</b>"
    document.write "<br>nodeType: <b>" & BOOKSnode.nodeType &_
                    " (" & BOOKSnode.nodeTypeString & ")</b>"
    document.write "<br>nodeValue: <b>" & BOOKSnode.nodeValue & "</b>"
```

```
    'Displaying XML content of the first BOOK
    msgbox firstBOOK.xml
//-->
</script>
</html>
```

Figure 4-6 displays a page of contents and a message box that is produced by NodeProperties.html when it is loaded using Internet Explorer 5.0.

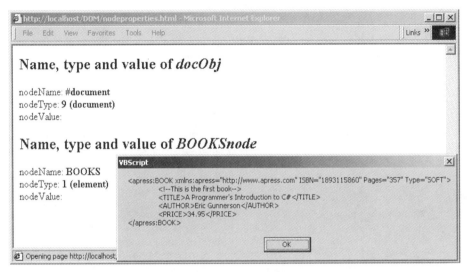

Figure 4-6. Display produced by NodeProperties.html using Internet Explorer 5.0

What Can We Do with a Node?

We have seen earlier how you can access the first child node of a given node by using the firstChild property. There are occasions when you would like to test if the node in question has any child node before addressing a specific child node. The hasChildNodes() method provides a way to check if a node contains any child node. It returns true if the answer is positive.

For example, if docObj and BOOKSnode are defined in NodeProperties.html, adding either of the following lines of script

```
    msgbox docObj.hasChildNodes()
    msgbox BOOKSnode.hasChildNodes()
```

yields the message box that is shown in Figure 4-7 in which the Boolean result is True since each of the nodes consists of at least one child node.

Figure 4-7. Response to hasChildNodes() *for* docObj *or* BOOKSnode

MSXML provides the following additional methods for the Node interface as listed in Table 4-5.

Table 4-5. MSXML Methods to the Node Interface

METHOD	DESCRIPTION
selectNodes (p)	This method returns a list of descendant nodes of this context node that matches the pattern specified by p, which is a valid XPath expression.
selectSingleNode (p)	This method returns the first descendant node of this context node that matches the pattern specified by p, which is a valid XPath expression.
transformNode (s)	This method returns the result, in string, of transformation applied on this node and its children using the supplied XSLT stylesheet DOM object, s.
transformNodeToObject (s, r)	This method processes this node and its children using the supplied XSLT stylesheet DOM object, s, and returns the resulting transformation in the supplied object, r.

Adding the following two lines of script in NodeProperties.html

```
msgbox "Title of first <BOOK>: " &_
        docObj.selectSingleNode("//TITLE").firstChild.nodeValue
```

yields the display that is shown in Figure 4-8.

Figure 4-8. Displaying the first title in the DOM object, docObj

Since <TITLE> is an element, its node value is null. In order to display the title, we must traverse down the tree shown in Figure 4-2 from the <TITLE> node of the first <BOOK> node, which gives us a text node next. The content of the text node is "A Programmer's Introduction to C#." Since the nodeValue of a text node displays the content of the node, we can use this property to print out the title of the book concerned.

We have seen how transformNode() is used in Chapter 3:

```
Response.write (xml.transformNode(xsl))
```

The DOM object (xml) representing an XML data document was transformed by the stylesheet represented as the DOM object, xsl. The result is a string, which is output as a stream from the server to the client.

By using transformNodeToObject() we are able to realize the same transformation and output the result to an object such as a DOM object as follows:

```
Set output = CreateObject(MSXML2.DOMDocument)
xml.transformNodeToObject (xsl, output)
```

Fundamentals of a NodeList

The NodeList interface is different from the Node interface in that it is representing a set of nodes instead of just one single node. There is only one property and one method defined for the NodeList interface by the World Wide Web Consortium (W3C) DOM Level 1. They are the length property and the item() method, and they are discussed in the next two subsections.

Size of a NodeList

Assuming that BOOKSnode represents the <BOOKS> element node of the tree that is shown in Figure 4-2, we can find out the number of <BOOK> child nodes that the tree contains by using the following line of script:

```
msgbox "No. of <BOOK> nodes under <BOOKS>: " &_
          BOOKSnode.selectNodes("BOOK").length
```

Figure 4-9. Display the number of <BOOK> nodes under the <BOOKS> node

The expression, BOOKSnode.selectNodes("BOOK"), returns a NodeList object, which is an ordered set of descendant nodes of the <BOOKS> node and which has the tag name, BOOK. The length property of a node list returns the number of nodes it contains, which is two in this case since there are two such <BOOK> nodes under the <BOOKS> node.

Getting to the Individuals of a NodeList

The item() method takes in a parameter, say i, which is used as the index of the requested node in a given node list. In short, it returns the $(i+1)^{th}$ node in the list for the specified index parameter, i, since the index starts with 0.

Using the same reference node that is indicated by BOOKSnode, as shown in Figure 4-5, consider the following lines of script:

```
Set BOOKnodes = BOOKSnode.selectNodes("BOOK")
msgbox BOOKnodes.item(1).xml
```

The script displays the subtree that is the second <BOOK> element of Bestpicks.xml.

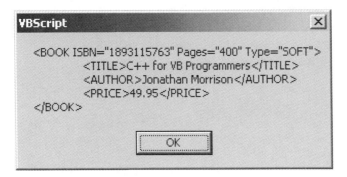

Figure 4-10. XML data for the second <BOOK> element in Bestpicks.xml

The expression, BOOKnodes.item(1), can be simplified to BOOKnodes(1).

Fundamentals of an Element Node

The Element node is a special case of node that extends the Node interface with an additional property and some other methods pertaining to elements. In addition, MSXML also defines some useful properties and methods to this interface.

Names of an Element Node

The first thing we can find out about an element node is its name.

Let's assume that the same definition applies to firstBOOK (as we have seen earlier), which is depicted in Figure 4-11.

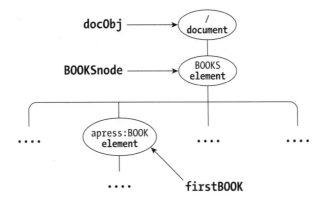

Figure 4-11. Reference to the first child node of the <BOOKS> node

Consider the following script fragment:

```
msgbox "nodeName:    " & firstBOOK.nodename & vbCRLF &_
       "tagName:     " & firstBOOK.tagname & vbCRLF &_
       "baseName:    " & firstBOOK.basename & vbCRLF &_
       "prefix:      " & firstBOOK.prefix & vbCRLF &_
       "namespaceURI: " & firstBOOK.namespaceURI
```

The properties that are displayed in Figure 4-12 refer to naming information of an element, in which the last three properties are MSXML extensions to the DOM Level 1 definition.

Figure 4-12. Naming information of the first book in Bestpicks.xml

Relating to Other Element Nodes

Let's try to traverse the DOM tree using firstBOOK as the reference node (Table 4-6).

Table 4-6. Examples of Traversal to Other Element Nodes from the Node Referenced by firstBOOK

DESCRIPTION	MESSAGE BOX SCRIPT & DISPLAY
Displaying the name of parent node of firstBOOK.	Msgbox firstBOOK.parentNode.nodeName
Displaying the contents of the node that is the next sibling (to the right) of firstBOOK.	Msgbox firstBOOK.nextSibling.xml 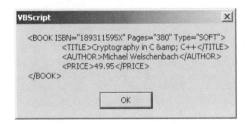
Displaying the contents of the node that is the last child element node of firstBOOK.	Msgbox firstBOOK.lastChild.xml 
Displaying the name of the Document node that represents the document containing firstBOOK.	Msgbox firstBOOK.ownerDocument.nodeName

Learning about Attributes of an Element Node

Let's investigate the attributes of firstBOOK (Table 4-7).

Table 4-7. Retrieving Information of Attributes of the Node Referenced by firstBOOK

DESCRIPTION	MESSAGE BOX SCRIPT & DISPLAY
Displaying the number of attributes associated with firstBOOK.	Msgbox "No. of attributes:" & firstBOOK.attributes.length
Displaying the value of the first attribute of firstBOOK.	Msgbox "First attribute:" & firstBOOK.attributes(0).nodeValue 
Displaying the value of the ISBN attribute of firstBOOK.	Msgbox "ISBN:" & firstBOOK.getAttribute("ISBN")

It should be highlighted that firstBOOK.attributes returns a NamedNodeMap object, which is an unordered list of nodes, whose individual nodes may be retrieved by their names, such as using the getAttribute() method.

Fundamentals of an Attr Node

We have just seen how an attribute of an element node is accessed. We look at some of the properties and methods of an Attr (i.e., attribute) node here.

Since the Attr interface extends the Node interface, most of the properties and methods that we discussed under the Node interface also apply to an Attr node.

Consider the following script fragment, which first sets a reference to the Pages attribute of firstBOOK using the getAttributeNode() method of an element node, and then displays some properties pertaining to the attribute node, as shown in Figure 4-13 and Figure 4-14, respectively:

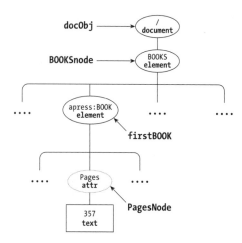

Figure 4-13. Reference to the Pages *attribute of the node referenced by* firstBOOK

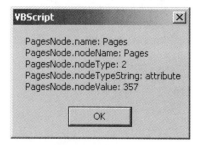

Figure 4-14. Naming information of the Pages *attribute of the node referenced by* firstBOOK

```
Set PagesNode = firstBOOK.getAttributeNode("Pages")
msgbox "PagesNode.name: "       & PagesNode.name & vbCRLF &_
       "PagesNode.nodeName: "   & PagesNode.nodeName & vbCRLF &_
       "PagesNode.nodeType: "   & PagesNode.nodeType & vbCRLF &_
       "PagesNode.nodeTypeString: " & PagesNode.nodeTypeString & vbCRLF &_
       "PagesNode.nodeValue: "  & PagesNode.nodeValue
```

The name property is an extended property to the Node interface. The rest of the properties are not new to us, as they had been mentioned earlier when we introduced the fundamentals of the Node interface.

Client-Side DOM Programming—Shopping Cart

In this section, we make use of a case study to demonstrate DOM programming on the client side. We introduce the use of more properties and methods of the various interfaces for accomplishing the functionality of the application.

We extend the application requirements to include the server-side DOM programming in a later section.

Client-Side Application Requirements

Let's implement a shopping cart that keeps track of the items selected by the user from a list of best-sellers of some bookstore. The shopping cart can expand or shrink as the user adds or drops items from his or her shopping cart.

The following describes the client-side requirements from the user's perspective:

1. The user is presented with a selection list of best-sellers from a bookstore.

2. The user can select an item and specify the quantity to add to the shopping cart. The user can remove the item from the cart by specifying the quantity to be zero.

3. The user can check out and submit the shopping cart to a backend server through clicking on a button.

To simplify our implementation, we will not provide a mechanism for the user to view the shopping cart since the coding techniques that are required for this functionality are similar to some of those that are used for implementing the three requirements specified in the preceding list. The user interface design is not of utmost concern here and we will try to keep a simple interface to avoid cluttering the essential code for manipulating the DOM objects, which is relevant to this chapter. Also, we will skip the script necessary for validating user's input, as that does not add much value to illustrating programming techniques with DOM.

Initialization

At this point, we can identify a few initialization tasks:

- Declaring global variables

- Loading Bestpicks.xml as a DOM tree

- Creating initial DOM tree for the shopping cart

- Invoking the loading of a form for user to do ordering

We will not show all of the global variables at once; instead we will mention them when they are introduced as the need arises.

We will put all the initialization script in a VBScript subroutine named `initialize`.

Loading an XML Document into a DOM Tree

To access the information enclosed in the XML document, Bestpicks.xml, we first create a DOM object and load it with data from the document. We will also initialize a variable (`BOOKSnode`) to point to the document root (`<BOOKS>` element):

```
Dim booksDoc, BOOKSnode
Sub initialize
    Set booksDoc = CreateObject("MSXML2.DOMDocument")
    booksDoc.async = false
    booksDoc.load "Bestpicks.xml"
    Set BOOKSnode = booksDoc.documentElement
End Sub
```

Here, `booksDoc` and `BOOKSnode` are declared as global variables as they should be accessible throughout most of the other subroutines.

Creating a DOM Tree for the Shopping Cart

We need to create the DOM tree for the shopping cart from scratch. This can be accomplished by the following code inserted into the `initialize` subroutine, where `orderDoc` and `ORDERSnode` are declared as global variables:

```
    Set orderDoc = CreateObject("Msxml2.DOMDocument")
    orderDoc.async = false
    orderDoc.loadXML "<?xml version='1.0'?>" &_
                    "<ORDERS></ORDERS>"
    Set ORDERSnode = orderDoc.documentElement
```

After the initialization, the cart will have the following DOM tree structure, as shown in Figure 4-15.

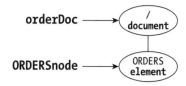

Figure 4-15. Initial DOM structure of the shopping cart (`orderDoc`)

We can also display the XML contents (Figure 4-16) using a message box during development, such as:

```
msgbox orderDoc.xml
```

*Figure 4-16. Initial XML content of the shopping cart (*orderDoc*)*

Invoking the Loading of an Order Form

We will make use of a subroutine loadOrderForm to load an order form. To invoke the loading, we merely include the following call statement as the last line of code in the initialize subroutine:

```
Call loadOrderForm
```

Creating an Order Form

We will obtain the information of the best sellers from Bestpicks.xml and present them as a selection list in an order form as shown in Figure 4-17.

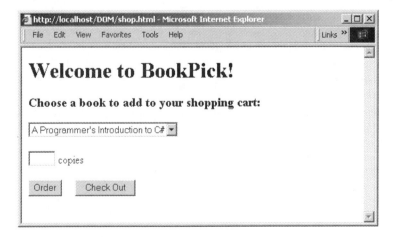

Figure 4-17. The order form

Traversing All BOOK Nodes of the DOM Tree

Since we need to present all the books, we need to traverse the entire DOM tree representing Bestpicks.xml in search of book element nodes. When the DOM tree was first created, the reference to the tree is the root node of the tree, that is, booksDoc, which is a Document node. To start traversing the tree, we need to reference the node representing the document root, <BOOKS>, which was accomplished in the initialization subroutine presented earlier. The object name used to reference the <BOOKS> node is BOOKSnode.

To iterate through each child node (which may be a <BOOK> node or an <apress:BOOK> node) of BOOKSnode in the DOM tree and present it as an option of a selection list, we first gather the list of child nodes using the childNodes property.

```
Set bestpicks = BOOKSnode.childNodes
```

We can insert this statement into the initialize subroutine.

> **NOTE** *We cannot collect all the nodes representing the books in the DOM tree based on a given element tag name by using either the DOM Level 1 method,* getElementsByTagName(), *or the* selectNodes() *method provided by MSXML. This is because not all the eligible book elements have the same tag name.*

We will now write the subroutine to load the order form. In this subroutine, we will construct a loop to perform information presentation n times where n is the number of books in the node list, bestpicks. We will present each title as an option in the selection list. Also, each option is associated with a value, which is the book's ISBN. The following shows the construction of the selection list:

```
Sub loadOrderform
    document.write "<p><form name='orderForm'>"
    document.write "<select name='selectedbook' size='1'>"
    lastBookIndex = bestpicks.length - 1
    for i = 0 to lastBookIndex
        document.write "<option value='" &_
                        bestpicks(i).getAttribute("ISBN") & "'>" &_
                        bestpicks(i).selectSingleNode("TITLE").text
```

```
      next
      document.write "</select> "
      document.write "</form> "
End Sub
```

Note that the text property used to display the title is an extension provided by MSXML. Without this property, the display of the title is achieved through a longer expression, such as the following:

```
bestpicks(i).selectSingleNode("TITLE").firstChild.nodeValue
```

Other Form Elements

To complete the form as shown previously in Figure 4-17, we need to add an input box for the user to specify the number of copies and two buttons. The first button is an order button to invoke the adding of the item to the shopping cart. The second button will lead to the submission of the shopping cart to the server for further processing.

Following is an example for coding the three items immediately after the output of the end-tag of the selection list (i.e., </select>):

```
document.write "<p><input type='text' name='num' " &_
               "size='3' maxlength='2'> copies"
document.write "<p><input type='button' name='order' value='Order'>" &_
               "   " &_
               "<input type='button' name='checkout' value='Check Out'>"
```

Note that we have assigned the name, order, to the order button. Hence, upon clicking on the button, the subroutine, order_onClick, will be invoked to add the selected book into the shopping cart. Similarly, clicking on the check-out button will invoke the subroutine, checkout_onClick.

Updating the Shopping Cart

This functionality is invoked through the clicking of the order button in the order form. That is, the subroutine for handling this task is order_onClick, which we have just introduced.

In this subroutine, we need to update the DOM object representing the shopping cart, which is referenced by orderDoc, based on the input of the user through the order form.

The shopping cart referenced by orderDoc is first checked to see if the selected item exists in the cart. If so, we merely need to update the number of copies. However, if the user specified a quantity of 0 or less for an existing item, we will remove the corresponding node of the selected book from the shopping cart.

If the selected book is not found in the DOM object for the shopping cart, we need to add the necessary book element into the DOM tree unless the user specified 0 copy for the selected book.

```
1  Sub order_onClick
2      orderISBN = document.orderForm.selectedbook.value
3      orderQtty = document.orderForm.num.value
4
5      Set bookOrders = ORDERSnode.childNodes
6      found = 0
7      for each order in bookOrders
8          if order.selectSingleNode("ISBN").text = orderISBN then
9              found = 1
10             if orderQtty > 0 then
11                 'update the number of copies ordered
12                 order.selectSingleNode("QTTY").text = orderQtty
13             else
14                 'remove the order
15                 ORDERSnode.removeChild order
16             end if
17             exit for
18         end if
19     next
20
21     if found = 0 and orderQtty > 0 then
22         'add in new ORDER node
23         Set newOrderElement = orderDoc.createElement("ORDER")
24         Set newISBNElement = orderDoc.createElement("ISBN")
25         Set newQttyElement = orderDoc.createElement("QTTY")
26
27         Set newISBN = orderDoc.createTextNode(orderISBN)
28         Set newQtty = orderDoc.createTextNode(orderQtty)
29
30         newISBNElement.appendChild(newISBN)   'create <ISBN>xxx</ISBN>
31         newQttyElement.appendChild(newQtty)   'create <QTTY>yy</QTTY>
32
33         newOrderElement.appendChild(newISBNElement)
34         newOrderElement.appendChild(newQttyElement)
35         ORDERSnode.appendChild(newOrderElement)
36     end if
37 End Sub
```

We will highlight the new features that are introduced in the preceding subroutine:

- Lines 7 to 19 handle the case when the selected book has already been added into the shopping cart. Line 12 updates the quantity ordered if the user keys in a positive number. Line 15 uses the `removeChild` method to drop the selected book from the shopping cart by removing the corresponding <ORDER> node from the DOM tree.

- Lines 21 to 36 handle the case when the selected book is not found in the existing cart and that the user specified a positive value for the quantity.

- Lines 23 to 25 use the `createElement` method to create three new elements: <ORDER>, <ISBN>, and <QTTY> with no content.

- Lines 27 and 28 use the `createTextNode` method to create two text nodes for holding the ISBN and quantity values captured from the order form.

- Line 30 uses the `appendChild` method to associate the text node created in line 27 to the <ISBN> element created in line 24 as a child node to the latter. Hence, if the user selected the first book whose ISBN is 1893115860, then line 30 will result in the following element: <ISBN>1893115860</ISBN>

- Similarly, if the user input the quantity as 3, then line 31 will result in the following element: <QTTY>3</QTTY>

Let's insert the following line of code for displaying the new order element immediately after line 34, as shown in Figure 4-18:

```
msgbox newOrderElement.xml
```

Figure 4-18. Contents of the new order just created

- Lines 33 and 34 use the <ISBN> and <QTTY> elements that were just created as building blocks to construct a higher-level <ORDER> element: <ORDER><ISBN>1893115860</ISBN> <QTTY>3</QTTY></ORDER>

- Finally, the new <ORDER> element constructed was appended as the last order under the <ORDERS> element referenced by ORDERSnode.

Checking Out

This functionality is invoked through clicking on the check out button in the order form and it involves the following final tasks to be developed on the client side:

- Prompts user to enter a user ID, which is then inserted as an attribute value of the <ORDERS> node in the DOM tree for the shopping cart.

- Creates an XMLHTTP object for delivering the shopping cart DOM object over the HTTP from the client browser to the targeted ASP script residing on an HTTP server.

- Waits for server's response and displays it on the browser.

- Re-initializes the DOM object representing the shopping cart.

Prompting for User ID

When the user chooses to check out, we would like the application to prompt the user for his user ID and insert into the DOM tree of the shopping cart as an attribute of the document root, which is <ORDERS> in our case.

We can make use of the inputBox() function to capture the user ID, as shown in Figure 4-19:

```
userID = inputBox ("Key in user ID:", "Check out")
```

VBScript: Check out ☒

Key in user ID:-

OK

Cancel

| |

Figure 4-19. Input box prompting for user ID

We will then create an attribute node with the userID value and associate that value with the <ORDERS> node that is referenced by the variable ORDERSnode, as shown in the following line:

```
ORDERSnode.setAttribute "userID", userID
```

If the user keys in the user ID Cust0001, the preceding will result in changing the start-tag to <ORDERS userID="Cust0001">, as shown in Figure 4-20.

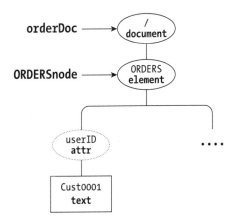

Figure 4-20. Adding the userID *attribute to the root element* ORDERS

Passing DOM Object to HTTP Server

First, we will create an XMLHTTP object to communicate with the backend HTTP server where the server script for processing the shopping cart can be reached.

This will enable us to pass an XML packet to the server using the HTTP connection between the client and the server.

The XMLHTTP object can request to open a connection with an HTTP server, specifying the HTTP request method, such as GET or POST, the resource it is looking for, such as an ASP script for processing the shopping cart, the asynchronization flag, as well as optional user id and password. If the asynchronization flag is set to false, then further execution will not occur at the client side until a response from the server is received. The final step is to send the XML packet out to the server using the send method.

An example of the corresponding code that is used for doing the tasks that were just described is shown in the following lines of script:

```
Set postObj = CreateObject ("MSXML2.XMLHTTP")
postObj.open "POST", "process.asp", false
postObj.send orderDoc
```

Displaying the Server's Response

If the response from the server is expected to be a text string, then we can retrieve the response through the responseText property of the XMLHTTP object. If we are expecting the response to be parsed XML content, we should use the responseXML property instead.

For example, if we want to display the server's text string response in a message box, we can achieve that through the following line of code:

```
msgbox postObj.responseText
```

Alternatively, we may want to receive the response as XML content and assign it to a newly created DOM object as shown here:

```
Set responseDoc = CreateObject ("MSXML2.DOMDocument")
Set responseDoc = postObj.responseXML
```

Re-initializing the Shopping Cart

After sending the shopping cart to the server, the content of the cart at the client side was not changed. If a different user would like to start ordering from the same ordering page left behind by the previous user, we need to make sure that the new user starts with an empty cart. To ensure that the cart is empty, we can include the following lines to re-initialize the shopping cart to its original state:

```
orderDoc.loadXML "<?xml version='1.0'?>" &_
                 "<ORDERS></ORDERS>"
Set ORDERSnode = orderDoc.documentElement
```

Complete Listing of the Client-Side Script

Now that we have completed the "bottom-up" discussion of the various functionalities that are performed on the client side, we present in Listing 4-2 the complete
listing of the source code for the client. We have also included appropriate inline
comments to help you understand the code as you glance through it:

Listing 4-2. Client-side script for shopping cart example

```
<html>
<head>
<script language="vbscript">
<!--
    Dim booksdoc, BOOKSnode, orderDoc, ORDERSnode
    Dim bestpicks

sub initialize
'Loading Bestpicks.xml
    Set booksDoc = CreateObject("Msxml2.DOMDocument")
    booksDoc.async = false
    booksDoc.load "Bestpicks.xml"
'Setting references to document root and list of books
    Set BOOKSnode = booksDoc.documentElement
    Set bestpicks = BOOKSnode.childNodes

'Creating new DOM tree for a shopping cart
    Set orderDoc = CreateObject("Msxml2.DOMDocument")
    orderDoc.async = false
    orderDoc.loadXML "<?xml version='1.0'?>" &_
                     "<ORDERS></ORDERS>"
    Set ORDERSnode = orderDoc.documentElement

'Loading the form for ordering
    call loadOrderForm
end sub
```

```
sub loadOrderForm
    document.write "<h3>Choose a book to add to your shopping cart:</h3>"
    document.write "<p><form name='orderForm'>"
    document.write "<select name='selectedbook' size='1'>"
    lastBookIndex = bestpicks.length - 1
    for i = 0 to lastBookIndex
        document.write "<option value='" & bestpicks(i).getAttribute("ISBN") &_
                        "'>" & bestpicks(i).selectSingleNode("TITLE").text
    next
    document.write "</select> "
    document.write "<p><input type='text' name='num' &_
                    "size='3' maxlength='2'> copies"
    document.write "<p><input type='button' name='order' value='Order'>" &_
                    "   " &_
                    "<input type='button' name='checkout' value='Check Out'>"
    document.write "</form>"
end sub

sub order_onClick
    orderISBN = document.orderForm.selectedbook.value
    orderQtty = document.orderForm.num.value

    Set bookOrders = ORDERSnode.childNodes
    found = 0
    for each order in bookOrders
        if order.selectSingleNode("ISBN").text = orderISBN then
            found = 1
            if orderQtty > 0 then
            'update the number of copies ordered
                order.selectSingleNode("QTTY").text = orderQtty
            else
            'remove the order
                ORDERSnode.removeChild order
            end if
            ' break
        end if
    next

    if found = 0 and orderQtty <> 0 then
        'add in new node
        Set newOrderElement = orderDoc.createElement("ORDER")
        Set newISBNElement = orderDoc.createElement("ISBN")
        Set newQttyElement = orderDoc.createElement("QTTY")
```

```
            Set newISBN = orderDoc.createTextNode(orderISBN)
            Set newQtty = orderDoc.createTextNode(orderQtty)

            newISBNElement.appendChild(newISBN)
            newQttyElement.appendChild(newQtty)

            newOrderElement.appendChild(newISBNElement)
            newOrderElement.appendChild(newQttyElement)
            ORDERSnode.appendChild(newOrderElement)
        end if
end sub

sub checkout_onClick
'Prompting for user ID
    userID = InputBox("Key in user ID:- ", "Check out")
    ORDERSnode.setAttribute "userID", userID
    msgbox orderDoc.xml

'Posting an XML packet to server and displaying server's string response
    Set postObj = CreateObject("Microsoft.XMLHTTP")
    postObj.open "POST", "process.asp", false
    postObj.send orderDoc
    msgbox postObj.responseText

'Reinitializing orderDoc and ORDERSnode
    orderDoc.loadXML "<?xml version='1.0'?>" &_
                    "<ORDERS></ORDERS>"
    Set ORDERSnode = orderDoc.documentElement
end sub

//-->
</script>
</head>

<body>
<h1>Welcome to BookPick!</h1>
<script language="VBScript">
    initialize
</script>
</body>
</html>
```

Server-Side DOM Programming—Shopping Cart

We will now move over to the server side to illustrate how the shopping cart is received and how the information is extracted from the XML packet sent to it through the HTTP protocol. We will then generate a string as a response to the client. We will name our ASP script, process.asp.

For our purposes there is no need to dwell further on the processing of the shopping cart's content, such as updating sales database table, generating invoices, and payment, which are no doubt essential in a real-life e-commerce transaction.

As such, we can simplify our ASP script to perform only the following:

- Sets the content type of the response to be generated to the client

- Creates a DOM instance and loads it with the shopping cart's contents

- Retrieves userID attribute information and total number of orders—each selected item is considered one order regardless of the quantity specified for the same selected item

- Generates an acknowledgement string

Before we end this section, we will also mention an important issue that involves validating XML content received by the server.

Setting the Content Type

The purpose of setting the content type is to insert a content-type field into the header of the HTTP response message to be sent to the client, specifying the type of content the client is receiving.

If our intention is to generate a string of plain text to be sent back to the client, we can use the following line to set the content type:

```
<% Response.ContentType = "text/plain" %>
```

If the application may send back either plain text or HTML content, then we should specify the following content type:

```
<% Response.ContentType = "text/html" %>
```

If we wish to send XML content back to the client, we should do the following:

```
<% Response.ContentType = "text/xml" %>
```

The content types just described are not exhaustive. It really depends on what you want to send back to the client as a response.

 NOTE *Response is an object specified in the ASP programming model for generating and sending response messages to the client.*

Receiving a DOM Object from the Client

We need to create a DOM instance and load it with the incoming XML content from the ASP Request object as illustrated in the following code:

```
<%
    Dim receivedDoc
    Set receivedDoc = Server.CreateObject (MSXML2.DOMDocument)
    receivedDoc.async = false
    receivedDoc.load Request
%>
```

After the loading is completed, we would have created a DOM tree of the shopping cart at the server side. We can apply the same programming techniques used at the client side to manipulate the tree.

Retrieving the Shopping Cart's Contents

This is a simple task as it involves only appropriate traversal of the DOM tree (receivedDoc) to access the information we would like to have.

Based on our requirements specification, we need to get the user ID and find out the number of orders made.

The first task is straightforward as we can simply use the selectSingleNode() method and specify the XPath expression for the userID attribute node in the document. To obtain the second piece of information, we must first collect a list of <ORDER> nodes, which can easily be done using the selectNodes() method. We can then use the length property of the node list to find out the number of orders the user had just made.

The code for achieving the retrieval of the userID attribute node and the <ORDER> node list is shown here:

```
<%
'Retrieving user ID
   Set idNode = receivedDoc.selectSingleNode("//@userID")
   userid = idNode.nodeValue
'Retrieving orders
   Set orderNodes = receivedDoc.selectNodes("//ORDER")
%>
```

Next, we will generate a response that makes use of this information we have just retrieved.

Generating a Response to the Client

For illustration purposes, we will generate an acknowledgement string, which will be displayed at the client side using a message box (decided by the client script), as shown in Figure 4-21.

Figure 4-21. Client display of sample response string generated by the server

Here is the code for generating the short string as shown in the preceding illustration :

```
<%
   if orderNodes.length < 2 then
      Response.write orderNodes.length & " order from " & userID
   else
      Response.write orderNodes.length & " orders from " & userID
   end if
%>
```

Complete Listing of the Server-Side ASP Script

Listing 4-3 shows the source code of the server-side script process.asp, in which you can see the complete listing instead of fragments:

Listing 4-3. Process.asp

```
<%
'Setting content type
    Response.ContentType = "text/html"

'Creating a new DOM object and loading contents from the ASP's Request object
    Set receivedDoc = CreateObject("MSXML2.DOMDocument")
    receivedDoc.async = false
    receivedDoc.load Request

'Retrieving userID and the orders
    Set idNode = receivedDoc.selectSingleNode("//@userID")
    userid = idNode.nodeValue
    Set orderNodes = receivedDoc.selectNodes("//ORDER")

'Generating acknowledgement string to user (i.e., client)
    if orderNodes.length < 2 then
        Response.write orderNodes.length & " order from " & userID
    else
        Response.write orderNodes.length & " orders from " & userID
    end if
%>
```

Useful Web Links

- DOM Level 1 at

    http://www.w3.org/TR/REC-DOM-Level-1/

- DOM Level 3 Core Specification Working Draft at

    http://www.w3.org/TR/2001/WD-DOM-Level-3-Core-20010913/

- Mathematical Markup Language at

    http://www.w3.org/TR/MathML2

- Basic DOM interfaces for Scalable Vector Graphics at

```
http://www.w3.org/TR/SVG/svgdom.html
```

- DOM interfaces for Synchronized Multimedia Integration Language at

```
http://www.w3.org/TR/smil-boston-dom/
```

- Xerces – DOM Paser at

```
http://www.w3.org/TR/2000/REC-xml-20001006
```

- Oracle XML Parser for Java v2 at

```
http://technet.oracle.com/tech/xml/parser_java2/
```

- XML DOM Objects/Interfaces supported in MSXML 3.0 at

```
http://msdn.microsoft.com/library/default.asp?url=/library/
  en-us/xmlsdk30/htm/xmmscxmldomobjects.asp
```

Summary

In this chapter, we introduced DOM programming by illustrating the properties and methods of the different types of interfaces that may be used to make accessing and manipulation of the XML data in an XML document possible. We also presented a mini-case study in which a shopping cart was created and manipulated on the client side, and illustrated how the server could receive and retrieve an XML DOM object from the client.

The concepts that we covered in this chapter should enable you to jumpstart an application using DOM programming. Since we are unable to examine all the APIs for DOM programming in one chapter, we encourage you to refer to the list in Appendix B. We also hope you find the list of links that we provided in the preceding section useful.

Support of XML in ActiveX Data Objects (ADO) 2.1 and Above

IN CHAPTER 4, WE SHOWED how you could access and manipulate data in an XML document using DOM programming. A natural question for you to ask next is how can we eventually keep the data in a permanent store. In the previous chapter, you saw how to serialize an XML DOM object into a stream and then save it into a text file. Aside from a text file, there may be other forms of permanent store, such as a database table or an Excel spreadsheet.

In this chapter, we interact with a data store, specifically a database. We first present Microsoft's strategy in data access and an introduction to ADO as a mechanism for the programmer to interact with the data store. We make use of the ADO object model to incorporate into ASP programming the ability for an application to access the data in a database and, finally, discuss the support for XML.

Universal Data Access

Universal Data Access is Microsoft's strategy for accessing data or information of varied data sources, such as relational databases from different vendors, as well as non-relational data sources, such as electronic mail, using a common set of programming interfaces.

The strategy is materialized via a repertoire of enabling technologies, which we look at next.

Microsoft Data Access Components

The Microsoft Data Access Components (MDAC) provide the components that enable the access to data or information in various types of data stores in a distributed environment where applications and data stores are remote to each other, such as across the Internet. These components include the Microsoft ActiveX Data Objects (ADO), OLE DB, and Open Database Connectivity (ODBC).

The following Web site provides the latest information on and a downloadable version of MDAC: `http://www.microsoft.com/data/`.

At the time of this writing, this Web site shows the latest version for download as MDAC 2.6.

Open Database Connectivity (ODBC)

The ODBC was designed to enable applications to access data primarily in relational data stores using the Structured Query Language (SQL). The same ODBC API for data access in an application can access SQL-based DBMSs of different vendors as long as there is an ODBC driver that enables the API in the application to interface with the underlying DBMS. ODBC reaped huge success as ODBC drivers were developed for most of the major relational database systems.

Some of the ODBC drivers supported in Windows 2000 are:

- Microsoft ODBC driver for Access (4.00.4403.02): ODBCJT32.DLL

- Microsoft ODBC driver for Oracle (2.573.7430.00): MSORCL32. DLL

- Microsoft ODBC driver for Visual FoxPro (6.01.8629.01): VFPODBC.DLL

- Microsoft ODBC driver for SQL Server 2000 (2000.81.7430.00): SQLSRV32.DLL

OLE DB

OLE DB is a successor to ODBC and is designed to provide COM interfaces for accessing other types of data store in addition to the relational databases. OLE DB is designed for relational and nonrelational information sources, including mainframe ISAM/VSAM and hierarchical databases; e-mail and file system stores; text, graphical, and geographical data; and custom business objects.

In the OLE DB architecture, components that are classified as *data providers* are responsible for accessing the data sources and thus exposing data to components that are termed *data consumers*, which use the data. Bridging the providers and the consumers are the OLE DB interfaces together with the *service components*, which are responsible for processing and transporting data.

In order to render continual support to the existing ODBC drivers for the great number of DBMSs, OLE DB also serves as a bridge from the application to the ODBC drivers, which is shown as the OLE DB for ODBC or Microsoft's MSDASQL in Figure 5-1.

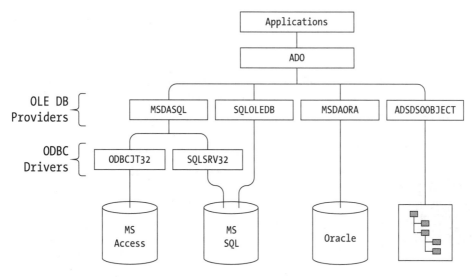

Figure 5-1. Overview of OLE DB architecture

Microsoft has developed the OLE DB providers for most of the major DBMSs as well as other data sources. Table 5-1 shows some of these data sources and the names of the providers.

Table 5-1. List of Data Sources and the Names of Corresponding OLE DB Providers

DATA SOURCE	NAME OF MICROSOFT OLE DB PROVIDER
Microsoft Access	Microsoft.Jet.OLEDB.4.0
Microsoft SQL Server	SQLOLEDB
DB2	DB2OLEDB
Oracle	MSDAORA
ODBC	MSDASQL
Microsoft Directory Services	ADSDSOOBJECT
Microsoft Indexing Service	MSIDXS
Microsoft DTS Packages	DTSPackageDSO
Microsoft Exchange	exoledb.datasource.1
Internet Publishing	MSDAIPP.DSO
Simple Data Sources	MSDAOSP

The simple data sources in Table 5-1 refer to data sources that require fundamental OLE DB support such as arrays in the memory or XML document. Support for XML is discussed later in this chapter.

ActiveX Data Objects (ADO)

The objective of the Microsoft ActiveX Data Objects (ADO) is to provide a consistent application programming interface (API) to data with supports for a variety of development needs such as the creation and operation of objects in a Web environment.

ADO is designed with performance and ease of use in mind. Lightweight, high-performance interface is achieved with implementation using a minimal number of layers between the application's front end and data store.

Figure 5-1 shows the role of ADO with respect to business applications and OLE DB providers, as well as the mechanism in providing backward compatibility for ODBC.

The ADO Object Model

There are five top-level objects in the ADO programming object model:

Connection

This object contains two collection objects:

- Errors, which can contain one or more Error objects

- Properties, which can contain one or more Property objects

Command

This object also defines two collection objects:

- Parameters, which can contain one or more Parameter objects

- Properties, which can contain one or more Property objects

Recordset

This object has two collection objects:

- Fields, which can contain one or more Field objects

- Properties, which can contain one or more Property objects

Record (ADO 2.5 and Above)

This object defines only one collection object:

- Fields, which can contain one or more Field objects

Stream (ADO 2.5 and Above)

We will next look at each of the objects with special emphasis on the Connection, Recordset, and Stream objects, which will help to lay the background knowledge to the case study at the end of this chapter to demonstrate the use of ADO objects in support for XML.

Connection Object

The Connection object represents a session established with a data source, hence, as its name implies, establishing a connection with the data source, which may be across a network. Besides establishing a connection using its Open method, the Connection object also provides the Execute method to retrieve information from the data source.

In this section, we focus on the use of these two methods. For reference to the other methods of the Connection object, navigate your browser to the library of the Microsoft MSDN site at `http://msdn.microsoft.com/library/`.

Connecting to Data Source: The Open Method

To create a Connection object in an ASP script, we use the CreateObject method of the ASP's Server object:

```
<%
    Dim conn
    Set conn = Server.CreateObject ("ADODB.Connection")
%>
```

To open a connection to a data source the Open method is used, which has the following syntax:

```
conn.Open ConnectionString, UserID, Password, ConnectOption
```

The ConnectionString parameter is a string that contains information for establishing a connection. It can contain one or more of the five types of information as listed in Table 5-2.

Table 5-2. Arguments Supported in the ConnectionString

CONNECTIONSTRING ARGUMENT	DESCRIPTION
Provider	Name of OLE DB provider to use for the connection.
File name	Name of file containing provider-specific information. This argument cannot coexist with the provider argument.
Remote Provider	Name of provider to use when opening a client-side connection for remote data services.
Remote Server	Location path of server to use when opening a client-side connection for remote data services.
URL	Absolute URL of a resource.

User ID and password can be specified to ensure authorized access to the data source.

The ConnectOption value determines whether the Open method should return after (i.e., synchronous) or before (i.e., asynchronous) the establishment of the connection. The possible ConnectOption values are adConnectUnspecified (default value) for synchronous connection and adAsyncConnect for asynchronous connection.

The parameters to the Open method can be specified separately as values delimited by commas or as a single string.

The following ASP script fragment shows the opening of a Connection object (conn) to a Microsoft SQL database, BooksCatalog.

```
<%
    conn.Open "Provider=SQLOLEDB;Server=dataServer;Database=BooksCatalog;" &_
            "User ID=sa;Password=;"
%>
```

Next is another script fragment to show the opening and closing of a Connection object using alternative names for some of the arguments in the connection string. In this script, a timeout value of 20 seconds for the establishment of connection is specified to overwrite the default value of 15 seconds. Notice also that we can check the connection status using the State property, which may have the value of either adStateOpen (with constant value 1), or adStateClosed (or 0).

```
<%
    conn.ConnectionString = "Provider=SQLOLEDB;DataSource=dataServer;" &_
                            "Initial Catalog=BooksCatalog;" &_
                            "UID=sa;Pwd=;"
    conn.ConnectionTimeout = 20
    conn.Open
    Response.Write conn.State
    conn.Close
%>
```

Aside from the arguments mentioned previously for use in a connection string, each provider may have its own provider-specific arguments.

Accessing Records in Data Source: The Execute Method

The Connection object provides the Execute method for executing an SQL statement, which may result in the return of a Recordset object. The Execute method may be invoked using one of the following ways depending on whether a Recordset is expected:

```
conn.Execute CommandText, RecordsAffected, Options
Set rs = conn.Execute (CommandText, RecordsAffected, Options)
```

The variable, rs, in the preceding statement represent a Recordset object. A Recordset object is used to hold records of the data source and it is discussed in greater detail later.

The first parameter, CommandText, can be an SQL statement, a database table, a stored procedure, a URL or a provider-specific command.

The second parameter, RecordsAffected, is optional and is used by the provider to return a numeric value indicating the number of records affected by the operation performed by the Execute method.

The third parameter is optional and it evaluates to a numeric value. It is a combination of one or more of the CommandTypeEnum and ExecuteOptionEnum values. The CommandTypeEnum values indicate how the provider should evaluate the first parameter, CommandText, while ExecuteOptionEnum specifies if an execution is performed asynchronously as well as the type of object returned.

The possible values of CommandTypeEnum and ExecuteOptionEnum are listed in Table 5-3 and Table 5-4, respectively. The numeric constant is given next to each constant name. Note that not all of the values are used for the Execute method defined for the Connection object.

Table 5-3. Possible CommandTypeEnum Values Used as Parameters for the Execute Method

COMMANDTYPEENUM	IMPLICATION
adCmdUnspecified (-1)	The type of CommandText is not specified.
adCmdText (1)	CommandText is a text string that is either an SQL command or a stored procedure call.
adCmdTable (2)	CommandText is the name of a database table. An SQL is generated internally to retrieve all columns for all records in the table specified as the CommandText parameter.
adCmdStoredProc (4)	CommandText is the name of a stored procedure.
adCmdUnknown (8)	The type of CommandText is unknown.
adCmdFile (256)	CommandText is the name of a file, typically acting as a persistent store for the contents of a Recordset object. This parameter value is used only for the Open and Requery methods.
adCmdTableDirect (512)	CommandText is the name of a database table. This parameter value is used only for the Open and Requery methods.

Table 5-4. Possible ExecuteOptionEnum Values Used as Parameters for the Execute Method

EXECUTEOPTIONENUM	IMPLICATION
adOptionUnspecified (-1)	The command is not specified.
adAsyncExecute (16)	The command is executed asynchronously.
adAsyncfetch (32)	Retrieval is performed asynchronously after an initial quantity (specified as the CacheSize property).
adAsyncfetchNonBlocking (64)	Retrieval is performed asynchronously without blocking subsequent fetching operations.
adExecuteNoRecords (128)	The CommandText parameter is an SQL command or stored procedure that does not return any row or record from the data source. If there is any returned, it is discarded.
adExecuteStream (1024)	The result of the command execution is returned as a stream.
adExecuteRecord (2048)	The result of the command execution is returned as a Record object.

Example of Accessing a Data Source Using the Connection Object

Let's work with a database named BooksCatalog, which consists of a table named books. Each record in the books table encapsulates the information about a book with unique ISBN. The table consists of the following fields:

- ISBN: The International Standard Book Number of a book

- Title: The title of a book

- Price: The list price of a book in US dollars

- CoverType: The cover type (hard or soft) of a book

- Pages: The number of pages in a book

We will write a fragment of ASP script that performs the following:

- Uses a Connection to establish a connection to the BooksCatalog database created on a Microsoft SQL 2000 Server using the Open method.

- Executes an SQL statement to retrieve all book records in the books table into a Recordset object for further manipulation, such as displaying the retrieved book information.

- Executes a second SQL statement that updates the price of the book with ISBN, 1-893115-86-0.

```
<!-- connExe.asp -->
<!--#include file="adovbs.inc"-->
<html>
<h3>Execute Method of the Connection Object</h3>
<%
    Option Explicit
    Dim conn
    Dim rs
    Set conn = Server.CreateObject ("ADODB.Connection")
    query = "UPDATE books SET Price='35.0' WHERE ISBN='1-893115-86-0'"

    conn.Open "Provider=SQLOLEDB;Server=dataServer;Database=BooksCatalog;" &_
              "uid=sa;password="
    Set rs = conn.Execute ("books", , adCmdTable)
    conn.Execute (query, , adCmdText)
%>
</html>
```

NOTE *The adovbs.inc file contains declarations and values of some important constants such as adCmdTable in order for the previous example to work without giving errors. Make sure this file is placed in the same directory as the ASP script, connExe.asp. It can be found in the Program Files\Common Files\System\ado directory of the drive where the Windows operating system (such as Windows 2000 Advanced Server) is installed.*

NOTE *The* Option Explicit *statement is included to enforce the declaration of all variables before they are used. This is a good practice when writing VBScript scripplets of considerable size as it facilitates maintenance of codes.*

The first Execute call results in a Recordset object that consists of all fields of all three books stored in the books database table. The second call to the Execute method will not return any row of record in the books table. However, the Price value of the second book, shown in Figure 5-2, will be updated to 35.

ISBN	Title	Price	CoverType	Pages
1-893115-76-3	C++ for VB Programmers	49.95	S	400
1-893115-86-0	A Programmer's Introduction to C#	34.95	S	357
1-893115-95-X	Cryptography in C & C++	49.95	S	380

Figure 5-2. Structure and original contents of the books *table*

Recordset Object

The ADO Recordset object is where the result of a query to a data source is held. It is also used to buffer the content of a record to be edited before an update or insertion operation to the data source is executed. It is most often used to hold information from a relational data source such as a relational database. The logical table structure of the Recordset object can be mapped directly to the records of a relational database, where each row in the Recordset corresponds to a record and the columns correspond to the fields of a record as used in the database. The Recordset object provides access to the data (i.e., records) via a *cursor* and protection of data via a *locking* mechanism.

As in a Connection object, a Recordset can be created in a back-end service using the ASP Server object as shown in the following code:

```
<%
    Dim rs
    Set rs = Server.CreateObject ("ADODB.Recordset")
%>
```

To create a Recordset in a script running at a Web client, we can write the following lines using VBScript:

```
<script language="VBScript">
    Dim rs
    Set rs = CreateObject ("ADODB.Recordset")
</script>
```

Some reasons for creating a Recordset object at a Web client include loading some XML structure such as an XML DOM object into a Recordset structure so that we can leverage on the existing Recordset methods to modify or edit data. The modified data held in a Recordset can then be sent back to the backend server to be updated into some database. We will see an example on the use of a client-side Recordset object in a Web-based application in the later part of this chapter.

In the next section, we explore the properties and methods of a Recordset object used directly with an SQL query in ASP scripts.

Properties and Methods

We shall first present some of the properties and methods defined for a Recordset object, which we use in the examples discussed in this section. The lists are shown in Table 5-5 and Table 5-6, respectively.

For a complete listing of the properties, methods, and events of a Recordset object, point your browser to http://msdn.microsoft.com/library/default.asp?url=/library/en-us/ado270/htm/mdobjodbrecpme.asp.

Table 5-5. Partial List of Properties of a Recordset Object

PROPERTIES	DESCRIPTION
AbsolutePosition	This property is the location of the current record in a Recordset object, where the first record has the AbsolutePosition value 1. It may take on any of the PositionEnum values predefined in adovbs.inc as mentioned previously.
ActiveCommand	This is the Command object that is associated with or created the Recordset in question.
ActiveConnection	This refers to the Connection object over which the Recordset object is opened.
BOF, EOF	BOF refers to the cursor position that is before the first record in a Recordset object. EOF refers to the cursor position that is after the last record.
CacheSize	This returns the number of records cached in local memory.
CursorLocation	This indicates the location of the cursor. It may take on any of the CursorLocationEnum values defined in adovbs.inc: adUseNone (1), adUseServer (2 - default), and adUseClient (3).
CursorType	This indicates the type of cursor used in a Recordset object. It may take on any of the CursorTypeEnum values defined in adovbs.inc: adOpenForwardOnly (0, default), adOpenKeyset (1), adOpenDynamic (2), and adOpenStatic (3).

(continued)

Table 5-5. Partial List of Properties of a Recordset Object (continued)

PROPERTIES	DESCRIPTION
Fields	A collection of Field objects where a Field corresponds to a column in the Recordset object.
LockType	This refers the type of lock applying on the Recordset object while operations or methods are being executed on the records in the Recordset object. It takes on any of the LockTypeEnum values: adLockReadOnly (1, default), adLockPessimistic (2), adLockOptimistic (3), adLockBatchOptimistic (4), adLockUnspecified (-1).
MaxRecords	This property refers to the maximum number of records to be returned to a Recordset from a query. The default value is 0, which indicates no limit to the number of records returned.
PageCount	This refers to the number of pages of records the Recordset object contains. Each except the last page has a size indicated by PageSize. The last page may have fewer records than other pages.
PageSize	This is the maximum number of records set for a page of the Recordset object.
Properties	This is a collection of Property objects that correspond to the properties specific to the data provider. These properties are also called dynamic properties as to be differentiated from the built-in properties of a Recordset object. All the other properties in Table 5-5 are built-in properties. Each dynamic property has a name, data type, value and attributes specific to the provider. The attributes are collectively represented as a value of the long data type. This value is the sum of one or more of the possible PropertyAttributesEnum values: adPropNotSupported (0), adPropRequired (1), adPropOptional (2), adPropRead (512), and adPropWrite (1024).
RecordCount	This returns the number of records in a Recordset object.
Source	This indicates the data source of a Recordset object. It may be a Command object, an SQL statement, name of a database table or a stored procedure.

(continued)

Table 5-5. Partial List of Properties of a Recordset Object (continued)

PROPERTIES	DESCRIPTION
State	This returns the state of the Recordset object. It takes on any of the ObjectStateEnum values: adStateClosed (0, default), adStateOpen (1), adStateConnecting (2), adStateExecuting (4), adStateFetching (8).
Status	This indicates the status of a record with respect to a batch operation such as the UpdateBatch method on a Recordset object.

Table 5-6. Partial List of Methods of a Recordset Object

METHODS	DESCRIPTION
Addnew Fields, FieldValues	This method creates a new record in a Recordset object and causes the cursor to point to the new record as the current record. The first parameter (Fields) is a list of one or more fields of the new record addressed by their names or ordinal positions. The second parameter (FieldValues) is the corresponding values of the fields specified in the first parameter.
Cancel	This method is called to terminate a previous asynchronous Open method.
CancelBatch AffectedRecords	This method cancels a pending batch update operation. It takes in an optional parameter, which can be any of the AffectEnum values that specifies the number of records that are affected: adAffectCurrent (1), adAffectGroup (2), adAffectAll (3), and adAffectAllChapters (4).
CancelUpdate	This method cancels all changes made to the current or new record in a Recordset object or a Record object before calling the update method.
Close	This closes an open Recordset object and all its dependents.
Delete AffectedRecords	This method deletes the current record or a group of records from a Recordset object depending on the parameter value, which can be any of the AffectEnum values as described previously for the CancelBatch method.

(continued)

Table 5-6. Partial List of Methods of a Recordset Object (continued)

METHODS	DESCRIPTION
MoveFirst	This method moves the cursor to point to the first record in a Recordset object.
MoveLast	This method moves the cursor to point to the last record in a Recordset object.
MoveNext	This method moves the cursor forward to point to the next record in a Recordset object. If the current cursor position is the last record, calling MoveNext will set the cursor to the position after the last record, rendering the property EOF to be true. Calling MoveNext when EOF is true will cause an error to occur.
MovePrevious	This method moves the cursor backward to point to the previous record in a Recordset object. If the current cursor position is the first record, calling MovePrevious will set the cursor to the position before the first record, rendering the property BOF to be true. Calling MovePrevious when BOF is true will cause an error to occur.
Open Source, ActiveConnection, CursorType, LockType, Options	This method creates a cursor used with a Recordset. All the parameters are optional. The Source parameter may be a Command object, a string of SQL statement, a database table, a stored procedure call, a URL, a file or a Stream object. The Options parameter is a numeric value that gives clues to the provider on how the Source parameter should be evaluated. Options is a combination of one or more of the CommandTypeEnum or ExecuteOptionEnum values. The possible CommandTypeEnum values are listed in Table 5-3 and the possible ExecuteOptionEnum values are listed in Table 5-4.

(continued)

Table 5-6. Partial List of Methods of a Recordset Object (continued)

METHODS	DESCRIPTION
Save Destination, PersistFormat	Destination may be a complete path to a file or a Stream object such as the ASP Response object. PersistFormat specifies the format in which the Recordset should be saved. It takes on one of the possible PersistFormatEnum values: adPersistADTG (0 – Microsoft Advanced Data adPersistADTG ≈ adPersistXML or ad PersistADO (1), and adPersistProviderSpecific (2).
Update Fields, FieldValues	This method updates the current record in a Recordset object. The parameters are optional. The first parameter specifies a list of one or more fields of the current record addressed by their names or ordinal positions. The second parameter specifies the corresponding values of the fields in the first parameter.
UpdateBatch AffectedRecords	This method performs all pending updates in a batch. The optional parameter can be any of the AffectEnum values as described for the CancelBatch method.

Querying Records in a Database

We will use the database, BooksCatalog, as depicted previously in Figure 5-2, to illustrate the use of a Recordset object. For easy reference, we will display the original contents of the books table again; this is where we will start working with the Recordset object.

ISBN	Title	Price	CoverType	Pages
1-893115-76-3	C++ for VB Programmers	49.95	S	400
1-893115-86-0	A Programmer's Introduction to C#	34.95	S	357
1-893115-95-X	Cryptography in C & C++	49.95	S	380

The ASP script in Listing 5-1 creates a connection to the BooksCatalog database, retrieves all books that contain the keyword, *Programmer*, in their titles, and displays each book retrieved in a separate line using HTML.

Listing 5-1. rsQuery.asp

```
<!-- rsQuery.asp -->
<!--#include file="adovbs.inc"-->
<html>
<h3>Books for Programmers</h3>
<%
    Dim conn
    Dim rs
    Set conn = Server.CreateObject ("ADODB.Connection")
    Set rs = Server.CreateObject ("ADODB.Recordset")
    query = "SELECT ISBN, Title FROM books WHERE Title LIKE '%Programmer%'"

    conn.Open "Provider=SQLOLEDB;Server=dataServer;Database=BooksCatalog;" &_
              "uid=sa;password="
    rs.Open query, conn, adOpenForwardOnly, adLockOptimistic, adCmdText

    while not rs.EOF
        Response.Write rs("ISBN") & "   " & rs("Title")
        rs.MoveNext
    wend
    rs.Close
    conn.Close
%>
</html>
```

In the Open statement of the Recordset, the last parameter value, adCmdText, indicates that the provider will interpret the source, "query," as the text of an SQL string.

If the ASP script is saved as rsQuery.asp and loaded from Internet Explorer 5.0, the search result will be as shown in Figure 5-3.

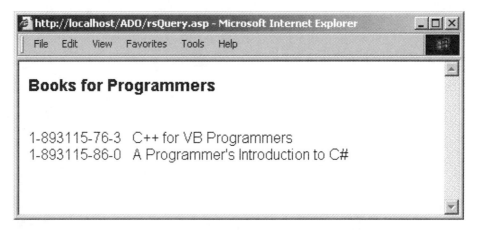

Figure 5-3. Query to the books *table using the search string, Programmer, for book titles*

In the previous ASP script, the statement

```
rs.Open query, conn, adOpenForwardOnly, adLockOptimistic, adCmdText
```

can be replaced by the following statements that set some of the relevant properties of the Recordset object, rs:

```
rs.ActiveConnection = conn
rs.CursorType = adOpenForwardOnly
rs.LockType = adLockOptimistic
rs.Open query
```

Inserting a Record in a Database

We will use the same database (BooksCatalog) to illustrate the insertion of a new record into the books table. The script in Listing 5-2 will accomplish the task:

Listing 5-2. rsInsert.asp

```
<!-- rsInsert.asp -->
<!--#include file="adovbs.inc"-->
<html>
<h3>Adding New Book to Catalog</h3>
<%
    Dim conn
    Dim rs
    Set conn = Server.CreateObject ("ADODB.Connection")
    Set rs = Server.CreateObject ("ADODB.Recordset")
```

```
        conn.Open "Provider=SQLOLEDB;Server=dataServer;Database=BooksCatalog;" &_
                  "uid=sa;password="
        rs.Open "books", conn, adOpenForwardOnly, adLockOptimistic, adCmdTable
        rs.Addnew
            rs("ISBN") = "1-893115-81-X"
            rs("Title") = "SQL Server: Common Problems, Tested Solutions"
            rs("Price") = "39.95"
            rs("CoverType") = "S"
            rs("Pages") = "598"
        rs.Update
        rs.Close
        conn.Close
%>
</html>
```

Notice that the Open statement of the Recordset contains the parameter value, adCmdTable, indicating that the provider will interpret the source, "books," as the name of a database table.

The resultant books table after the insertion is shown in Figure 5-4.

ISBN	Title	Price	CoverType	Pages
1-893115-76-3	C++ for VB Programmers	49.95	S	400
1-893115-81-X	SQL Server: Common Problems, Tested Solutions	39.95	S	598
1-893115-86-0	A Programmer's Introduction to C#	34.95	S	357
1-893115-95-X	Cryptography in C & C++	49.95	S	380

Figure 5-4. The books *table showing the new book added as the second record*

An alternative to the preceding script is to use the Execute method of a Command or a Connection object to perform the insertion of a new record, in which case, we don't need to execute the Open method of the Recordset explicitly. However, we need to first formulate the SQL statement in a string before executing it via the Connection object, conn, as in the following listing:

```
sql = "INSERT INTO books (ISBN, Title, Price, CoverType, Pages) " &_
      "VALUES ('1-893115-81-X', " &_
      "'SQL Server: Common Problems, Tested Solutions', " &_
      "39.95, 'S', 598)"
Set rs = conn.Execute (sql)
```

One disadvantage of not opening the Recordset object explicitly is that the resultant Recordset would assume the default cursor type (i.e., move forward only) and other relevant values.

Deleting a Record from a Database

We will show in Listing 5-3 how the book with ISBN 1-893115-81-X can be deleted using the Delete method of the Recordset object.

Listing 5-3. rsDelete.asp

```
<!-- rsDelete.asp -->
<!--#include file="adovbs.inc"-->
<html>
<h3>Deleting Book from Catalog</h3>
<%
    Dim conn
    Dim rs
    Set conn = Server.CreateObject ("ADODB.Connection")
    Set rs = Server.CreateObject ("ADODB.Recordset")
    query = "SELECT * FROM books WHERE ISBN='1-893115-81-X'"

    conn.Open "Provider=SQLOLEDB;Server=dataServer;Database=BooksCatalog;" &_
             "uid=sa;password="
    rs.Open query, conn, adOpenKeyset, adLockOptimistic, adCmdText
    rs.Delete adAffectCurrent
    rs.Close
    conn.Close
%>
</html>
```

The default parameter value, adAffectCurrent, of the rs.Delete method used in the previous script indicates that the deleting operation affects only the current record, which is the only record (with ISBN 1-893115-81-X) in the Recordset returned from the rs.Open statement just before the deletion statement.

If the rs.Open and rs.Delete statements in the preceding script are replaced by

```
rs.Open "books", conn, adOpenForwardOnly, adLockOptimistic, adCmdTable
rs.Delete
```

only the first book of the books table is deleted.

Command Object

The Command object specifies the statement for manipulating the data such as insertion of data into a database table or directory. In the case of a relational database, this can simply be a string of SQL statement.

The Command object has a Dialect property that can be set to the CommandText or CommandStream value. The former constant value indicates that the Command object contains an executable command, such as an SQL statement, while the latter indicates that the object can be used to hold other more complex command or query structures, such as the XML template query that we discuss in Chapter 6.

The Command object defines an Execute method with the following syntax for returning a Recordset result:

```
Set rs = cmd.Execute (RecordsAffected, Parameters, Options)
```

and the following for returning a non-Recordset result:

```
cmd.Execute (RecordsAffected, Parameters, Options)
```

The first parameter, RecordsAffected, is optional and is used by the provider to return a numeric value to indicate the number of records affected by the operation performed by the Execute method.

The second parameter, Parameters, is an optional list of values used together with the input CommandText or CommandStream.

The third parameter is optional and it evaluates to a numeric value. It is a combination of one or more of the CommandTypeEnum and ExecuteOptionEnum values that have been discussed earlier and listed in Table 5-3 and Table 5-4.

As with the Recordset object, the Command object can be associated with an opened connection, where the Command object's Name property can be used to indicate the Command object as a method on the connection.

We have seen various ways of performing a query to a relational database using the Connection and Recordset objects. What makes the use of the Command object in executing a query different from the other two objects is that we are able to define and *persist* a statement using a Command object and re-execute the statement.

In this next section, we show the similarity between using the Connection and Command objects, as well as how the latter are used to create a prepared statement.

Querying a Database Using the Execute Method

The Execute method for the Command object has the same format as that discussed for the Connection object. The ASP fragment in Listing 5-4 shows how a Command object is created and used to query the BooksCatalog database for books whose prices are below $40.

Listing 5-4. `cmdExe.asp`

```
<!-- cmdExe.asp -->
<!--#include file="adovbs.inc"-->
<html>
<h3>Querying Books (<$40) from Catalog</h3>
<%
    Dim conn
    Dim cmd
    Dim rs
    Set conn = Server.CreateObject ("ADODB.Connection")
    Set cmd = Server.CreateObject ("ADODB.Command")
    Set rs = Server.CreateObject ("ADODB.Recordset")

    cmd.ActiveConnection = conn
    cmd.CommandText = "SELECT * FROM books WHERE Price < 40"
    cmd.CommandType = adCmdText

    Set rs = cmd.Execute
    while not rs.EOF
        Response.write rs("Title") & "<br>"
        rs.MoveNext
    wend
%>
</html>
```

If the state of the BooksCatalog database appears as shown in Figure 5-2 previously, the output generated by cmdExe.asp is as shown in Figure 5-5.

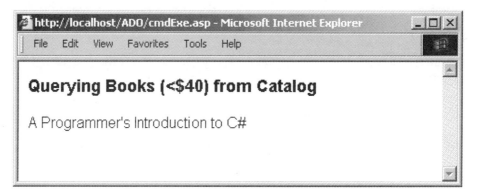

Figure 5-5. Querying books using the Execute method of a Command object

Persisting SQL Statement

To *persist* an SQL statement is to create a *prepared SQL statement* as in contrast to the dynamic SQL statements that we have been using so far in this chapter. The latter is appropriate in applications where the same SQL statement is seldom re-invoked. Each time such an SQL statement is invoked, it involves an overhead in parsing the statement and creating a data access plan.

For applications that execute a similarly structured SQL statement multiple times, differing only in the parameter values each time the SQL statement is executed, the base SQL statement can be *prepared* once and executed many times. In this case, the parsing and access plan creation need to be performed only once, with *parameter placeholders* that can be substituted with the actual values during run-time.

For example, if we expect the user in a browsing session to invoke queries multiple times for books whose price is less than x dollars, where x may vary in each query, then the use of a prepared SQL statement is appropriate.

To prepare a statement ready for invocation, it involves a few steps that we can illustrate using an ASP script:

1. Set the base statement. For our requirement for finding books less than x, the variable parameter value is denoted by the ? symbol:

```
Set cmd.CommandText = "SELECT * FROM books WHERE Price < ?"
```

NOTE *CommandText is a property of the Command object. For a full list of properties and methods of the Command object, refer to* http://msdn.microsoft.com/library/default.asp?url=/library/en-us/ado270/htm/mdobjcommandpme.asp.

2. Define the type of parameter value we are expecting. In our case we will call this parameter priceParam and we will use the CreateParameter method to create a Parameter object to embody it. (Note that if we have more than one ? in the base statement, we need to uniquely identify each of them.) Now, if we expect the price limit to be a single-precision, floating-point number, we can describe the parameter for holding the price limit as follows:

```
Dim paramObject
Set paramObject = cmd.CreateParameter("priceParam", adSingle, _
                                      adParamInput, 4, 0)
```

173

NOTE *adSingle describes the data type; adParamInput is a parameter direction indicator specifying that the parameter is to be input for processing by the provider; 4 is the length; 0 is a value assigned to the parameter.*

NOTE *For a full list of data types, refer to* http://msdn.microsoft.com/library/ default.asp?url=/library/en-us/ado270/htm/ mdcstdatatypeenum.asp.

NOTE *For a full list of parameter direction indicators, refer to* http://msdn.microsoft.com/library/ default.asp?url=/library/en-us/ado270/htm/ mdcstparameterdirectionenum.asp.

3. Add the Parameter object embodying the pricing parameter to the Parameters collection of the Command object:

```
cmd.Parameters.Append paramObject
```

To invoke the prepared statement, we need to perform the following steps:

1. Assign the runtime value of `priceParam` in the Parameters collection of the Command object, `cmd`, that represents the prepared statement.

2. Execute the Command object using the Execute method.

The following is a fragment of an ASP script that performs what was just described, with the assumption that the actual price limit value (denoted by the variable `priceLimit`) is retrieved from a form passed in to the script:

```
cmd.Parameters("priceParam").Value = Request.Form("priceLimit")
Set rs = cmd.Execute
```

Record Object

The Record object can be viewed as a single-row Recordset object. It is used with Document Source Providers such as the OLE DB provider for Internet Publishing.

This object is used to map to a document-based data source such as a report with special layout or an e-mail message. The RecordType property identifies the type of the Record object, which may be adSimpleRecord that refers to a file, or adCollectionRecord that refers to a folder.

To open a Record object to associate with a data source, the Open method is used. Other methods include CopyRecord, DeleteRecord, GetChildren, MoveRecord, Cancel, and Close methods.

We will not focus on the Record object other than to introduce it briefly to make the chapter more complete. For reference to the purpose of the various properties and use of methods of the Record object, point your browser to the MSDN library Web site of Microsoft at `http://msdn.microsoft.com/library/`.

Stream Object

A *stream* is a sequence of data bytes, which may be text or binary. The ADO Stream object is used to encapsulate such a stream.

Each object, such as a file, pointed to by a URL has an associated Stream object that can be opened, read from, written to, as well as closed. Each Record object is also associated with a Stream object. Besides the two default Stream objects, we can instantiate one in an application for holding data.

An example for instantiating a Stream object is for storing information used by providers such as the Microsoft OLE DB Provider for Internet Publishing.

Another example would be for receiving retrieved information from a data source provider in formats (e.g., XML format) other than the Recordset format. In addition, a Stream object can be used to store data of a Record or Recordset object saved in XML format.

As mentioned earlier, a Command object may contain a CommandStream instead of CommandText, in which case, a Stream object is used as the source containing the command for execution. An example of CommandStream would be the XML UpdateGrams, which can be used as a source of command against the Microsoft OLE DB Provider for SQL Server 2000.

Our focus here will be using the Stream object in support of the XML data.

Creating a Stream Object

The ASP script used to create a Stream object follows:

```
<%
    Dim strm
    Set strm = Server.CreateObject ("ADODB.Stream")
%>
```

Similarly, a Stream object can be created in a Web client for storing data in binary or XML format. The following shows a script fragment for creating it at a client:

```
<script language="VBScript">
    Dim strm
    Set strm = CreateObject ("ADODB.Stream")
</script>
```

Opening a Stream Object

The Open method of a Stream object, strm, has the following syntax:

```
strm.Open Source, Mode, OpenOptions, Username, Password
```

A Stream can be associated with a source referenced by some URL, or with a Record or Recordset object. If the *Source* parameter is not specified, this is an instantiated Stream object.

The Mode parameter can take on any of the ConnectModeEnum values listed in Table 5-7.

Table 5-7. Possible ConnectModeEnum Values Used as Parameters for the Open Method of a Stream Object

CONNECTMODEENUM	IMPLICATION
adModeUnknown (0)	Default, indicating access permissions are unknown or cannot be determined.
adModeRead (1)	Read-only mode.
adModeWrite (2)	Write-only mode.
adModeReadWrite (3)	Read/write mode.
adModeShareDenyRead (4)	Denying read access in opening a connection.
adModeShareDenyWrite (8)	Denying write access in opening a connection.
adModeShareDenyExclusive (12)	Disallowing opening of a connection.
adModeShareDenyNone (16)	Allowing opening of a connection with any mode—no denial of any access permission.
adModeRecursive (0x400000)	Used in conjunction with adModeShareDenyRead, adModeShareWrite, adModeShareDenyExclusive to propagate restrictions to all subrecords of a Record object.

The OpenOptions parameter can take on any of the StreamOpenOptionsEnum values listed in Table 5-8.

Table 5-8. Possible StreamOpenOptionsEnum Values Used as Parameters for the Open Method of a Stream Object

STREAMOPENOPTIONSENUM	IMPLICATION
adOpenStreamUnspecified (-1)	Default, indicating Stream object is opened with default options.
adOpenStreamAsync (1)	Stream object is opened using asynchronous mode.
adOpenStreamFromRecord (4)	Opening Stream object where Source is an opened Record object.

The last two optional parameters of the Open method specify the authorized user id and password for opening the Stream object.

Loading Content into a Stream Object

An opened Stream object, `strm`, may be populated with content in several ways:

- Loading contents to a Stream object from a file. After loading, the current position is set to 0—i.e., the first byte of the stream.

    ```
    strm.LoadFromFile filename
    ```

- Saving contents of a Recordset object, `rs`, into a Stream object. The format in which the Recordset object should be saved can be specified in the second parameter, persistFormat.

    ```
    rs.Save strm, persistFormat
    ```

- Writing binary data to a Stream object. The source is a variant containing the binary data to be copied to the stream, `strm`.

    ```
    strm.Write Source
    ```

- Writing binary data to a Stream object. The WriteText method takes in a first parameter, which is a string containing the text data to be copied to the stream, `strm`. A second option can be specified to indicate if a line separator character is to be appended to the back of the string after it is copied to the stream. If a separator is needed, the parameter should be set to adWriteLine (a constant with value 1); otherwise, it has the default value adWriteChar (0).

    ```
    strm.WriteText Source, Options
    ```

Reading Content from a Stream Object

The Read or ReadText method is used to read the content of a Stream object. The latter is valid only for text content. The reading operation starts from the location indicated by the Position property of the Stream object, and it is only in the forward direction. The two reading methods return a variant object, depending on the content read.

The syntax is shown next for each of the two methods of a Stream, `strm`, where the data is returned to a variant, `result`:

```
result = strm.Read(NumBytes)
result = strm.ReadText(NumChars)
```

NumBytes and NumChars indicate the number of bytes and characters to be read and are optional parameters. The default is reading all bytes and characters (adReadAll)—that is, until `strm.EOS` (end of stream)—starting from the location, `strm.Position`. For text stream, reading can be done line by line, based on the line separators.

Saving Content of a Stream Object

The SaveToFile method is used to save binary data of a Stream object, e.g., `strm`, to a specified file:

```
strm.SaveToFile Filename, SaveOptions
```

The SaveOptions parameter can be a combination of any of the SaveOptionsEnum values listed in Table 5-9.

Table 5-9. Possible SaveOptionsEnum Values Used as Parameters for SaveToFile Method of a Stream Object

SAVEOPTIONSENUM	IMPLICATION
adSaveCreateNoExist (1)	Default, indicating a new file is created if the specified file, Filename, does not already exist.
adSaveCreateOverWrite (2)	If the specified file, Filename, already exists, its content will be overwritten.

Closing a Stream Object

To close an opened Stream, the Close method is used:

```
strm.Close
```

Error Handling

Let's introduce the ADO Error object and the ADO Errors collection for handling errors encountered during data access operations.

A Connection object has an Errors collection, which consists of 0 or more Error objects. Each of the Error objects in the collection can be addressed as Errors(i) or Errors.Item(i), where i is an index value that starts from 0.

The Errors Collection

An Errors collection has two properties:

- Count: The number of Error objects in the Errors collection

- Item: For referencing an individual Error object in the Errors collection

Methods of the Errors collection:

- Clear: Removes all Error objects from the Errors collection

- Refresh: Updates the Error objects with information from the provider

The Error Object

An Error object has the following properties:

- Description: Description of the error

- HelpContext: ContextID in the help file associated with the error

- Helpfile: Name of the help file associated with the error

- NativeError: Provider-specific error code of the error

- Number: Unique ADO number that identifies the error

- Source: Name of object or application that generated the error originally

- SQLState: 5-character code for the error if the error occurred during an SQL command

Error Checking

We demonstrate error checking in an ASP script after making a query to the books table of the BooksCatalog database. We have planted a small error in the SQL statement by specifying an erroneous field name, Titl, for the books table. The listing for the ASP script is shown in Listing 5-5.

Listing 5-5. errorCheck.asp

```
<!-- errorCheck.asp -->
<!--#include file="adovbs.inc"-->
<%
    Dim conn
    Dim rs
    Set conn = Server.CreateObject("ADODB.Connection")
    Set rs = Server.CreateObject("ADODB.Recordset")

    conn.Open "Provider=SQLOLEDB;Server=dataServer;Database=BooksCatalog;" &_
            "User ID=sa;Password=;"
    sql = "SELECT Titl FROM books"

    On Error Resume Next
    Set rs = conn.Execute (sql)

    if conn.Errors.Count <> 0 then
        Response.write conn.Error.Count & " Errors:" & "<br>"
        for each e in conn.Errors
            Response.write "   -[" & e.NativeError & "] " &_
                            e.Description & "<br>"
        next
    else
        while not rs.EOF
            Response.write rs("Title") & "<br>"
            rs.MoveNext
        wend
    end if
    rs.Close
    conn.Close
%>
```

The On Error Resume Next statement will avoid the termination of code execution and displaying of error messages voluntarily when a runtime error occurs. It allows execution to resume with the next statement after the line generating the error. It is then the programmer's responsibility to insert appropriate code to handle the errors. In the preceding code, we "handle" the error by displaying the total number of errors captured in the Errors collection at that point in time, as well as displaying the NativeError and Description properties of each error.

Figures 5-6 and 5-7, respectively, show the difference in browser displays with and without the error handling code.

Figure 5-6. Result of loading errorCheck.asp

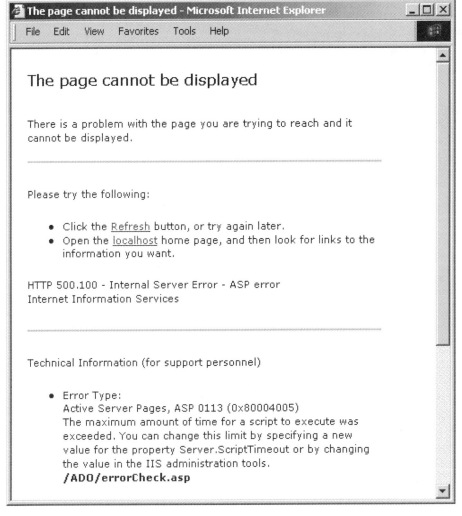

Figure 5-7. Resultant display if error handling is not incorporated into errorCheck.asp

Case Study: Updating Book Prices Using Three-Tier Architecture

In this section, we illustrate the use of a stream in XML format to transport the contents of a Recordset over the HTTP link between a Web client and Web server.

The client first requests a list of books priced above $40. To simplify the programming, the user is not given the liberty to choose individual books to reduce their prices. If the user decides to slash down prices, the discount applies to all the books that cost more than $40. The user is allowed to reduce the prices by 50¢ at a time.

Next, the user invokes the sending of the list of books with their updated pricing information back to the Web server, which in turn executes a batch update command to update all the records that were retrieved earlier—that is, books costing more than $40.

Figure 5-8 illustrates the sequence of events for granting a discount to chosen books. The different formats for holding books' information at each stage in the event sequence are described.

The two main data formats used are the Recordset and Stream. Consider sending a stream from the Web server to the client as described in step 6 in Figure 5-8. The Stream object is written from the server to the client via the ASP Response object and when it reaches the client, it is loaded into a DOM object before being loaded into a Recordset object created at the client.

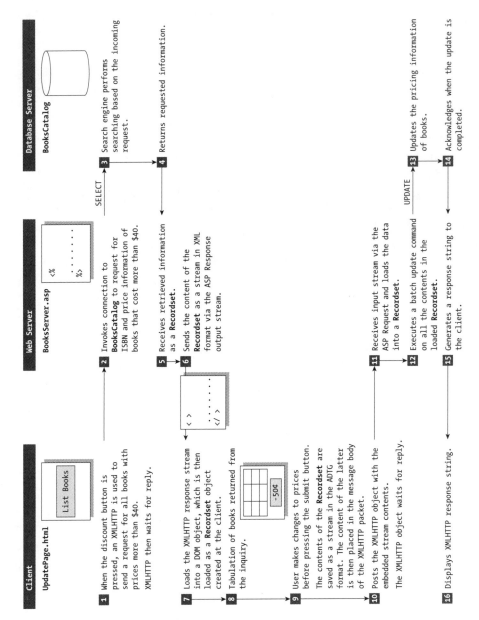

Figure 5-8. Three-tier architecture used for updating prices of selected books

For the sending of a stream from the client to the Web server, the Recordset operated on at the client is saved as a stream and sent via the XMLHTTP to the Web server (step 10). When the stream reaches the server, the receiving ASP script at the server retrieves the stream through the ASP Request object, which can be opened as a Recordset object (step 11).

The Data Store

We will continue to use the BooksCatalog database that was shown earlier in
Figure 5-2. For convenience of reference, the current state of the books table is
presented here:

ISBN	Title	Price	CoverType	Pages
1-893115-76-3	C++ for VB Programmers	49.95	S	400
1-893115-86-0	A Programmer's Introduction to C#	34.95	S	357
1-893115-95-X	Cryptography in C & C++	49.95	S	380

Web Page for the Client: UpdatePage.html

From Figure 5-8, the client side is responsible for performing the following tasks:

- Providing a button to invoke a request to the Web server via an XMLHTTP
  object for a list of books that cost more than $40.

- Receiving the list of requested books into a DOM object, and then opening
  the latter as a Recordset object.

- Displaying the books' information in a table.

- Providing a button to invoke reduction of book prices by 50¢.

- Updating the prices of the books and refreshing the screen with the new
  pricing information.

- Providing a button to invoke a request, via an XMLHTTP object, to a server
  to update the books with their new prices.

- Receiving response to the update request.

User Interface

We implement three buttons in the application:

- A button labeled List Books is used to invoke step 1 of the event
  sequence that is shown in Figure 5-8. This button should not appear in
  subsequent stages.

- A button labeled – 50¢ is used to impose a reduction of prices of all the books listed each time it is clicked.

- A button labeled Submit to send the new prices of the books to the Web server where a batch update will be initiated to update the prices in the database.

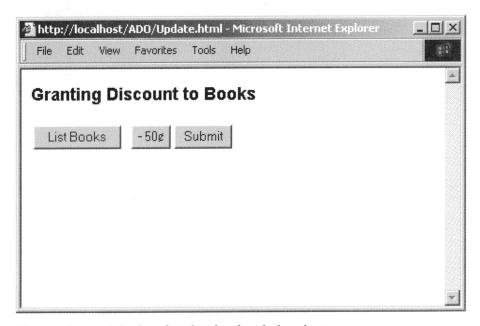

Figure 5-9. Initial display of Update.html with three buttons

There will be no effect in clicking the last two buttons if the first button has not been clicked first.

An area denoted by the identifier BooksArea situated after the page heading but before the buttons is designated as the location to list the books with original prices above $40. The area (BooksArea) and buttons can be implemented using the following code fragment in UpdatePage.html:

```
<h3>Granting Discount to Books</h3>
<div id="BooksArea"></div>
<table border="0">
    <tr>
        <td width="200"><div id="ListButtonArea">
            <button name="getBooks">List Books</button>
        </div></td>
        <td><button name="updatePrice">- 50¢</button></td>
```

```
    <td><button name="sendToServer">Submit</button></td>
  </tr>
</table>
```

Listing Books

When the List Books button is clicked, the subprogram, getBooks_onClick, is invoked. This subprogram will create a few objects: Recordset, XML DOM, and XMLHTTP. The XMLHTTP object is used to send an HTTP request using the GET method and with the variable, req, whose value is set to getbooks. The value of req is used to differentiate the two types of requests sent to the ASP script, BooksServer.asp.

The getBooks_onClick subprogram will handle the tasks denoted by steps 1 and 7 that were shown in Figure 5-8 previously. In addition, it will call another subprogram, which we will name displayBooks, to handle the task of tabulating the books returned from the server and which is denoted as step 8 in Figure 5-8.

Following is the source code for getBooks_onClick:

```
Sub getBooks_onClick
    Dim xmlDOM
    Dim xmlhttp

    Set rsClient = CreateObject("ADODB.Recordset")
    Set xmlDOM = CreateObject("MSXML2.DOMDocument")
    Set xmlhttp = CreateObject("MSXML2.XMLHTTP")

    'Initiates a request to BooksServer.asp via XMLHTTP object
    xmlhttp.Open "GET", "BooksServer.asp?req=getBooks", false
    xmlhttp.Send

    'Loads returned stream (via xmlhttp.responseText) into DOM document
    xmlDOM.LoadXML xmlhttp.responseText

    rsClient.Open xmlDOM
    displayBooks
End Sub
```

In the preceding code, we assume that the object named rsClient is declared globally.

The next piece of source code shows how the books' information that has been collected into the Recordset object (rsClient) in the getBooks_onClick subprogam, can be displayed in a table:

```
Sub displayBooks
    displayString = "<p><table border='1' cellpadding='7'>" &_
                    "<tr><th>ISBN</th> <th>Price</th></tr>"

    while not rsClient.EOF
        displayString = displayString &_
                    "<tr><td>" & rsClient("ISBN") & "</td>" &_
                    "<td>" & rsClient("Price") & "</td></tr>"
        rsClient.MoveNext
    wend

    displayString = displayString & "</table>"
    BooksArea.innerHTML = displayString
    ListButtonArea.innerHTML = ""
End Sub
```

The last line of code in the subprogram is responsible for causing the List Books button to vanish. The area for displaying the button was set to an empty string, i.e., not displaying anything.

The display in response to the clicking of the List Books button is shown in Figure 5-10. Note that the List Books button does not appear. The user is now left with only two steps left in the discount granting process.

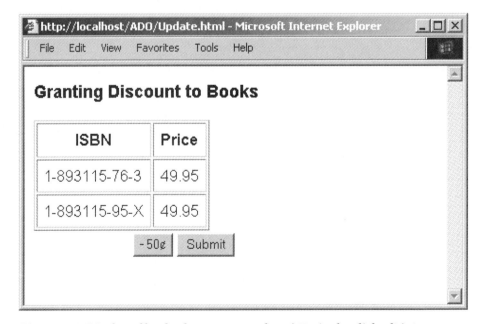

Figure 5-10. Display of books that cost more than $40 via the click of List Books *button*

Reducing Prices of Books

When the button labeled – 50¢ is clicked, the subprogram, updatePrice_onClick, is invoked. The subprogram scans through all the records in the Recordset, rsClient, to check if the current price of the book is more than $40 before deducting $0.50 from the price.

The updatePrice_onClick subprogram handles changing of pricing as described in step 9 of Figure 5-8, and is listed next:

```
Sub updatePrice_onClick
    if ListButtonArea.innerHTML = "" then
        'Update prices in the record set, rsClient
        rsClient.MoveFirst
        while not rsClient.EOF
            if rsClient("Price") > 40 then
                rsClient("Price") = rsClient("Price") - 0.5
            end if
            rsClient.MoveNext
        wend
        rsClient.MoveFirst
        displayBooks
    end if
End Sub
```

Before we iterate through the records inside rsClient, we need to first set the cursor to the Recordset to point to the first record using the MoveFirst method. Also, after the prices are updated in rsClient, the cursor to rsClient is again set to the beginning of rsClient before the subprogram, displayBooks, is called to display the new pricing information.

If the user clicks the button labeled – 50¢ twice, the resultant display will be as shown in Figure 5-11.

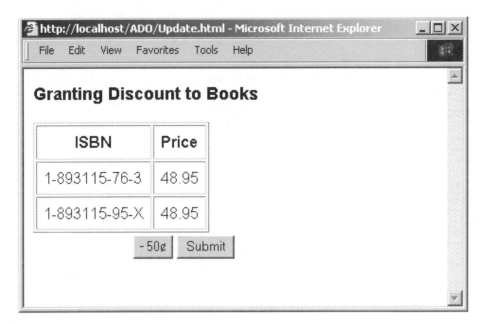

Figure 5-11. Display of new book prices after the button labeled − 50¢ is clicked twice

Submitting Updated Prices to Web Server

So far, the changes to the book prices are modified only locally on the client by updatePrice_onClick. We need to click the button labeled Submit to post the contents in the Recordset, rsClient, to the Web server, which in turn will invoke an update request to the BooksCatalog database with the new pricing information. This task is denoted in Figure 5-8 as step 10.

The subprogram, sendToServer_onClick in UpdatePage.html is responsible for transforming the contents of rsClient into a stream, which is then posted in the message body of the XMLHTTP object to the Web server. Besides, the subprogram also takes care of step 16 in Figure 5-8 for receiving response from the server.

The source code of the sendToServer_onClick subprogram is listed next:

```
Sub sendToServer_onClick
    Dim xmlhttp
    Dim stream

    if ListButtonArea.innerHTML = "" then
        'Prepares a Stream object to transmit Recordset content
        Set stream = CreateObject("ADODB.Stream")
        stream.Mode = adModeRead   'adModeRead=1
        stream.Open                     'instantiates a stream
```

```
        rsClient.Save stream, adpersistADTG
        rsClient.Close

        Set xmlhttp = CreateObject ("MSXML2.XMLHTTP")
        xmlhttp.Open "POST", "BooksServer.asp?req=update", false
        xmlhttp.Send stream.Read(stream.Size)

        'Displays response from server
        BooksArea.innerHTML = xmlhttp.responseText

        'Clears the rest of the buttons
        UpdateButtonArea.innerHTML = ""
        SendButtonArea.innerHTML = ""
    end if
End Sub
```

The if-statement is to ensure that the List Books button had been clicked before proceeding with passing information to the server to update pricing information.

The mode of the Stream object is set to read-only as denoted by the constant value adModeRead. You may want to refer to Table 5-7 for other possible mode values. Since the Open method of the Stream object is called without a source, it implies that we would like to instantiate rather than open one that is associated with an existing object such as a Record or Recordset object.

The Save method of the Recordset is used to save the contents into a stream in the Microsoft's Advanced Data TableGram binary format as specified by the second parameter value, adpersistADTG. We show the use of the Save method with another possible format specification, adpersistXML, later in another ASP script, to enable saving of Recordset data in the XML format. It is not used here since we will not be dealing with an XML stream anymore. The next immediate request would be updating the Recordset contents with the database.

As on the previous occasion, the client communicates with the server via the XMLHTTP object.

In our example, the script called at the server will return a simple acknowledgment string that is shown in Figure 5-12 upon successful update of the Recordset contents.

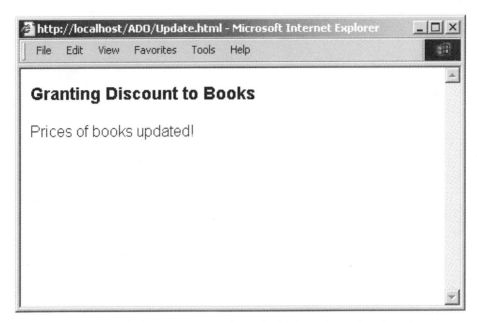

Figure 5-12. Acknowledgment message from the Web server to the client browser

After two deductions of prices on books that originally cost more than $40, the books table of the BooksCatalog database would show the contents that appear in Figure 5-13.

ISBN	Title	Price	CoverType	Pages
1-893115-76-3	C++ for VB Programmers	48.95	S	400
1-893115-86-0	A Programmer's Introduction to C#	34.95	S	357
1-893115-95-X	Cryptography in C & C++	48.95	S	380

Figure 5-13. The books *table showing reduced prices of the first and third books*

ASP Script on the Web Server: BooksServer.asp

We will use only one ASP source file to cater to the two different invocations from the client. To differentiate the two invocations, we require the client to submit a req variable, whose value is set to either getBooks or update to mark the two distinctive purposes of calling the ASP script.

If the ASP script, BooksServer.asp, finds that the value of req is getBooks, it will invoke a SELECT SQL statement to the provider to retrieve all the books with prices above $40. If the req value is not getBooks, the script will issue a batch update request to the provider, which will in turn carry out the update operations accordingly.

The listing of BooksServer.asp is shown in Listing 5-6.

Listing 5-6. BooksServer.asp

```asp
<!--#include file="adovbs.inc"-->
<%
    Response.Expires = 0
    Dim conn
    Dim rs

    Set conn = Server.CreateObject("ADODB.Connection")
    Set rs = Server.CreateObject("ADODB.Recordset")

    conn.Open "Provider=SQLOLEDB;Server=dataServer;Database=BooksCatalog;" &_
            "User ID=sa;Password=;"

    if Request.QueryString("req") = "getBooks" then
        'Retrieves books
        sql =  "SELECT ISBN, Price FROM books WHERE Price > 40"
        rs.ActiveConnection = conn
        rs.CursorLocation = adUseClient
        rs.CursorType = adOpenStatic
        rs.LockType = adLockBatchOptimistic
        rs.Open sql
        rs.Save response, adPersistXML
        rs.Close
    else
        'Updates prices
        rs.Open Request
        On Error Resume Next
        rs.Activeconnection = conn
        rs.Updatebatch
        rs.Close
        if conn.Errors.Count = 0 then
            Response.Write "Prices of books updated!"
        else
            Response.Write "Problems encountered in price update!"
        end if
    end if
    conn.Close
%>
```

Retrieving Books

BooksServer.asp will retrieve books if `req` is determined to have the value, `getBooks`. The SQL statement for the retrieval operation is formulated in the string denoted by `sql` in the listing of BooksServer.asp. The result is a set of records held in the Recordset, `rs`. Before the Open method is executed, some of the relevant parameters are first set.

The cursor location parameter is set to the constant value adUseClient to indicate the use of a client-side cursor.

The cursor type value is set to adOpenStatic to indicate that the data remains static in the Recordset, disregarding changes made by other users. This cursor type supports both forward and backward movements.

The lock type is set to adLockbatchOptimistic to lock the data during a batch update operation, which is shown as the second half of the code in BooksServer.asp.

The Save method is used to put the Recordset data into the Response stream of the ASP programming model, in the XML format. The recipient of the Response stream is the client, which will receive a stream of data in the XML format. The stream can then be loaded into an XML DOM object, and indeed that was what we did in the getBooks_onClick subprogram running on the client side.

Batch Updating of Book Prices

According to Listing 5-7, if the value of `req` is not `getBooks`, a batch update operation is performed on the Recordset, `rs`.

A possible runtime error that may occur for this batch update is when one of the records in the Recordset, `rs`, requested for update has been deleted by some other user. The provider will return the error via the Errors collection.

Upon successful update, the script will send back an appropriate message. Otherwise, a brief message indicating a problem occurring during update is sent back to the client.

 NOTE The Expires property of the Response object is set to 0 to ensure that a fresh copy of BooksServer.asp is invoked instead of from the cache.

Useful Web Links

- OLE DB Providers at
  `http://msdn.microsoft.com/library/default.asp?url=/library/`
  `en-us/acdata/ac_8_qd_12_15ma.asp`

- ADO Object Model at
  `http://msdn.microsoft.com/library/default.asp?url=/library/`
  `en-us/ado270/htm/mdmscadoobjmod.asp`

- ADO: Objects/Properties/Collections/Methods/Event at
  `http://msdn.microsoft.com/library/default.asp?url=/library/`
  `en-us/ado270/htm/mdmscadoapireference.asp`

Summary

In this chapter, we introduced the use of ADO to access the data sources, in particular the SQL server. The major objects of the ADO programming model were discussed. Appropriate examples were used to illustrate the access and manipulation of the data in a database on the SQL server. The Stream object was specifically highlighted with its support for holding data in XML format.

We also ended the chapter with a three-tier Web-based application in which data was put into a Recordset after being retrieved from the database, transformed into an XML stream, and sent to the client where the stream was loaded into a DOM object and eventually a client-side Recordset. Modified client-side Recordset data was then sent back to the Web server as a stream using the XMLHTTP object where a batch update is invoked.

CHAPTER 6

XML Support in SQL Server 2000

IN CHAPTER 5, WE SHOWED HOW YOU can access and manipulate data using Microsoft's ADO technology. You have seen specifically how XML data can be delivered from one party to the other via the Stream object of the ADO programming model.

In this chapter, we focus on the SQL Server 2000's support for XML so that data can be retrieved from the database and returned in the XML format. The features we will look at include:

- Retrieving or updating data in XML format using the FOR XML clause in SQL query statement, the OpenXML, and the XPath query language

- Accessing the SQL Server 2000 via HTTP

- Support for the XML-Data Reduced (XDR) schema and query for data against the schema

Additional Software Installation and Configuration

Before we look into the use of the repertoire of features that we can use with SQL Server 2000 to empower our applications, we should first highlight the necessary additional software to be installed as well as the database and other tools that we will be working with.

XML for Microsoft SQL Server 2000 Web Release 2

The SQL Server 2000 does not come with all the XML support features that we are going to discuss in this chapter. To see the examples of this chapter work, you need to navigate to the MSDN Code Center to download the *XML for Microsoft SQL Server 2000 Web Release 2 (SQLXML 2.0) Beta 2* that was released in May 2001.

The Web Release 1 of the software includes two main support features for XML, namely *Updategrams* and *Bulk load*. Web Release 2 has added XSD mapping schema, a host of other advanced features, as well as attempts to improve the performance.

The downloaded installation file is *SQLXML.exe* and is about 4.8MB in size.

BooksCatalog Database

All our examples are based on the BooksCatalog database that we used in Chapters 4 and 5. However, in order to incorporate some complex features for demonstration, we include one more field to the original books table that was used in the previous two chapters. In addition, we have another table that keeps record of all the authors of a given book in the books table. We shall name the additional table the authors table.

Tables 6-1 and 6-2, respectively, summarize the fields of the two tables used in the BooksCatalog database that we are using in this chapter.

Table 6-1. Column Fields of the books *Table of the BooksCatalog Database*

FIELD	DATA TYPE
ISBN	Unicode character string of variable length, *nvarchar*
Title	Unicode character string of variable length, *nvarchar*
Price	*money* type
CoverType	Unicode character ('S' for soft, 'H' for hard), *nvarchar*
Pages	Integer, *int*
CoverImage	Binary data of variable length, *varbinary*

Table 6-2. Column Fields of the authors *Table of the BooksCatalog Database*

FIELD	DATA TYPE
ISBN	Unicode character string of variable length, *nvarchar*
Author	Unicode character string of variable length, *nvarchar*

Figure 6-1 shows the contents of the books table, while Figure 6-2 shows the contents of the authors table.

ISBN	Title	Price	CoverType	Pages	CoverImage
1-893115-06-2	A Visual Basic 6 Programmer's Toolkit	39.95	S	400	\<Binary\>
1-893115-76-3	C++ for VB Programmers	49.95	S	400	\<Binary\>
1-893115-86-0	A Programmer's Introduction to C#	34.95	S	357	\<Binary\>
1-893115-95-X	Cryptography in C & C++	49.95	S	380	\<Binary\>

Figure 6-1. The books *table of the BooksCatalog database*

ISBN	Author
1-893115-06-2	Eric Smith
1-893115-06-2	Hank Marquis
1-893115-76-3	Jonathan Morrison
1-893115-86-0	Eric Gunnerson
1-893115-95-X	Michael Welschenbach

Figure 6-2. The authors *table of the BooksCatalog database*

SQL Query Analyzer

We will make use of the SQL Query Analyzer that comes with the SQL Server 2000 in the section where we discuss the use of the FOR XML clause in a SELECT statement. This section illustrates how this component of the SQL Server 2000 is invoked and how we can feed in an SQL statement and obtain the results in three different forms: *grid, file,* and *text.*

Invoking the SQL Query Analyzer

There are two ways to invoke the SQL Query Analyzer. You may first invoke the *SQL Server Enterprise Manager* and under the Tools menu of the manager window, choose to invoke the SQL Query Analyzer.

Alternatively, the SQL Query Analyzer can be started by pressing the key sequence Start > Programs > Microsoft SQL Server > Query Analyzer.

You will be prompted to enter the SQL server to connect to, as well as the security requirement. Once the necessary information is provided, the SQL Query Analyzer window will appear as shown in Figure 6-3.

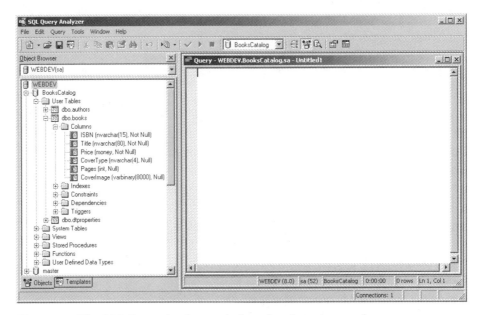

Figure 6-3. The SQL Query Analyzer window showing two panels

The SQL Query Analyzer in Figure 6-3 has chosen to work with the BooksCatalog database as reflected in the menu bar of the window. There are a few subwindows or panels in the main display window of the SQL Query Analyzer. Figure 6-3 shows an *Object Browser* on the left and a *Query* panel on the right. We can unfold the details of the BooksCatalog database that we are going to work with in the Object Browser, and to the level of columns design as shown in the figure.

Executing an SQL Statement and Specifying Results Format

Under the Query menu, you should be able to see three options regarding the format of the results returned by the execution of the query:

- Results in Text

- Results in Grid

- Results to File

We will choose the grid format to start with. Type the following in the Query panel of the SQL Query Analyzer window that was shown previously in Figure 6-3:

```
SELECT ISBN, Title
FROM books
WHERE Title LIKE '%Programmer%'
```

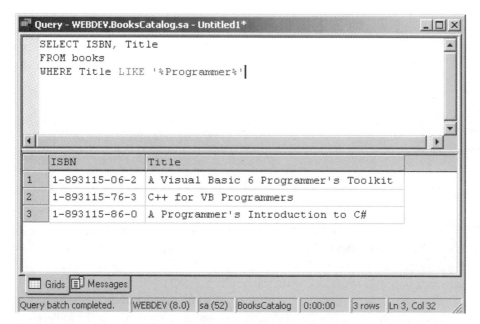

Figure 6-4. Executing a SELECT statement and displaying results in the grid format

Press the F5 function key to execute the statement. The results will be shown in a results panel below the Query panel as shown in Figure 6-4. The format of the results is a grid.

Change the format of results to text and execute the query again using the F5 key. The results are as shown in Figure 6-5.

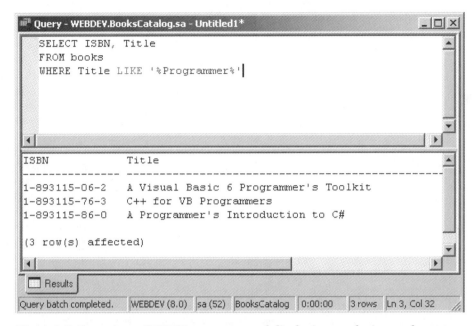

Figure 6-5. Executing a SELECT statement and displaying results in text format

The third option is to save the results into a file as text contents. If this option is used, you will be prompted for a file name and location to save the file in. The default extension of this resultant file is *.rpt*. If the file is opened in a text editor, the same text contents as that shown in the results panel of Figure 6-5 will be displayed.

One common problem you may face is that the row contents might be truncated after a preset number of characters is displayed in each row. This preset number can be edited by invoking Tools >Options, which will present a dialog window as shown in Figure 6-6. The default value for the number of characters displayed in a row is 512. The valid range for the value is 30 to 8192.

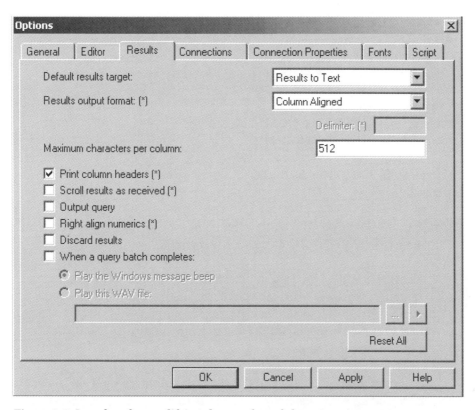

Figure 6-6. Interface for modifying the number of characters in a row

Retrieving and Transforming Rowset Data into XML Data

In this section, we look at how we can retrieve XML data using the SELECT statement with the FOR XML clause. We also introduce the OpenXML rowset provider, and last but not least, the use of XPath query language in making SQL queries.

There are three different types of XML *mode* that can be used with a FOR XML clause:

- RAW

- AUTO

- EXPLICIT

The following shows the general syntax for a simple SELECT statement with a FOR XML clause:

```
SELECT <fields>
FROM <tables>
[WHERE <conditions>]
[GROUP BY <field or expression>]
[HAVING <condition on GROUP BY result>]
[ORDER BY <fields> [ASC|DESC]]
[FOR XML <RAW | AUTO[, ELEMENTS] | EXPLICIT>
    [, XMLDATA] [, BINARY BASE64]]
```

Aside from the XML mode, the FOR XML clause can include the following specifications:

- **XMLDATA**: Indicates the return of an inline schema that is specified using Microsoft's XML-Data Reduced (XDR) schema

- **ELEMENTS**: This is used together with the AUTO XML mode to cause the column field to be returned as a child element instead of an attribute

- **BINARY BASE64**: Specifies that columns with binary data should be encoded in Base64 format

In the rest of this section, we focus on the FOR XML clause and explain the effects of the different options that can be specified for the clause. We make use of the Query Analyzer of the SQL Server 2000 for illustrating the output obtained using the different XML modes and other clause specifications.

FOR XML RAW Extension

The RAW XML extension causes each row of data retrieved from the database to be returned as a single element with the name *row*, where the retrieved column fields from the data source are returned as attributes of the <row> element. If *n* records from the data source satisfy the query criteria, then *n* <row> elements will be returned.

A Simple Retrieval Example

Create the following query in the Query panel of the SQL Query Analyzer window that was shown previously in Figure 6-4:

```
SELECT ISBN, Title
FROM books WHERE Title LIKE '%Programmer%' FOR XML RAW
```

Execute the query using text result format. The following results will be displayed:

```
XML_F52E2B61-18A1-11d1-B105-00805F49916B
<row ISBN="1-893115-06-2" Title="A Visual Basic 6 Programmer's Toolkit"/>
<row ISBN="1-893115-76-3" Title="C++ for VB Programmers"/>
<row ISBN="1-893115-86-0" Title="A Programmer's Introduction to C#"/>

(3 row(s) affected)
```

NOTE *Appropriate indentation and new-line characters have been inserted manually into the original results generated by the SQL Query Analyzer presented in this chapter to make them more readable.*

The first line contains a Globally Unique Identifier (GUID), which follows the XML_ prefix. The query results in three <row> elements, in which the attributes, ISBN and Title, represent the columns or fields retrieved by the query statement. The last line indicates the number of rows retrieved. For subsequent displays of results, we will not display the first and last lines in order to focus on the XML-related results.

It should be highlighted that if there is no value returned for a column in a particular row, the attribute will not appear in the corresponding <row> element.

Notice that the multiple <row> elements do not form a well-formed XML document, as there is no unique root element encompassing these elements. We discuss how to get around this problem later. In the meantime, we first look at what is being returned using the various types of queries using the FOR XML RAW clause.

Changing Default Attribute Names

In the previous example, the attribute names simply follow the column names used in the books table of the BooksCatalog database. We can choose to use different names as shown in the following query:

```
SELECT ISBN AS bookISBN, Title AS bookTitle
FROM books
WHERE Title LIKE '%Programmer%'
FOR XML RAW
```

Execute the preceding query using the SQL Query Analyzer and the following results will be returned:

```
<row bookISBN="1-893115-06-2" bookTitle="A Visual Basic 6 Programmer's
Toolkit"/>
<row bookISBN="1-893115-76-3" bookTitle="C++ for VB Programmers"/>
<row bookISBN="1-893115-86-0" bookTitle="A Programmer's Introduction to C#"/>
```

Using GROUP BY and Aggregate Functions

Consider a simple query that counts the number of rows returned from the authors table based on the ISBN. This is also a count of number of authors for every unique book in our database. Hence, all the books in our books table would return a count of 1 except for the book with ISBN 1-893115-06-2, which consists of two authors. Figure 6-2 showed the contents of the authors table.

The query to accomplish the aforementioned mission is as shown in the following, with the help of the COUNT() function and the GROUP BY clause:

```
SELECT ISBN, COUNT(*) AS AuthorsCount
FROM authors
GROUP BY ISBN
```

Figure 6-7 shows the results of the query preceding returned as a grid.

	ISBN	AuthorsCount
1	1-893115-06-2	2
2	1-893115-76-3	1
3	1-893115-86-0	1
4	1-893115-95-X	1

Figure 6-7. Counting number of authors for each book using COUNT() and GROUP BY

We can transform the tabulated results into XML data by simply appending the FOR XML RAW clause:

```
SELECT ISBN, COUNT(*) AS AuthorsCount
FROM authors
GROUP BY ISBN
FOR XML RAW
```

The results follow:

```
<row ISBN="1-893115-06-2" AuthorsCount="2"/>
<row ISBN="1-893115-76-3" AuthorsCount="1"/>
<row ISBN="1-893115-86-0" AuthorsCount="1"/>
<row ISBN="1-893115-95-X" AuthorsCount="1"/>
```

Retrieving Binary Data

In this subsection, we try to retrieve the cover image of the book with ISBN 1-893115-06-2 as part of the XML data. The image was prepared as a JPEG file, which is shown in Figure 6-8.

Figure 6-8. Cover image of the book with ISBN 1-893115-06-2

The image of the cover is stored in the CoverImage field of the books table, where the field is declared to be of the varbinary type, which indicates binary data field with variable length.

Let us try to execute the following using the SQL Query Analyzer:

```
SELECT ISBN, CoverImage
FROM books
WHERE ISBN = '1-893115-06-2'
FOR XML RAW
```

The query results in the following error message:

```
Server: Msg 6829, Level 16, State 1, Line 1
FOR XML EXPLICIT and RAW modes currently do not support addressing binary data as
URLs in column 'CoverImage'. Remove the column, or use the BINARY BASE64 mode, or
create the URL directly using the 'dbobject/TABLE[@PK1="V1"]/@COLUMN' syntax.
```

Do not let the message discourage you. What the message means is simply that if the RAW mode is used, you need to use one of two alternatives for handling binary data.

The first way to retrieve binary data is through the specification of the Base64 encoding system. We can modify the query to the following:

```
SELECT ISBN, CoverImage
FROM books
WHERE ISBN = '1-893115-06-2'
FOR XML RAW, BINARY BASE64
```

Run the query again and you should see the following:

```
<row ISBN="1-893115-06-2" CoverImage="/9j/4AAQSkZ   ...   jOP//Z"/>
```

The value of CoverImage is displayed in the Base64 encoded format. Note that the resultant <row> element was not shown in its entirety. You may notice that we have replaced the encoded content with ellipsis (. . .) to spare you more pages of encoded content, which appear meaningless to most of us, as it does not show the complete Base64 string representing the graphical content of the book cover. The original binary contents of the book cover have a size of more than 5KB and it would indeed take more than two pages to display the complete binary contents.

One point to highlight is that in order to obtain the entire encoded image content, you need to set the "maximum characters per column" value of the Options dialog window that was shown previously in Figure 6-6 to a sufficiently large value.

Instead of retrieving contents as part of the XML data, we can set the CoverImage attribute in the <row> element to a URL reference from which the actual binary data can be retrieved. Try executing the following SQL query:

```
SELECT ISBN, 'dbobject/books[@ISBN='+ISBN+']/@CoverImage' CoverImage
FROM books
WHERE ISBN = '1-893115-06-2'
FOR XML RAW
```

The purpose of the string enclosed within the single quotation marks in the first line of the query is to explicitly create a URL reference, as compared to automatic generation that we will see with the AUTO XML mode later. The URL reference is a URL relative to the virtual root of the database concerned. The syntax for creating a URL is:

```
Dbobject/tableName[@primaryKey=valueInText]/@columnName
```

Dbobject is a default virtual name for database objects such as database tables or views. We will look at creation of virtual names for database objects in the section on accessing the SQL server via HTTP.

We need to specify a primary key for the table concerned in such a query. Hence, specifying an explicit URL reference is applicable only for database tables that consist of at least one primary key. Also the valueInText value should be expressed as a string. If the value is numeric, casting the value to a text string is necessary. The casting syntax is:

```
'Dbobject/tableName[@primaryKey='+CAST(primaryKey AS nvarchar(length))+']
/@columnName'
```

An example of casting a primary key would be as follows:

```
'Dbobject/products[@serialID='+CAST(serialID AS nvarchar(40))+']
/@productName'
```

The result of executing the query with URL reference for the book with ISBN 1-893115-06-2 is shown next:

```
<row ISBN="1-893115-06-2" CoverImage="dbobject/books[@ISBN=1-893115-06-2]
/@CoverImage"/>
```

Requesting XML-Data Schema

For a query that expects the return of an XML-Data schema, we need to append the XMLDATA specification as shown in the query that follows:

```
SELECT ISBN, Title
FROM books
ORDER BY ISBN
FOR XML RAW, XMLDATA
```

Executing the preceding query gives the following return:

```
<Schema name="Schema1" xmlns="urn:schemas-microsoft-com:xml-data"
xmlns:dt="urn:schemas-microsoft-com:datatypes">
<ElementType name="row" content="empty" model="closed">
    <AttributeType name="ISBN" dt:type="string"/>
    <AttributeType name="Title" dt:type="string"/>
    <attribute type="ISBN"/>
    <attribute type="Title"/>
</ElementType>
</Schema>
<row xmlns="x-schema:#Schema1" ISBN="1-893115-06-2" Title="A Visual Basic 6
Programmer's Toolkit"/>
<row xmlns="x-schema:#Schema1" ISBN="1-893115-76-3" Title="C++ for VB
Programmers"/>
<row xmlns="x-schema:#Schema1" ISBN="1-893115-86-0" Title="A
Programmer's Introduction to C#"/>
<row xmlns="x-schema:#Schema1" ISBN="1-893115-95-X" Title="Cryptography in C
&amp; C++"/>
```

NOTE *An overview of Microsoft XML-Data Reduced (XDR) schema is given in Appendix C.*

FOR XML AUTO Extension

A query using the AUTO XML mode returns results as attributes within an element whose name is that of the table from which the data is drawn. If more than one table is used, nested elements are formed, where the parent element's name is that of the table of the first column returned.

Consider the following query:

```
SELECT books.ISBN, Author, Title
FROM books, authors
WHERE books.ISBN=authors.ISBN
FOR XML AUTO
```

The results appear in the following section:

```
<books ISBN="1-893115-06-2" Title="A Visual Basic 6 Programmer's
Toolkit">
    <authors Author="Eric Smith"/>
    <authors Author="Hank Marquis"/>
</books>
<books ISBN="1-893115-76-3" Title="C++ for VB Programmers">
    <authors Author="Jonathan Morrison"/>
</books>
<books ISBN="1-893115-86-0" Title="A Programmer's Introduction to C#">
    <authors Author="Eric Gunnerson"/>
</books>
<books ISBN="1-893115-95-X" Title="Cryptography in C &amp; C++">
    <authors Author="Michael Welschenbach"/>
</books>
```

Hierarchy of Nested XML Elements

In the previous query, the column field, ISBN, could be drawn either from the books table or the authors table. In such circumstances, the SELECT statement must specify explicitly the table from which to obtain the field. In the preceding example, we specify it as the books table. As a result, the parent or outermost element derives its name from the books table and the child element from the authors table according to the sequence in which columns are specified in the SELECT statement.

To illustrate the ordering of elements in hierarchy, consider the following query:

```
SELECT Author, books.ISBN
FROM books, authors
WHERE books.ISBN=authors.ISBN
FOR XML AUTO
```

The corresponding results appear in the following section:

```
<authors Author="Eric Smith">
   <books ISBN="1-893115-06-2"/>
</authors>
<authors Author="Hank Marquis">
   <books ISBN="1-893115-06-2"/>
</authors>
<authors Author="Jonathan Morrison">
   <books ISBN="1-893115-76-3"/>
</authors>
<authors Author="Eric Gunnerson">
   <books ISBN="1-893115-86-0"/>
</authors>
<authors Author="Michael Welschenbach">
   <books ISBN="1-893115-95-X"/>
</authors>
```

If the wildcard * is used in the query to indicate returning of all columns, the hierarchy of the elements depends on the order of the columns returned by the SQL engine. We will consider returning all the information concerning the book and authors of the book with ISBN 1-893115-95-X using different orders.

The following query will cause the columns in the books table to be returned before those of the authors table:

```
SELECT *
FROM books, authors
WHERE books.ISBN='1-893115-95-X' AND authors.ISBN='1-893115-95-X'
FOR XML AUTO
```

The result of the query is displayed here:

```
<books ISBN="1-893115-95-X" Title="Cryptography in C &amp; C++"
Price="49.9500" CoverType="S" Pages="380">
   <authors ISBN="1-893115-95-X" Author="Michael Welschenbach"/>
</books>
```

Notice that CoverImage does not appear as an attribute of the <books> element because we have intentionally left this field empty for this book record in the books table. The objective is to keep our output simple. We will discuss handling of binary data for CoverImage using AUTO mode in a later part of this section.

If we change the order of specification as follows, we will change the order in which the columns are returned:

```
SELECT *
FROM authors, books
WHERE books.ISBN='1-893115-95-X' AND authors.ISBN='1-893115-95-X'
FOR XML AUTO
```

The corresponding result follows:

```
<authors ISBN="1-893115-95-X" Author="Michael Welschenbach">
    <books ISBN="1-893115-95-X" Title="Cryptography in C &amp; C++"
           Price="49.9500" CoverType="S" Pages="380"/>
</authors>
```

Using Alias Names

As with the RAW XML mode, we can choose to give an alias name to any of the resultant attributes instead of using the column names. We can also choose a different name for the element other than the default table name.

Consider the following query:

```
SELECT books.ISBN, Author, Title AS BookTitle
FROM books As Books, authors As Authors
WHERE books.ISBN=authors.ISBN
FOR XML AUTO
```

We show only the first parent element and its contents in the returned results here:

```
<Books ISBN="1-893115-06-2" BookTitle="A Visual Basic 6 Programmer's
Toolkit">
    <Authors Author="Eric Smith"/>
    <Authors Author="Hank Marquis"/>
</Books>
```

Observe that the <books> element has been renamed as <Books>, <authors> as <Authors> and the attribute name Title has been changed to BookTitle.

Mapping Columns to Elements

Instead of the default mapping of the retrieved columns into attributes, we can opt to map them into subelements of the default element hierarchy. This is accomplished using the ELEMENTS specification.

Run the following query using the SQL Query Analyzer:

```
SELECT books.ISBN, Author, Title AS BookTitle
FROM books, authors
WHERE books.ISBN=authors.ISBN
FOR XML AUTO, ELEMENTS
```

The result displayed next shows only the first top-level element and its content so that we can more clearly observe the change in the resultant structure compared to the previous two cases.

```
<books>
    <ISBN>1-893115-06-2</ISBN>
    <BookTitle>A Visual Basic 6 Programmer's Toolkit</BookTitle>
    <authors>
        <Author>Eric Smith</Author>
    </authors>
    <authors>
        <Author>Hank Marquis</Author>
    </authors>
</books>
```

Using Computed Column

Queries that expect the return of some computed column will not be able to associate a table with these returned values. In such cases, they are embedded as an attribute of the element at the deepest level.

Consider the query with the computed column (Price + 5) to be returned as NewPrice:

```
SELECT books.ISBN, Price, Author, Price+5 AS NewPrice
FROM books, authors
WHERE books.ISBN=authors.ISBN
FOR XML AUTO
```

The first outermost element and its content are shown next, where NewPrice is an attribute of the <authors> element, which is a sub-element of the <books> element:

```
<books ISBN="1-893115-06-2" Price="39.9500">
    <authors Author="Eric Smith" NewPrice="44.9500"/>
    <authors Author="Hank Marquis" NewPrice="44.9500"/>
</books>
```

Consider yet another query with the first column (authors.ISBN) retrieved from the authors table instead of the books table:

```
SELECT authors.ISBN, Price, Author, Price+5 AS NewPrice
FROM books, authors
WHERE books.ISBN=authors.ISBN
FOR XML AUTO
```

The first two outermost elements that correspond to the information presented in the first outermost element of the previous query are presented here for comparison:

```
<authors ISBN="1-893115-06-2" Author="Eric Smith">
    <books Price="39.9500" NewPrice="44.9500"/>
</authors>
<authors ISBN="1-893115-06-2" Author="Hank Marquis">
    <books Price="39.9500" NewPrice="44.9500"/>
</authors>
```

Notice that the computed column, NewPrice, is now an attribute of the <books> element, which is at a deeper level than the <authors> element this time around.

Using GROUP BY and Aggregate Functions

You have seen how we can use the FOR XML RAW to transform retrieved and computed data into XML data using aggregate functions and GROUP BY clause. The XML-like data is structured into <row> elements with retrieved columns mapped onto attributes within the <row> elements.

If you think you can change the element name from row to the appropriate table name or its alias by simply modifying the FOR XML RAW with GROUP BY to FOR XML AUTO with GROUP BY, you are in for a surprise. In fact, you will encounter an error message announcing that the AUTO XML mode does not support GROUP BY and aggregate functions currently.

The get-around is to use a nested query. The nested query consists of an inner query that is without the FOR XML AUTO clause, and it is responsible for yielding a result table that contains the desired values returned by functions as well as GROUP BY specification. The outer query will incorporate the FOR XML AUTO clause to shape the result into XML data.

We demonstrate the nested query on retrieving the number of authors for each unique book in our database. The nested query is as shown next:

```
SELECT ISBN, AuthorsCount
FROM (SELECT ISBN, COUNT(*) AS AuthorsCount
      FROM authors
      GROUP BY ISBN) AuthorsInfo
FOR XML AUTO
```

The inner query is the SELECT statement enclosed within the parentheses immediately after the first FROM keyword. It returns a result that is a table as illustrated in Figure 6-7. The execution of the nested query results in the return of XML data structured in the following manner:

```
<AuthorsInfo ISBN="1-893115-06-2" AuthorsCount="2"/>
<AuthorsInfo ISBN="1-893115-76-3" AuthorsCount="1"/>
<AuthorsInfo ISBN="1-893115-86-0" AuthorsCount="1"/>
<AuthorsInfo ISBN="1-893115-95-X" AuthorsCount="1"/>
```

To create subelements under <AuthorsInfo> that list all the authors of a particular book as retrieved from the authors table, we need to modify the outer query to include the Author column, as well as including the authors table in the outer FROM specification. The modified query will look like this:

```
SELECT AuthorsInfo.ISBN, AuthorsCount, Author
FROM (SELECT ISBN, COUNT(*) AS AuthorsCount
      FROM authors
      GROUP BY ISBN) AuthorsInfo, authors As BookAuthor
WHERE AuthorsInfo.ISBN=BookAuthor.ISBN
FOR XML AUTO
```

This new nested query will yield the following results:

```
<AuthorsInfo ISBN="1-893115-06-2" AuthorsCount="2">
   <BookAuthor Author="Eric Smith"/>
   <BookAuthor Author="Hank Marquis"/>
</AuthorsInfo>
<AuthorsInfo ISBN="1-893115-76-3" AuthorsCount="1">
   <BookAuthor Author="Jonathan Morrison"/>
</AuthorsInfo>
<AuthorsInfo ISBN="1-893115-86-0" AuthorsCount="1">
   <BookAuthor Author="Eric Gunnerson"/>
</AuthorsInfo>
<AuthorsInfo ISBN="1-893115-95-X" AuthorsCount="1">
   <BookAuthor Author="Michael Welschenbach"/>
</AuthorsInfo>
```

Retrieving Binary Data

We will execute a similar SELECT statement for retrieving the cover image for the book with ISBN 1-893115-06-2 as we have done with the RAW mode, except that here we shall specify the use of the AUTO mode in the SQL query:

```
SELECT ISBN, CoverImage
FROM books
WHERE ISBN = '1-893115-06-2'
FOR XML AUTO
```

The result consists of only a single element:

```
<books ISBN="1-893115-06-2" CoverImage="dbobject/books[@ISBN='1-893115-06-
2']/@CoverImage"/>
```

Notice that it did not complain as in the case with the RAW XML mode. Also, a URL reference is generated by default, which points to the place from which the binary data can be loaded.

> **NOTE** dbobject *is used to refer to a database object, such as a table or view, and in this case, the* books *table. We will revisit it later under the section on Accessing SQL Server Using HTTP.*

If you want the binary data to be returned as Base64 encoded data, use the Base64 specification that follows:

```
SELECT ISBN, CoverImage
FROM books
WHERE ISBN = '1-893115-06-2'
FOR XML AUTO, BINARY BASE64
```

FOR XML EXPLICIT Extension

The EXPLICIT XML mode provides us with the most flexibility in structuring the results. We are able to control the outcome with more specific details even to the level of the individual columns. When using this mode, we need to write our query by including two meta-data columns as the first two columns in the result set, which we call a *universal table*. This internal result set, i.e., the universal table, is in turn processed and transformed into an XML document.

The SELECT clause of a query using the EXPLICIT mode should specify the integer numbers for two meta-data columns, named *Tag* and *Parent*, used eventually to form the hierarchical structure (parent and child elements) of the data. The first number uniquely identifies the current element in the level concerned. Each Tag number corresponds to exactly one element name.

The second number denoted by Parent specifies the hierarchical level of the parent of the current element. The Parent number indicates the depth of the current element. For example, if the Parent value is 0 or null, it means the current element is at the top level or level 1. Hence, the two meta-data columns represent a parent-child relationship, and that helps to build up the hierarchical structure.

Formulating a Query Using EXPLICIT XML Mode

In general, the entire query consists of a few steps:

1. Specify the database to access using the USE clause.

2. Formulate a query using the SELECT statement to specify the meta-data column, the various data columns from the relevant database tables to be mapped onto elements and attributes, as well as user-given element and attribute names with structural information. The purpose of this step is to provide structural information for constructing the XML tree.

3.   Perform a UNION ALL operation to collate the results of the query for meta-data with the results returned from a subsequent query for data from the database tables.

4.   Formulate a normal query for data without all the additional structural specifications, but with the FOR XML EXPLICIT clause.

NOTE   *The UNION operator collates the results from two or more queries into a single result set that consists of all the rows of results of all the queries involved in the union. The ALL option includes duplicate rows in the combined result set, which are removed from the result set by default.*

Let's take a look at forming a query using the EXPLICIT mode to retrieve information about books and authors:

```
1    USE BooksCatalog
2    SELECT 1 AS Tag, NULL AS Parent,
3        books.ISBN AS [Book!1!bookISBN],
4        books.Title AS [Book!1!bookTitle],
5        NULL AS [Author!2!Name]
6    FROM books
7    UNION ALL
8    SELECT 2, 1,
9        books.ISBN,
10       Title,
11       authors.Author
12   FROM books, authors
13   WHERE books.ISBN = authors.ISBN
14   ORDER BY [Book!1!bookISBN], [Author!2!Name]
15   FOR XML EXPLICIT
```

Line 1 specifies the database to use.

Lines 2 through 6 form the first query, the objective of which is to build up the overall hierarchical structure of the result set, also called universal table, and which corresponds to an element. This element has a tag number as specified by the Tag meta-data. Aside from the two meta-data columns, Tag and Parent, the SELECT clause also specifies other data columns to be included in the result set, or universal table. Each data column can be associated with a specification of its *universal table column name.*

The general format of the universal table column name specification is given here:

```
[ElementName!TagNumber!AttributeName!Directive]
```

The specification includes information of the column's hierarchical location, as well as the name or alias of its containing element (e.g., Book and Author for elements with Tag numbers 1 and 2 respectively) and the attributes (e.g., bookISBN, bookTitle and Name) that are mapped onto the data column eventually. Besides, an optional directive can be appended.

The ElementName and TagNumber parameters are straightforward. They indicate the name and tag number of the containing element of the current column data. The third parameter, AttributeName, requires further explanation.

If no Directive is specified, then AttributeName is the name of the attribute that is mapped to that particular column in question. However, the use of Directive may change our interpretation of this parameter. For example, if the Directive value is element, then the name denoted by AttributeName is taken as the name of the subelement used for the column concerned. That is, the column is now mapped onto an element instead of an attribute. We will discuss more about the various possible Directive values in a later section.

Notice that the second SELECT statement that starts at line 8 does not contain column naming for the universal table. This has been done in the first SELECT statement.

The results of the two SELECT statements need to combine to construct the universal table needed for conversion into the XML format. This can be accomplished using the UNION ALL statement shown in line 7.

The results of the query presented in the previous 15 lines follow:

```
<Book bookISBN="1-893115-06-2" bookTitle="A Visual Basic 6 Programmer's
Toolkit">
    <Author Name="Eric Smith"/>
    <Author Name="Hank Marquis"/>
</Book>
<Book bookISBN="1-893115-76-3" bookTitle="C++ for VB Programmers">
    <Author Name="Jonathan Morrison"/>
</Book>
<Book bookISBN="1-893115-86-0" bookTitle="A Programmer's Introduction to
C#">
    <Author Name="Eric Gunnerson"/>
</Book>
<Book bookISBN="1-893115-95-X" bookTitle="Cryptography in C &amp; C++">
    <Author Name="Michael Welschenbach"/>
</Book>
```

In the next section, we show the structure of the universal table that we will obtain for our example query. We then explain how the universal table is processed to obtain the XML data displayed here.

Universal Table

Lines 2 through 6 of the previous example construct a hierarchical structure with the top-level elements that have a tag number value of 1. These top-level elements would have been given a default name as the table name of the first data column in the SELECT clause if the FOR XML AUTO were used. The clue for the elements' hierarchical status is the Parent's tag value, which is specified as NULL in line 2. This top-level element is assigned the Tag value 1. The Tag value can be any value as long as it is uniquely mapped onto an element name.

Structure also takes form for three data columns, which are mapped into attributes. The first two data columns, ISBN and Title from the books table, are specified to be the attributes of the top-level element, which is assigned the name Book. As the two data columns are from the books table, which forms the current element, their values will be filled up at this stage. The third data column, authors.Author, will assume the value NULL. Table 6-3 shows the partial universal table at this point of parsing the query.

Table 6-3. Partial Universal Table after Building the Top-Level Element

TAG	PARENT	[BOOK!1!BOOKISBN]	[BOOK!1!BOOKTITLE]	[AUTHOR!2!NAME]
1	NULL	1-893115-06-2	A Visual Basic 6 Programmer's Toolkit	NULL
1	NULL	1-893115-76-3	C++ for VB Programmers	NULL
1	NULL	1-893115-86-0	A Programmer's Introduction to C#	NULL
1	NULL	1-893115-95-X	Cryptography for C & C++	NULL

Lines 8 through 13 attempt to structure the next level of element denoted by the Tag value 2. It is a subelement of the previous element constructed—i.e., the parent of the current element with Tag 2 is the element with Tag value 1 and element name Book.

The second SELECT statement starting from line 8 will insert additional information into the universal table. Also, the final universal table has its row sequenced according to the order specified in the ORDER BY clause in line 14, which in this case, is the ISBN (denoted by [Book!1!ISBN]) followed by the author's name (denoted by [Author!2!Name]). We are now able to fill in the rest of the universal table, which also includes the previous version (that was shown in

Table 6-3) since we specify combining the two sets through the use of the UNION ALL clause.

Table 6-4. Universal Table of the Query Retrieving Book and Author Information

TAG	PARENT	[BOOK!1!BOOKISBN]	[BOOK!1!BOOKTITLE]	[AUTHOR!2!NAME]
1	NULL	1-893115-06-2	A Visual Basic 6 Programmer's Toolkit	NULL
2	1	1-893115-06-2	A Visual Basic 6 Programmer's Toolkit	Eric Smith
2	1	1-893115-06-2	A Visual Basic 6 Programmer's Toolkit	Hank Marquis
1	NULL	1-893115-76-3	C++ for VB Programmers	NULL
2	1	1-893115-76-3	C++ for VB Programmers	Jonathan Morrison
1	NULL	1-893115-86-0	A Programmer's Introduction to C#	NULL
2	1	1-893115-86-0	A Programmer's Introduction to C#	Eric Gunnerson
1	NULL	1-893115-95-X	Cryptography for C & C++	NULL
2	1	1-893115-95-X	Cryptography for C & C++	Michael Welschenbach

Using Directive in a Universal Table Column Name

You have seen how to name a column in the universal table in the previous query example. We present the naming specification again later, but use a more generic name for the third parameter:

```
dataColumn AS [ElementName!TagNumber!DataName!Directive]
```

We have intentionally chosen to use the name `DataName` rather than the name `AttributeName` for the third parameter in the column naming specification for the universal table. This is because it can actually be the name of an attribute or an element or even not needed, depending on the directive value.

An example of the use of the Directive parameter would be the following, using the BooksCatalog database:

```
books.Title AS [Book!1!bookTitle!element]
```

In this section, we look at the possible values of the last parameter, `Directive`, and how it affects the mapping of the data column into either attribute, subelement, or character data of the containing element.

First, we should put down some ground rules regarding the naming specification:

- If Directive is not present, the DataName value must be specified and it would represent the name of the attribute that maps onto the current data column.

- If the Directive value is CDATA, ELEMENT, XML, or XMLTEXT, the DataName value is used as the name of the subelement of the containing element, where the name of the latter is indicated by ElementName.

- If both DataName and Directive are not specified, then the column data retrieved constitutes the content of the element whose name is given by ElementName.

Table 6-5 and Table 6-6 tabulate the possible values of Directive and their functions. The former expects the data column retrieved to be mapped into an attribute, and the directive values are used to describe the attribute type. The latter group of directive values define how the retrieved data is mapped into the XML data, for example, as element or text content in an XML document.

Table 6-5. Using Directive to Specify the Attribute Type

DIRECTIVE VALUE	FUNCTION
ID	This is used to specify an attribute with ID type. This is effective only if XMLDATA is also specified in the FOR XML clause to request for XDR schema to be returned. The attribute with ID type can then be referenced via other attributes with the IDREF or IDREFS type.
IDREF	This specifies the type of an attribute to be the IDREF. Such an attribute is assigned a value that is an ID attribute value. As with the ID attribute type, if XMLDATA is not specified, this directive would have no effect.
IDREFS	This is similar to IDREF except that the attribute in question can assume more than one ID attribute value. Again, if XMLDATA is not specified, this directive would have no effect.
HIDE	The data column is mapped into an attribute, which however, is not displayed in the XML output.

It should be highlighted that the declaration of ID, IDREF, IDREFS will not cause any syntactical difference. They are used to validate the use of attribute of ID type. Hence, they become meaningful only when validation is used. The latter is possible if a schema is provided, which is why the XMLDATA specification is necessary in order to generate the XDR schema to accomplish the validation process.

Table 6-6. Using Directive to Define Mapping between Data Column and Final XML Data

DIRECTIVE VALUE	FUNCTION
CDATA	The retrieved data is wrapped within the XML CDATA wrapper `<![CDATA[ . . . ]]>`. When this directive is specified, no `DataName` should be specified. No entity encoding is applied on the retrieved data. The directive can only be used with the data column that is defined with one of the following data types: `varchar`, `nvarchar`, `text`, and `ntext`.
ELEMENT	This directive causes a subelement to be generated with the name `DataName`, and with the retrieved data being its content. Entity encoding is applied on the resultant element data. For example, the apostrophe character retrieved from the database will be changed to `&apos;` in the XML element data.
XML	This directive creates the same effects as the `ELEMENT` directive except that no entity encoding is applied on the resultant element data.
XMLTEXT	This is used in conjunction with a retrieved column whose data is XML text such as `<tagname attr='var'>contents</tagname>`. If no `DataName` is specified, the attribute will be appended as an attribute of the containing element, namely <ElementName>, and the `contents` of the retrieved data will be inserted at the beginning of the containment of <ElementName>. No entity encoding is applied on the final enclosed contents within the <ElementName> element. If `DataName` is used, the entire XML text retrieved will become the first child element of the <ElementName> element, with, however, tagname being replaced by `DataName`. For this directive to work correctly, the column concerned should be designed with one of the following data types: `char`, `nchar`, `text`, `ntext`, `varchar`, `nvarchar`.

Some Examples Using Directives

We now show some of the directives in action. As the ID, IDREF, and IDREFS directives will not cause differences in the XML output, we only demonstrate the use of the HIDE directive shown in Table 6-5 and the rest of the directives listed in Table 6-6.

Assume that we need only to use the Title of the books table to perform ordering or sequencing in line 14 of the previous query, but not requiring it as part of the resultant XML data. In this case, we can use the HIDE directive on the books.Title column, as follows, by modifying line 4 of the query:

```
4          books.Title AS [Book!1!!HIDE],
```

Notice that no DataName is supplied since the Title will not appear anywhere in the resultant XML data. We will supply a name only if there is more than one such column name, [Book!1!!HIDE], in our universal table and we need to uniquely differentiate one or more of the hidden columns; otherwise, the name [Book!1!!HIDE] used subsequently in the query will always refer to the first column that has such a naming specification. Another line that needs modification is line 14. One possible new ORDER BY clause is:

```
14   ORDER BY [Book!1!!HIDE], [Author!2!Name]
```

Alternatively, we can use the following line 14 if [Book!1!!HIDE] cannot uniquely identify the intended column:

```
14   ORDER BY books.Title, [Author!2!Name]
```

The result generated by the modified query follows:

```
<Book bookISBN="1-893115-06-2"><Author Name="Eric Smith"/><Author Name="Hank
Marquis"/></Book>
<Book bookISBN="1-893115-86-0"><Author Name="Eric Gunnerson"/></Book>
<Book bookISBN="1-893115-76-3"><Author Name="Jonathan Morrison"/></Book>
<Book bookISBN="1-893115-95-X"><Author Name="Michael Welschenbach"/></Book>
```

Before we proceed to present more examples, let's consider a query that returns simple data of just one book since our focus is on the use of directives rather than the ordering of data as in the previous query. We modify the new query subsequently by introducing some of the directives that were discussed previously in Table 6-6 to show their effects:

```
1    USE BooksCatalog
2    SELECT 1 AS Tag, NULL AS Parent,
3           books.ISBN AS [Book!1!bookISBN],
4           books.Title AS [Book!1!bookTitle],
5           NULL AS [Author!2!Name]
6    FROM books
7    WHERE books.ISBN='1-893115-06-2'
8    UNION ALL
9    SELECT 2, 1,
10          books.ISBN,
11          Title,
12          authors.Author
13   FROM books, authors
14   WHERE books.ISBN='1-893115-06-2' AND books.ISBN=authors.ISBN
15   ORDER BY [Book!1!bookISBN], [Author!2!Name]
16   FOR XML EXPLICIT
```

The outcome of the query is:

```
<Book bookISBN="1-893115-06-2" bookTitle="A Visual Basic 6 Programmer's
Toolkit">
   <Author Name="Eric Smith"/>
   <Author Name="Hank Marquis"/>
</Book>
```

We shall now demonstrate the effect of the CDATA directive by modifying line 4 of the query to the following, taking note that no DataName should be specified:

```
4           books.Title AS [Book!1!!CDATA],
```

The outcome of the modified query is:

```
<Book bookISBN="1-893115-06-2">
   <![CDATA[A Visual Basic 6 Programmer's Toolkit]]>
   <Author Name="Eric Smith"/>
   <Author Name="Hank Marquis"/>
</Book>
```

Notice that the title of the book has been changed into character data of the <Book> element and is wrapped within the XML CDATA wrapper. Also, the apostrophe character is not converted to an entity reference.

Next, modify line 4 of the query to the following:

```
4          books.Title AS [Book!1!bookTitle!ELEMENT],
```

The outcome of the modified query is:

```
<Book bookISBN="1-893115-06-2">
   <bookTitle>A Visual Basic 6 Programmer's Toolkit</bookTitle>
   <Author Name="Eric Smith"/>
   <Author Name="Hank Marquis"/>
</Book>
```

Let us try yet another modification to line 4 of the query:

```
4          books.Title AS [Book!1!bookTitle!XML],
```

The new outcome of the query is:

```
<Book bookISBN="1-893115-06-2">
   <bookTitle>A Visual Basic 6 Programmer's Toolkit</bookTitle>
   <Author Name="Eric Smith"/>
   <Author Name="Hank Marquis"/>
</Book>
```

The difference between the previous two directives, ELEMENT and XML, is that the former uses entity encoding in the character content while the latter does not.

Before we demonstrate the effect of the XMLTEXT directive, we need to make an assumption regarding the contents stored under the Title column of the books database table. For the book with ISBN 1-893115-06-2, assume that the contents of its Title column is an XML text string as shown here:

```
<title rating="Good">A Visual Basic 6 Programmer's Toolkit</title>
```

To integrate this XML data into the rest of the XML data structure we can modify line 4 as follows:

```
4          books.Title AS [Book!1!!XMLTEXT],
```

In this case, we will obtain the following result:

```
<Book bookISBN="1-893115-06-2" rating="Good">
   A Visual Basic 6 Programmer's Toolkit
   <Author Name="Eric Smith"/>
   <Author Name="Hank Marquis"/>
</Book>
```

Alternatively, we may want to create an additional child element for the title information by including a name, such as bookTitle, in the naming specification:

```
4          books.Title AS [Book!1!bookTitle!XMLTEXT],
```

The corresponding result follows:

```
<Book bookISBN="1-893115-06-2">
   <bookTitle rating="Good">
      A Visual Basic 6 Programmer's Toolkit
   </bookTitle>
   <Author Name="Eric Smith"/>
   <Author Name="Hank Marquis"/>
</Book>
```

Providing Rowset Data from XML Data Using the OPENXML Provider

We have spent quite a bit of time discussing how data retrieved from the database can be transformed into XML data from its default rowset format. In this section, we do the reverse. We present XML data in a relational or rowset structure. The OPENXML function is used to provide a rowset view of XML data loaded into the memory so that we can use the familiar SQL statements such as SELECT, INSERT, and UPDATE to manipulate the data originally stored in an XML document. It is hence also called a rowset data provider.

Attaining the previous objective of working with XML data via a view with a rowset structure typically involves these steps:

- Invoke the system stored procedure, sp_xml_preparedocument, to load the XML text or data into the memory and performs parsing for optimal query performance. This procedure returns a handle that is used subsequently to locate the in-memory data. From this point onward, the data will reside in the memory until the connection is terminated or when another cleaning-up process is called.

- Formulate a query against the in-memory data using the OPENXML function, which creates a view of the data in a rowset format.

- Execute the system stored procedure, sp_xml_removedocument, to remove the in-memory data and thus release the memory resource.

We elaborate each of these steps next.

Loading XML Document into Memory

The procedure that creates an internal representation of an XML document before the data can be consumed via a Transact-SQL statement is sp_xml_preparedocument, which has the following syntax:

```
sp_xml_preparedocument @hdoc OUTPUT
    [, xmlTextData]
    [, xpathNamespaces]
```

Table 6-7. Parameters Used in sp_xml_preparedocument

PARAMETER	DESCRIPTION
hdoc	This is the handle that is returned by sp_xml_preparedocument, and it points to the in-memory document created. This parameter is an integer.
xmlTextData	This is the original XML document that contains data that we are interested in accessing. It is in text format, which may take the form of one of the following formats: char, nchar, text, ntext, varchar, nvarchar. The default for this parameter is NULL if it is not specified.
xpathNamespaces	This is the declaration of namespaces for the prefixes used in the XPath expression in OPENXML. It is a text parameter that takes one of the formats: char, nchar, text, ntext, varchar, nvarchar. The default value for this parameter is <root xmlns:mp="urn:schemas-microsoft-com:xml-metaprop">.

Writing Transact-SQL Using OPENXML

After we obtain a handle to the internal representation of the XML document that we are interested in, we can write Transact-SQL statements against this internal representation as though we are dealing with rowset data of a database. We can accomplish this by expressing the internal structure via the OPENXML, whose syntax is shown next:

```
OPENXML (@hdoc, XPathPattern, Flags)
   [WITH (SchemaDeclaration | TableName)]
```

hdoc Parameter

This is an input parameter to OPENXML that has a data type int. It is the handle to the internal representation of the XML document concerned. It is created via sp_xml_preparedocument.

XPathPattern Expression

This is an XPath expression that identifies the nodes of the internal representation that are to be processed as rows. This second input parameter has an SQL data type of nvarchar.

> **NOTE** *The* nvarchar *data type indicates a Unicode character string of variable length, up to a maximum of 4000 characters. Other Unicode character string data types include* nchar *and* ntext. *For more information on SQL data types, visit the MSDN library Web site of Microsoft.*

Flags Parameter

This optional parameter specifies the mapping to be used between the XML data and the in-memory rowset. It also specifies how the *spill-over* columns should be filled. Table 6-8 shows the possible Flags values and what each value implies. This specification can combine two or more of the possible values whenever it is appropriate. Each value has the data type, byte.

Table 6-8. Flags Parameter Values

BYTE VALUE OF FLAGS	DESCRIPTION
0	This is the default Flags value. It implies that attribute-centric mapping is used—i.e., attributes with the specified column names of the internal representation are used.
1	If this value is used alone, it specifies attribute-centric mapping as in the case of 0 value. It can combine with, i.e., added to, the value 2 or 8, or both. When combined with the other values, the behavior dictated by this value takes precedence.
2	When used alone, this value specifies element-centric mapping—i.e., elements with the specified names of the internal representation are used. If it is combined with 1 and both an attribute and an element are found to have a specified name, the attribute will be used as it is given the precedence over element.
8	This flag can be used with 1 or 2. It implies that the consumed data should not be copied to the overflow meta-property, @mp:xmltext. Without this flag, all data is copied to @mp:xmltext.

WITH Clause

The WITH clause is used to give a rowset format to the XML data, using either a schema declaration or an existing table.

SchemaDeclaration Expression

A WITH clause that specifies a schema declaration can be presented in greater detail as follows:

```
WITH ( ColName ColType [ColXPathPattern | MetaProperty]
       [, ColName ColType [ColXPathPattern | MetaProperty]] ... )
```

Table 6-9. Components of the SchemaDeclaration in the WITH Clause

PARAMETER	DESCRIPTION
ColName	This is the column name in the rowset view provided by the OPENXML.
ColType	This is the SQL data type specification of the column in the rowset.
ColXPathPattern	This is an optional XPath expression for mapping the XML nodes into the columns. This may be used to overwrite the mapping specified by the Flags parameter.
MetaProperty	This is used to extract meta-information such as the XML node's relative position or namespace information.

TableName

This is the name of an existing table that has the desired schema.

Removing In-Memory XML Representation

The procedure that removes an existing internal representation of an XML document is sp_xml_removedocument, which has the following syntax:

```
sp_xml_removedocument @hdoc
```

The only parameter used, hdoc, is the handle that points to the internal representation.

Example of Using OPENXML

In our example, we consider an XML text string that stores the information of two books. The ISBN and Title of each book are stored as attributes of the <Book> element. The authors are stored as child elements of the <Book> element.

In the first version of the example, we use the Flags value of 1 for the OPENXML function. Try the following using the SQL Query Analyzer:

```
1   DECLARE @hdoc int
2   DECLARE @doc varchar(1000)
3   SET @doc = '
```

```
4    <APressBooks>
5       <Book ISBN="1-893115-59-3" Title="C# and the .NET Platform">
6          <Author>Andrew Troelsen</Author>
7       </Book>
8       <Book ISBN="1-893115-53-4" Title="Visual Basic For Testers">
9          <Author>Mary Romero Sweeney</Author>
10      </Book>
11   </APressBooks>'
12   EXEC sp_xml_preparedocument @hdoc OUTPUT, @doc
13   SELECT * FROM
14   OPENXML (@hdoc, '/APressBooks/Book', 1)
15   WITH (ISBN nvarchar(15), Author nvarchar(30))
16   ORDER BY ISBN
17   EXEC sp_xml_removedocument @hdoc
```

The results of the previous example when saved into a file look like the following:

```
ISBN             Author
---------------  ------------------------------
1-893115-53-4    NULL
1-893115-59-3    NULL

(2 row(s) affected)
```

The Flags 1 (line 14) indicates that if the query specifies a column name, such as ISBN in line 15, it is indeed an attribute in the XML document, and its value will be returned. Notice that the column name, Author, in line 15, has no corresponding attribute in the XML document. It is actually an element, as shown in lines 6 and 9. In this case, the result would be NULL for Author.

Let's modify the Flags parameter of OPENXML to (1+2), i.e., 3, as follows:

```
14   OPENXML (@hdoc, '/APressBooks/Book', 3)
```

Execute the query again and you should see the following result:

```
ISBN             Author
---------------  ------------------------------
1-893115-53-4    Mary Romero Sweeney
1-893115-59-3    Andrew Troelsen

(2 row(s) affected)
```

Aside from the SELECT statement that we show in this example, we can use the OPENXML function to provide a rowset view to other Transact-SQL statements such as INSERT and UPDATE.

Unconsumed Columns

Consider lines 14 and 15 of the previous query using the OPENXML function again:

```
14  OPENXML (@hdoc, '/APressBooks/Book', 1)
15  WITH (ISBN nvarchar(15), Author nvarchar(30))
```

Either the Flags value in line 14 is 1 or 3, it is observed that the output consists of only two columns, ISBN and Author. The ISBN column corresponds to an attribute of the <Book> element that we are looking at (specified as an XPath expression in line 14), and the Author column corresponds to a child element of the <Book> element. Depending on the Flags value, these columns may or may not have the value NULL.

There is one more piece of information in the <Book> element that is not displayed—namely the Title attribute. This attribute is called an *unconsumed column*, sometimes also known as an *overflow* column or *spill-over* column.

Unconsumed columns are copied to a meta-property of OPENXML: @mp:xmltext. To display all the unconsumed columns, simply extend line 15 with one more column name with appropriate type and with the meta-property name @mp:xmltext.

For example, we may want to specify an unconsumed column with the name Unconsumed as shown next:

```
15  WITH (ISBN nvarchar(15), Author nvarchar(25),
            Unconsumed nvarchar(40) '@mp:xmltext')
```

In order to display only unconsumed column data (i.e., Title in our example) under the third column, Unconsumed, we need to include the value 8 in the Flags parameter value of line 14. Assuming that we would like to display the values for the ISBN attribute and Author child element of <Book>, we must then include values 1 and 2 as well in the Flags parameter of the OPENXML function.

After taking into consideration the requirements discussed previously, we modify line 14 to the following:

```
14   OPENXML (@hdoc, '/APressBooks/Book', 11)
```

Run the query in the SQL Query Analyzer again and the following will be obtained:

```
ISBN             Author                  Unconsumed
---------------  ----------------------  ---------------------------------------
1-893115-53-4    Mary Romero Sweeney      <Book Title="Visual Basic For Testers"/>
1-893115-59-3    Andrew Troelsen          <Book Title="C# and the .NET Platform"/>

(2 row(s) affected)
```

As you can observe by now in our example, the overflow meta-property, @mp:xmltext, can be used to store the entire contents of each <Book> element if the value 8 is not used as part of the Flags parameter of the OPENXML, or it is just used for the unconsumed data, which you choose to store for recording purposes.

Accessing SQL Server Using HTTP

We have been testing bits and pieces of SQL queries using the SQL Query Analyzer. In this section, we show you how to access the Microsoft SQL Server 2000 using HTTP, and thus provide you with the ability to access the database over the Internet!

Before we can accomplish this via HTTP access, we must first create a virtual directory, also called *virtual root*, to expose a database. We show how this can be done using the *IIS Virtual Directory Management for SQL Server Utility*. After setting up the virtual root, we then discuss the accessing of the SQL Server using HTTP and the virtual root created.

IIS Virtual Directory Management for SQL Server Utility

Just as a virtual directory is created to map onto a physical directory that holds Web pages, scripts, or presentation media, we can also create a virtual directory to map to a database. The resultant directory is used in a path for query to the database concerned. We also show the use of virtual directories to hold the queries formulated as a template and the schemas used in some queries.

The management utility can be invoked via the press of the key sequence, Start > Programs > Microsoft SQL Server > Configure SQL XML Support in IIS.

For example, in the default Web site of a server named WEBDEV, the initial setting of the various parameters appear in the right panel of the management window, as shown in Figure 6-9.

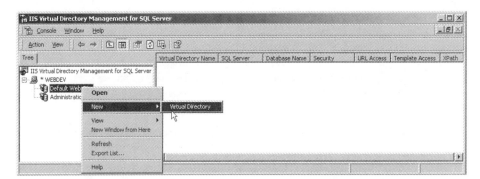

Figure 6-9. Window layout of the IIS Virtual Directory Management for SQL Server

Right-click the Default Web Site and choose the New option followed by the Virtual Directory item. This leads us to the dialog window of New Virtual Directory Properties. Create an alias name, BooksDB, that maps into some directory say, D:\VirtualDB, as shown in Figure 6-10. Note that you can choose any directory you like for the actual directory to map to.

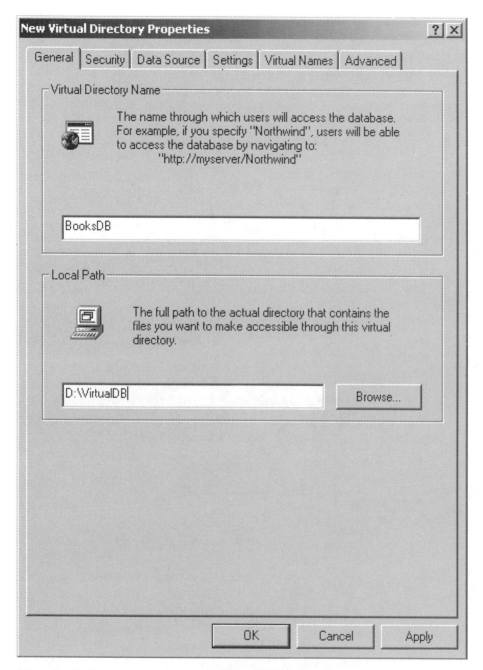

Figure 6-10. Creating a new virtual directory, BooksDB

Next, click the Security tab of the dialog window that is shown in Figure 6-10. Consider the security you need for accessing the SQL Server. If you allow only users in the intranet to access the database, the safest mode is to choose the

Windows Integration Authentication option. If you allow anyone out there in the Internet to access the database, an appropriate account needs to be set up to allow authorized access.

The third step is to specify our data source as captured in Figure 6-11.

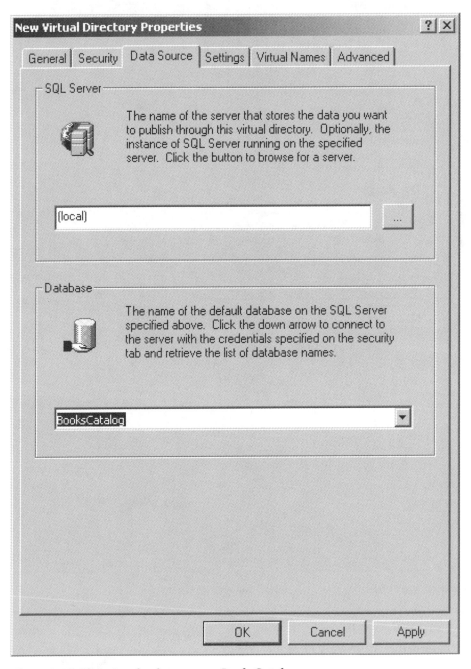

Figure 6-11. Choosing the data source, BooksCatalog

Next, click the Settings tab to set the appropriate types of access you allow to
the SQL Server, as shown in Figure 6-12.

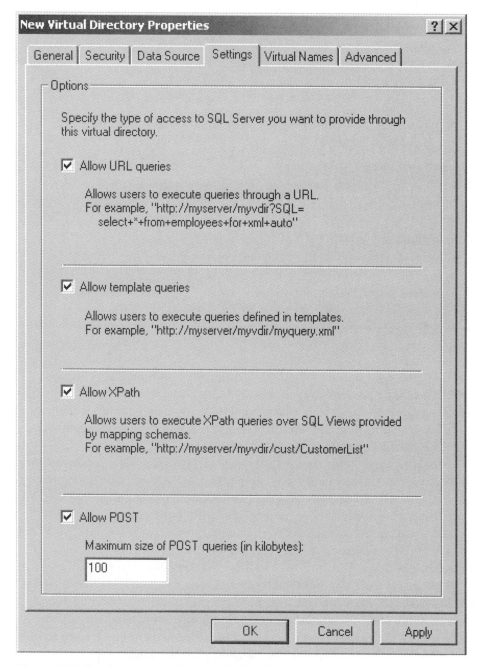

Figure 6-12. Setting access options to the database

Tab Virtual Names next and choose to define a new virtual name by clicking the New button. The dialog box that is shown in Figure 6-13 appears to allow you to create a virtual name for various types of items, including dbobject, schema, and template.

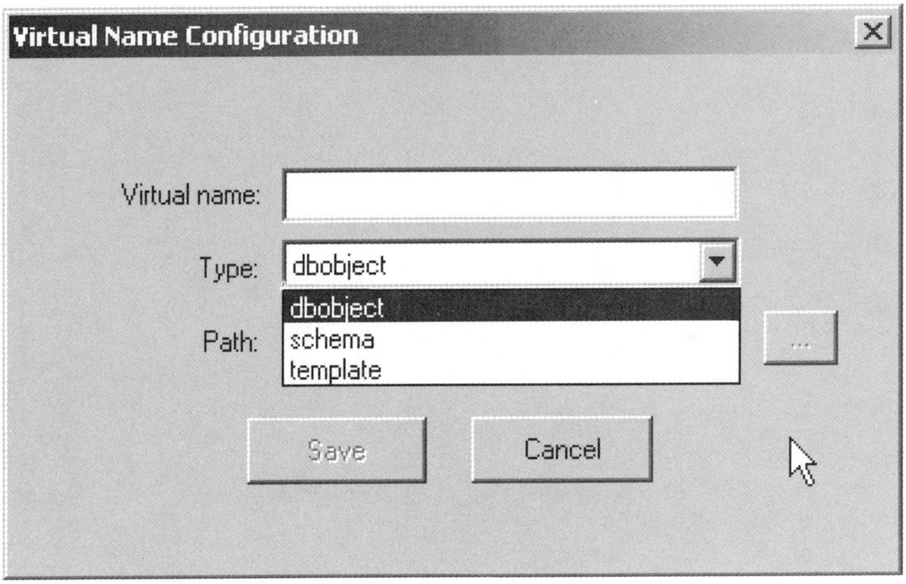

Figure 6-13. Defining new virtual name

The virtual name created will be specified as part of the URL to either access a database object (e.g., table or view) directly, to execute an XPath query against a mapping schema file, or to execute a template file depending on the type associated with the virtual name.

For our example, first choose the dbobject type to allow direct access to our BooksCatalog database objects such as the books and authors tables. Assign the virtual name say, BooksObject. Click the Save button to save the setting.

Next, create a virtual name, BooksSchema, for the schema type. Specify a directory path say, D:\VirtualDB\Schemas, for storing the schemas. Last, create a third virtual name, BooksTemplate, for the template type. Similarly, let's specify a directory, D:\VirtualDB\Templates, for storing our templates.

We will not make any modification to the Advanced dialog window at this stage.

Click the OK button to complete the setting up of a virtual root directory. Note that the BooksCatalog database is now exposed through the virtual root directory, BooksDB. The window contents that appeared previously in Figure 6-9 are refreshed to update the setup information as shown in Figure 6-14.

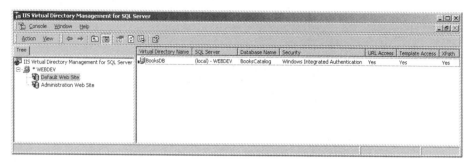

Figure 6-14. Updated IIS Virtual Directory Management for SQL Server utility window

In the rest of this section, we show examples of the different types of queries (indicated in Figure 6-12) that we can formulate.

Direct URL Queries

If the `Allow URL queries` option that was shown in Figure 6-12 is checked during the registration of the virtual root, we can access the SQL server by executing an SQL query via a URL specification.

The URL will specify the IIS server's name and the virtual root that we have registered (e.g., BooksDB in our earlier example). We can then append necessary parameters to formulate our query as well as returned data. The full syntax for the direct URL query is shown next, where the portions enclosed within [and] are optional:

```
http://IISserver/virtualroot?sql=sql_string[&root=docElement][&xsl=styleFile]
[&outputencoding=encoding_scheme][&contenttype=content_type]
```

Table 6-10. Parameters of the Direct URL Query

PARAMETER	DESCRIPTION
sql	This parameter specifies the SQL query string to execute, which may include a FOR XML clause if XML data is expected.
root	This parameter is used to specify the name of the document root element embodying the XML data returned from the query if the FOR XML clause is used in the query string. Without the root specification, an error will occur since the result will not be a well-formed XML document.
xsl	This parameter allows one to specify the stylesheet file to be applied on the returned XML document.
outputencoding	This parameter is used to change the character encoding for the output from the default encoding, UTF-8.
contentType	This parameter specifies the content type value as used in the HTTP header.

Type the following in the Address box of Internet Explorer 5.0. The result that is returned appears in a single-column rowset format, as shown in Figure 6-15.

```
http://webdev/BooksDB?sql=SELECT+Title+FROM+books
```

The name of the IIS Server used for running our examples in this chapter is given the name, webdev. If you are launching the browser in the same host machine as your IIS Server, you can also type the following:

```
http://localhost/BooksDB?sql=SELECT+Title+FROM+books
```

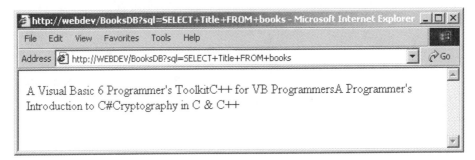

Figure 6-15. Direct URL query for retrieving titles from the books *database table*

The + character in the query string is used to indicate a space character. %20 will replace a space character found in the query string, where 20 is the underlying encoding code value for the space character expressed in hexadecimal format.

In the next example, we execute a query with a FOR XML AUTO clause together with the specification of the document root element to obtain the XML output that is presented in Figure 6-16. The URL query is:

```
http://webdev/BooksDB?sql=SELECT+Title+FROM+books+FOR+XML+AUTO&root=BooksDoc
```

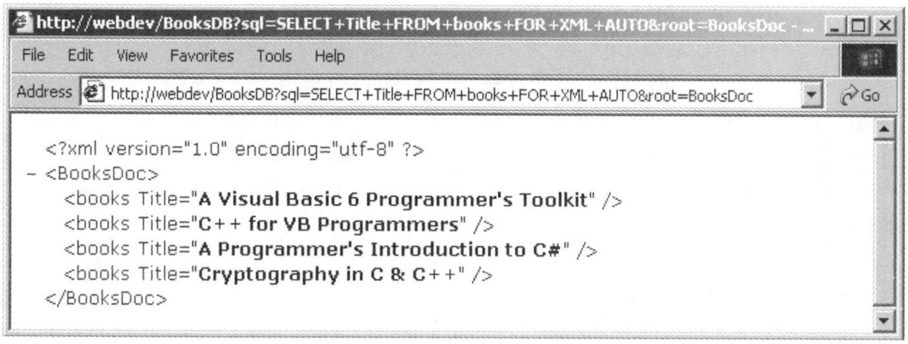

Figure 6-16. Direct URL query for retrieving book titles using a FOR XML clause

Aside from invoking a query to access the SQL Server via a browser's Address box, a direct URL query can be specified within an HTML document. The following HTML document (directURL.html) consists of a hotlink (the word here), which, upon clicking it, will yield the same results as shown in Figure 6-16:

```
<html>
<!-- directURL.html -->
<h3>Click <a href="http://webdev/BooksDB?sql=SELECT Title from books FOR XML
AUTO&root=BooksDoc">here</a> to view book titles!</h3>
</html>
```

Template Queries

A *template* is a valid XML document that consists of one or more SQL statements that are executed when the template is specified in the URL query. The contents of a template can be saved in an XML file (with .xml extension), or it can be assigned in the form of a string.

The template parameter can be used in place of the sql parameter in the URL specification, in which case, we are required to append the template content as a string when specifying a URL to visit, which is cumbersome and gives rise to security concerns.

Specifying the direct query string (through the `sql` parameter as discussed in the previous section) or the template content string (via the `template` parameter) in the URL directly will expose the SQL query content in the Address box as well as Internet Explorer 5.0 window's title, even though they may be invoked via a link within some document, as in the case of directURL.html. If confidentiality of the query content is a concern, the direct URL query method that displays the SQL query content is obviously not acceptable.

The template query method provides two alternatives in executing a query. The first alternative requires you to specify the query string in a template format via the template parameter and invoke its execution in the same way you execute a direct URL as discussed in the previous section. This alternative method has the same security threats as the direct URL query method for executing a query using the sql parameter. The second alternative of executing a template requires you to specify only the name of the file you use to save the actual content of a template.

Template Containing an SQL Query

Before using a template to carry out the SQL statements that it contains, let's first look at a simple template (queryTemplate.xml):

```
<DocROOT xmlns:sql="urn:schemas-microsoft-com:xml-sql">
    <sql:query>
        SELECT Title, Author
        FROM books, authors
        WHERE books.ISBN=authors.ISBN AND
              books.Price>35 AND books.Price&lt;40
        FOR XML AUTO
    </sql:query>
</DocROOT>
```

In a template, the <sql:query> element is used to create an SQL query. The namespace of the prefix, sql, is specified in the first line as an attribute value within the document root element, <DocROOT>. The name of the document root element is user-given, and in this case, it is <DocROOT>. You may also recall in Chapter 1 that entity reference for the less than comparator should be used when used in the parsed data content of an XML element unless it is specified as CDATA. Hence, the entity reference, <, is used in place of the < symbol.

Type the preceding template and save as queryTemplate.xml under the templates folder specified during the set-up step shown previously in Figure 6-13. You'll recall that we have also defined a virtual name,

BooksTemplate, which is of the `template` type, and the templates folder is
D:\VirtualDB\Templates.

Now, type the following in the Address box of Internet Explorer 5.0 to test out
the effect, as shown in Figure 6-17:

```
http://webdev/BooksDB/BooksTemplate/queryTemplate.xml
```

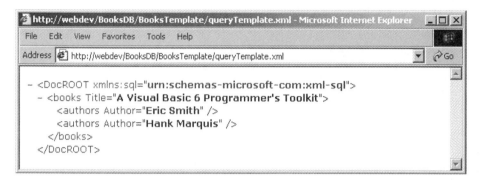

*Figure 6-17. Retrieving book titles and authors using a template
(queryTemplate.xml)*

Alternatively, we may specify the contents of queryTemplate.xml as the value
of the `template` parameter in the URL specification:

```
http://webdev/BooksDB?template=<DocROOT+xmlns:sql="urn:schemas-microsoft-
com:xml-sql">+<sql:query> .. . .... </sql:query>+</DocROOT>
```

> **NOTE** *In this case, you will see the actual SQL query embed-
> ded within the template string in its entirety in the Address
> box as well as Internet Explorer 5.0 window's title, as with
> the case of a direct URL query. This method, while it works
> fine and returns the results as requested, is obviously cum-
> bersome and error-prone. Also, the security concern that was
> discussed earlier applies here, too.*

Aside from the <sql:query> element, other useful elements that can be used
in a template are <sql:header>, <sql:param>, and <sql:xpath-query>. The last of
the three will be discussed under the section on XPath queries.

We demonstrate the use of <sql:header> and <sql:param> in the following example:

```
<DocROOT xmlns:sql="urn:schemas-microsoft-com:xml-sql">
    <sql:header>
        <sql:param name="minPrice">35</sql:param>
    </sql:header>
    <sql:query>
        SELECT Title, Author
        FROM books, authors
        WHERE books.ISBN=authors.ISBN AND
              books.Price>CAST(@minPrice AS money) AND books.Price&lt;40
        FOR XML AUTO
    </sql:query>
</DocROOT>
```

The parameter, `minPrice`, is predefined with the value 35 in the header section. The default type of the parameter is `nvarchar`, which will cause a type mismatch problem in the WHERE clause since books.Price has the SQL data type, `money`. As such, the `CAST` function is used to convert the data type of the parameter value denoted by `@minPrice`, into the SQL `money` type for comparison. This new template query will yield the same results as were shown in Figure 6-17.

If we would like to transform the XML data, which appeared previously in Figure 6-17, into a more presentable HTML document, we could include an XSLT document as an attribute in the <DocRoot> in the preceding example. For example, if the XSLT document is named booklist.xsl located in the folder D:\VirtualDB\xsl, then the first line of the template will look like this:

```
<DocROOT xmlns:sql="urn:schemas-microsoft-com:xml-sql"
         sql:xsl="../xsl/booklist.xsl">
```

Template Containing Execution of a Stored Procedure

Let us consider a simple stored procedure for retrieving books that have a price lower than $40.

You can create a stored procedure (Figure 6-18) by following the steps here:

1. Invoke the SQL Server Enterprise Manager.

2. Highlight the database to be used, e.g., BooksCatalog.

3. Display a pop-up menu by right-clicking the selected database.

4. Choose New > Stored Procedure.

Type the following into the text area labeled Text:

```
CREATE PROCEDURE getCheapBooks @budget nvarchar(7) AS
    SELECT Title, Price
    FROM books AS cheapbook
    WHERE Price < CAST(@budget AS money)
    ORDER BY Title
    FOR XML AUTO
GO
```

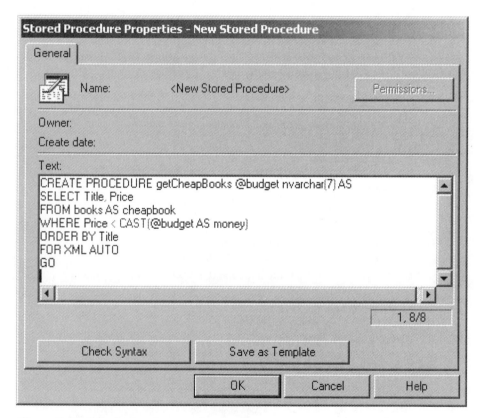

Figure 6-18. Creating a new stored procedure

You may click the Check Syntax button to check the syntax before clicking the Save as Template button to save the stored procedure as getCheapBooks.

Next, create the following template to make use of the stored procedure and save it as say, cheapBooksTemplate.xml, under the templates folder:

```
<Books xmlns:sql="urn:schemas-microsoft-com:xml-sql">
    <sql:query>
        SELECT Title, Author
        FROM books, authors
        WHERE books.ISBN=authors.ISBN
        FOR XML AUTO
    </sql:query>
    <sql:header>
        <sql:param name="maxPrice">40</sql:param>
    </sql:header>
    <sql:query>
        EXEC getCheapBooks @maxPrice
    </sql:query>
</Books>
```

We have included two queries in cheapBooksTemplate.xml. The first query is to list out all the titles and their authors, and the second to accomplish our original objective of listing the titles whose price is lower than $40. The results appear in Figure 6-19.

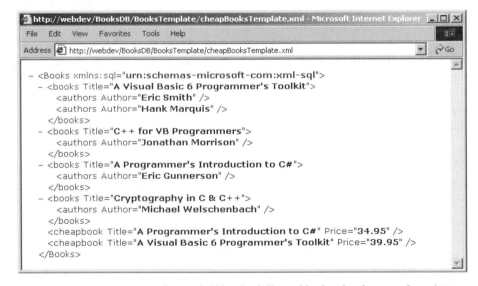

Figure 6-19. Retrieving authors of all books followed by books cheaper than $40

XPath Queries

An XPath query, which is a valid XPath expression, can be specified as part of a direct URL query or in a template query. The XPath query is executed against an annotated mapping schema file, also specified as part of the URL. The schema provides the structure to a view of the data from a selected relational database.

Only a subset of the XPath language is implemented in Microsoft SQL Server 2000. The features supported are listed in Table 6-11.

Table 6-11. Subset of the XPath Language Implemented in SQL Server 2000

FEATURE	ITEMS
Axes	attribute, child, parent, self
Boolean-valued predicates (including successive and nested predicates)	one or more condition expressions enclosed within [and]
Boolean operators	AND, OR
Boolean functions	true(), false(), not()
Relational operators	=, !=, <, <=, >, >=
Arithmetic operators	+, -, *, div
Conversion functions	number(), string(), Boolean()
XPath variables	—

NOTE *For more information on the XPath language and the Microsoft XDR schema, please refer to Chapter 2 and Appendix C, respectively.*

Specifying an XPath Query in a URL

When using an XPath query in a direct URL query, the query forms part of the URL and is represented as an XPath expression that returns a single-column value from the database. When accessing the database object (e.g., the books table of the BooksCatalog database) using the direct URL query, we make use of a virtual name of the dbobject type. The syntax of the URL looks like this:

```
http://IISserver/virtualroot/dbobject_virtualname/xpath_query
```

The line that follows shows the use of an XPath query in a URL for retrieving the title of the book with ISBN 1-893115-86-0:

```
http://webdev/BooksDB/BooksObject/books[@ISBN='1-893115-86-0']/@Title
```

The previous URL uses the setup that we have demonstrated using the IIS Virtual Directory Management for SQL Server. The substring in bold is the XPath query string.

Type the URL in Internet Explorer 5.0 and the result is returned as displayed in Figure 6-20.

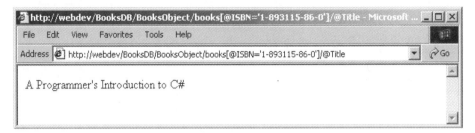

Figure 6-20. Using XPath query in URL to retrieve title of the book with ISBN 1-893115-86-0

To obtain an XML document instead of a rowset value from the database, we need to specify a schema:

```
http://IISserver/virtualroot/schema_virtualname[/relative-path-to-schema]
/schemaFile/xpath_query[?root=rootvalue[&xsl=styleFile]]
```

The optional relative path is the location path of the folder holding the XDR schema file to be used. The path can be relative to the schemas folder associated with the virtual name declared with the schema type during the registration of the virtual root. For example, we have associated the schemas folder, D:\VirtualDB\Schemas, with the virtual name BooksSchema of schema type via the dialog window that was previously shown in Figure 6-13. The order of specification of the two optional parameters, root and xsl, is interchangeable.

Consider the following XDR schema:

```
<?xml version="1.0"?>
<Schema xmlns="urn:schemas-microsoft-com:xml-data"
        xmlns:dt="urn:schemas-microsoft-com:datatypes"
        xmlns:sql="urn:schemas-microsoft-com:xml-sql">
    <ElementType name="Book" sql:relation="books">
        <AttributeType name="ISBN" dt:type="string" />
        <AttributeType name="Title" dt:type="string" />
        <AttributeType name="Price" dt:type="float" />
        <attribute type="ISBN" />
        <attribute type="Title" />
```

```
        <attribute type="Price" />
    </ElementType>
</Schema>
```

Save the previous XDR schema as catalog.xml in the schemas folder.

Enter the following URL in the Address box of Internet Explorer 5.0 and you are returned the results that appear in Figure 6-21:

```
http://webdev/BooksDB/BooksSchema/catalog.xml/Book[@Price<40.0]?root=Catalog
```

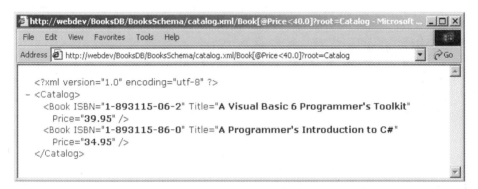

Figure 6-21. Using XPath query in URL to retrieve books with `Price<40.0`

It should be highlighted that the less than symbol < must be specified as it is as shown in the Address box of Figure 6-21. If you try to escape it by using <, an error will be encountered that has status code HTTP 500 (Internal server error).

Specifying an XPath Query in a Template

To specify an XPath query in a template, we use the <sql:xpath-query> element tag, where the XDR schema is indicated as a value of the attribute mapping-schema.

An example follows that uses the XDR schema, catalog.xml. It will yield the same XML results as the output that was displayed in Figure 6-21.

```
<Catalog xmlns:sql="urn:schemas-microsoft-com:xml-sql">
    <sql:xpath-query mapping-schema="../Schemas/catalog.xml">
        /Book[@Price&lt;40]
    </sql:xpath-query>
</Catalog>
```

Save the preceding template as CatalogTemplate.xml into the templates folder with the virtual name, BooksTemplate. To execute the XPath query in CatalogTemplate.xml, type the following URL and template file specification in the Internet Explorer 5.0's Address box:

```
http://webdev/BooksDB/BooksTemplate/CatalogTemplate.xml
```

A point to highlight here is the use of < in place of the < symbol to indicate a less-than comparator. An error will occur if < is used.

We modify the template slightly so that the upper price limit can be changed dynamically during execution time instead of being fixed as 40. We do this by replacing the 40 with a parameter name say, maxPrice, declared using a <sql:param> element. The parameter is initialized to 50.

Modify CatalogTemplate.xml to the following:

```
<Catalog xmlns:sql="urn:schemas-microsoft-com:xml-sql">
    <sql:header>
        <sql:param name="maxPrice">50</sql:param>
    </sql:header>
    <sql:xpath-query mapping-schema="../Schemas/catalog.xml">
        /Book[@Price&lt;$maxPrice]
    </sql:xpath-query>
</Catalog>
```

In the Address box of Internet Explorer 5.0, append the actual value for maxPrice to the end of the URL and template specification:

```
http://webdev/BooksDB/BooksTemplate/CatalogTemplate.xml?maxPrice=40
```

Posting Templates

So far in our discussion of using template queries, we have seen two methods for invoking a template through a URL specification:

- Appending a template query string, i.e., the cumbersome template query contents become part of the URL specification

- Using a virtual name of template type, which serves as a location reference to the template file that is specified as part of the URL specification

In the first method, the template contents are sent as a query string to the Web server using the default HTTP method, GET. That is, the template is part of the HTTP header in the HTTP request packet sent to the server. In this section, we see an alternative way of passing the template via the HTTP POST method. In this case, the template is found in the HTTP message instead of the header of the HTTP request packet sent to the server.

We can accomplish this in two ways, which we discuss next.

Posting a Template Through an HTML Form

Create a virtual directory, say http://localhost/SQLXML, on the IIS Server for holding HTML pages. Next, create the following HTML document (Listing 6-1) and save it as postCatalogTemplate.html under the virtual directory that we have just created:

Listing 6-1. postCatalogTemplate.html

```
1    <html>
2    <h3>Searching Book By ISBN</h3>
3    <form action="http://webdev/BooksDB" method="POST">
4    Enter ISBN:
5        <input type="text" name="bookISBN" value="" size="15">
6
7    <input type="hidden" name="contentType" value="text/xml">
8    <input type="hidden" name="template"
9        value='<Catalog xmlns:sql="urn:schemas-microsoft-com:xml-sql">
10               <sql:header>
11                   <sql:param name="bookISBN">0</sql:param>
12               </sql:header>
13               <sql:query>
14                   SELECT ISBN, Title, Price
15                   FROM books AS Book
16                   WHERE ISBN=@bookISBN
17                   FOR XML AUTO
18               </sql:query>
19               </Catalog>'>
20
21     <input type="submit" value="Search!">
22    </form>
23    </html>
```

The HTML document contains a <form> element (lines 3 to 22). The form in turn contains four input objects named bookISBN, contentType, and template, as well as a submit button (line 21). The two parameter names, contentType and template, are reserved names and they are used to refer to the content type value as used in an HTTP header and the template query as understood by the SQL Server 2000.

The submission of the preceding form will cause the sending of an HTTP packet with the URL specified as shown in line 3, together with the three parameters, bookISBN, contentType, and template, delivered in the HTTP message portion.

Enter the following URL in the Address box of Internet Explorer 5.0 to load the HTML form:

```
http://localhost/SQLXML/postCatalogTemplate.html
```

Enter an ISBN, for example, 1-893115-06-2, to the HTML form, as shown in Figure 6-22.

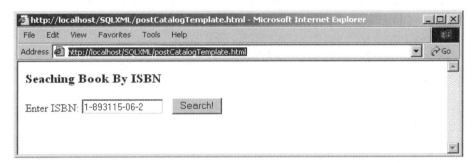

Figure 6-22. Input form in postCatalogTemplate.html

When the button labeled Search! is clicked, the three parameter values mentioned earlier are sent in an HTTP request to the targeted URL—i.e., SQL Server 2000 named webdev. The template content is processed and the XML data is returned as shown in Figure 6-23.

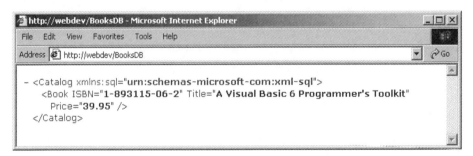

Figure 6-23. Retrieving book information using a template sent via an HTTP form

If we do not want to leave the returned XML data as it is in the client browser, we can use an xsl parameter to specify an XSLT stylesheet to transform the XML data into a desired format. For example, we can add in a statement in line 6 to

make use of a stylesheet say, catalog.xsl, that is located in the folder
D:\VirtualDB\xsl, as follows:

```
6    <input type="hidden" name="xsl" value="xsl/catalog.xsl" />
```

The value specified for the location of the stylesheet is relative to the current
directory specified as the virtual directory http://webdev/BooksDB in line 3.

Listing 6-2 is a possible stylesheet used as catalog.xsl for our example.

Listing 6-2. catalog.xsl

```
<?xml version="1.0" encoding="ISO-8859-1"?>
<xsl:stylesheet xmlns:xsl="http://www.w3.org/1999/XSL/Transform" version="1.0">
<xsl:template match="/">
    <HTML>
    <HEAD>
        <STYLE>TH {background-color:#DDCCDD}</STYLE>
    </HEAD>
    <BODY>
    <TABLE border="1" width="450">
        <TR><TD colspan="3" align="center"><H3>BOOKS</H3></TD></TR>
        <TR><TH>ISBN</TH><TH>Title</TH><TH>Price</TH></TR>
        <xsl:apply-templates select="/Catalog" />
    </TABLE>
    </BODY>
    </HTML>
</xsl:template>

<xsl:template match="Catalog">
    <xsl:for-each select="Book">
    <TR>
        <TD><xsl:value-of select="@ISBN" /></TD>
        <TD><xsl:value-of select="@Title" /></TD>
        <TD><xsl:value-of select="@Price" /></TD>
    </TR>
    </xsl:for-each>
</xsl:template>
</xsl:stylesheet>
```

Since we expect the output to be in HTML format after the transformation
performed by catalog.xsl, we need to modify line 7 of postCatalogTemplate.html
to the following:

```
7    <input type="hidden" name="contentType" value="text/html">
```

The result of transforming the original XML output shown in Figure 6-23 based on the stylesheet, catalog.xsl, is given in Figure 6-24.

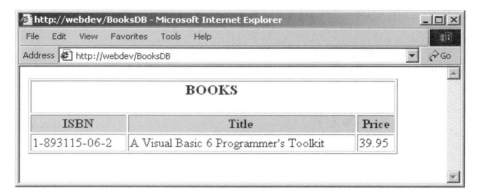

Figure 6-24. Formatting retrieved book information in XML into HTML format

Posting a Template via an XMLHTTP Object

Chapter 4 described how an XMLHTTP object could be used to deliver an XML document over the HTTP to a target server. In this section, we load the content of a template query into a DOM object, which in turn rides on the HTTP over to the SQL Server.

In the example that we show in this section, we merely display the returned response string from the server using a message box in VBScript on the client, since data transformation and presentation are not the emphasis here. Chapter 3 provides good coverage on how to transform the XML data into a more presentable form.

Consider the following example and save it as poster.html (Listing 6-3) under the virtual directory, http://localhost/SQLXML/.

Listing 6-3. poster.html

```
<html>
<head>
<script language="vbscript">
<!--
    Dim doc, poster

    Sub search_onClick
    'Creating and populating a new DOM tree with template query contents
    Set doc = CreateObject("Msxml2.DOMDocument")
    doc.async = false
    doc.loadXML "<Catalog xmlns:sql='urn:schemas-microsoft-com:xml-sql'>" &_
                "<sql:header>" &_
```

```
            "<sql:param name='bookISBN'>" &_
                searchform.bookISBN.value &_
            "</sql:param>" &_
            "</sql:header>" &_
            "<sql:query>" &_
                "SELECT ISBN, Title, Price FROM books AS Book " &_
                "WHERE ISBN=@bookISBN FOR XML AUTO" &_
            "</sql:query>" &_
            "</Catalog>"

    'Posting an XMLHTTP packet to server and displaying server's string response
    Set poster = CreateObject("Microsoft.XMLHTTP")
    poster.open "POST", "http://webdev/BooksDB", false
    poster.setRequestHeader "Content-type", "application/xml"
    poster.send doc
    msgbox poster.responseText
    End Sub
//-->
</script>
</head>

<body>
<h3>Welcome to Book Search!</h3>
<form name="searchform" method="POST">
Enter ISBN:
    <input type="text" name="bookISBN" value="" size="15">
 <input type="button" name="search" value="Search!">
</form>
</body>
</html>
```

To test the script, enter the following in the Address box of Internet Explorer 5.0:

```
http://localhost/SQLXML/poster.html
```

Enter an ISBN, for example, 1-893115-06-2, to the HTML form. The result will be similar to that shown previously in Figure 6-23.

Persisting Changes Using Updategram

An Updategram is used for persisting changes, which are made to an XML view, to the database. Updategram is executed through an XML template and uses the namespace, *urn:schemas-microsoft-com:xml-updategram.*

When using an Updategram, we need to specify the before- and after-transaction XML instances. The changes from the before-view and the after-view are used to generate the appropriate Transact-SQL statement such as INSERT, UPDATE or DELETE, sometimes based on a specified annotated XDR schema. The annotated XDR schema is used to map the XML data into data in relational tables.

You may realize that the intended purpose for using Updategrams, as mentioned previously, can also be accomplished using the OPENXML function that was discussed earlier. A basic difference is that in the latter, the entire XML document corresponding to a view or an entire database table needs to be loaded into the memory. In the case of Updategram, only the XML data corresponding to the affected rows in the database needs to be presented in the Updategram. Hence, if the update affects only a relatively small portion of a view of a database table, Updategram can indeed help save the memory resources. This shall become clearer as we illustrate the use of Updategram with a couple of examples that follow.

A Simple Example to Insert, Delete, and Update

We present our first example of Updategram for performing the following tasks:

- Updating the specification of cover type of a book

- Inserting a new book

The tasks are accomplished via Listing 6-4.

Listing 6-4. simpleGram.xml

```
<Catalog xmlns:updg="urn:schemas-microsoft-com:xml-updategram">
<updg:sync>
   <updg:before>
      <books ISBN="1-893115-06-2" CoverType="S" />
   </updg:before>
   <updg:after>
      <books ISBN="1-893115-06-2" CoverType="H" />
   </updg:after>

   <updg:before>
   </updg:before>
   <updg:after>
      <books ISBN="1-893115-80-1"
             Title="A Programmer's Guide to Jini Technology"
             Pages="375"
```

```
            Price="$39.95"
            CoverType="S" />
    </updg:after>
</updg:sync>
</Catalog>
```

Save the Updategram (Listing 6-4) as simpleGram.xml into the templates
folder (D:\VirtualDB\Templates in our case) with the virtual name
BooksTemplate, under the virtual root BooksDB. Call the template via Internet
Explorer 5.0 by entering the following URL in the Address box:

```
http://webdev/BooksDB/BooksTemplate/simpleGram.xml
```

You will see a single line displayed in Internet Explorer 5.0 after the successful transaction:

```
<Catalog xmlns:updg="urn:schemas-microsoft-com:xml-updategram" />
```

The original contents of the books database table (that was presented
previously in Figure 6-1) have now changed to the contents that are shown in
Figure 6-25. Notice the insertion of a new book (third record) and the change of
cover type of the first book from S to H.

ISBN	Title	Price	CoverType	Pages	CoverImage
1-893115-06-2	A Visual Basic 6 Programmer's Toolkit	39.95	H	400	<Binary>
1-893115-76-3	C++ for VB Programmers	49.95	S	400	<Binary>
1-893115-80-1	A Programmer's Guide to Jini Technology	39.95	S	375	<Binary>
1-893115-86-0	A Programmer's Introduction to C#	34.95	S	357	<Binary>
1-893115-95-X	Cryptography in C & C++	49.95	S	380	<Binary>

Figure 6-25. Contents of the books *database table after executing simpleGram.xml*

Understanding the Code

Let's take a closer look at the code of the Updategram.

The <updg:sync> element is used to denote a transaction, which in turn, may
consist of one or more pairs of the <updg:before> and <updg:after> elements.
The entire transaction denoted by the <updg:sync> element is performed only if
all the Transact-SQL statements corresponding to all the enclosed before- and
after-instances are successfully carried out. If there is one single step that fails, all
the other steps enclosed in the <updg:sync> will be rolled back.

An empty <updg:before> element paired with a non-empty <updg:after>
element implies an insertion of record to the database. On the other hand,
a before-after pair that contains a non-empty <updg:before> element and an

empty <updg:after> element implies deletion of the record represented in the before-instance from the database.

The sequence of specifying the <updg:before> and <updg:after> elements is important. The after-instance must follow the before-instance in a before-after-instances-pair. An empty <updg:before> or <updg:after> element may be omitted completely from the <updg:sync> content.

Another observation is that the <books> element is mapped to a record or row in the books table. Each of the attributes in the <books> element is mapped to a column of the row concerned. Indeed this is the implicit mapping that is used in the Updategram unless an annotated mapping schema is explicitly specified as an attribute value in the <updg:sync> element that we will discuss in greater detail later.

Some Possible Errors

In our example, we have specified an update to the CoverType field of the books record with ISBN 1-893115-06-2. Before the update is carried out, the appropriate record is first identified in the database table, and its contents should match those specified in the first <updg:before> element. If the record has been modified or no appropriate record can be identified, an error is said to occur and none of the Transact-SQL statements implied in the Updategram will be honored.

For example, if the original value of the CoverType field of the book with ISBN 1-893115-06-2 is not S, an MSSQL error message with the following description will be shown in the browser:

```
SQLOLEDB Error Description: Empty update, no updatable rows found
Transaction aborted
```

Notice the value of the Price field of the record to be inserted as specified in the content of the second <updg:after> element is given as $39.95. The $ prefix is important because it is used to indicate that the XML data value 39.95 of type nvarchar should be converted to the SQL data type, money. Without the $ prefix, an error message appears, which is similar to the one that is shown in Figure 6-26.

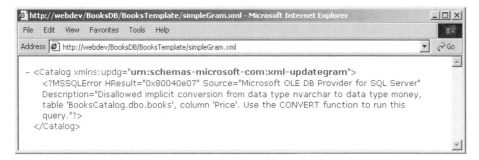

Figure 6-26. Error in converting XML data into SQL money *data type for the Price column*

If simpleGram.xml is loaded a second time after it was successfully executed the first time (which resulted in an update to the books table that was shown previously in Figure 6-25, i.e., the cover type of the book with ISBN 1-893115-06-2 is changed to H and a new record is added into the books table for a book with ISBN 1-893115-80-1), the following complaints will appear in the browser, as shown in Figure 6-27.

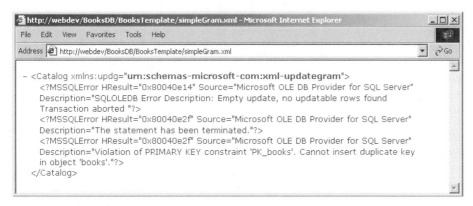

Figure 6-27. Errors in type conversion and insertion of duplicate record

One of the problems was mentioned earlier—no record of the state as depicted within the first <updg:before> could be found in the books table. The second problem occurred because there was an attempt to insert a duplicate record with the primary key value 1-893115-80-1 into the books table.

Using Single Before-After Pair to Handle Multiple Transact-SQL Statements

In simpleGram.xml, each before-after pair generates an appropriate Transact-SQL statement—one is an UPDATE while the other is INSERT. We could have used just one before-after pair to generate both the SQL statements, in which case, we need to assign a unique identifier to each (<books>) element representing a unique record in the database table. We make use of the updg:id attribute to accomplish the job.

Save the following Updategram as multipleSQLsGram.xml (Listing 6-5) into the templates folder:

Listing 6-5. multipleSQLsGram.xml

```
&lt;<Catalog xmlns:updg="urn:schemas-microsoft-com:xml-updategram">
<updg:sync>
   <updg:before>
      <books updg:id="book1" ISBN="1-893115-06-2" CoverType="H" />
   </updg:before>
   <updg:after>
      <books updg:id="book1" ISBN="1-893115-06-2" CoverType="S" />
      <books updg:id="book2"
            ISBN="1-893115-53-4"
            Title="Visual Basic for Testers"
            Pages="350"
            Price="$39.95"
            CoverType="S" />
   </updg:after>
</updg:sync>
</Catalog>
```

If the previous Updategram is executed, we will see that the cover type of the book with ISBN 1-893115-06-2 is changed back to S, and that a sixth book is added into the books database table, as shown in Figure 6-28.

ISBN	Title	Price	CoverType	Pages	CoverImage
1-893115-06-2	A Visual Basic 6 Programmer's Toolkit	39.95	S	400	<Binary>
1-893115-53-4	Visual Basic for Testers	39.95	S	350	<Binary>
1-893115-76-3	C++ for VB Programmers	49.95	S	400	<Binary>
1-893115-80-1	A Programmer's Guide to Jini Technology	39.95	S	375	<Binary>
1-893115-86-0	A Programmer's Introduction to C#	34.95	S	357	<Binary>
1-893115-95-X	Cryptography in C & C++	49.95	S	380	<Binary>

Figure 6-28. Contents of the books *table after executing multipleSQLsGram.xml*

If the updg:id attribute were omitted, the following error message would display:

```
All updategram nodes with siblings must have ids, either user specified ones
or mapping schema based key field id
```

Using Multiple <updg:sync> Blocks in an Updategram

The other extreme is to enclose only a single before-after pair within each <updg:sync> element. The advantage is that any failure with a before-after pair will not affect the other Transact-SQL statements in other before-after instances since each <updg:sync> element is considered an independent transaction.

Create and save the following Updategram (Listing 6-6) as multipleSyncGram.xml:

Listing 6-6. multipleSyncGram.xml

```
<Catalog xmlns:updg="urn:schemas-microsoft-com:xml-updategram">
<updg:sync>
    <updg:before>
        <books ISBN="1-893115-06-2" CoverType="S" />
    </updg:before>
    <updg:after>
        <books ISBN="1-893115-06-2" CoverType="H" />
    </updg:after>
</updg:sync>

<updg:sync>
    <updg:before>
    </updg:before>
    <updg:after>
        <books ISBN="1-893115-80-1"
               Title="A Programmer's Guide to Jini Technology"
               Pages="375"
               Price="$39.95"
               CoverType="S" />
    </updg:after>
</updg:sync>
</Catalog>
```

Executing the preceding Updategram on the books table (whose state was shown previously in Figure 6-28) will cause the cover type of the book with ISBN 1-893115-06-2 to be changed to H despite an error occurring in executing the second Transact-SQL statement. An error message will be displayed to indicate a failure in inserting the book with ISBN 1-893115-80-1 since the book is already in the books table.

Using Annotated XDR Schema in Updategrams

We mentioned in the explanation of our first Updategram example, simpleGram.xml, that an implicit mapping schema is applied on the Updategram when it is executed.

We now show the use of an annotated XDR schema to help define the relationship between elements, subelements, and attributes when they involve more than one database table. The schema also allows the specification of data types of the elements or attributes that map to their corresponding fields in the database tables.

The following Updategram (Listing 6-7), schemaGram.xml, creates a record or row for the author of the book with ISBN 1-893115-80-1. This row will be inserted into the authors table.

Listing 6-7. schemaGram.xml

```
<Catalog xmlns:updg="urn:schemas-microsoft-com:xml-updategram">
<updg:sync mapping-schema="booksSchema.xml">
    <updg:before>
       <Book ISBN="1-893115-80-1" />
    </updg:before>

    <updg:after>
       <Book ISBN="1-893115-80-1">
           <AuthorOfBook Name="Jan Newmarch" />
       </Book>
    </updg:after>
</updg:sync>
</Catalog>
```

A few pieces of information are missing and they are going to be filled in by an annotated XDR schema, explicitly specified via the mapping-schema attribute of the <updg:sync> element. They include the mapping of <Book> and <AuthorOfBook> to the appropriate table rows, as well as the relationship between the two in the database.

Let's look at the schema, booksSchema.xml (Listing 6-8), which provides the necessary mapping for running the Updategram, schemaGram.xml, correctly. The contents of the annotated schema, booksSchema.xml, are shown next:

Listing 6-8. booksSchema.xml

```xml
<?xml version="1.0"?>
<Schema xmlns="urn:schemas-microsoft-com:xml-data"
        xmlns:dt="urn:schemas-microsoft-com:datatypes"
        xmlns:sql="urn:schemas-microsoft-com:xml-sql">
    <ElementType name="Book" sql:relation="books">
        <AttributeType name="ISBN" />
        <attribute type="ISBN" />
        <element type="AuthorOfBook">
            <sql:relationship key-relation="books" key="ISBN"
                              foreign-relation="authors" foreign-key="ISBN" />
        </element>
    </ElementType>

    <ElementType name="AuthorOfBook" sql:relation="authors">
        <AttributeType name="Name" />
        <attribute type="Name" sql:field="Author" />
    </ElementType>
</Schema>
```

Let's take a look at the first <ElementType> element in the preceding schema. The `sql:relation` attribute is used to indicate a database table (in this case, the `books` table) whose rows the <Book> elements are mapped to. Similarly, in the second <ElementType> element, we specify that the <AuthorOfBook> element is to map to a row in the `authors` database.

Let's keep our focus on the second <ElementType> element with name, AuthorOfBook. There is a specification of an attribute, `Name`, for the <AuthorOfBook> element used in the Updategram or any valid XML document using this schema. This attribute is mapped to the column or field, Author, in the `authors` table using `sql:field`.

According to the preceding schema, the <AuthorOfBook> element can be found as a child element within a <Book> element. They are related according to the relationship specified using the <sql:relationship> tag. In our example, it is indicated that a row (i.e., <Book>) in the books table is related to a row (i.e., <AuthorOfBook>) in the `authors` table based on the ISBN value.

If we place both the Updategram, schemaGram.xml, and the annotated XDR schema, booksSchema.xml, in our templates folder, D:\VirtualDB\Templates, we can execute the Updategram by entering the following in the Address box of Internet Explorer 5.0:

```
http://webdev/BooksDB/BooksTemplate/schemaGram.xml
```

This will result in the creation of a new row in the authors table of the BooksCatalog database, as shown in Figure 6-29.

ISBN	Author
1-893115-06-2	Eric Smith
1-893115-06-2	Hank Marquis
1-893115-76-3	Jonathan Morrison
1-893115-80-1	Jan Newmarch
1-893115-86-0	Eric Gunnerson
1-893115-95-X	Michael Welschenbach

Figure 6-29. Insertion of a new row in the authors *table after executing schemaGram.xml*

Posting an Updategram

Aside from executing an Updategram by specifying it directly in the Address box of Internet Explorer 5.0, we can also execute it by posting the Updategram via an HTML form or an XMLHTTP object as in the case of a template. This is not surprising since we can view an Updategram as a special form of a template.

We will wrap up the Updategram section by showing an example of an Updategram executed via an HTML form. The Updategram attempts to insert an author record using the ISBN and author's name entered by the user via the HTML form. The HTML document containing the HTML form is shown in Listing 6-9.

Listing 6-9. insertAuthor.html

```
<html>
<h3>Adding Author for Book</h3>
<form action="http://webdev/BooksDB" method="POST">
Enter ISBN:
    <input type="text" name="bookISBN" value="" size="15">
<br>
Enter Author's name:
    <input type="text" name="authorName" value="" size="40">
<input type="hidden" name="contentType" value="text/xml">
<input type="hidden" name="template"
        value='<Catalog xmlns:updg="urn:schemas-microsoft-com:xml-updategram">
                <updg:header>
                    <updg:param name="bookISBN">0</updg:param>
                    <updg:param name="authorName">0</updg:param>
                </updg:header>
                <updg:sync mapping-schema="booksSchema.xml">
```

```
                   <updg:before>
                      <Book ISBN="$bookISBN" />
                   </updg:before>

                   <updg:after>
                      <Book ISBN="$bookISBN">
                         <AuthorOfBook Name="$authorName" />
                      </Book>
                   </updg:after>
                </updg:sync>
                </Catalog>'>
<br><br>
 <input type="submit" value="Insert!">
</form>
</html>
```

Save Listing 6-9 as insertAuthor.html and place it in the same templates folder as the XDR schema, booksSchema.xml.

Invoke Internet Explorer 5.0 and load the HTML page, insertAuthor.html. Enter an ISBN value and an author's name as shown in Figure 6-30.

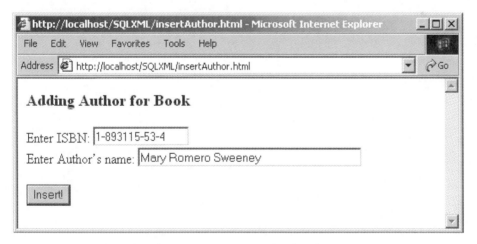

Figure 6-30. Input to the HTML page, insertAuthor.html

A new row is inserted into the authors table as presented in Figure 6-31.

ISBN	Author
1-893115-06-2	Eric Smith
1-893115-06-2	Hank Marquis
1-893115-53-4	Mary Romero Sweeney
1-893115-76-3	Jonathan Morrison
1-893115-80-1	Jan Newmarch
1-893115-86-0	Eric Gunnerson
1-893115-95-X	Michael Welschenbach

Figure 6-31. Contents of the authors *table after inserting an author through insertAuthor.htm.*

Useful Web Links

For more information, we recommend you read:

- Base64 Encoding Format at
  `http://www.freesoft.org/CIE/RFC/1521/7.htm`

- XML for Microsoft SQL Server 2000 Web Release 2 at
  `http://msdn.microsoft.com/downloads/default.asp`

- Data types for Microsoft SQL Server at
  `http://msdn.microsoft.com/library`

- FOR XML Clause at
  `http://msdn.microsoft.com/library/default.asp?url=/library/
  en-u/xmlsql/ac_openxml_lhd8.asp`

- OPENXML Function at
  `http://msdn.microsoft.com/library/default.asp?url=/library/
  en-u/tsqlref/ts_oa-oz_5c89.asp`

- Accessing SQL Server Using HTTP at
  `http://msdn.microsoft.com/library/default.asp?url=/library/
  en-u/xmlsql/ac_xml1_59m4.asp`

Summary

In this chapter, we looked at the support for XML that is incorporated into SQL Server 2000 as well as some of the features that are provided through the XML for Microsoft SQL Server 2000 Web Release.

The features that we discussed here are by no means exhaustive. You should refer to the site for the MSDN library for more references and frequent updates.

CHAPTER 7

Simple API
for XML (SAX)

BY NOW YOU SHOULD BE FAMILIAR WITH how XML documents are processed. Until now, two methods of manipulating XML documents have been discussed:

- Document Object Model (DOM)

- Extensible Stylesheet Language Transformation (XSLT)

Both methods allow information from an XML document to be retrieved or perhaps allow its structure to be modified. However, the DOM is more suitable for retrieving information from an XML document rather than transforming its structure, while XSLT is designed for transforming the format of an XML document, although it can also be used for information retrieval (albeit a bit awkwardly).

In this chapter, we look at yet another alternative—the Simple API for XML (SAX). SAX is simply an interface for manipulating elements in an XML document, much like DOM and XSLT. However, unlike the DOM, SAX uses an event-driven programming model. A program written using SAX will examine an XML document and upon encountering the various components like attributes and elements, it will trigger events so that the programmer can respond to it.

SAX was developed collaboratively by the members of the XML-DEV mailing list that was released on Monday, May 11, 1998 (SAX 1). The birth of SAX was due to the quest for a common Java-based XML API for parsing XML documents, which at that time had numerous XML parsers with their proprietary APIs. Interested readers can check out the following link for a detailed history of SAX: http://www.megginson.com/SAX/SAX1/history.html.

On Friday, May 5, 2000, SAX 2.0 was released. The MSXML3 Parser supports SAX2.

An Alternative to DOM

To compare DOM and SAX, let's use programming as an analogy. In procedural programming, commands that typically execute in a linear fashion are found (as in C or Pascal programming). This can be likened to DOM, which also processes the elements in an XML document in linear fashion. Now, compare this traditional processing model with the event-driven model (Visual Basic and Java are good examples). The codes that are written in an event-driven programming language are not executed sequentially. Rather, they are fired (or activated) when certain events happen, and therefore the code is written to service these specific events. Programming SAX is like event-driven programming—when certain elements are located, events would be fired.

Using SAX with Microsoft Visual Basic 6.0

Before we get into the details of SAX, let's look at a very simple example to see how SAX works. For illustration purposes, we use Microsoft Visual Basic 6.0 (VB6).

Creating a New Project

The first step is to create a new STANDARD EXE project in VB.

Adding Reference to the MSXML3

Next, add a reference to the MSXML3 parser, as shown in Figure 7-1.

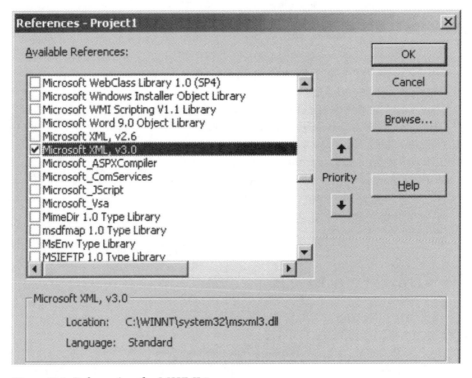

Figure 7-1. Referencing the MSXML3 parser

Loading the XML Document to Be Processed

In this step, we prepare the document that we want SAX to process. The code for the XML document appears in Listing 7-1.

Listing 7-1. Books.xml

```
<?xml version="1.0"?>
<BOOKS>
  <BOOK Pages="357" Type="SOFTCOVER">
    <TITLE>A Programmer's Introduction to C#</TITLE>
    <AUTHOR>Eric Gunnerson</AUTHOR>
    <ISBN>1893115860</ISBN>
    <SYNOPSIS>Eric Gunnerson, the test lead for and member of
              Microsoft's C# design team, has written a
              comprehensive C# tutorial for programmers to help
              them get up to speed
    </SYNOPSIS>
    <PRICE>$34.95</PRICE>
  </BOOK>
  <BOOK Pages="380" Type="SOFTCOVER">
    <TITLE>Cryptography in C &amp; C++</TITLE>
    <AUTHOR>Michael Welschenbach</AUTHOR>
    <ISBN>189311595X</ISBN>
    <SYNOPSIS>Detailed treatment of public key cryptography with
              detailed coverage of the RSA algorithm that is now
              in the public domain </SYNOPSIS>
    <PRICE>$49.95</PRICE>
  </BOOK>
  <BOOK Pages="400" Type="SOFTCOVER">
    <TITLE>C++ for VB Programmers</TITLE>
    <AUTHOR>Jonathan Morrison</AUTHOR>
    <ISBN>1893115763</ISBN>
    <SYNOPSIS>Morrison teaches VB programmers how to use C++
              while addressing their Visual Basic knowledge–making
              the transition as easy as possible.
    </SYNOPSIS>
    <PRICE>$49.95</PRICE>
  </BOOK>
</BOOKS>
```

In the default Form 1 Load event, add the following code that appears in Listing 7-2.

Listing 7-2. Adding codes to the form_load event

```
Private Sub Form_Load()
    Dim SAXReader As New SAXXMLReader
    '--For handling parsing events--
    Dim contentHandler As New contentHandler
    Set SAXReader.contentHandler = contentHandler
    '--Parse the XML document--
    SAXReader.parseURL ("c:\inetpub\apress\chapter 7 codes\books.xml")
End Sub
```

Next, add a Class Module to your project and name it *contentHandler*. This Class Module is shown in Figure 7-2.

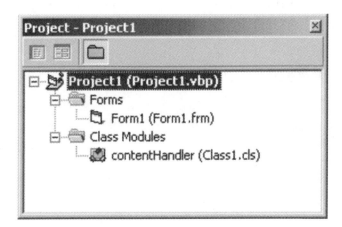

Figure 7-2. Adding a class module to the project

Implementing the Method in the Abstract Class (IVBSAXContentHandler Interface)

Within the contentHandler class module, add the following line at the top of the class module:

```
Implements IVBSAXContentHandler
```

Once the IVBSAXContentHandler interface is implemented, you can simply select the list of methods to code against by clicking on the drop-down list. Select the IVBSAXContentHandler object from the drop-down list; the list of methods appears in the drop-down list on the right. This process is illustrated in Figure 7-3.

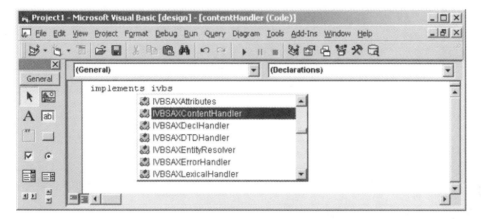

Figure 7-3. Implementing the IVBSAXContentHandler interface

Select the methods that are to be implemented and add in your codes as shown in Listing 7-3. This step is illustrated in Figure 7-4.

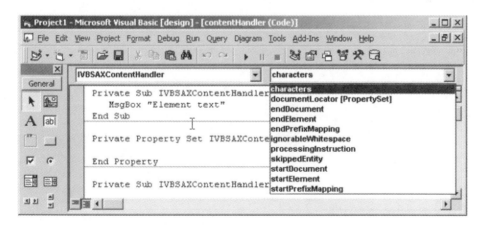

Figure 7-4. Implementing the abstract classes

Once all the methods have been selected, add the following code (shown in bold) to it.

Listing 7-3. Adding codes to the selected methods

```
Private Sub IVBSAXContentHandler_characters(strChars As String)
    '--displays the element text in a message box--
    MsgBox "Element text"
End Sub


Private Property Set IVBSAXContentHandler_documentLocator(ByVal RHS As
 MSXML2.IVBSAXLocator)

End Property


Private Sub IVBSAXContentHandler_endDocument()
    '--end of the XML document encountered--
    MsgBox "End of XML document"
End Sub


Private Sub IVBSAXContentHandler_endElement(strNamespaceURI As String,
 strLocalName As String, strQName As String)
    '--displaying the end tag of an element in a message box--
    MsgBox "End of element detected. Element is </" & strLocalName & ">"
End Sub


Private Sub IVBSAXContentHandler_endPrefixMapping(strPrefix As String)

End Sub


Private Sub IVBSAXContentHandler_ignorableWhitespace(strChars As String)

End Sub


Private Sub IVBSAXContentHandler_processingInstruction(strTarget As
 String, strData As String)

End Sub


Private Sub IVBSAXContentHandler_skippedEntity(strName As String)

End Sub
```

```
Private Sub IVBSAXContentHandler_startDocument()
    '--start of XML document encountered--
    MsgBox "Start of XML document"
End Sub

Private Sub IVBSAXContentHandler_startElement(strNamespaceURI As String,
 strLocalName As String, strQName As String, ByVal oAttributes As
 MSXML2.IVBSAXAttributes)
    '--displaying the start tag of an element--
    MsgBox "Start of element detected. Element name is <" & _
            strLocalName & ">"
    '--if the element contains attributes . . .
    If oAttributes.length > 0 Then    '--print all the attributes in it
        For i = 0 To oAttributes.length - 1
            MsgBox "Attribute: " & oAttributes.getLocalName(i) & _
                        "=" & oAttributes.getValue(i)
        Next i
    End If
End Sub

Private Sub IVBSAXContentHandler_startPrefixMapping(strPrefix As String,
 strURI As String)

End Sub
```

Methods in IVBSAXContentHandler

Table 7-1 describes the different methods available in the IVBSAXContentHandler interface and when they are invoked.

Table 7-1. Methods in the IVBSAXContentHandler Interface

METHODS	DESCRIPTION
StartElement()	Invoked when the reader encounters the start of an element.
EndElement()	Invoked when the reader encounters the end of an element.
StartDocument()	Invoked when the reader starts reading from the beginning of a document. It is only invoked once.
EndDocument()	Invoked when the reader has reached the end of a document. It is only invoked once.
StartPrefixMapping()	Invoked when a new namespace prefix is encountered.
EndPrefixMapping()	Invoked when the end of a namespace prefix is encountered.
SkippedEntity()	Invoked once for each entity skipped in the document.
ProcessingInstruction()	Invoked once for each processing instruction found.
Characters()	Invoked when character data is found.
IgnorableWhiteSpace()	Not supported in current implementation.

Running the Program

To run the program, press the F5 function key. As the program runs, various message boxes will pop up. Some of them are shown in Figure 7-5.

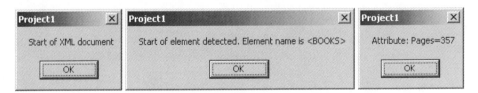

Figure 7-5. Displaying the events fired using the message box

How SAX Works

Now that you have seen SAX in action, let's take a moment to look at how SAX processes an XML document (Figure 7-6).

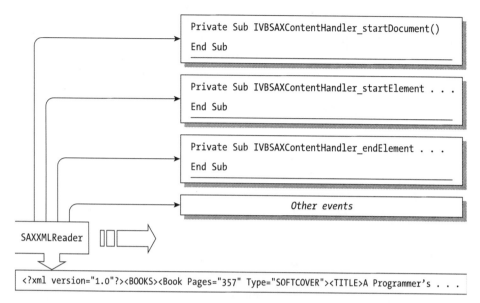

```
Private Sub IVBSAXContentHandler_startDocument()
End Sub
```

```
Private Sub IVBSAXContentHandler_startElement . . .
End Sub
```

```
Private Sub IVBSAXContentHandler_endElement . . .
End Sub
```

Other events

SAXXMLReader

`<?xml version="1.0"?><BOOKS><Book Pages="357" Type="SOFTCOVER"><TITLE>A Programmer's . . .`

Figure 7-6. SAX processing model

As illustrated in Figure 7-6, the SAXXMLReader reads the XML document sequentially, starting from the beginning till the end. As it reads the document, it looks for special characters like the beginning of an element character (<), attributes, and all characters of interest. As these characters are found, it fires the appropriate events so that the necessary processing can be carried out. For instance, we might be looking for the author in the preceding example. When the startElement event is fired, we can write codes to check if the <Author> element is found. If it is found, we wait for the next event to be fired when the content of the <Author> element is found. We can then retrieve the author's name.

NOTE *A quick comparison between DOM and SAX: At this moment, it is important to realize that SAX does not require the whole XML document to be loaded like DOM does. It simply reads the XML document and raises the appropriate events.*

SAX in MSXML3

Microsoft implements SAX2 as a COM object. The Microsoft COM/C++ implementation of SAX2 includes a number of interfaces that map to the Java-based SAX2 standard. These interfaces are exposed through the MSXML parser. Beside the C++ implementation, Microsoft has also created wrappers for the C++/COM interfaces for Microsoft Visual Basic.

Table 7-2 lists the interfaces that are supported by the MSXML3.

Table 7-2. Interfaces Supported by the MSXML3

INTERFACE	DESCRIPTION
IMXAttributes	Creates and edits attributes collection.
IMXReaderControl	Provides control on reader behaviors like abort, suspend, or resume parsing.
IMXWriter	APIs that allow XML documents to be created.
IVBSAXAttributes	Provides access to attributes using index, namespace-qualified name, and prefixed name.
IVBSAXContentHandler	Receives notification of the various components in an XML document. This is the main interface to implement when creating SAX applications.
IVBSAXDeclHandler	Enables a SAX application to implement an optional extension handler for receiving information about DTD declarations in an XML document.
IVBSAXDTDHandler	For handling DTDs.
IVBSAXEntityResolver	For resolving external entities.
IVBSAXErrorHandler	For handling errors in processing.
IVBSAXLexicalHandler	Enables a SAX application to implement an optional extension handler for receiving information from the SAX reader, such as comments, the document type declaration, CDATA sections, and the start and end of an entity within a document.
IVBSAXLocator	Associates a SAX event with a document location.
IVBSAXXMLFilter	Similar to IVBSAXXMLReader except that it obtains its events from another IVBSAXXMLReader rather than a primary source, such as an XML document or a database.
IVBSAXXMLReader	To manage and execute the parsing of an XML document.

NOTE *For a full description of the interfaces, please refer to the documentation provided by the MSXML 3.0 SDK release, downloadable from* msdn.microsoft.com/xml/default.asp.

In Listing 7-3 previously, the IVBSAXContentHandler interface was used:

```
Implements IVBSAXContentHandler
```

The IVBSAXContentHandler interface receives notification of the logical content of a document. This is the main interface that you should implement when creating SAX applications.

You'll recall from Listing 7-2:

```
Private Sub Form_Load()
    Dim SAXReader As New SAXXMLReader
    '--For handling parsing events--
    Dim contentHandler As New contentHandler
    Set SAXReader.contentHandler = contentHandler
    '--Parse the XML document--
    SAXReader.parseURL ("c:\inetpub\apress\chapter 7 codes\books.xml")
    Exit Sub
End Sub
```

First, a new instance of the *SAXXMLReader* is created. The SAXXMLReader, as its name implies, reads an XML document and raises events.

```
Dim SAXReader As New SAXXMLReader
```

Next, an instance of the *contentHandler* class is created. The contentHandler class will implement the abstract methods in the class for handling the events raised by the SAXXMLReader.

```
Dim contentHandler As New contentHandler
```

Next, the contentHandler property of the SAXXMLReader object is set to the contentHandler class created earlier. In doing so, the events raised by the SAXXMLReader will be serviced by the contentHandler class.

```
Set SAXReader.contentHandler = contentHandler
```

And lastly, the XML document is parsed and loaded:

```
SAXReader.parseURL ("c:\inetpub\apress\chapter 7 codes\books.xml")
```

The IVBSAXContentHandler interface supports the following methods (Table 7-3), which correspond to the events that are triggered by the SAXXMLReader.

Table 7-3. Methods Supported by the IVBSAXContentHandler Interface

EVENT	DESCRIPTION
characters	Receives notification of character data.
endDocument	Receives notification of the end of a document.
startDocument	Receives notification of the beginning of a document.
endElement	Receives notification of the end of an element.
startElement	Receives notification of the beginning of an element.
ignorableWhitespace	Receives notification of ignorable white space in element content. This method is not called in the current implementation because the SAX2 implementation is non-validating.
endPrefixMapping	Ends the scope of a prefix-URI namespace mapping.
StartPrefixMapping	Begins the scope of a prefix-URI namespace mapping.
ProcessingInstruction	Receives notification of a processing instruction.
SkippedEntity	Receives notification of a skipped entity.

Source – MSXML 3.0 documentation

The IVBSAXContentHandler interface also supports the properties that are listed in Table 7-4.

Table 7-4. Properties Supported by the IVBSAXContentHandler Interface

PROPERTY	DESCRIPTION
DocumentLocator	Receives an interface pointer to the IVBSAXLocator Interface, which provides methods for returning the column number, line number, PublicId, or SystemID for a current document event.

Source – MSXML 3.0 documentation

Our earlier example implemented some of the preceding methods:

```
Private Sub IVBSAXContentHandler_characters(strChars As String)
Private Sub IVBSAXContentHandler_endDocument()
Private Sub IVBSAXContentHandler_endElement(strNamespaceURI As String,
    strLocalName As String, strQName As String)
Private Sub IVBSAXContentHandler_startDocument()
Private Sub IVBSAXContentHandler_startElement(strNamespaceURI As String,
    strLocalName As String, strQName As String, ByVal oAttributes As
 MSXML2.IVBSAXAttributes)
```

Error Handling in SAX

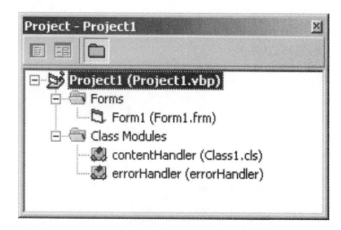

Figure 7-7. Adding the error-handling class module

To implement error handling in SAX, add a new class module and name it *ErrorHandler,* as illustrated in Figure 7-7.

The codes for the ErrorHandler class are:

```
Implements IVBSAXErrorHandler
```

```
Private Sub IVBSAXErrorHandler_error(ByVal oLocator As
MSXML2.IVBSAXLocator, strErrorMessage As String, ByVal nErrorCode As
Long)

End Sub

Private Sub IVBSAXErrorHandler_fatalError(ByVal oLocator As
MSXML2.IVBSAXLocator, strErrorMessage As String, ByVal nErrorCode As
Long)
    '--displaying the error message using the message box--
    MsgBox strErrorMessage
End Sub

Private Sub IVBSAXErrorHandler_ignorableWarning(ByVal oLocator As
MSXML2.IVBSAXLocator, strErrorMessage As String, ByVal nErrorCode As
Long)

End Sub
```

We also need to add the following code for error handling (shown in bold) to the default form:

```
Private Sub Form_Load()
    Dim SAXReader As New SAXXMLReader
    '--For handling parsing events--
    Dim contentHandler As New contentHandler
    Dim errorHandler As New errorHandler

    Set SAXReader.contentHandler = contentHandler
    Set SAXReader.errorHandler = errorHandler

    '--Parse the XML document--
    On Error Resume Next
    SAXReader.parseURL ("c:\inetpub\apress\chapter 7 codes\books.xml")

    Exit Sub
End Sub
```

The IVBSAXErrorHandler interface supports the methods that are listed in Table 7-5.

Table 7-5. Methods Supported by the IVBSAXErrorHandler Interface

METHODS	DESCRIPTION
error	Receives notification of a recoverable error.
fatalError	Receives notification of a non-recoverable error.
ignorableWarning	Receives notification of a warning.

However, the current SAX2 implementation does not support the error() and ignorableWarning() methods. To see how errors are handled, let's cause a deliberate error on our XML document:

```
<?xml version="1.0"?>
<BOOKS>
  <BOOK Pages="357" Type="SOFTCOVER">
    <TITLE>A Programmer's Introduction to C#<TITLE> <!-- / missing -->
    <AUTHOR>Eric Gunnerson</AUTHOR>
    <ISBN>1893115860 </ISBN>
```

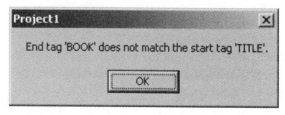

Figure 7-8. Error message displayed by the error handler

. . .

We have omitted the / in the end tag of the <TITLE> element. When the application is run, the error message shown in Figure 7-8 is displayed:

The preceding dialog box is fired by the *fatalError* event:

```
Private Sub IVBSAXErrorHandler_fatalError(ByVal oLocator As
 MSXML2.IVBSAXLocator, strErrorMessage As String, ByVal nErrorCode As
 Long)
   MsgBox strErrorMessage
End Sub
```

Using SAX

Let's now see a real-life example of SAX using the same XML document that we described earlier (except with the <ISBN> element appearing before the <TITLE> element, for reasons that we shall see shortly). The code appears in Listing 7-4.

Listing 7-4. BooksISBN.xml

```
<?xml version="1.0"?>
<BOOKS>
  <BOOK Pages="357" Type="SOFTCOVER">
     <ISBN>1893115860</ISBN>
     <TITLE>A Programmer's Introduction to C#</TITLE>
     <AUTHOR>Eric Gunnerson</AUTHOR>
     <SYNOPSIS>Eric Gunnerson, the test lead for and member of
               Microsoft's C# design team, has written a
               comprehensive C# tutorial for programmers to help
               them get up to speed
     </SYNOPSIS>
     <PRICE>$34.95 </PRICE>
   </BOOK>

  <BOOK Pages="380" Type="SOFTCOVER">
     <ISBN>189311595X</ISBN>
     <TITLE>Cryptography in C &amp; C++</TITLE>
     <AUTHOR>Michael Welschenbach</AUTHOR>
     <SYNOPSIS>Detailed treatment of public key cryptography with
               detailed coverage of the RSA algorithm that is now
               in the public domain
     </SYNOPSIS>
     <PRICE>$49.95</PRICE>
   </BOOK>

  <BOOK Pages="400" Type="SOFTCOVER">
     <ISBN>1893115763</ISBN>
     <TITLE>C++ for VB Programmers</TITLE>
     <AUTHOR>Jonathan Morrison</AUTHOR>
     <SYNOPSIS>Morrison teaches VB programmers how to use C++ while
               addressing their Visual Basic knowledge--making the
               transition as easy as possible.
     </SYNOPSIS>
     <PRICE>$49.95</PRICE>
   </BOOK>
</BOOKS>
```

We want to search for a title based on the ISBN.

 NOTE *In a real-life situation, this XML document could be much larger than just containing three titles. In fact the XML document might well be generated from a database server (or ADO) and persisted as XML.*

To locate a title, we simply look for the appearance of the <ISBN> element, and once the ISBN matches, the content of the <TITLE> element would be displayed. The following code snippets in Listing 7-5 accomplish this.

Listing 7-5. Codes for displaying the title of a book based on the ISBN

```
Implements IVBSAXContentHandler
Dim ISBNFound As Boolean
Dim titleFound As Boolean
Dim displayTitle As Boolean
Dim title As String

Private Sub IVBSAXContentHandler_characters(strChars As String)
    '--finding the title with the right ISBN--
    If ISBNFound And strChars = "189311595X" Then
     titleFound = True
    End If
    If displayTitle Then
        title = title & strChars
    End If
End Sub

Private Sub IVBSAXContentHandler_endElement(strNamespaceURI As String,
 strLocalName As String, strQName As String)
    '--displaying the found title in a message box--
    If displayTitle Then
        MsgBox title
        End '--title found; aborts the processing--
    End If
End Sub

Private Sub IVBSAXContentHandler_startElement(strNamespaceURI As String,
```

```
strLocalName As String, strQName As String, ByVal oAttributes As
MSXML2.IVBSAXAttributes)
    '--keeping a lookout for the ISBN and TITLE elements--
    If strLocalName = "ISBN" Then
        ISBNFound = True
    End If
    If titleFound And strLocalName = "TITLE" Then
        displayTitle = True
    End If
End Sub
```

What the code does is to look for the <ISBN> element and check to see if its content is "189311595X." If it is located, we proceed to look out for the <TITLE> element and save the title of the book into a variable called "title." Finally we print out the title of the book in the *endElement* event. There is a good reason for doing that. Be aware that the line

```
Cryptography in C &amp; C++
```

will fire off the characters event three times as shown in Figure 7-9.

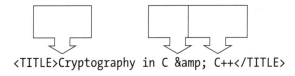

```
<TITLE>Cryptography in C &amp; C++</TITLE>
```

Figure 7-9. This content will fire three events

Thus, you need to print the title at the endElement event. Once the title is located and printed, the program ends and the SAXXMLReader will abort the processing of the XML document.

Limitations of SAX

From the previous example, it is not too difficult to see that you have to take care of maintaining the context of the document you are manipulating. While DOM provides the ability to refer to child elements using nodes traversal technique,

SAX does not provide that kind of feature. Instead, the responsibility is yours to maintain the information that you need.

Also, the structure of the XML document is important. You'll recall that in this example, we have deliberately shifted the <ISBN> element to appear *before* the <TITLE> element. If the <ISBN> element appears *after* the <TITLE> element, this will make the search process less efficient, as illustrated in Figure 7-10.

<ISBN> appears *before* <TITLE>

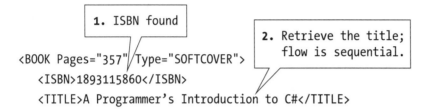

<ISBN> appears *after* <TITLE>

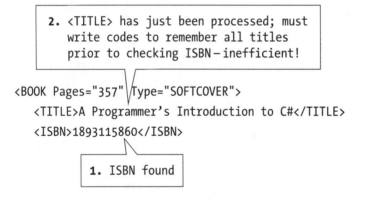

Figure 7-10. Structure of XML document affects the efficiency of SAX processing

Though these are the limitations, using SAX in this case slashes the processing time (as compared to using DOM). This is because the processing is aborted as soon as the title is found; there is no need to process the whole document.

When Do You Use SAX?

Now that you have seen how SAX works, let's examine the uses for which SAX is suited.

Advantages of SAX

The advantages of using SAX are:

- Handles large XML documents

- Able to retrieve small amounts of information

- Processing can be stopped immediately

SAX Is Suitable for Large Documents

While DOM requires the whole XML document to be loaded into main memory, SAX does not. This makes SAX particularly suitable for handling large XML documents as only a portion of the XML document is handled at any one time. This cuts down on the memory requirements.

SAX Is Good for Retrieving Small Amounts of Information

Using our previous application as an example, imagine you now have an XML document that contains a few hundred titles. If you want to simply extract the price of a title, it is clearly more efficient to use SAX than DOM as there is no need to wait for the whole XML document to be loaded in memory.

SAX Allows Processing to Be Aborted When Necessary

When a price of a title has been found, the processing of the XML document can be stopped immediately. This is a real nice feature of SAX.

Disadvantages of SAX

As in the real world, there is no free lunch. SAX has its share of limitations. Most notably, they are:

- Can't access document elements directly

- Can't search a document easily

SAX Does Not Allow Direct Access to Document Elements

As SAX processes an XML document sequentially, it does not allow access to elements that have been processed earlier. This is a severe limitation compared to DOM, which allows nodes to be accessed directly.

Complex Searches Are Not Easy to Implement

As illustrated earlier in the example where we searched for a specific title of a book, there is little support from SAX in letting me know the contextual information of a particular section of the document. The developer will have to implement his/her own data structure to maintain that information.

Some Uses of SAX

Choosing between DOM and SAX is not always a clear-cut matter. However, there are some obvious cases where the use of SAX is clearly superior over DOM. Here are some of the possible uses:

- Scanning for an item in an XML document. In such cases, it is definitely more efficient to use SAX, as the search can be aborted as soon as the required item is found. An example would be an inventory system where the product information is stored in XML format. Searches for production details like price and quantity can really benefit from the use of SAX.

- Manipulating a large XML document. When manipulating a large XML document, using DOM will result in the whole document being loaded into memory. This results in increased loading and processing time to build the tree in memory. Using SAX will avoid the overheads. An example would be Web application. As Web applications are inherently concurrent, using SAX frees up a lot of memory constraints that would be incurred with DOM.

Useful Web Links

- Microsoft XML SDK at http://msdn.microsoft.com/xml/default.asp

- History of SAX at http://www.megginson.com/SAX/SAX1/history.html

Summary

In this relatively short chapter, we have seen the alternative to processing XML documents. The Simple API for XML (SAX). SAX, as its name implies, is a really simple API. While not touted as a replacement for DOM, SAX is useful in cases in which fast retrieval of information is needed. However, SAX is not a complete cure for XML document processing.

In the next chapter, we take a look at the XML Schema Definition (XSD) and the support provided by the latest MS XML parser.

CHAPTER 8

XML Schemas

MOST OF US WHO ARE INVOLVED in XML development are all too familiar with using Document Type Definition (DTD) to enforce the structure of XML documents. Basically, a DTD is a schema that defines the content model of an XML document. However, DTD has some shortcomings.

- First, a DTD is not an XML document. It does not allow DTD to be easily processed by XML parsers.

- Second, DTD does not support data typing. All content is treated as strings. This lack of support for data types means that additional workload must be placed on applications handling the XML document to verify the content of the XML document.

Consider the following code in Listing 8-1:

Listing 8-1. XML document containing an internal DTD

```
<?xml version="1.0" encoding="UTF-8"?>
<!DOCTYPE Product [
    <!ELEMENT Name (#PCDATA)>
    <!ELEMENT Price (#PCDATA)>
    <!ELEMENT Product (Name, Price)>
]>
<Product>
    <Name>LCD Monitor</Name>
    <Price>500</Price>
</Product>
```

There is no way a DTD can validate that the price is a numeric value; hence <Price> will be validated as correct. The following document in Listing 8-2 will still be validated correctly:

Listing 8-2. DTD does not support data types

```
<?xml version="1.0" encoding="UTF-8"?>
<!DOCTYPE Product [
```

```
<!ELEMENT Name (#PCDATA)>
<!ELEMENT Price (#PCDATA)>
<!ELEMENT Product (Name, Price)>
]>
<Product>
         <Name>LCD Monitor</Name>
         <Price>xyz</Price>
</Product>
```

Due to all of these reasons, DTD is slowly being phased out. In the meantime, several alternate solutions have been proposed:

- Microsoft Extensible Data Reduced (XDR) Schema Language (XDR is discussed in Appendix C)

- Document Content Description (DCD)

- XML Schema Definition Language (XSD)

An ideal XML schema should have the following features:

- Supports data types

- Uses XML syntax

- Able to be processed by XML processors

- Supports elements of global and local scope (for example, the use of identical element names)

The W3C's XML Schema Definition Language (XSD) was formally approved as a Recommendation on May 2, 2001. In this chapter, we discuss the W3C's XSD.

 CAUTION *Do not confuse the term XML schema with W3C's XML Schema. An XML schema is basically a set of rules that defines the structure of an XML document. The W3C's XML Schema is also one that has been drafted and recommended for adoption by vendors to enhance the functionality and interoperability of the Web.*

XML Schema and XDR Schema

Before the W3C's XSD was approved as a Recommendation, Microsoft implemented an interim solution to XSD—the Extensible Data Reduced (XDR) Schema Language. XDR was supported in many Microsoft products like BizTalk server, Office 2000, Internet Explorer 5.0 and SQL Server. However, Microsoft is expected to support the W3C's XSD in its future release of its products.

CAUTION   *The MSXML release 4 supports the XSD and XDR languages. MSXML3, however, supports only XDR.*

The W3C's XML Schema specification can be found on W3C's Web site. There are three parts to the specification (please refer to the end of this chapter for links to more information on the W3C's XML Schema):

- XML Schema Part 0: Primer

- XML Schema Part 1: Structures

- XML Schema Part 2: Data types

The *XML Schema Part 0: Primer* is an easy to read description of the XML Schema. *XML Schema Part 1: Structures* and *XML Schema Part 2: Data types* provide the complete description of the XML Schema language.

First Look at XML Schema

Before we dive deep into the details of XML Schema, let us illustrate XSD using a simple example. Consider the XML document that is shown in Listing 8-3.

Listing 8-3. Magazine.xml

```
<?xml version="1.0"?>
<Magazines>
    <Magazine Price="5.95">
        <Title>SQL Server magazine</Title>
        <Publisher>Penton</Publisher>
    </Magazine>
```

```
    <Magazine Price="4.95">
        <Title>Web Techniques</Title>
        <Publisher>CMP</Publisher>
    </Magazine>
    <Magazine Price="5.00">
        <Title>Wireless Business and Technology</Title>
        <Publisher>Sys-con media</Publisher>
    </Magazine>
    <Magazine Price="5.95">
        <Title>MSDN</Title>
        <Publisher>CMP</Publisher>
    </Magazine>
</Magazines>
```

The corresponding XML Schema for the preceding XML document is shown in Listing 8-4.

Listing 8-4. Magazine.xsd

```
<?xml version="1.0"?>
<xsd:schema xmlns:xsd="http://www.w3.org/2001/XMLSchema">
<xsd:element name="Magazines" type="MagazineType"/>
    <xsd:complexType name="MagazineType">
        <xsd:sequence>
            <xsd:element name="Magazine" type="MagazineDetails"
                         minOccurs="0" maxOccurs="unbounded"/>
        </xsd:sequence>
    </xsd:complexType>
    <xsd:complexType name="MagazineDetails">
        <xsd:sequence>
            <xsd:element name="Title" type="xsd:string"/>
            <xsd:element name="Publisher" type="xsd:string"/>
        </xsd:sequence>
        <xsd:attribute name="Price" type="xsd:float"/>
    </xsd:complexType>
</xsd:schema>
```

Note that the Schema file is also an XML document, which has the advantage of allowing XML parsers to process it. You might also have noticed the use of the "xsd" prefix. The use of the "xsd" prefix is similar to using the "xsl" prefix for XSLT stylesheets. Although using "xsd" as a prefix is the norm, you can use any prefix you want by modifying the namespace declaration.

Validating Against a Schema Using MSXML4

MSXML3 does not support the W3C Schema. At the time of writing, the MSXML4 has just been released. The MSXML4 supports the W3C Schema. In this section, we discuss how you can use the MSXML4 to validate an XML document against a Schema. We show our example in Visual Basic 6. For examples using other languages, please refer to the documentation provided with MSXML4.

We will use the examples that are shown in Listings 8-3 and 8-4. To demonstrate validating documents with namespaces, we have added a namespace in the magazine.xml document.

```
<?xml version="1.0"?>
<m:Magazines xmlns:m="urn:Mags">
    <Magazine Price="5.95">
       <Title>SQL Server magazine</Title>
       . . .
```

Listing 8-5 shows the code for XML Schema validation.

Listing 8-5. Validating an XML document against an XML Schema using VB6
```
Private Sub Form_Load()
  '--Create a schema cache--
  Dim xmlschema As New MSXML2.XMLSchemaCache40
  '--and add magazines.xsd to it--
  xmlschema.Add "urn:Mags", App.Path & "\magazine.xsd"
  '--Create an XML DOMDocument object--
  Dim xmldom As New MSXML2.DOMDocument40

  '--Assign the schema cache to the DOM document schemas collection.--
  Set xmldom.schemas = xmlschema
  '--Load magazines.xml document--
  xmldom.async = False
  xmldom.Load App.Path & "\magazine.xml"

  '--check for error--
  If xmldom.parseError.errorCode <> 0 Then
     MsgBox xmldom.parseError.errorCode & " " & xmldom.parseError.reason
  Else
     MsgBox "No Error"
  End If
End Sub
```

If the XML document does not conform to the rules that are specified in the Schema, an error message would be displayed. For example, if the price contains a nonnumeric, such as

```
<Magazine Price="A.95">
```

the XML document would display an error message:

"-1072897661 The attribute: 'Price' has an invalid value according to its data type."

Dissecting the Schema

Let's now dissect the Schema and see how it defines the model of our XML document.

We start the XML Schema by first declaring the <xsd:schema> root element. Also note the XSD namespace that we use. This namespace conforms to the latest W3C's recommendation of XML Schema on May 2, 2001.

```
<?xml version="1.0"?>
<xsd:schema xmlns:xsd="http://www.w3.org/2001/XMLSchema">
```

Next, we define the <Magazines> root element with the <xsd:element> element. The type attribute indicates that the <Magazines> element belongs to a complex type (more on this shortly) named MagazineType. This is very similar to declaring a variable to be of a certain data type in a programming language.

```
<xsd:element name="Magazines" type="MagazineType"/>
```

We then go on to declare the complex type MagazineType. All elements that contain attributes and child elements are known as complexType. Within the <xsd:complexType> element, we use the <xsd:sequence> element to list the sequence in which child elements must appear.

```
<xsd:complexType name="MagazineType">
   <xsd:sequence>
      <xsd:element name="Magazine" type="MagazineDetails" minOccurs="0"
                   maxOccurs="unbounded"/>
   </xsd:sequence>
</xsd:complexType>
```

So the preceding declaration means that <Magazines> contains child element(s) called <Magazine>. The minOccurs attribute indicates the minimum number of time (0 in this case; i.e., this element is optional) this element must appear while the maxOccurs attribute indicates the maximum number of time (any number in this case) this element can appear.

Table 8-1 lists some of the values possible for the minOccurs and maxOccurs attributes.

Table 8-1. Possible Values for the minOccurs *and* maxOccurs *Attributes*

MINOCCURS	MAXOCCURS	DESCRIPTION
0	1	Element is optional, but only one at most can be present
1	1	One and only one occurrence of the element
0	Unbounded	Can have any number of occurrences of the element
1	Unbounded	Element must appear at least once
4	9	Element must appear at least four times, subject to a maximum of nine

The <Magazine> element belongs to another complex type called MagazineDetails.

```
<xsd:complexType name="MagazineDetails">
    <xsd:sequence>
        <xsd:element name="Title" type="xsd:string"/>
        <xsd:element name="Publisher" type="xsd:string"/>
    </xsd:sequence>
    <xsd:attribute name="Price" type="xsd:float"/>
</xsd:complexType>
</xsd:schema>
```

The declaration for the MagazineDetails complex type is very similar to the previous one, except for the declaration of the Price attribute. In addition, the <Title> and <Publisher> elements are known as *simple type,* as they contain neither child elements nor attributes. The type attribute in <xsd:element> and <xsd:attribute> allows data types to be specified. This is one huge advantage XML Schema has over DTD.

Based on the first look at XML Schema, we can see that an XML Schema is itself an XML document, unlike a DTD (which has its own syntax for describing content model). An interesting thing (or irony!) to note is that an XML Schema has its own DTD! The official location for the DTD can be found at http://www.w3.org/2001/XMLSchema.dtd.

Hey! Who says DTD is dead?

Rearranging the Schema

The previous example takes the top-down approach of creating a schema. That is, examine the XML document from top to bottom and as elements and attributes are encountered, declare them in the schema. This approach, though simple to use, is not very suitable for large documents. Schemas created using this approach are often complicated and difficult to understand.

To solve this problem, let's rewrite our schema (Listing 8-6).

Listing 8-6. Magazine1.xsd

```
<xsd:schema xmlns:xsd="http://www.w3.org/2001/XMLSchema">


<xsd:element name="Title" type="xsd:string"/>
<xsd:element name="Publisher" type="xsd:string"/>
<xsd:attribute name="Price" type="xsd:float"/>


<xsd:element name="Magazine">
    <xsd:complexType>
        <xsd:sequence>
            <xsd:element ref="Title"/>
            <xsd:element ref="Publisher"/>
        </xsd:sequence>
        <xsd:attribute ref="Price"/>
    </xsd:complexType>
</xsd:element>

<xsd:element name="Magazines">
    <xsd:complexType>
        <xsd:sequence>
            <xsd:element ref="Magazine" minOccurs="0" maxOccurs="unbounded"/>
        </xsd:sequence>
    </xsd:complexType>
</xsd:element>

</xsd:schema>
```

Let's now dissect the schema.

First, we declare all the simple type elements first:

```
<xsd:element name="Title" type="xsd:string"/>
<xsd:element name="Publisher" type="xsd:string"/>
<xsd:attribute name="Price" type="xsd:float"/>
```

We then declare the <Magazine> element as a complex type. Note that we use the `ref` attribute to reference the simple type elements declared earlier.

```
<xsd:element name="Magazine">
    <xsd:complexType>
        <xsd:sequence>
            <xsd:element ref="Title"/>
            <xsd:element ref="Publisher"/>
        </xsd:sequence>
        <xsd:attribute ref="Price"/>
    </xsd:complexType>
</xsd:element>
```

And finally, we declare the <Magazines> root element:

```
<xsd:element name="Magazines">
    <xsd:complexType>
        <xsd:sequence>
            <xsd:element ref="Magazine" minOccurs="0" maxOccurs="unbounded"/>
        </xsd:sequence>
    </xsd:complexType>
</xsd:element>
```

Compared to the last example, this schema is much more readable and organized. We first start with the most basic elements and progressively declare more complex elements.

Sequencing

Previous examples have illustrated ordering the elements using the <xsd:sequence> element. The <xsd:sequence> element enforces the order in which all the elements appear. Sometimes, you may not want to enforce the order. To do so, use the <xsd:all> element.

```
<xsd:all>
    <xsd:element ref="Title"/>
    <xsd:element ref="Publisher"/>
</xsd:all>
```

For example, the preceding <xsd:all> element allows either the <Title> or <Publisher> element to appear first.

XML Schema Data Types

One of the strengths of the XSD is its support of data types. Data types in XSD can be classified as:

- Primitive data types

- Derived data types

Let's examine them in more detail.

Primitive Data Types

Primitive data types are the basic types in which other data types derive on. Some of the primitive data types are:

- String: Characters strings in XML

- Boolean: True or false, 1 or 0

- Float: Corresponds to the IEEE single-precision 32-bit floating point type

- Double: Corresponds to IEEE double-precision 64-bit floating point type

- Decimal: Represents arbitrary precision decimal numbers

Derived Data Types

As the name implies, derived data types are types that derive from the primitive data types. Examples of derived data types are:

- integer: Represents a sequence of digits with optional + or – sign. It is derived from the decimal type.

- long: Represents a range of numbers (-9223372036854775808 to 9223372036854775807). It is derived from integer.

- int: Represents a range of numbers (from -2147483648 to 2147483647). It is derived from long.

As you can see, a derived data type can both derive from a primitive data type or it can derive from another derived data type.

XML Schema Simple Types

In the earlier example (Listing 8-6), we saw the declaration of simple types using something like this:

```
<xsd:element name="Title" type="xsd:string"/>
```

And to make use of that simple type, we simply reference the simple type using the ref attribute:

```
<xsd:element ref="Title"/>
```

However, there are times when you want to use the same simple type but with a different tag name, for example "BookTitle." In this case, it is useful to define the "Title" element as a simple type using the <simpleType> element:

```
<xsd:simpleType name="TitleType">
    <xsd:restriction base="xsd:string"/>
</xsd:simpleType>
```

To make use of the simple type but with a different tag name, you can now reference it like this:

```
<xsd:element name="BookTitle" type="TitleType"/>
```

Using the <xsd:simpleType> element allows simple types to be reused.

Restricting Range

In the first example (shown previously in Listing 8-6), we declare the price of a magazine as a floating-point number:

```
<xsd:attribute name="Price" type="xsd:float"/>
```

However, we want to further impose some restrictions on the range of values that can be permitted. For example, the price must be greater than zero and not exceed $40 (it is not very likely to have such an expensive magazine). In this case, we need to further restrict the "xsd:float" data type. Consider the example:

```
<xsd:simpleType name="priceType">
    <xsd:restriction base="xsd:float">
        <xsd:minExclusive value="0" />
        <xsd:maxInclusive value="40"/>
    </xsd:restriction>
</xsd:simpleType>
```

Here we use the <xsd:simpleType> element to define a simple type called priceType. Within this simple type, we impose a restriction on the range of values permissible using the <xsd:minExclusive> and <xsd:maxInclusive> facet elements. A facet element defines constraints for a data type.

We also need to change the declaration for the <Price> element to use the new type:

```
<xsd:attribute name="Price" type="priceType"/>
```

With this restriction, our magazine price must be more than 0 (minExclusive) and less than or equal to 40 (minInclusive).

Enumeration

We might also want to restrict the list of publishers to three. In this case, we define another simple type element, like this:

```
<xsd:simpleType name="publisherType">
    <xsd:restriction base="xsd:string">
        <xsd:enumeration value="Penton"/>
        <xsd:enumeration value="CMP"/>
        <xsd:enumeration value="Sys-con media"/>
    </xsd:restriction>
</xsd:simpleType>
```

We used the <xsd:enumeration> element to set the allowable values for the "publisherType" element. Just like before, we need to modify the declaration for the <Publisher> element to use the new publisherType:

```
<xsd:element name="Publisher" type="publisherType"/>
```

So in this case, Publishers are limited to three—Penton, CMP, and Sys-con media.

Deriving New Simple Types

Simple types can be extended from another simple type. The following example illustrates this.

Suppose we have the AgeType derived from the short data type, with a minimum value of 0 and maximum value of 150

```
<xsd:simpleType name="AgeType">
   <xsd:restriction base="xsd:short">
      <xsd:minInclusive value="0"/>
      <xsd:maxInclusive value="150"/>
   </xsd:restriction>
</xsd:simpleType>
```

We want to have another type called AgeGroup1, which extends on the AgeType simple type. We shall impose another restriction, which states that the maximum value for this type cannot exceed 12. Here is the definition:

```
<xsd:simpleType name="AgeGroup1">
   <xsd:restriction base="AgeType">
   <xsd:maxInclusive value="12"/>
   </xsd:restriction>
</xsd:simpleType>
```

As usual, change the type attribute to AgeGroup1:

```
<xsd:element name="Age" type="AgeGroup1"/>
```

So the following text content for <Age> is invalid:

```
<Age>13</Age>
```

since it is more than 12.

XML Schema Complex Types

We have seen the use of complexType in the earlier sections. We shall now take a closer look.

Consider the following XML document for storing shipping and ordering information (Listing 8-7):

Listing 8-7. XML document for storing shipping and ordering information

```xml
<?xml version="1.0" encoding="UTF-8"?>
<OrderInfo>
    <ShipTo>
        <Name>Wei Meng Lee</Name>
        <Phone>065-4606872</Phone>
        <Address>
            <Street1>Ngee Ann Polytechnic</Street1>
            <Street2>535 Clementi Road</Street2>
            <Street3>Singapore</Street3>
            <Postal>599489</Postal>
        </Address>
    </ShipTo>
    <BillTo>
        <Name>Sales @ Apress</Name>
        <Phone>510-5495930</Phone>
        <Address>
            <Street1>Apress L.P.</Street1>
            <Street2>901 Grayson Street Suite 204</Street2>
            <Street3>Berkeley, CA</Street3>
            <Postal>94710</Postal>
        </Address>
    </BillTo>
</OrderInfo>
```

Obviously, there are a couple of repeating elements. Both the <ShipTo> and <BillTo> elements contain the <Name>, <Phone>, and <Address> elements. If you are familiar with object-oriented programming, then the notion of creating classes and deriving objects from them will come to mind. The W3C XML Schema allows us to define data types by giving the simple type or complex type a name attribute. The XML Schema for the preceding XML document appears in Listing 8-8 as follows:

Listing 8-8. Schema for the XML document in Listing 8-7

```xml
<?xml version="1.0" encoding="UTF-8"?>
<xsd:schema xmlns:xsd=http://www.w3.org/2001/XMLSchema
    elementFormDefault="qualified">

<xsd:simpleType name="StreetType">
    <xsd:restriction base="xsd:string">
        <xsd:maxLength value="30"/>
```

```
        </xsd:restriction>
    </xsd:simpleType>

    <xsd:simpleType name="PostalType">
        <xsd:restriction base="xsd:string">
            <xsd:maxLength value="6"/>
        </xsd:restriction>
    </xsd:simpleType>

    <xsd:complexType name="AddressType">
        <xsd:sequence>
            <xsd:element name="Street1" type="StreetType"/>
            <xsd:element name="Street2" type="StreetType"/>
            <xsd:element name="Street3" type="StreetType"/>
            <xsd:element name="Postal" type="PostalType"/>
        </xsd:sequence>
    </xsd:complexType>

    <xsd:simpleType name="PhoneType">
        <xsd:restriction base="xsd:string">
            <xsd:pattern value="[0-9]{3}-[0-9]{7}"/>
        </xsd:restriction>
    </xsd:simpleType>

    <xsd:complexType  name="Contact">
        <xsd:sequence>
            <xsd:element name="Name"/>
            <xsd:element name="Phone" type="PhoneType"/>
            <xsd:element name="Address" type="AddressType"/>
        </xsd:sequence>
    </xsd:complexType>

    <xsd:element name="OrderInfo">
        <xsd:complexType>
            <xsd:sequence>
                <xsd:element name="ShipTo" type="Contact"/>
                <xsd:element name="BillTo" type="Contact"/>
            </xsd:sequence>
        </xsd:complexType>
    </xsd:element>
</xsd:schema>
```

The first thing to note is that we have an additional attribute, name, in the <xsd:simpleType> element:

```
<xsd:simpleType name="StreetType">
    <xsd:restriction base="xsd:string">
        <xsd:maxLength value="30"/>
    </xsd:restriction>
</xsd:simpleType>
```

The preceding simple type element defines a data type called "StreetType." This is analogous to defining a class in an object-oriented programming language. Next comes the restriction element that expresses that this data type is derived from "xsd:string." Within the restriction element is the facet. The facet

```
<xsd:maxLength value="30"/>
```

states that the maximum length of this element is 30 characters.

Besides the simple type definition, we also have complex type definitions:

```
<xsd:complexType name="AddressType">
    <xsd:sequence>
        <xsd:element name="Street1" type="StreetType"/>
        <xsd:element name="Street2" type="StreetType"/>
        <xsd:element name="Street3" type="StreetType"/>
        <xsd:element name="Postal" type="PostalType"/>
    </xsd:sequence>
</xsd:complexType>
```

Here, the "AddressType" element is defined to contain four elements, three of which reference the "StreetType" type and one of which references the "PostalType" type. Also note that the <xsd:complexType> element has the name attribute. The inclusion of this name attribute allows this type to be reused and is known as a *named data type*. Complex type elements that do not contain the name attribute are known as *anonymous data types*.

The "PhoneType" type contains an interesting facet:

```
<xsd:simpleType name="PhoneType">
    <xsd:restriction base="xsd:string">
        <xsd:pattern value="[0-9]{3}-[0-9]{7}"/>
    </xsd:restriction>
</xsd:simpleType>
```

The <xsd:pattern> element specifies the specific pattern that the element must contain. The pattern is specified in the value attribute. The value attribute contains a *regular expression.* In our example, we specify that the phone number must start with three digits followed by a - and then followed by another seven digits.

To make use of the new data types, simply reference them using the type attribute as illustrated in the example:

```
<xsd:complexType  name="Contact">
   <xsd:sequence>
      <xsd:element name="Name"/>
      <xsd:element name="Phone" type="PhoneType"/>
      <xsd:element name="Address" type="AddressType"/>
   </xsd:sequence>
</xsd:complexType>
```

Mixed Content

How do you define mixed content in an XML document? Consider the following code that is shown in Listing 8-9:

Listing 8-9. Mixed content in an XML document

```
<?xml version="1.0"?>
<Synopsis>
   <Author>Eric Gunnerson</Author>, the test lead for and member of Microsoft's
 C# design team, has written a comprehensive <Topic>C#</Topic> tutorial for
 programmers to help them get up to speed.
</Synopsis>
```

Here the <Synopsis> element contains both child elements as well as text. Within the <Synopsis> element are <Author> and <Topic>. The Schema for the preceding XML document is shown in Listing 8-10.

Listing 8-10. Schema for the XML document in Listing 8-9

```
<?xml version="1.0" encoding="UTF-8"?>
<xsd:schema xmlns:xsd="http://www.w3.org/2001/XMLSchema">
   <xsd:element name="Author" type="xsd:string"/>
   <xsd:element name="Topic" type="xsd:string"/>
   <xsd:element name="Synopsis">
      <xsd:complexType mixed="true">
```

```
            <xsd:choice minOccurs="0" maxOccurs="unbounded">
                <xsd:element ref="Author"/>
                <xsd:element ref="Topic"/>
            </xsd:choice>
        </xsd:complexType>
    </xsd:element>
</xsd:schema>
```

To indicate that the <Synopsis> element is of mixed content, we add the mixed attribute to the <xsd:complexType> element.

```
    <xsd:complexType mixed="true">
```

We then declare the elements that can appear within the <Synopsis> element.

```
<xsd:choice minOccurs="0" maxOccurs="unbounded">
    <xsd:element ref="Author"/>
    <xsd:element ref="Topic"/>
</xsd:choice>
```

Note that we use the <xsd:choice> element to encapsulate the two elements. The <xsd:choice> element allows one and only one of the elements contained within it to be present in the XML instance document. In our example, it essentially means that either <Author> or <Topic> can appear, in any sequence, and with unlimited occurrences. The following is valid:

```
<Author>Eric Gunnerson</Author>, the test lead for and member of
Microsoft's C# design team, has written a comprehensive <Topic>C#</Topic>
tutorial for programmers to help them get up to speed. <Author>Andrew
Troelsen</Author> has also written a book on C#.
```

You might be tempted to use the <xsd:sequence> element, for example:

```
<xsd:sequence minOccurs="0" maxOccurs="unbounded">
    <xsd:element ref="Author"/>
    <xsd:element ref="Topic"/>
</xsd:sequence>
```

However, if you use the <xsd:sequence> element, then both the <Author> and <Topic> elements must appear in pairs, like this:

```
<Author>Eric Gunnerson</Author>, the test lead for and member of
Microsoft's C# design team, has written a comprehensive <Topic>C#</Topic>
```

tutorial for programmers to help them get up to speed. <Author>Daniel Appleman</Author> is the president of Desaware, Inc., a developer of add-on products and components for Microsoft Visual Development Tools including <Topic>Visual Basic</Topic>.

Empty Elements

For elements that do not have any content, that is, empty elements, you simply define a <xsd:complexType> within the element definition like this:

```
<xsd:element name="Empty">
  <xsd:complexType/>
</xsd:element>
```

The schema defines an empty element called <Empty/>.

Defining and Declaring Elements and Attributes

Till this point, we have frequently used the terms *declare* and *define*. But what is the distinction between them? A *declaration* describes the structure of an XML document. A *definition* creates new types to be used by other elements.

The following example illustrates a definition:

```
<xsd:simpleType name="PhoneType">
  <xsd:restriction base="xsd:string">
    <xsd:pattern value="[0-9]{3}-[0-9]{7}"/>
  </xsd:restriction>
</xsd:simpleType>
```

Here, we are defining a new type, which is based on the string primitive data type.

The following is a declaration:

```
<xsd:element name="Phone" type="PhoneType"/>
```

We are declaring an element called "Phone," which is of the "PhoneType" type.

Groupings

W3C Schema allows elements and attributes to be grouped so that they can be used as a "container." Consider the following example of an attributes group:

```
<?xml version="1.0" encoding="UTF-8"?>
<Library>
    <Magazine Publisher="Penton" Price="5.95" PubDate="2000-12-01">
        <Name>SQL Magazine</Name>
    </Magazine>
    <Book Publisher="Apress" Price="32.95" PubDate="2001-09-25">
        <Name>Microsoft XML Programming</Name>
    </Book>
</Library>
```

In the preceding example, both the <Magazine> and <Book> elements contain the same set of attributes. Rather than defining the attributes twice, it is neater to group them, as shown in the following Schema (Listing 8-11):

Listing 8-11. Grouping attributes in a Schema

```
<?xml version="1.0" encoding="UTF-8"?>
<xsd:schema xmlns:xsd="http://www.w3.org/2001/XMLSchema">

<xsd:attributeGroup name="AttributeGroup">
    <xsd:attribute name="Publisher" type="xsd:string"/>
    <xsd:attribute name="Price" type="xsd:number"/>
    <xsd:attribute name="PubDate" type="xsd:date"/>
</xsd:attributeGroup>

<xsd:element name="Magazine">
    <xsd:complexType>
        <xsd:sequence>
            <xsd:element name="Name"/>
        </xsd:sequence>
        <xsd:attributeGroup ref="AttributeGroup"/>
    </xsd:complexType>
</xsd:element>

<xsd:element name="Book">
    <xsd:complexType>
        <xsd:sequence>
            <xsd:element name="Name"/>
```

```
        </xsd:sequence>
        <xsd:attributeGroup ref="AttributeGroup"/>
    </xsd:complexType>
</xsd:element>

<xsd:element name="Library">
    <xsd:complexType>
        <xsd:sequence>
            <xsd:element ref="Magazine"/>
            <xsd:element ref="Book"/>
        </xsd:sequence>
    </xsd:complexType>
</xsd:element>

</xsd:schema>
```

We first define an attribute group using the <xsd:attributeGroup> element. Within it, we declare all the attributes belonging to the group.

```
<xsd:attributeGroup name="AttributeGroup">
    <xsd:attribute name="Publisher" type="xsd:string"/>
    <xsd:attribute name="Price" type="xsd:number"/>
    <xsd:attribute name="PubDate" type="xsd:date"/>
</xsd:attributeGroup>
```

To make use of the attribute group, we use the same <xsd:attributeGroup> element with the ref attribute.

```
<xsd:element name="Magazine">
    <xsd:complexType>
        <xsd:sequence>
            <xsd:element name="Name"/>
        </xsd:sequence>
        <xsd:attributeGroup ref="AttributeGroup"/>
    </xsd:complexType>
</xsd:element>
```

Besides using the <xsd:attributeGroup> element to group attributes, you can also group elements using the <xsd:group> element. Its usage is similar to that of using the <xsd:attributeGroup> element, except that for element group definition you need to use the <xsd:sequence> element to enforce the order of the elements.

Linking Schemas and Redefining Definitions

Schemas might be shared among various people. To facilitate sharing, you can include an external Schema by using the <xsd:include> element. For example, we can include another Schema by using:

```
<?xml version="1.0" encoding="UTF-8"?>
<xsd:schema xmlns:xsd="http://www.w3.org/2001/XMLSchema">
    <xsd:include schemaLocation="Address.xsd"/>
    <xsd:complexType name="AddressType">
        <xsd:sequence>
            <xsd:element name="Street1" type="StreetType"/>
            <xsd:element name="Street2" type="StreetType"/>
        <xsd:element name="Street3" type="StreetType"/>
            <xsd:element name="Postal" type="PostalType"/>
        </xsd:sequence>
    </xsd:complexType>
    . . .
```

In this example, the definition for StreetType and PostalType are defined in the XSD file Address.xsd.

You can also redefine a definition from the loaded Schema. For example, you might want to redefine the PostalType to contain at most four characters:

```
<?xml version="1.0" encoding="UTF-8"?>
    <xsd:schema xmlns:xsd="http://www.w3.org/2001/XMLSchema">
        <xsd:redefine schemaLocation="Address.xsd">
            <xsd:simpleType name="PostalType">
                <xsd:restriction base="xsd:string">
                    <xsd:maxLength value="4"/>
                </xsd:restriction>
            </xsd:simpleType>
        </xsd:redefine>
    <xsd:complexType name="AddressType">
        <xsd:sequence>
            <xsd:element name="Street1" type="StreetType"/>
            <xsd:element name="Street2" type="StreetType"/>
        <xsd:element name="Street3" type="StreetType"/>
            <xsd:element name="Postal" type="PostalType"/>
        </xsd:sequence>
    </xsd:complexType>
    . . .
```

Here, we use the <xsd:redefine> element to change the definition of the "PostalType" type.

Documenting the Schema Using `<annotation>`

Documentation is an often-overlooked area in software development. Until this point, we have not really talked about documenting your Schema. To document your Schema, you may use the <!-- and --> pair, since an XSD document is actually an XML document. For example:

```
<!-- Declaring a complex type -->
<xsd:complexType name="MagazineDetails">
    <xsd:sequence>
        <xsd:element name="Title" type="xsd:string"/>
        <xsd:element name="Publisher" type="xsd:string"/>
    </xsd:sequence>
    <xsd:attribute name="Price" type="xsd:float"/>
</xsd:complexType>
```

However, applications processing your XML Schema might not be able to access the comment, since an XML parser can choose to ignore the comments in an XML document. In that case, the comment is not accessible for further processing (say, for documentation purposes). To document your Schema, consider the following example:

```
. . .
<xsd:annotation>
    <xsd:documentation xml:lang="en">
        Declaring a complex type
    </xsd:documentation>
    <xsd:appinfo>
        Declaration for the Synopsis element
    </xsd:appinfo>
</xsd:annotation>
<xsd:complexType name="MagazineDetails">
    <xsd:sequence>
        <xsd:element name="Title" type="xsd:string"/>
        <xsd:element name="Publisher" type="xsd:string"/>
    </xsd:sequence>
    <xsd:attribute name="Price" type="xsd:float"/>
</xsd:complexType>
. . .
```

The <xsd:annotation> element contains two child elements:

- <xsd:appinfo>

- <xsd:documentation>

The <xsd:appinfo> element is for the XML parsers to process the comments while the <xsd:documentation> element allows you to add in comments for human consumption.

Tools for Validating XML Schemas

At the time of writing, there aren't many tools out in the market that are able to validate an XML document against an XML Schema. Most tools, if available, do not support the latest XSD recommendation from W3C. Apart from using the MSXML Preview Release 4, you can use XMLSpy version 4.0 from Altova (www.xmlspy.com). XMLSpy is an Integrated Development Environment for XML that includes all major aspects of XML in one powerful and easy-to-use product. XMLSpy features support for:

- XML document editing and validation

- W3C's XSD Recommendation

- XSLT

In this section, we briefly explain how you can validate an XML document against an XML Schema using XMLSpy 4.0.

Creating the XML Schema

A common question that is often asked is which comes first—XML document or XML Schema? Well, creating XML documents and Schema can be likened to creating databases. In creating database applications, the first thing to do is to design the database before populating the database. Similarly, it is natural that you first design your XML Schema before you create your XML document.

XMLSpy provides an IDE to create XML Schemas easily. Figure 8-1 shows an XML Schema that is created in XMLSpy.

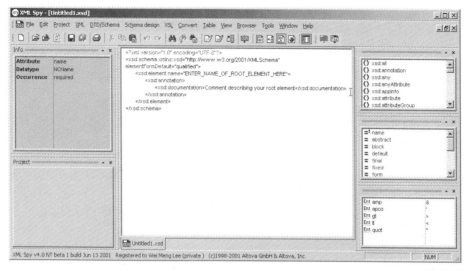

Figure 8-1. Creating an XML Schema in XMLSpy

We won't be going into details on how to create an XML Schema using XMLSpy. For more information, you can refer to the documentation that comes with XMLSpy.

Creating an XML Document Based on an XML Schema

Once the XML Schema is created, you can create XML documents based on that Schema. When you create a new XML document, XMLSpy will ask if you have an existing DTD or Schema that you may want to use as shown in Figure 8-2.

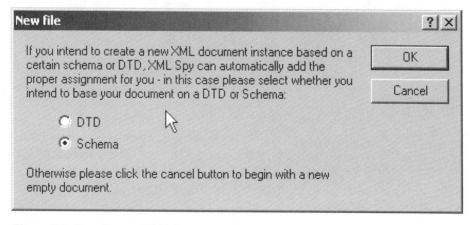

Figure 8-2. Creating an XML document

When a Schema is selected, XMLSpy will automatically generate an XML template that is based on the Schema. Figure 8-3 shows the template.

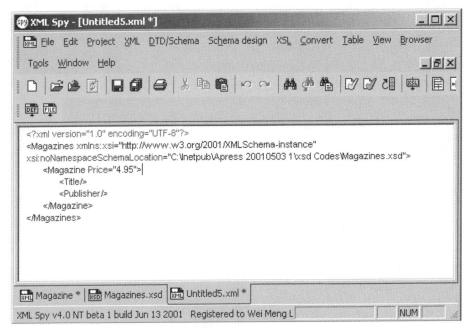

Figure 8-3. Template for XML document

To validate the XML document against the XML Schema, simply click on the "Validate File button," as shown in Figure 8-4.

Figure 8-4. Validating an XML document

Using an XML Document to Generate an XML Schema

Although we said that it is more logical to create an XML Schema before you create the XML document, XMLSpy enables you to generate an XML Schema that is based on an XML document, as shown in Figure 8-5.

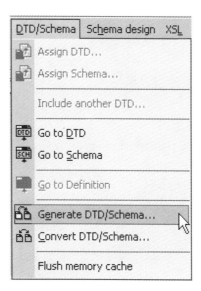

Figure 8-5. Generating an XML Schema

Once an XML Schema is generated, you can simply assign it to the XML document, as shown in Figure 8-6.

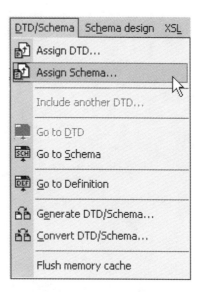

Figure 8-6. Assigning an XML Schema to an XML document

Generating an XML Schema from an XML document is helpful to beginners who are getting started with XML Schema.

Useful Web Links

- XML Schema Part 0: Primer at `http://www.w3.org/TR/xmlschema-0/`

- XML Schema Part 1: Structures at `http://www.w3.org/TR/xmlschema-1/`

- XML Schema Part 2: Data types at `http://www.w3.org/TR/xmlschema-2/`

- XMLSpy Web site at `http://www.xmlspy.com`

- Download MSXML4 at `http://msdn.microsoft.com/xml`

Summary

That's it! In this chapter, we provided an overview of how XML Schema is being used to replaceDTD for validating XML documents. We showed you how to define the structure of an XML document using simpleType and complexType elements. In addition, we showed you how to use XMLSpy from Altova for validating purposes.

Through the many examples that we presented in this chapter, we hope we have provided you with a jump start to getting XML Schema to work for you. Have fun!

CHAPTER 9

The Wireless Markup Language (WML)

LATELY, MOBILE APPLICATIONS HAVE become the buzzword. As we are moving toward the "information at your fingertips" era, people are expecting information to be available everywhere and anywhere they go. We are no longer satisfied accessing the Internet only by sitting in front of the computer, but we also want to be able to access the Internet through our mobile devices like mobile phones and Personal Digital Assistants (PDAs). And that is exactly the role of the Wireless Application Protocol (WAP) Forum.

The WAP Forum is an industry association comprising over 500 members. The aim of the forum is to help develop open specifications for wireless information communications and foster interoperability among players in the wireless industry.

Some of the members of the WAP Forum include:

- Ericsson

- Nokia

- Microsoft

- NTT DocoMo, Inc.

- NEC Corporation

Architecture of WAP

The Wireless Application Protocol (WAP) is an open specification that allows wireless devices to access information instantly through leveraging the current technology (and investment) made on the Internet. Figure 9-1 shows the WAP architecture.

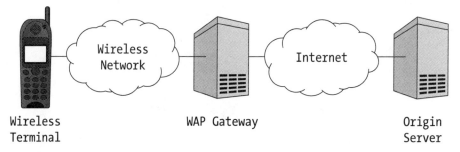

Figure 9-1. WAP architecture

There are three components of interest to us:

- Origin Server: Also commonly known as the Web server, this is the location where wireless applications written in the Wireless Markup Language (WML) and WMLScript are stored.

- WAP gateway: The gateway provides the linkage between the *Wireless Terminal* and the *Origin Server*. The gateway will encode the WML decks into WAP binaries and WMLScript files into WMLScript bytecodes.

- Wireless Terminal: This is the WAP device. It may be a handset, a PDA or any WAP-enabled wireless device. The Wireless Terminal contains *micro-browsers* to display the WAP application.

Function of the WAP Gateway

The roles of a WAP gateway are to

- Connect the mobile device to the Internet and intranet applications.

- Translate requests from the WAP protocol stack (WSP, WTP, WTLS and WDP) to the WWW protocol stack (HTTP and TCP/IP).

- Translate WAP content into binary content to be sent to the mobile device.

- Translate HTML encoding to WML encoding (only applies to some WAP gateways).

Components of WAP

WAP is a communications protocol and application environment. It is designed to work with most wireless networks, such as CDPD, CDMA, GSM, PDC, PHS, TDMA, FLEX, ReFLEX, iDEN, TETRA, DECT, DataTAC, and Mobitex.

 NOTE *Check out Motorola's online glossary of wireless network technologies at* http://www.motorola.com/ies/telematics/htmls/glossary.html.

WAP contains a suite of protocols as shown in Figure 9-2.

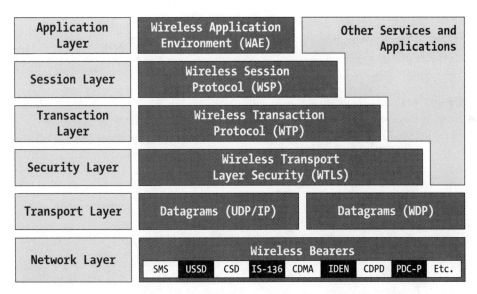

Figure 9-2. WAP Protocol stack (taken from the WAP Forum's WAP brochure)

Table 9-1 lists the protocols that the WAP Protocol stack contains.

Table 9-1. Protocols Contained in the WAP Protocol Stack

PROTOCOLS	DESCRIPTION
Wireless Application Environment (WAE)	The WAE specifies the application framework for wireless applications and services to run on wireless devices.
Wireless Session Protocol (WSP)	The WSP provides the WAE with a consistent interface for maintaining sessions. Two session services are supported: connection-oriented and connectionless services.
Wireless Transaction Protocol (WTP)	The WTP is a transaction-oriented protocol that provides the WAE with the services necessary for interactive browsing (request and response).
Wireless Transport Layer Security (WTLS)	The WTLS provides WAP applications and services with an interface for secure connections.
Datagrams (UDP/IP and Wireless Datagram Protocol)	The WDP provides non-reliable transport protocol with support for message segmentation and reassembly. The transport layer can also make use of UDP over IP (if supported).

Understanding the Wireless Markup Language (WML)

Name change: Openwave was previously known as Phone.com.

To develop wireless applications and services using WAP, the WAP forum defines the Wireless Markup Language (WML), which is an XML application.

Besides the WAP Forum, different vendors can extend the language by specifying unique Document Type Definitions (DTDs). For example, Openwave has extended the standard WML specification and developers are able to make use of these extended WML features by using the Openwave's DTD (we will look at the Document Type Declaration in a moment). However, for the reason of compatibility this is not a good option, unless you have control over the devices that the user is using.

You might be thinking, why do we need another markup language. Isn't HTML doing a good job for the Web browsers? Why don't WAP browsers support HTML?

> **NOTE** *This chapter discusses WAP version 1.1/1.2. At the time of this writing, WAP 2.0 had just been announced. However, it will be some time before WAP 2.0 compliant emulators and handsets become available.*

Rationale for WML

WML is designed with the constraints of small narrowband devices in mind. What this means is that a WML document (known as a deck) must be relatively small in size in order for it to be transmitted from a server to the devices quickly using a low bandwidth medium. Current WAP devices have speed ranging from 9600 kbps to 14400 kbps. WML content is also designed to be displayed in a small and limited screen size. The processing power and user input on a WAP device are also major considerations for the design of WML. Hence, if you look at a typical HTML page, you would realize that it is not very suitable for a device with limited capability.

Structure of a WML Document: Decks and Cards

Let's now take a look at the structure of a WML document (Listing 9-1).

Listing 9-1. WMLDeck.wml

```
<?xml version="1.0"?>
<!DOCTYPE wml PUBLIC "-//WAPFORUM//DTD WML 1.1//EN"
  "http://www.wapforum.org/DTD/wml_1.1.xml">
<wml>
    <card id="card1" title="Welcome">
      <p>
          WML - Wireless Markup Language <br/>
          <a href="#card2">Next Card</a>
      </p>
    </card>
    <card id="card2" title="">
      <p>
          WML is based on XML
      </p>
    </card>
</wml>
```

An example of a WML deck is shown in Figure 9-3.

Figure 9-3. Displaying a WML deck on an emulator

A WML document is known as a WML *deck*. Within a deck, there can be one or more *cards*, as shown in Figure 9-4. This figure shows the WML deck loaded using the WAP emulator provided by Openwave.

A deck is the basic unit that is transferred between the WAP gateway and the Origin Server.

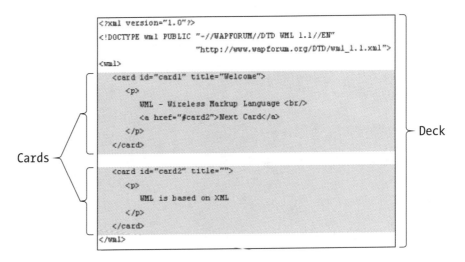

Figure 9-4. Structure of a WML deck

Let's dissect the WML deck and see the individual elements within it.

XML PI

As mentioned, WML is based on XML and hence the first line of a WML deck is the XML Processing instruction.

Document Type Declaration

The next line is the Document Type Declaration for WML. Note that this DTD must be typed exactly as shown, or else WAP gateways will report an encoding error.

```
<!DOCTYPE wml PUBLIC "-//WAPFORUM//DTD WML 1.1//EN"
  "http://www.wapforum.org/DTD/wml_1.1.xml">
```

To use the extended WML defined by Openwave, use the DTD:

```
<!DOCTYPE wml PUBLIC "-//PHONE.COM//DTD WML 1.1//EN"
  "http://www.phone.com/dtd/wml11.dtd" >
```

Some gateways actually expect to see the Document Type Declaration on the same line as the XML PI. In such cases, simply make sure that the XML PI and Document Type Declaration are on the same line.

WML Root Element

The root element of a WML deck is <wml>. All element names used in WML are in small caps.

Card

Within the <wml> element, the <card> element defines the start of a card. A card can be likened to a screen of information, though many times the content of a card often exceed the height of the physical screen. Within the <card> element, the **id** attribute defines a unique name for referencing the card. The **title** attribute contains the title to be displayed on the screen of the device.

*Title: The UP.SDK does not display the title as indicated in the **title** attribute.*

Paragraph and Anchor Elements

Next come the <p> and <a> elements. The <p> element specifies the start of a paragraph while the <a> element specifies an anchor link. In some ways, WML is quite similar to HTML. You can also use <b> and <i> to format a string in bold and italic respectively.

Setting the MIME Type

Before you try out the examples in this chapter, you have to set the following MIME type on your system (Table 9-2).

Table 9-2. List of MIME Strings

EXTENSION	MIME
.WML	text/vnd.wap.wml
.WMLS	text/vnd.wap.wmlscript
.WBMP	image/vnd.wap.wbmp

The three MIME types in Table 9-2 simply indicate to the emulator (or device) that the content that it is receiving is WML, WMLScript, and WBMP, respectively.

NOTE *We only need the WML MIME string. If you are using WMLScript and WBMP images, then the other MIME strings are needed.*

Setting a New MIME Type under IIS 5.0

To set a new MIME type under IIS 5.0, follow these steps:

1. Select the Web site, right click on it and select **Properties**.

2. Select the HTTP Header tab. Under the MIME Map section click on File Types. The File Types dialog box appears, as shown in Figure 9-5.

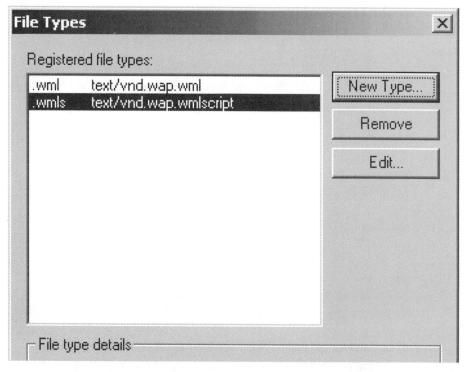

Figure 9-5. Adding new MIME types in IIS 5.0

3. Click on the New Type button to add the two new MIME types.

Setting a New MIME Type under Microsoft Personal Web Server

To set a new MIME type under Microsoft Personal Web Server, follow these steps:

1. Double-click on My Computer.

2. Choose View>Folder Options.

3. Click on the File Types tab.

4. Add the two new MIME types.

How WML Decks Are Processed

Here are the steps for processing a WML deck:

1. The WML document is stored in the *Origin Server*. Origin Servers are conventional Web servers that you are already familiar with. We can either have a WML document saved in its native format (with the .wml extension) or we can use server-side technologies to generate WML content on the fly so as to create dynamic WAP applications. Microsoft Active Server Pages (ASP) and Java Servlets are two popular server-side technologies.

2. The *Wireless Terminal* will make a connection over the wireless network to the WAP gateway.

3. The Wireless Terminal specifies a URL to fetch a WML document. The WAP gateway is connected to the Web using the HTTP protocol and it fetches the required WML document from the Origin Server.

4. Once the required WML document is fetched from the Origin Server, the WAP gateway encodes the WML document into WAP binary. If the fetched document does not conform to the WML specification, an error will occur.

5. The WAP gateway will create a WAP response containing the WAP binary and sends it to the Wireless Terminal.

6. The Wireless Terminal will parse the received WAP binary and renders the deck and cards on the Wireless Terminal.

WBXML

Tokenizer: Some WAP toolkits use the term "compiler" to describe the tools used to convert WML decks into WAP binary. The term used by the WAP Forum is "Tokenizer."

Because of the slow transmission speed of the wireless medium and the limited memory capacity of most wireless devices, it is not feasible to transmit the WML deck in plain text format. Therefore, the WML deck is "encoded" into a binary format known as WAP Binary XML format (WBXML).

The WBXML is a compact binary representation of the WML deck. The aim of WBXML is to reduce the size of the XML documents, thus increasing the throughput of narrowband devices like mobile devices. We won't be describing in detail how the tokenization of the WML deck is performed, but do want to show you a very simple deck—before and after tokenization.

Figure 9-6 shows the WML deck after it has been tokenized into WBXML format (shown using the WinHex editor).

```
WMLDeck.bin                                                              _ □ ×
Offset    0  1  2  3  4  5  6  7   8  9  A  B  C  D  E  F
00000000  01 04 6A 00 7F E7 55 03  63 61 72 64 31 00 36 03   ▮.j.▮çU.card1.6.
00000010  57 65 6C 63 6F 6D 65 00  33 01 60 03 57 4D 4C 20   Welcome.3.`.WML
00000020  2D 20 57 69 72 65 6C 65  73 73 20 4D 61 72 6B 75   - Wireless Marku
00000030  70 20 4C 61 6E 67 75 61  67 65 20 00 26 DC 4A 03   p Language .&ÜJ.
00000040  23 63 61 72 64 32 00 01  03 4E 65 78 74 20 43 61   #card2...Next Ca
00000050  72 64 00 01 01 01 E7 55  03 63 61 72 64 32 00 36   rd....çU.card2.6
00000060  01 60 03 57 4D 4C 20 69  73 20 62 61 73 65 64 20   .`.WML is based
00000070  6F 6E 20 58 4D 4C 20 00  01 01 01                  on XML ....
```

Figure 9-6. WML deck tokenized

 NOTE *The WinHex editor can be downloaded from* http://www.winhex.com/winhex/index-m.html. *It allows you to edit binary files and shows these files in hexadecimal.*

Before tokenization, the size of the WML deck is 422 bytes. After tokenization, the size is 123 bytes. Notice the huge reduction in file size.

Testing WML Applications

At this moment, there are quite a number of emulators freely available for download. These emulators can greatly assist in the development process. Some of the emulators available are:

- Openwave's UP.Simulator

- Nokia WAP Toolkit

- Ericsson WapIDE

- Motorola Mobile ADK

However, before you deploy your WAP application, it is important that you test out your application on real handsets. Testing on real handsets will reveal problems that cannot be replicated with an emulator. For example, real devices generally do not support cookies, but emulators normally support them.

In this chapter, we are using the UP.Simulator from Openwave. You can download the UP.Simulator from `http://www.openwave.com`.

Tailoring WAP Content with XML and XSLT

If all the Internet devices in this world understood and displayed a common markup language *uniformly*, life as a developer would be much simpler (well, maybe not since there is now no need for developers like us . . .).

In the real world, different devices understand different markup languages. For example, Web browsers understand HTML and mobile devices understand markup languages like WML or cHTML.

cHTML:
Compact HTML is the markup language supported by the immensely popular iMode phones from NTT Docomo, Japan.

To make matters worse, within the same family of device there might be varying levels of conformance. The browser war between Microsoft Internet Explorer and Netscape Navigator is an excellent example. With the advent of WAP, developers are painfully realizing the importance and necessity of tailoring mobile content for wireless devices.

Using XML for Content

Rather than code your content using the target markup language directly, a better solution is to use XML. By using XML to code the content of your application, there is no presentation information to worry about. Only when it comes to displaying on the device do we apply a stylesheet to transform it into the target markup language. Figure 9-7 illustrates the process.

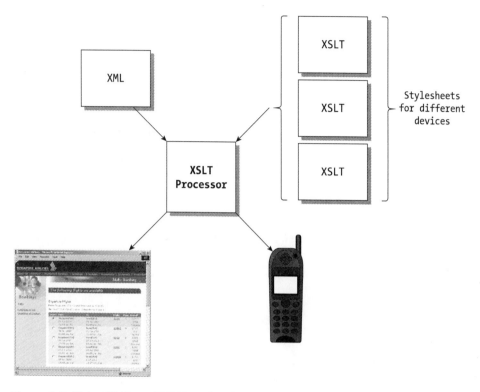

Figure 9-7. Using XML and XSLT to develop WAP applications

Let's consider the example that we presented earlier in Chapter 3. We have the following XML document describing a book (Listing 9-2).

Listing 9-2. Books.xml

```
<?xml version="1.0"?>
<BOOKS>
  <BOOK Pages="357" Type="SOFTCOVER">
    <TITLE>A Programmer's Introduction to C#</TITLE>
    <AUTHOR>Eric Gunnerson</AUTHOR>
    <ISBN>1893115860</ISBN>
    <SYNOPSIS>Eric Gunnerson, the test lead for and member of
              Microsoft's C# design team, has written a
              comprehensive C# tutorial for programmers to help
              them get up to speed</SYNOPSIS>
```

```
        <PRICE>34.95</PRICE>
    </BOOK>
</BOOKS>
```

Transforming XML into HTML and WML

Since our book information is coded in XML, we need to perform some transformation depending on the type of browsers used. If we have a Web browser, we can simply convert it into HTML using a stylesheet as shown in Listing 9-3.

Listing 9-3. HTML of books.xml

```
<?xml version="1.0"?>
<xsl:stylesheet xmlns:xsl="http://www.w3.org/1999/XSL/Transform"
 version="1.0">
<xsl:template match="/">
<html>
<body>
    <table cellspacing="0" border="1">
        <font face="Arial,Helvetica,Univers,Zurich BT" color="#69002f"
        size="-1">
         <b><xsl:value-of select="BOOKS/BOOK/TITLE"/></b></font><br/>
         <tr>
             <td width="175" bgColor="#f4f4ef">
             <font face="Arial,Helvetica,Univers,Zurich BT" size="-2">
             by <xsl:value-of select="BOOKS/BOOK/AUTHOR"/></font><BR/>
             </td>
         </tr>
         <tr>
             <td width="175" bgColor="#e5e5d8">
             <font face="Arial,Helvetica,Univers,Zurich BT" size="-2">
             <xsl:value-of select="BOOKS/BOOK/@Type"/>,
             <xsl:value-of select="BOOKS/BOOK/@Pages"/> PAGES</font><BR/>
             </td>
         </tr>
         <tr>
             <td width="175" bgColor="#f4f4ef">
             <font face="Arial,Helvetica,Univers,Zurich BT" size="-1">
             <b>ISBN:</b>
             <xsl:value-of select="BOOKS/BOOK/ISBN"/></font><BR/>
             </td>
         </tr>
```

```
        <tr>
            <td width="175" bgColor="#e5e5d8">
            <font face="Arial,Helvetica,Univers,Zurich BT" size="-1">
            <b>PRICE: $</b>
            <xsl:value-of select="BOOKS/BOOK/PRICE"/></font><BR/>
            </td>
        </tr>
    </table>
</body>
</html>
</xsl:template>
</xsl:stylesheet>
```

To transform the XML document using the stylesheet, we simply add a processing instruction at the top of the XML document and the Web browser will automatically perform the transformation, as shown in Figure 9-8.

```
<?xml version="1.0"?>
<?xml:stylesheet type="text/xsl" href="HTML.xsl"?>
<BOOKS>
  . . .
```

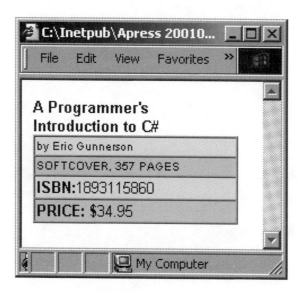

Figure 9-8. XML transformed into HTML

However, not all devices have the ability to perform transformation. Most mobile devices, like handsets, have limited capabilities. In such cases, letting the devices perform the transformation is not a feasible solution. Such transformation must be performed on the server side before it reaches the devices end. Before we look at how transformation is done on the server side, let's look at the stylesheet for transforming the previous XML document into WML (Listing 9-4).

Listing 9-4. WML.xsl

```
<?xml version="1.0"?>
<xsl:stylesheet xmlns:xsl="http://www.w3.org/1999/XSL/Transform" version="1.0">
<xsl:template match="/">
    <xsl:text disable-output-escaping="yes">
        &lt;!DOCTYPE wml PUBLIC "-//WAPFORUM//DTD WML 1.1//EN"
        "http://www.wapforum.org/DTD/wml_1.1.xml"&gt;
    </xsl:text>
    <wml>
        <card id="card1" title="Books">
            <p>
                <b><xsl:value-of select="BOOKS/BOOK/TITLE"/></b><br/>
                by <i><xsl:value-of select="BOOKS/BOOK/AUTHOR"/></i><br/>
                <b>Type:</b><xsl:value-of select="BOOKS/BOOK/@Type"/><br/>
                <b>Pages:</b><xsl:value-of select="BOOKS/BOOK/@Pages"/><br/>
                <b>ISBN:</b> <xsl:value-of select="BOOKS/BOOK/ISBN"/><br/>
                <b>PRICE: $$</b><xsl:value-of select="BOOKS/BOOK/PRICE"/><br/>
            </p>
        </card>
    </wml>
</xsl:template>
</xsl:stylesheet>
```

Transformation Using ASP

Since the transformation must be performed on the server side, we create an ASP file to transform the XML document to WML on the server side (Listing 9-5).

Listing 9-5. Books.asp

```
<%
    Set xml = Server.CreateObject("MSXML2.DOMDocument")
    xml.async = false
    xml.load (Server.MapPath("Books.xml"))
    Set xsl = Server.CreateObject("MSXML2.DOMDocument")
    xsl.async = false
    xsl.load (Server.MapPath("WML.xsl"))
```

```
    Response.ContentType = "text/vnd.wap.wml"
    Response.write (xml.transformNode(xsl))
%>
```

When the Books.asp file is loaded, an XML document appears, as shown in Figure 9-9.

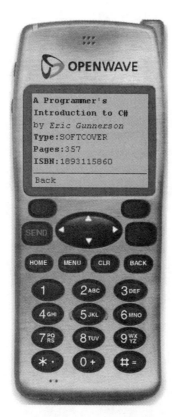

Figure 9-9. Displaying the XML document on a WAP device (emulator)

Differentiating Web from WAP Browsers

If you load the previous Books.asp file from a Web browser, you will get a dialog box similar to the one that is shown in Figure 9-10.

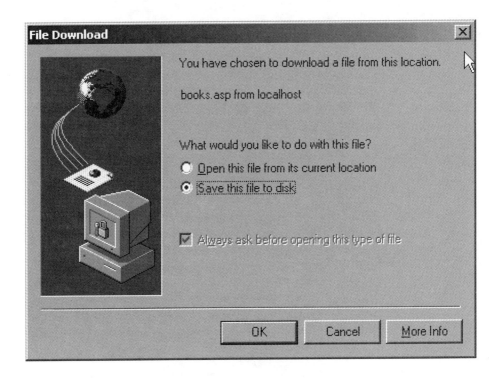

Figure 9-10. Loading Books.asp using a Web browser

This is due to the fact that the Books.asp file is generating WML codes with the WML MIME type. To solve this problem, the server-side codes need to be able to differentiate between the types of browsers being used on the client side.

To detect the kind of browser requesting the file, you can check the environment variable HTTP_USER_AGENT. The following codes in Listing 9-6 show how you can customize your transformation depending on browser type.

Listing 9-6. Books1.asp

```
<%
    Set xml = Server.CreateObject("MSXML2.DOMDocument")
    xml.async = false
    xml.load (Server.MapPath("Books.xml"))
    Set xsl = Server.CreateObject("MSXML2.DOMDocument")
    xsl.async = false

    if InStr(Request.ServerVariables("http_user_agent"),"Mozilla") then
        xsl.load (Server.MapPath("HTML.xsl"))
    else
```

```
    xsl.load (Server.MapPath("WML.xsl"))
    Response.ContentType = "text/vnd.wap.wml"
  end if
  Response.write (xml.transformNode(xsl))
%>
```

Of special interest to us is the ability to detect the type of browser requesting the file. When a device requests a document, it sends information about itself to the Origin Server. Information about the type of browser is stored in this particular environment variable called HTTP_USER_AGENT. The ServerVariables collection of the Request object in ASP allows you to access the environment variable:

```
if InStr(Request.ServerVariables("http_user_agent"),"Mozilla") then
    xsl.load (Server.MapPath("HTML.xsl"))
else
    xsl.load (Server.MapPath("WML.xsl"))
    Response.ContentType = "text/vnd.wap.wml"
end if
```

If the HTTP_USER_AGENT contains the keyword "Mozilla," we can safely assume that the user is using a Web browser. Else we simply assume that the user is using a WAP device. For WAP devices, we also need to set the MIME type explicitly using the ContentType property of the Response object.

NOTE   *We are simplifying the process here. A better way is to use a combination of HTTP_USER_AGENT and HTTP_ACCEPT to test for the different devices. Some WAP micro-browsers, like Microsoft Mobile Explorer (MME), sends "Mozilla" as its user agent string, which may confuse our ASP file here into thinking it is a Web browser.*

Using the Microsoft XSL ISAPI

Microsoft realizes the importance and usefulness of customizing content using XSLT stylesheets. However, as we mentioned earlier, not all devices have the ability to perform transformation on the client side. And as such, we have to resort to server-side transformation. As you have seen in the last section, selecting the appropriate stylesheet for server-side transformation is not an easy task—it involves a lot of work on the part of the developer.

The Microsoft XSL Internet Server Application Programming Interface (ISAPI) Filter is a tool that simplifies the task of selecting the right stylesheet to apply to an XML document. It accomplishes the following tasks:

- Simplifies the task of performing server-side XSL transformations

- Automatically selects and executes stylesheets based on browser characteristics

- Stylesheet caching for improved performance

In this section, we take a closer look at the Microsoft XSL ISAPI and see how it can help transform XML documents into the desired markup language.

Obtaining and Installing MS XSL ISAPI

The MS XSL ISAPI version 2.1 is available for free download from Microsoft's Web site at `http://msdn.microsoft.com/downloads` (Figure 9-11). To download the MS XSL ISAPI filter, type **MS XSL ISAPI** inside the search box to bring you to the download page.

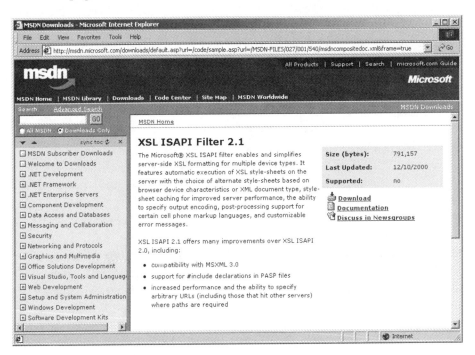

Figure 9-11. Downloading the XSL ISAPI Filter 2.1

Once the MS XSL ISAPI is downloaded, simply extract the files into a folder on your hard disk. For example, we have selected "C:" and the following folders are automatically created, as shown in Figure 9-12.

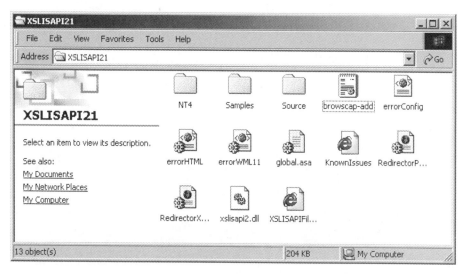

Figure 9-12. Files and folders in C:\xslisapi21

Registering the XSLISAPI2.dll

The next step would be to register the new DLL. To register the DLL for MS XSL ISAPI, simply change to the directory containing the extracted file and type the following command in the Command Window:

```
C:\XSLISAPI>regsvr32 xslisapi2.dll
```

Installing the Filter in IIS

In order for IIS to use the filter, you need to register this under the IIS Administration tool. To do so, select the Web site that you are planning to house the XML documents, click on Properties, and click on the ISAPI Filters tab. Click on the Add button and add the DLL as shown in Figure 9-13.

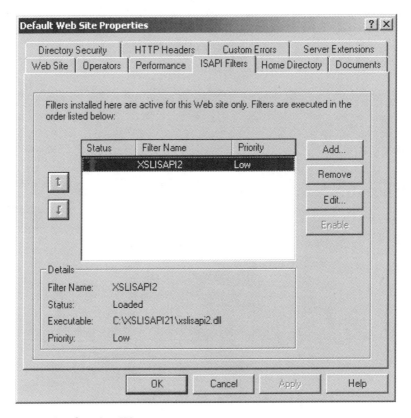

Figure 9-13. Configuring IIS

That's it! You can now test if your filter is installed correctly.

Testing Your Installation

To test your installation, open your Web browser and type
`http://localhost/xslisapi/samples/install/installtext.xml` (Figure 9-14).

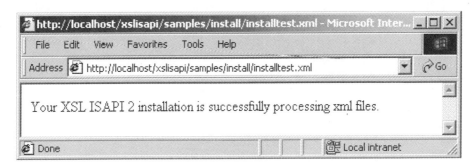

Figure 9-14. Testing your installation

If you see a successful message, then your filter is installed correctly. Else, check the documentation that comes with it and make sure you follow the steps illustrated earlier carefully.

Adding Additional Browser Information

The last configuration step that you need to perform is adding entries to your browscap.ini file. Your browscap.ini is located (by default) in

```
C:\winnt\system32\inetsvr\browscap.ini
```

Add the following entries (in boldface) to your browscap.ini file:

```
. . .
[Mozilla/?.0 (compatible; Opera/3.0;*)]
parent=Opera unknown system

[Mozilla/?.0 (*;US) Opera*]
parent=Opera unknown system

[*Opera*]
parent=Opera unknown system

; Unwired Planet SDK Simulator v 3.1 for WML
[UP.Browser/3.0-UPG1 UP.Link/3.1]
browser=Phone.com
target-markup=HDML 3.0
content-type=text/x-hdml

; Unwired Planet SDK Simulator v 3.2 for HDML
[UP.Browser/3.0-UPG1 UP.Link/3.2]
browser=Phone.com WML 1.0 simulator
target-markup=WML1.0
content-type=text/x-wap.wml

; Unwired Planet SDK Simulator v 3.2 for WML
[UP.Browser/3.1-UPG1 UP.Link/3.2]
browser=Phone.com simulator
target-markup=WML1.1
content-type=text/vnd.wap.wml

; Ericsson SDK Simulator R320s for WML
```

```
[WapIDE-SDK/2.0; (R320s (Arial))]
browser=Ericsson R320s
target-markup=WML1.1
content-type=text/vnd.wap.wml

; Openwave browser
[OWG1 UP/4.1.20a UP.Browser/4.1.20a-XXXX UP.Link/4.1.HTTP-DIRECT]
browser=Openwave UP.SDK
target-markup=WML1.1
content-type=text/vnd.wap.wml

;;;;;;;;;;;;;;;;;;;;;;;;;;;
;;; Default Browser    ;;;
;;;;;;;;;;;;;;;;;;;;;;;;;;;
[*]
browser=Default
Version=0.0
majorver=#0
minorver=#0
frames=False
  . . .
```

Rewriting Our XML Document

We are now ready to use the XSL ISAPI filter for transformation. Let's modify our Books.xml document (Listing 9-7).

Listing 9-7. Books.xml

```xml
<?xml version="1.0"?>
<?xml-stylesheet type="text/xsl" server-config="/config.xml" href="HTML.xsl"?>
<BOOKS>
  <BOOK Pages="357" Type="SOFTCOVER">
    <TITLE>A Programmer's Introduction to C#</TITLE>
    <AUTHOR>Eric Gunnerson</AUTHOR>
    <ISBN>1893115860</ISBN>
    <SYNOPSIS>Eric Gunnerson, the test lead for and member of
              Microsoft's C# design team, has written a
              comprehensive C# tutorial for programmers to help
              them get up to speed</SYNOPSIS>
    <PRICE>34.95</PRICE>
  </BOOK>
</BOOKS>
```

Note that we have some additional attributes within the <?xml-stylesheet?> PI:

- server-config: specifies the configuration file to look into for stylesheet selection.

- href: specifies the stylesheet to load if the file specified in the server-config attribute cannot be found.

Listing 9-8 displays the code for the configuration file.

Listing 9-8. config.xml

```xml
<?xml version="1.0"?>
<server-styles-config>
    <device browser="MSIE" version="6.0b">
        <stylesheet href="/HTML.xsl"/>
    </device>
    <device target-markup="WML1.1">
        <content-type type="text/vnd.wap.wml"/>
        <stylesheet href="/WML.xsl"/>
    </device>
</server-styles-config>
```

The configuration file (saved in the root of the Web publishing directory) contains the <server-styles-config> root element. It contains two child elements called <device>.

The XSL ISAPI uses the ASP BrowserType object to compare each attribute with the corresponding device property in the browscap.ini database. It first compares the value that is obtained from the environment variable http_user_agent with the [HTTPUserAgentHeader] specified in the browscap.ini database, as shown in Figure 9-15.

Figure 9-15. Dissecting the browscap.ini file

The XSL ISAPI filter will then evaluate each <device> element (in sequence) to match the corresponding browser features located in the browscap.ini file.

NOTE *The browscap.ini file is a simple ASCII text file containing a list of all well-known browsers and their specific characteristics. Typical browser characteristics that are maintained for each browser include whether the browser supports frames, ActiveX controls, JavaScript, sound, etc. The browscap.ini file is maintained by Cyscape, Inc. (*http://www.cyscape.com/browscap/*), and can be downloaded free of charge.*

For example, if the user were using Internet Explorer 6.0, then the entry in browscap.ini that matches this would be:

```
[Mozilla/4.0 (compatible; MSIE 6.0b; Windows NT 5.0; COM+ 1.0.2204; .NET
CLR 1.0.2914)]
browser=MSIE
Version=6.0b
    . . .
```

In this case, since there is a match, the first <device> element would be selected and the stylesheet specified by the <stylesheet> element (/HTML.xsl) would be used.

The evaluation sequence is as follows:

- The <device> elements are evaluated from top to bottom, with the first match winning.

- If a property doesn't exist in browscap.ini for the requesting browser, a value of "undefined" is used.

- A <device> element without any attributes is considered an automatic match, and its stylesheet child elements are selected.

- If no <device> elements match, the XML is sent, untouched, to the browser, with a content type of "text/xml."

- If there is a <device> match, but that <device> element doesn't contain any <stylesheet> child elements, the XML is sent, untouched, to the browser.

Customizing content for the various devices would simply involve modifying your config.xml file. Compared to using ASP for server-side transformation, the XSL ISAPI allows stylesheets to be selected automatically.

Useful Web Links

- WAP Forum at http://www.wapforum.org

- Openwave at http://www.openwave.com

- Ericsson WAP IDE at http://www.ericsson.com/wap

- Nokia WAP Toolkit at http://www.nokia.com/wap

Summary

In this chapter, we took a quick look at an application of XML—the WML. While we did not delve into too much detail, we have shown how XML and XSLT can be used to customize content for different kinds of devices. The Microsoft XSL ISAPI is one of the tools that help to ease the burden of detecting the kinds of devices accessing a document.

In the next chapter, we look at another application of XML and see how XML can be used to support distributed computing.

CHAPTER 10

Simple Object Access Protocol (SOAP) and Web Services

THE INTERNET IS RESHAPING the way in which we compute today. With the advancement of Web and networking technologies, the trend is moving toward distributed computing. The capabilities of an application are no longer constrained by the processing power of a single machine, but rather they are distributed by cooperation of many different machines each providing a specific service. Software is now being seen as a collection of services, and these services can be provided by another party and made available through the network. In this chapter, we take a look at one way in which XML can be used in distributed computing. We take a closer look at the Simple Object Access Protocol (SOAP) and build a sample application using the Microsoft SOAP Toolkit.

Introduction to SOAP

The Simple Object Access Protocol (SOAP) is an XML-based protocol for exchanging information between distributed systems. It uses XML as the transmission format, as illustrated in Figure 10-1.

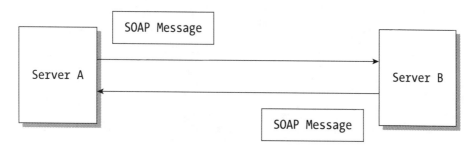

Figure 10-1. Exchanging messages using XML

A SOAP message is an XML document that contains information to be transmitted between one system to another. It is designed to be a *simple and lightweight protocol for accessing objects* on remote servers via XML messages. An example of such a message might be information on how to activate a remote procedure call on the target machine. When the target machine has finished processing what is required, it may send back the SOAP messages to the originating machine. The returned SOAP message may contain results of the processing.

Systems may utilize the HTTP transfer protocol to carry SOAP messages to the destination server. Such an arrangement has its benefit. By using the HTTP protocol, SOAP messages are easily transported between systems, as firewalls do not normally block access to the HTTP port. And by transferring messages in text-based XML, servers that are running on a different platform can still communicate. While it is common that SOAP utilizes HTTP as the transmission protocol, it is perfectly feasible to utilize other protocols.

SOAP 1.1

The current version of SOAP stands at version 1.1. Let's now take a look at a typical SOAP request message.

Listing 10-1. A SOAP message transported by HTTP—request

```
POST /TimeService HTTP/1.1
Host: www.timeserver.com
Content-Type: text/xml; charset="utf-8"
Content-Length: nnnn
SOAPAction: "Some-URI"

<SOAP-ENV:Envelope
   xmlns:SOAP-ENV="http://schemas.xmlsoap.org/soap/envelope/"
   SOAP-ENV:encodingStyle="http://schemas.xmlsoap.org/soap/encoding/">
   <SOAP-ENV:Body>
       <m:GetTime xmlns:m="Some-URI">
           <country>SIN</country>
       </m:GetTime>
   </SOAP-ENV:Body>
</SOAP-ENV:Envelope>
```

The SOAP request message that is shown in Listing 10-1 simply sends a request (GetTime) to the TimeService server.

```
<m:GetTime xmlns:m="Some-URI">
```

Besides sending the request, the SOAP message also includes a parameter:

```
<country>SIN</country>
```

When the server receives the request for the GetTime service, it will execute the required object and return the result in a SOAP response message. The SOAP response message is shown in Listing 10-2.

Listing 10-2. A SOAP message transported by HTTP—response
```
HTTP/1.1 200 OK
Content-Type: text/xml; charset="utf-8"
Content-Length: nnnn

<SOAP-ENV:Envelope
  xmlns:SOAP-ENV="http://schemas.xmlsoap.org/soap/envelope/"
  SOAP-ENV:encodingStyle="http://schemas.xmlsoap.org/soap/encoding/"/>
   <SOAP-ENV:Body>
       <m:GetTimeResponse xmlns:m="Some-URI">
            <Time>23:59</Time>
       </m:GetTimeResponse>
   </SOAP-ENV:Body>
</SOAP-ENV:Envelope>
```

The SOAP response message contains the result of the processing. The result is encapsulated within the <Time> element.

Components of a SOAP Message

Based on the preceding SOAP messages, you'll notice the following characteristics:

- SOAP messages are coded in XML. Also note that the SOAP messages do not contain a PI or a DTD.

- SOAP Namespace. SOAP messages define two namespaces:

  - SOAP Envelope: `http://schemas.xmlsoap.org/soap/envelope`

  - SOAP Serialization: `http://schemas.xmlsoap.org/soap/encoding`

- SOAP messages contain the following components, as shown in Figure 10-2:

  - SOAP Envelope (mandatory)

  - SOAP Header (optional)

  - SOAP Body (mandatory)

SOAP **Envelope**	
SOAP **Header** SOAP **Body**	`<SOAP-ENV:Envelope` `xmlns:SOAP-ENV=http://schemas.xmlsoap.org/soap/envelope/` `SOAP-` `ENV:encodingStyle="http://schemas.xmlsoap.org/soap/encoding/">` `    <SOAP-ENV:Body>` `        <m:GetTime xmlns:m="Some-URI">` `            <country>SIN</country>` `        </m:GetTime>` `    </SOAP-ENV:Body>` `</SOAP-ENV:Envelope>`

Figure 10-2. Structure of a SOAP message

The SOAP message Body contains information about the service(s) required. Note that however, SOAP does not dictate how the service is to be executed on the server. It simply governs the message format. Also, note that SOAP does not define how the messages are transported, it is up to the developer to decide.

For a full description of SOAP, please refer to the SOAP specification at W3C. The URL of the specification is listed at the end of the chapter.

NOTE *Since SOAP is based on XML, machines running on different platforms are able to intercommunicate and interoperate. This is the key feature of SOAP.*

Web Services

Recently, a new term has sprung up in the computing world: Web services. A Web service is defined as a programmable logic residing on a server, accessible through standard Internet protocols. The vision of Web services is not new, in fact it is an extension of the concepts of Remote Procedure Call (RPC) and Distributed Computing.

To better understand what a Web service is all about, let's consider an example. Most of us are familiar with Web applications. A Web application basically is a composition of two components:

- Data, which is the component of most interest to you

- User Interface (UI), which makes the presentation of the data appealing to you

Most of the time we are really interested in the data. And often we want to integrate the data from a Web application into our own application. Now, take away the UI portion and we have what we call a Web service.

With Web services, the application that you use might be made up of various pieces of application logic, which are distributed on the network. The key point about a Web service is that it allows seamless *integration* between your application and other Web services. The diagram in Figure 10-3 illustrates the process.

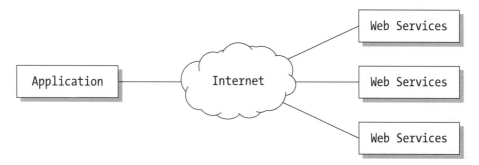

Figure 10-3. Web services provide the application logic to an application.

To ensure cross-platform compatibility, Web services do not make use of proprietary protocols like Distributed Component Object Model (DCOM), Remote Method Invocation (RMI), and Internet Inter-ORB Protocol (IIOP). Instead, Web services make use of ubiquitous Web protocols like HTTP and data format like XML for data interchange. SOAP is a natural fit as it makes use of XML for message transfer. Its text-based format ensures that communicating applications are platform agnostic. Furthermore, the use of HTTP as a transport protocol eliminates the most common security problem—firewalls. Firewalls typically restrict access to most ports in a system other than port 80, the default port of HTTP. By transporting XML messages using HTTP, security problems arising from firewalls are reduced, as shown in Figure 10-4.

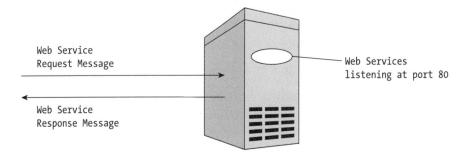

Figure 10-4. A Web service listening at a specific port on the computer and waiting for requests

Web Services Description Language (WSDL)

Having a Web service listening at port 80 of a server is just one side of the story. In order for the Web service to be consumed, some ground rules must be laid. The Web Services Description Language (WSDL) is an XML document that specifies the Web services offered by a server. The WSDL file can be likened to a contract, which accurately describes how the two parties (Web service provider and Web service consumer) communicate and interoperate. Specifically, the WSDL file specifies the message format expected by the Web service so that the Web service can process that service and return the appropriate result back to the consumer. Thus, the WSDL shields the Web service consumer from the inner workings of the Web service, as shown in Figure 10-5.

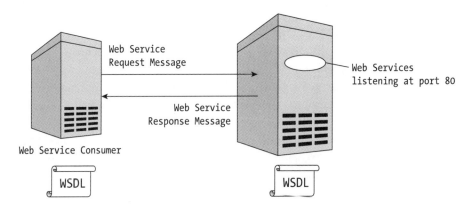

Figure 10-5. WSDL defines a contract to which both the Web service provider and the Web service consumer adhere.

NOTE   *A Web service consumer is one who uses the service provided by a Web service.*

Hence, in order to consume a Web service, the consumer needs to first of all download the WSDL file provided by the Web service and then format a SOAP request message to the Web service.

Let's now consider an example of a WSDL file.

Listing 10-3. A sample WSDL file

```
<?xml version='1.0' encoding='UTF-8' ?>
<definitions  name ='FlightsInfo'  targetNamespace = 'http://tempuri.org/wsdl/'
    xmlns:wsdlns='http://tempuri.org/wsdl/'
    xmlns:typens='http://tempuri.org/type'
    xmlns:soap='http://schemas.xmlsoap.org/wsdl/soap/'
    xmlns:xsd='http://www.w3.org/2001/XMLSchema'
    xmlns:stk='http://schemas.microsoft.com/soap-toolkit/wsdl-extension'
    xmlns='http://schemas.xmlsoap.org/wsdl/'>
  <types>
    <schema targetNamespace='http://tempuri.org/type'
      xmlns='http://www.w3.org/2001/XMLSchema'
      xmlns:SOAP-ENC='http://schemas.xmlsoap.org/soap/encoding/'
      xmlns:wsdl='http://schemas.xmlsoap.org/wsdl/'
      elementFormDefault='qualified'>
    </schema>
  </types>
  <message name='FlightSchedules.searchFlights'>
    <part name='flyFrom' type='xsd:string'/>
    <part name='flyTo' type='xsd:string'/>
    <part name='depdate' type='xsd:string'/>
  </message>
  <message name='FlightSchedules.searchFlightsResponse'>
    <part name='Result' type='xsd:string'/>
    <part name='flyFrom' type='xsd:string'/>
    <part name='flyTo' type='xsd:string'/>
    <part name='depdate' type='xsd:string'/>
  </message>
  <portType name='FlightSchedulesSoapPort'>
    <operation name='searchFlights' parameterOrder='flyFrom flyTo depdate'>
```

```
          <input message='wsdlns:FlightSchedules.searchFlights' />
          <output message='wsdlns:FlightSchedules.searchFlightsResponse' />
      </operation>
  </portType>
  <binding name='FlightSchedulesSoapBinding'
               type='wsdlns:FlightSchedulesSoapPort' >
      <stk:binding preferredEncoding='UTF-8'/>
      <soap:binding style='rpc' transport='http://schemas.xmlsoap.org/soap/http' />
      <operation name='searchFlights' >
        <soap:operation soapAction=
                  'http://tempuri.org/action/FlightSchedules.searchFlights' />
        <input>
          <soap:body use='encoded' namespace='http://tempuri.org/message/'
                 encodingStyle='http://schemas.xmlsoap.org/soap/encoding/' />
        </input>
        <output>
          <soap:body use='encoded' namespace='http://tempuri.org/message/'
                 encodingStyle='http://schemas.xmlsoap.org/soap/encoding/' />
        </output>
      </operation>
  </binding>
  <service name='FlightsInfo' >
      <port name='FlightSchedulesSoapPort'
               binding='wsdlns:FlightSchedulesSoapBinding' >
        <soap:address location='http://win2000as/FlightsInfo.ASP' />
      </port>
  </service>
</definitions>
```

Close inspection of the WSDL file reveals the following elements:

- Types

- Message

- PortType

- Binding

- Service

Let's take a closer look at each element and see their uses.

Types

The <Types> element defines the data types definitions used for the message exchange. For maximum interoperability, the XML Schema (XSD) is used.

```
<types>
  <schema targetNamespace='http://tempuri.org/type'
    xmlns='http://www.w3.org/2001/XMLSchema'
    xmlns:SOAP-ENC='http://schemas.xmlsoap.org/soap/encoding/'
    xmlns:wsdl='http://schemas.xmlsoap.org/wsdl/'
    elementFormDefault='qualified'>
  </schema>
</types>
```

The <Types> element contains the <schema> child elements, which declare all the namespaces used.

Message

The <message> element refers to the message structure that is passed between the Web service consumer and the Web service provider.

```
<message name='FlightSchedules.searchFlights'>
  <part name='flyFrom' type='xsd:string'/>
  <part name='flyTo' type='xsd:string'/>
  <part name='depdate' type='xsd:string'/>
</message>
<message name='FlightSchedules.searchFlightsResponse'>
  <part name='Result' type='xsd:string'/>
  <part name='flyFrom' type='xsd:string'/>
  <part name='flyTo' type='xsd:string'/>
  <part name='depdate' type='xsd:string'/>
</message>
```

In the example used, we have two messages. The first <message> defines the message structure that the consumer must pass to the Web service, whereas the second <message> element defines the resultant message returned by the Web service. The <part> element defines the individual components that comprise the message.

PortType

The <portType> element defines a set of abstract operations via the <operation> element.

```
<portType name='FlightSchedulesSoapPort'>
  <operation name='searchFlights' parameterOrder='flyFrom flyTo depdate'>
    <input message='wsdlns:FlightSchedules.searchFlights' />
    <output message='wsdlns:FlightSchedules.searchFlightsResponse' />
  </operation>
</portType>
```

In our example, we have one operation named "searchFlights" with input parameters "flyFrom," "flyTo", and "depDate." It also describes whether the service is a *one-way* operation or *request-response* operation (two-way operation). A one-way operation processes only input whereas in a request-response operation, there are both input and output.

Binding

The <binding> element specifies the protocol to use.

```
<binding name='FlightSchedulesSoapBinding'type='wsdlns:FlightSchedulesSoapPort' >
  <stk:binding preferredEncoding='UTF-8'/>
  <soap:binding style='rpc' transport='http://schemas.xmlsoap.org/soap/http' />
  <operation name='searchFlights' >
    <soap:operation
soapAction='http://tempuri.org/action/FlightSchedules.searchFlights' />
    <input>
      <soap:body use='encoded' namespace='http://tempuri.org/message/'
            encodingStyle='http://schemas.xmlsoap.org/soap/encoding/' />
    </input>
    <output>
      <soap:body use='encoded' namespace='http://tempuri.org/message/'
            encodingStyle='http://schemas.xmlsoap.org/soap/encoding/' />
    </output>
  </operation>
</binding>
```

In this example, the <binding> has two child elements, <soap:binding> and <operation>. The <soap:binding> element specifies whether the operation is a remote procedure call (RPC) or a document-oriented operation. It also specifies the transport protocol used (HTTP in this case).

Service

The <service> element contains a set of ports defined by the <port> element.

```
<service name='FlightsInfo' >
  <port name='FlightSchedulesSoapPort'
binding='wsdlns:FlightSchedulesSoapBinding' >
    <soap:address location='http://win2000as/FlightsInfo.ASP' />
  </port>
</service>
```

The <port> element defines an endpoint by specifying an address for a service. In this case, it is pointing to `http://win2000as/FlightsInfo.asp`.

Creating a Web Service

Until now, we have only talked about Web services in abstract terms. In reality, a Web service is a piece of application logic (or simply a program) that sits on a server waiting to be executed. This application can be in the form of a COM object or a simple JavaScript program. Let's now walk through the steps we need to perform in order to get a Web service up and running:

- Develop the application logic. An example would be to develop a COM object encapsulating the application logic.

- Create a contract for the Web service using WSDL.

- Deploy the Web service on a Web server.

Sounds simple, huh? Well, if you think creating the WSDL file is a fun thing to do, then it may sound trivial. But in reality, creating the WSDL file is not for the faint-hearted. Fortunately for those of you who are planning to deploy Web services using Microsoft Windows, Microsoft provides the SOAP Toolkit to help developers deploy Web services painlessly (well, at least not as painful as expected). We talk more about the SOAP Toolkit later in this chapter.

Consuming a Web Service

To consume a Web service, you may write an application in languages like Visual Basic or JavaScript. Your application may also be in the form of Web pages coded in server-side technologies like ASP or JSP. In order to communicate correctly with the Web service, your application needs to download the WSDL file and understand it so that the correct messages expected by the Web service can be constructed. You also need to understand from the WSDL file the results returned by the Web service so that you can use them.

The Microsoft SOAP Toolkit also provides a convenient way for developers to consume Web services.

Developing Web Services Using the Microsoft SOAP Toolkit Version 2.0

We have spent a good part of the chapter explaining to you what is SOAP and how it helps to create Web services. We are sure you are now quite excited to get your hands dirty and try creating a Web service yourself. As we mentioned earlier, Microsoft provides the SOAP Toolkit to help developers deploy and consume Web services. In this part of the chapter, we develop a simple Web service using the SOAP Toolkit.

Obtaining and Installing the Microsoft SOAP Toolkit 2.0

The Microsoft SOAP Toolkit for Visual Studio is available for download at `http://msdn.microsoft.com/xml`.

The installation of the SOAP Toolkit is straightforward. After installation, the Toolkit can be found in the directory c:\program files\MSSOAP. Several subfolders are created in this folder. The most important subfolder is the *Binaries* folder, as shown in Figure 10-6. It contains two tools to make Web services development painless. The first, *wsdlgen*, is the WSDL generator that generates a WSDL file based on the COM object that you wish to expose as a Web service. The second, MsSoapT, traces the SOAP messages that are exchanged between the consumer and the Web service.

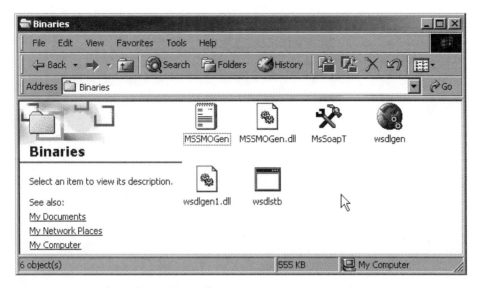

Figure 10-6. Tools in the SOAP Toolkit

Providing Web Services Using the SOAP Toolkit: A Case Study

In this section, we look at how we can build a Web service easily using the SOAP Toolkit. We build a COM object that encapsulates the application logic to access a database and expose it as a Web service. The SOAP Toolkit will then generate the WSDL contract based on this COM object. We then proceed to build a Web service consumer to consume that service. Let's first look at the business scenario and understand how it will benefit from a Web service.

Scenario

Most airlines provide flight schedules on their Web sites. A good example is Singapore's national carrier, Singapore Airlines. Singapore Airlines provides a useful Web site (Figure 10-7), which, along with other useful information, includes a flight scheduler system that allows customers to check flight schedules.

Figure 10-7. Singapore Airlines' Web site

To check for a flight schedule, the customer simply enters the relevant information like departure and return (if necessary) dates as well as the destination, as shown in Figure 10-8. Based on this information, the system will display the flight information that satisfies the criteria.

Figure 10-8. Using the flight scheduler

Figure 10-8 shows the date on which the tickets are required. Figure 10-9 shows the result that is returned by the system.

Figure 10-9. Result returned by the flight scheduler

Existing Solutions

While the existing system is useful, it can be extended further. Travel agents are normally linked up with the airlines via a dedicated system to retrieve flight information. Such a dedicated system makes use of dedicated consoles, which are often text-based.

> **CAUTION** *The use of Singapore Airlines in this chapter is purely for illustrative purposes. The actual system that links travel agents and the airline is much more involved than the examples illustrated in this chapter.*

Aside from travel agents, airlines normally have connections with corporations that allow them to buy tickets at a special price. An example would be the Human Resource (HR) department of a company that makes travel arrangements for staff going on overseas meetings, conferences, etc. The HR department itself might have a system for managing such matters. But when it comes to checking for flight schedules, HR would still need to check with the airlines or Web site for flight availability. Of course, the relevant information can still be extracted from the Web site. For example, HR might build a system to query the Singapore Airlines' Web site and based on the HTML returned, perform *screen-scrapping* to extract the relevant data. While this approach sounds feasible, there is a strong *coupling* between the HR system and Singapore Airlines' Web site. Any changes in Singapore Airlines' Web site is going to render the HR system useless, as the screen-scrapping utility must be updated to reflect the changes.

Proposed Solution Using Web Services

With most companies connected to the Web, Singapore Airlines could make use of Web services to publish its flight information. The flight scheduling system can be exposed as a Web service so that all interested parties can simply connect to it and integrate with their existing system.

The proposed Web service is as shown in Figure 10-10.

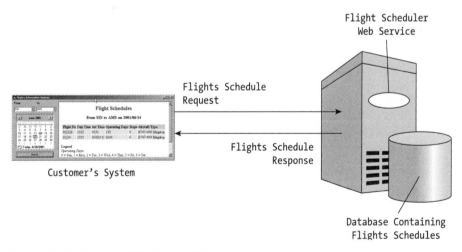

Figure 10-10. Proposed FlightInfo Web service

For our case study, we will be building the following components:

- Database containing flight information

- COM object accessing database for flight information. The output will be an XML string that contains information on flight information

- WSDL contract generated using the SOAP Toolkit

- Web consumer to consume the Web service

Database Structure

For our case study, we have created a simple table in SQL Server 2000. Figure 10-11 displays the schema for the Schedules table.

	Column Name	Data Type	Length	Allow Nulls
🔑	ind	int	4	
	FlyFrom	char	3	✓
	FlyTo	char	3	✓
	FlyDate	char	10	✓
	FlightNo	varchar	5	✓
	DepTime	char	4	✓
	ArrTime	char	4	✓
	AddDays	tinyint	1	✓
	Operating	varchar	7	✓
	Stops	tinyint	1	✓
	AircraftType	varchar	50	✓

Figure 10-11. Schema for the Schedules *table*

The table contains information on flight schedules.

NOTE *We assume readers are familiar with table creation in Microsoft SQL Server 2000.*

Table 10-1 contains some sample data.

Table 10-1. Sample Data in the Schedules *Table*

IND	FLYFROM	FLYTO	FLYDATE	FLIGHTNO	DEPTIME	ARRTIME	ADDDAYS	OPERATING	STOPS	AIRCRAFTTYPE
1	SIN	AMS	2001/06/14	SQ328	2325	0630	0	135	0	B747-400 Megatop
2	SIN	AMS	2001/06/14	SQ24	2335	0640	1	0246	0	B747-400 Megatop
3	AMS	SIN	2001/06/14	SQ23	1230	0635	0	1246	0	B747-400 Megatop
4	AMS	SIN	2001/06/14	SQ327	1300	0705	1	035	0	B747-400 Megatop
5	SFO	SIN	2001/05/25	SQ1	0150	1130	0	0123456	1	B747-400 Megatop
6	SFO	SIN	2001/05/25	SQ15	1600	0245	0	0123456	1	A340-300E Celestar

Creating the COM Object

We use Microsoft Visual Basic 6.0 to create a COM object to expose as a Web service on the server.

First, create a new ActiveX DLL project, as shown in Figure 10-12.

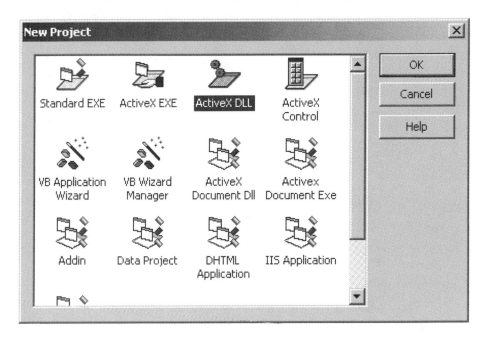

Figure 10-12. Creating a new ActiveX DLL project

Next, name the project and the class files in the project as shown in Figure 10-13.

Figure 10-13. Naming the ActiveX DLL files

The FlightSchedules.cls Class file contains a method named searchFlights(). Listing 10-4 includes the code for the function.

Listing 10-4. Function to search for the appropriate flights, which returns the result as an XML string

```
Public Function searchFlights(flyFrom As String, flyTo As String, depdate
 As String) As String
    Dim conn As New Connection
    Dim rs As New Recordset
    Dim connStr, sql, xmlStr As String
    Dim discount As Integer
        '---database connection string---
        connStr = "Provider=SQLOLEDB.1;Password=secret;Persist Security
Info=True;User ID=sa;Initial Catalog=FlightSchedules;Data
Source=WIN2000AS"

        conn.Open connStr
        '---retrieving the relevant flights info based on the inputs---
        sql = "SELECT * FROM Schedules WHERE FlyFrom='" & flyFrom & _
              "' AND FlyTo='" & flyTo & "' AND FlyDate='" & depdate & "'"
        Set rs = conn.Execute(sql)
        '---construct the XML result string---
        xmlStr = "<?xml version='1.0'?>"
        xmlStr = xmlStr & "<FlightsInfo>"
        xmlStr = xmlStr & "<From>" & flyFrom & "</From>"
        xmlStr = xmlStr & "<To>" & flyTo & "</To>"
        xmlStr = xmlStr & "<Date>" & depdate & "</Date>"
```

```
            While Not rs.EOF
                xmlStr = xmlStr & "<Flight>"
                xmlStr = xmlStr & "<FlightNo>" & rs("FlightNo") & "</FlightNo>"
                xmlStr = xmlStr & "<DepTime>" & rs("DepTime") & "</DepTime>"
                If CInt(rs("AddDays")) = 0 Then
                    xmlStr = xmlStr & "<ArrTime>" & rs("ArrTime") & "</ArrTime>"
                Else
                    xmlStr = xmlStr & "<ArrTime>" & rs("ArrTime") & "(+" & _
                             rs("AddDays") & ")</ArrTime>"
                End If
                xmlStr = xmlStr & "<Operating>" & rs("Operating") & _
                         "</Operating>"
                xmlStr = xmlStr & "<Stops>" & rs("Stops") & "</Stops>"
                xmlStr = xmlStr & "<AircraftType>" + rs("AircraftType") & _
                         "</AircraftType>"
                xmlStr = xmlStr & "</Flight>"
                rs.MoveNext
            Wend
            xmlStr = xmlStr & "</FlightsInfo>"
            '---return the XML result string---
            searchFlights = xmlStr
    End Function
```

The method takes in three input parameters:

- The departing airport

- The destination airport

- Departure date

Based on these three input parameters, all matching flights are retrieved from the table. The results are then formatted as an XML string and sent back to the client. Listing 10-5 shows an XML string containing two such matching flights.

Listing 10-5. A sample XML result string that contains matching flight information

```
<?xml version='1.0'?>
<FlightsInfo>
    <From>SIN</From>
    <To>AMS</To>
    <Date>2001/06/14</Date>
```

```
<Flight>
    <FlightNo>SQ328</FlightNo>
    <DepTime>2325</DepTime>
    <ArrTime>0630</ArrTime>
    <Operating>135</Operating>
    <Stops>0</Stops>
    <AircraftType>B747-400 Megatop</AircraftType>
</Flight>
<Flight>
    <FlightNo>SQ24</FlightNo>
    <DepTime>2335</DepTime>
    <ArrTime>0640(+1)</ArrTime>
    <Operating>0246</Operating>
    <Stops>0</Stops>
    <AircraftType>B747-400 Megatop</AircraftType>
</Flight>
</FlightsInfo>
```

That's it! To complete this section, we have to compile the project into a DLL.

Compiling the COM Object

Once the codes are created, compile the COM component (DLL).

 CAUTION *Make sure that the DLL is compiled with the "Retained in Memory" and "Unattended execution" options.*

Also, once a COM component is compiled and used, any attempt to modify the codes and recreate the DLL will encounter an error message, as shown in Figure 10-14.

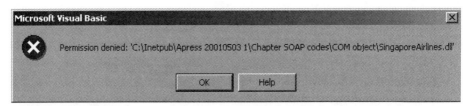

Figure 10-14. Attempting to overwrite a COM object while it is in use

In this case, apart from rebooting your machine in order to release the DLL, you can do the following:

At the command prompt, type the following line to stop IIS.

```
C:\>net stop iisadmin /y
```

Next recompile the COM component. Now the DLL can be overwritten. Restart IIS by typing the following:

```
C:\>net start w3svc
```

Generating the WSDL, WSML, and Listener Files

Once the COM object is created, we can now create the next set of files needed to expose it as a Web service. To do so, we use the *wsdlgen* utility that comes with the SOAP Toolkit, as shown in Figure 10-15.

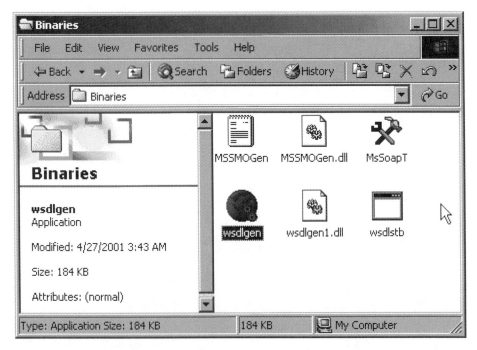

Figure 10-15. Using the wsdlgen utility to generate the next set of files

First, name your WSDL and WSML files **FlightsInfo** (see Figure 10-16). Also, specify the location of your COM object. Click on Next.

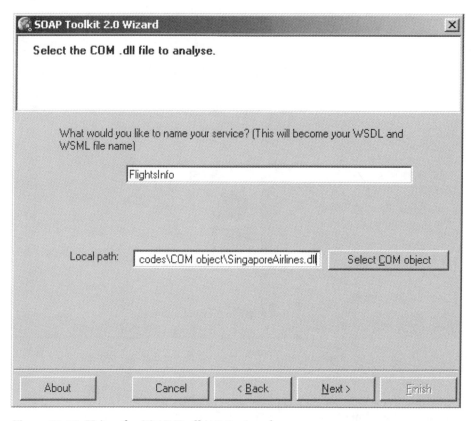

Figure 10-16. Using the SOAP Toolkit 2.0 wizard

The next step is to select the method(s) to expose as a Web service. Since our COM object only contains a single method searchFlights(), selecting the FlightsInfo checkbox will check all the checkboxes in Figure 10-17.

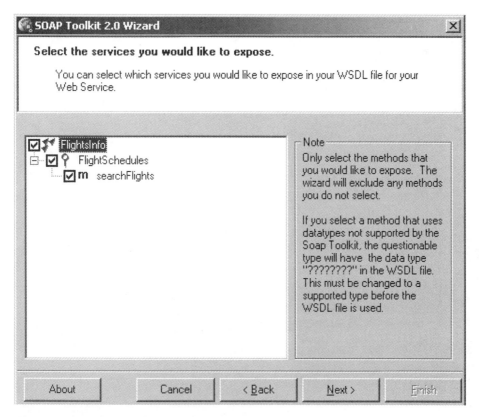

Figure10-17. Selecting the services to "expose"

The next screen (Figure 10-18) allows you to set the listener location as well as listener type and the version of XSD to support. In our example, we are exposing our Web service on our local machine, Win2000as.

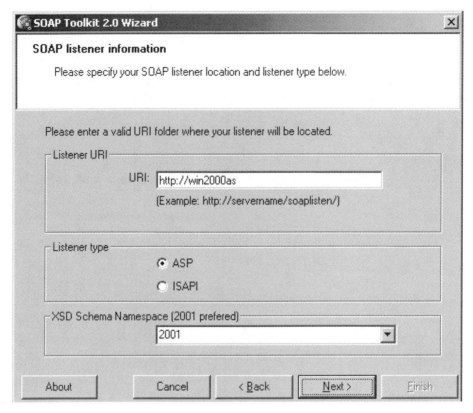

Figure 10-18. Selecting the listener and XSD type

The last step is to specify the path to store all the generated files, as shown in Figure 10-19.

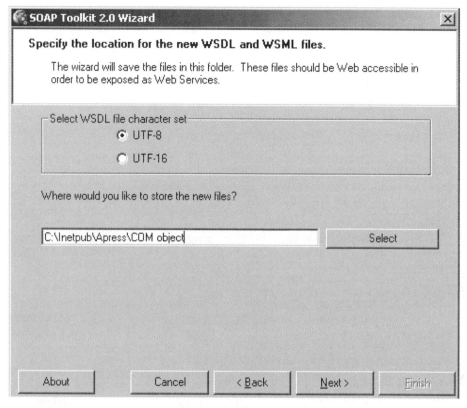

Figure 10-19. Setting the path to store the WSDL and WSML files

On our Web server, we have mapped our home directory `http://win2000as/` to c:\inetpub\Apress\Com Object.

Here are the files generated by the *wsdlgen* utility:

- FlightsInfo.wsdl

- FlightsInfo.wsml

- FlightsInfo.asp

WSDL File

As highlighted in the earlier section, the WSDL file is the contract for using the Web service. In this case, the SOAP Toolkit has automatically generated the WSDL that is based on the COM object. Listing 10-6 includes the code.

Listing 10-6. FlightsInfo.wsdl

```xml
<?xml version='1.0' encoding='UTF-8' ?>
 <!-- Generated 05/24/01 by Microsoft SOAP Toolkit WSDL File Generator,
   Version 1.00.623.1 -->
<definitions  name ='FlightsInfo'   targetNamespace =
 'http://tempuri.org/wsdl/'
 xmlns:wsdlns='http://tempuri.org/wsdl/'
 xmlns:typens='http://tempuri.org/type'
 xmlns:soap='http://schemas.xmlsoap.org/wsdl/soap/'
 xmlns:xsd='http://www.w3.org/2001/XMLSchema'
 xmlns:stk='http://schemas.microsoft.com/soap-toolkit/wsdl-extension'
 xmlns='http://schemas.xmlsoap.org/wsdl/'>
  <types>
    <schema targetNamespace='http://tempuri.org/type'
      xmlns='http://www.w3.org/2001/XMLSchema'
      xmlns:SOAP-ENC='http://schemas.xmlsoap.org/soap/encoding/'
      xmlns:wsdl='http://schemas.xmlsoap.org/wsdl/'
      elementFormDefault='qualified'>
    </schema>
  </types>
  <message name='FlightSchedules.searchFlights'>
    <part name='flyFrom' type='xsd:string'/>
    <part name='flyTo' type='xsd:string'/>
    <part name='depdate' type='xsd:string'/>
  </message>
  <message name='FlightSchedules.searchFlightsResponse'>
    <part name='Result' type='xsd:string'/>
    <part name='flyFrom' type='xsd:string'/>
    <part name='flyTo' type='xsd:string'/>
    <part name='depdate' type='xsd:string'/>
  </message>
  <portType name='FlightSchedulesSoapPort'>
    <operation name='searchFlights' parameterOrder='flyFrom flyTo depdate'>
      <input message='wsdlns:FlightSchedules.searchFlights' />
      <output message='wsdlns:FlightSchedules.searchFlightsResponse' />
    </operation>
  </portType>
  <binding name='FlightSchedulesSoapBinding'
type='wsdlns:FlightSchedulesSoapPort'>
    <stk:binding preferredEncoding='UTF-8'/>
    <soap:binding style='rpc' transport='http://schemas.xmlsoap.org/soap/http' />
    <operation name='searchFlights' >
      <soap:operation
```

```
soapAction='http://tempuri.org/action/FlightSchedules.searchFlights' />
      <input>
        <soap:body use='encoded' namespace='http://tempuri.org/message/'
                encodingStyle='http://schemas.xmlsoap.org/soap/encoding/' />
      </input>
      <output>
        <soap:body use='encoded' namespace='http://tempuri.org/message/'
                encodingStyle='http://schemas.xmlsoap.org/soap/encoding/' />
      </output>
    </operation>
  </binding>
  <service name='FlightsInfo' >
    <port name='FlightSchedulesSoapPort'
 binding='wsdlns:FlightSchedulesSoapBinding' >
      <soap:address location='http://win2000as/FlightsInfo.ASP' />
    </port>
  </service>
</definitions>
```

We have already seen this WSDL file in the earlier section on WSDL.

WSML File

The Web Service Meta Language (WSML) file is specific to the current implementation of the SOAP Toolkit. It is used to map services that are described in the WSDL file to methods available in a COM object. Listing 10-7 includes the code.

Listing 10-7. FlightsInfo.wsml

```
<?xml version='1.0' encoding='UTF-8' ?>
 <!-- Generated 05/24/01 by Microsoft SOAP Toolkit WSDL File Generator,
 Version 1.00.623.1 -->
<servicemapping name='FlightsInfo'>
  <service name='FlightsInfo'>
    <using PROGID='FlightsInfo.FlightSchedules' cachable='0'
 ID='FlightSchedulesObject' />
    <port name='FlightSchedulesSoapPort'>
      <operation name='searchFlights'>
        <execute uses='FlightSchedulesObject' method='searchFlights'
 dispID='1610809344'>
          <parameter callIndex='1' name='flyFrom' elementName='flyFrom' />
          <parameter callIndex='2' name='flyTo' elementName='flyTo' />
          <parameter callIndex='3' name='depdate' elementName='depdate' />
```

```
                    <parameter callIndex='-1' name='retval' elementName='Result' />
                </execute>
            </operation>
        </port>
    </service>
</servicemapping>
```

The WSML file contains the <servicemapping> element that contains the <service> child element. The <service> element contains information on the COM component to be used (as indicated by the PROGID) as well as the method(s) to invoke (as indicated by the <operation> element).

ASP Listener

Since the Web server is providing a service, there must be "someone" on the Web server to "listen" for incoming requests and to send back the results. This is the function of the ASP file that was created automatically by the *wsdlgen* utility, which is included in Listing 10-8.

Listing 10-8. FlightsInfo.asp

```
<% @ LANGUAGE=VBScript %>
<%
Option Explicit
On Error Resume Next
Response.ContentType = "text/xml"
Dim SoapServer
If Not Application("SoapServerInitialized") Then
  Application.Lock
  If Not Application("SoapServerInitialized") Then
    Dim WSDLFilePath
    Dim WSMLFilePath
    WSDLFilePath = Server.MapPath("FlightsInfo.wsdl")
    WSMLFilePath = Server.MapPath("FlightsInfo.wsml")
    Set SoapServer = Server.CreateObject("MSSOAP.SoapServer")
    If Err Then SendFault "Cannot create SoapServer object. " & Err.Description
    SoapServer.Init WSDLFilePath, WSMLFilePath
    If Err Then SendFault "SoapServer.Init failed. " & Err.Description
    Set Application("FlightsInfoServer") = SoapServer
    Application("SoapServerInitialized") = True
  End If
  Application.UnLock
End If
```

```
Set SoapServer = Application("FlightsInfoServer")
SoapServer.SoapInvoke Request, Response, ""
If Err Then SendFault "SoapServer.SoapInvoke failed. " & Err.Description
Sub SendFault(ByVal LogMessage)
  Dim Serializer
  On Error Resume Next
  ' "URI Query" logging must be enabled for AppendToLog to work
  Response.AppendToLog " SOAP ERROR: " & LogMessage
  Set Serializer = Server.CreateObject("MSSOAP.SoapSerializer")
  If Err Then
    Response.AppendToLog "Could not create SoapSerializer object. " & _
        Err.Description
    Response.Status = "500 Internal Server Error"
  Else
    Serializer.Init Response
    If Err Then
      Response.AppendToLog "SoapSerializer.Init failed. " & Err.Description
      Response.Status = "500 Internal Server Error"
    Else
      Serializer.startEnvelope
      Serializer.startBody
      Serializer.startFault "Server", "The request could not be processed due
      to a problem in the server. Please contact the system administrator. " & _
      LogMessage
      Serializer.endFault
      Serializer.endBody
      Serializer.endEnvelope
      If Err Then
        Response.AppendToLog "SoapSerializer failed. " & Err.Description
        Response.Status = "500 Internal Server Error"
      End If
    End If
  End If
  Response.End
End Sub
%>
```

Much of these are plumbing codes needed to get the Web service to work.

Creating the Web Service Consumer—SOAP Client

At this point, the Web service is up and running. It is listening at port 80, waiting for any incoming requests for that service. So now we are going to create a client to make use of that Web service. Again, we will make use of VB 6 and create a new EXE project.

Here is our project information, as shown in Figure 10-20.

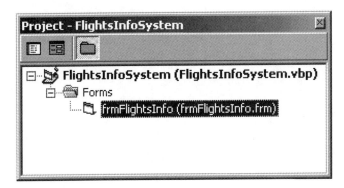

Figure 10-20. FlightsInfoSystem project

Our client consists of only one form, as shown in Figure 10-21.

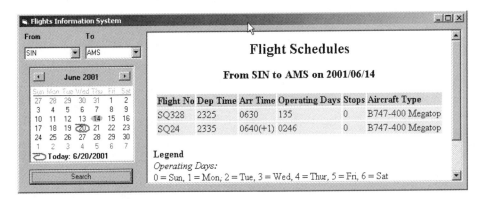

Figure 10-21. Flight information system form

This is how our client would work:

- User selects the departure and destination city, followed by the date of departure.

- The Web service Client uses the SOAP client component provided to communicate with the Web service.

- The Client receives the XML result returned by the Web service.

- The Client applies an XSLT stylesheet to the XML result to transform the result into HTML.

- The HTML is then displayed in the WebBrowser control in the client window.

Referencing the SOAP Type Library

The first step would be to reference the necessary libraries. Since our client uses the SOAP Toolkit, we need to reference the SOAP Type Library. Also, we need to reference the Microsoft XML 3.0 library, as we would be manipulating XML strings returned from the Web service, as shown in Figure 10-22.

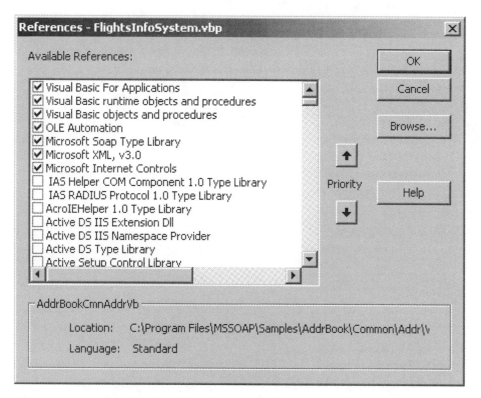

Figure 10-22. Referencing the SOAP Type Library

Creating an Instance of the SOAPClient

To make use of the SOAPClient provided by the SOAP Toolkit, we need to create an instance of it in the (general) section of the Visual Basic form, as shown in Figure 10-23.

Figure 10-23. Using the SOAPClient object

Initializing the SOAPClient Object

When the form is first loaded, the SOAPClient object must be initialized. The SOAPClient object is initialized with the WSDL file, Service Name, and Port from the server providing the Web service. The Service Name and Port are derived from the WSDL file.

```
Private Sub Form_Load()
    On Error Resume Next
    '---Initialise the SOAP client---
    SoapClient.mssoapinit "http://win2000as/FlightsInfo.wsdl", "FlightsInfo",
    "FlightSchedulesSoapPort"
    If SoapClient.detail <> "" Then
        MsgBox SoapClient.detail
        End
    End If
    WebBrowser1.Navigate "http://www.singaporeair.com"
End Sub
```

The **detail** property of the SOAPClient object will contain error messages if the SOAPClient fails in its attempt to connect to the Web service. For example, if the Web server is stopped, the SOAPClient's detail property will return the following error:

```
WSDLReader:Loading of the WSDL file failed HRESULT=0x80070057 -
    WSDLReader:XML Parser failed at linenumber 0, lineposition 0, reason is:
    The system cannot locate the resource specified.
    HRESULT=0x1
```

NOTE *You can access the WSDL contract by using the Web browser with URL:* `http://<servername>/FlightsInfo.wsdl;` *for example:* `http://win2000as/flightsinfo.wsdl.`

Consuming the Web Service

After the user has supplied the necessary information (departure airport, destination airport, and date), it is now time to consume the Web service provided by the server.

```
Private Sub cmdSearch_Click()

Dim xmldoc As New MSXML2.DOMDocument30
Dim xsldoc As New MSXML2.DOMDocument30
Dim seldate As String

    '---creates the selected date---
    seldate = selectedDate.Year & "/" & Format(selectedDate.Month, "0#") & "/" &_
    Format(selectedDate.Day, "0#")

    '---load the XML result returned from the Web service---
    xmldoc.async = False

    On Error Resume Next
    xmldoc.loadXML SoapClient.searchFlights(ComboFrom, ComboTo, seldate)
    If SoapClient.detail <> "" Then
        MsgBox SoapClient.detail & ". Please try again."
    End If

    '--load the XSL stylesheet for transforming the XML result into HTML---
    xsldoc.async = False
    xsldoc.Load "c:\Flights.xsl"

    '---writes the result into c:\---
    Open "c:\output.html" For Output As #1
    Print #1, CStr(xmldoc.transformNode(xsldoc))
    Close 1
    '---loads the HTML result into the Web browser---
    WebBrowser1.Navigate "c:\output.html"

End Sub
```

What we did was first format the date according to the one expected by the Web service. We then call the Web service using the SOAPClient object's SearchFlights() method. The result of the Web service is then loaded into the XML DOM object:

```
xmldoc.loadXML SoapClient.searchFlights(ComboFrom, ComboTo, seldate)
```

If there were any error, it would be contained within the SOAPClient object's detail property.

```
If SoapClient.detail <> "" Then
    MsgBox SoapClient.detail & ". Please try again."
End If
```

If not, we proceed to transform the XML result into HTML using the stylesheet that we have created (see next section). The result of the transformation is then saved onto the local hard disk and then loaded by the Web Browser control.

Stylesheet for XSL Transformation

Because the Web service is formatted as an XML string, we need a stylesheet to format the result into a viewable format. HTML is a natural choice as we can then make use of the Web Browser control to display it. The stylesheet in Listing 10-9 transforms the XML result into HTML.

Listing 10-9. Flights.xsl

```
<?xml version="1.0"?>
<xsl:stylesheet xmlns:xsl="http://www.w3.org/1999/XSL/Transform" version="1.0">
<xsl:template match="/">
<html>
<center>
<h2>Flight Schedules</h2>
    <h3>From <xsl:value-of select="FlightsInfo/From"/> to
    <xsl:value-of select="FlightsInfo/To"/> on
    <xsl:value-of select="FlightsInfo/Date"/></h3>
    <table border="0">
    <tr bgcolor="#E5E5D8">
        <td><b>Flight No</b></td><td><b>Dep Time</b></td>
        <td><b>Arr Time</b></td><td><b>Operating Days</b></td>
        <td><b>Stops</b></td><td><b>Aircraft Type</b></td>
    </tr>
```

```
<xsl:for-each select="FlightsInfo/Flight">
<tr  bgcolor="#F4F4EF">
   <td><xsl:value-of select="FlightNo"/></td>
   <td><xsl:value-of select="DepTime"/></td>
   <td><xsl:value-of select="ArrTime"/></td>
   <td><xsl:value-of select="Operating"/></td>
   <td><xsl:value-of select="Stops"/></td>
   <td><xsl:value-of select="AircraftType"/></td>
</tr>
</xsl:for-each>
</table>
</center>
<br/><b>Legend</b><br/>
<i>Operating Days: </i><br/>
0 = Sun, 1 = Mon, 2 = Tue, 3 = Wed, 4 = Thur, 5 = Fri, 6 = Sat <br/>
<i>Arrival Times:</i><br/>
+1 Arrival next day<br/>
+2 Arrival two days later<br/>
</html>
</xsl:template>
</xsl:stylesheet>
```

Chapter 3 covers XSLT in more detail.

Using the Web Service

Now that everything is in place, let's try out our Web service! Assuming we need to find the flight from Singapore (SIN) to Amsterdam (AMS) departing on June 14, 2001, we simply select the From and To list boxes (be sure to populate the list boxes with some sample country codes) and select the date (Figure 10-24). To search for flights departing on that day, click on the Search button. The result will be shown on the Web browser control.

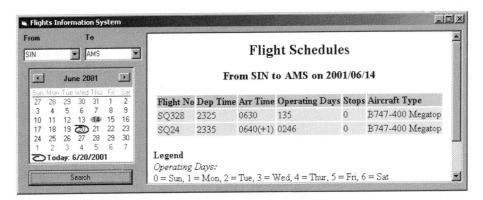

Figure 10-24. Testing the Web service

How It All Works

The MS SOAP Toolkit provides the SOAP Server, which takes care of processing the incoming requests and responding with the results.

Let's summarize the various steps involved in the process, as illustrated in Figure 10-25.

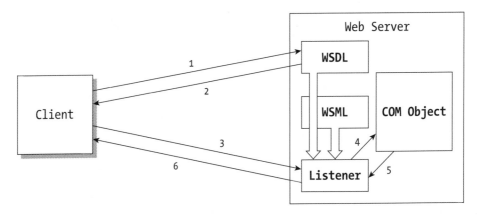

Figure 10-25. How the SOAP Toolkit works

1. Client instantiates the SOAPClient object and requests the WSDL file.

2. Web server sends back the WSDL file to client.

3. Client uses the information in the WSDL file to build SOAP messages and sends the request to the ASP listener.

4.   The listener instantiates the SOAPServer object and loads the WSDL and
     WSML files. The listener then executes the COM object whose methods
     are mapped to the WSDL file.

5.   The COM object returns the result to the listener.

6.   The listener packages the result as a SOAP message and sends the SOAP
     message as a response back to the client.

Tracing the SOAP Messages

The Microsoft SOAP Toolkit comes with a trace utility to see the SOAP messages
that are being exchanged between the client and the server.

The trace utility is located in the Binaries subfolder of the SOAP folder
(Figure 10-26).

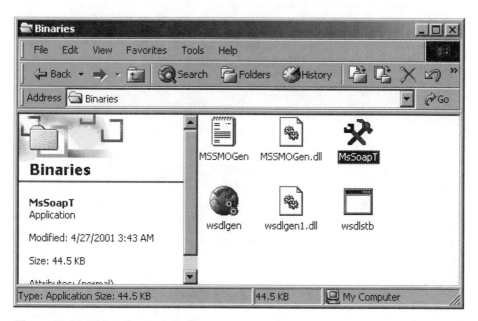

Figure 10-26. Using the trace utility

To use the trace utility, double click on the MsSoapT icon. To view the SOAP
messages in text form, select File > New > Formatted Trace (Figure 10-27). The
other option, Unformatted Trace, will display the SOAP messages in hexadecimal.

Figure 10-27. Setting up the trace

Once this option is selected, you will be prompted to supply the information that is shown in Figure 10-28.

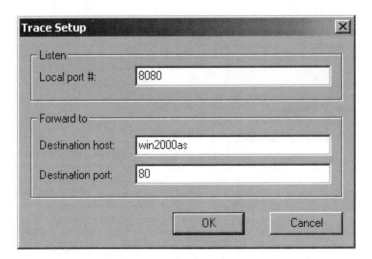

Figure 10-28. Setting the port number to sniff

- The **Local port #** represents the port number in which the Trace utility will listen to.

- **Destination host** is the machine hosting the Web service.

- The **Destination port** represents the port number that the Web service will listen to.

For the trace to work, we need to modify the <soap:address> element in the WSDL file to reflect the change in port number, as shown in Figure 10-29.

```
...
<port name='FlightSchedulesSoapPort'
binding='wsdlns:FlightSchedulesSoapBinding' >
   <soap:address location='http://win200as:8080/FlightsInfo.ASP' />
</port>
...
```

> Port changed from 80 (default) to 8080

Figure 10-29. Modifying the <soap:address> element

That's it! Run the Web service again and look at the Trace window, as shown in Figure 10-30.

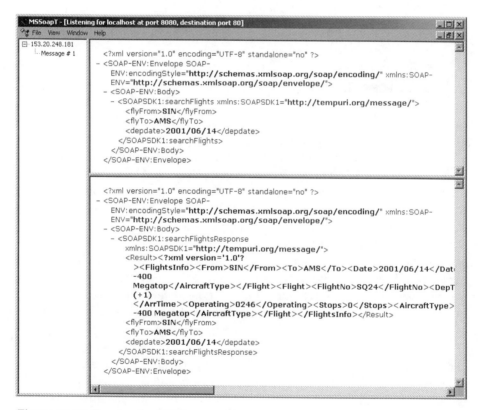

Figure 10-30. Tracing the SOAP messages

The top right window shows the SOAP request message. Notice the three parameters that were passed to the Web service: "flyFrom," "flyTo,, and "depdate".

The bottom right window shows the SOAP response message returned by the Web service. Note the XML result in boldface.

The diagram in Figure 10-31 shows how the MsSoapT works.

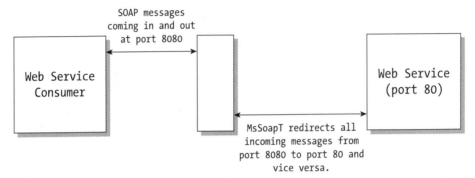

Figure 10-31. Tracing using MsSoapT

Web Services Security

Before we end the chapter on SOAP and Web services, let's briefly talk about securing Web services. There are times when you would want to restrict access of your Web service to a selected few. In an intranet, it is possible to use the Internet Protocol Security (IPSec) to restrict access to a Web service based on the IP address of machines in the network. However, as Web services are often deployed for the Internet, it is not always possible to know the IP address of a machine beforehand. As such, IPSec is not useful in such situations.

It is worthwhile noting that since Web services typically use HTTP as a transport protocol, securing Web services is no different from securing Web sites. You can use the often-tried approach of securing Web sites. For example, if the Web server is using the Microsoft Internet Information Server (IIS), you can make use of the various authentication methods available in IIS. Such methods may be *Basic authentication* or *Integrated Windows authentication.*

For a more detailed description of the various methods to secure your Web site, please refer to http://www.microsoft.com/technet/iis/authmeth.asp.

Alternatively, you can also create your own authentication mechanism. That is, the Web service consumer needs to specify the access information (IDs and passwords) to access a particular Web service and transmit them in the SOAP messages. This approach is the most flexible. However, since XML messages are plain text, this method might not be secure. To solve this problem, you might want to use Secure Socket Layer (SSL), instead of HTTP. The downside to using SSL is in performance, since SSL is significantly slower than HTTP.

Securing Our Example Web Service

To secure the Web service that we developed earlier, let's use the Basic Authentication method. We first need to secure the Web site that provides the Web service; next, we need to specify the login credentials in our Web consumer.

Securing the Web Server

To secure the Web server, follow these steps:

1. Select the Web site/virtual directory to secure and then click on Properties.

2. Select the Directory Security tab.

3. Under Anonymous access and authentication control, click on Edit.

4. Uncheck Anonymous access and check Basic authentication (password is sent in clear text), as shown in Figure 10-32.

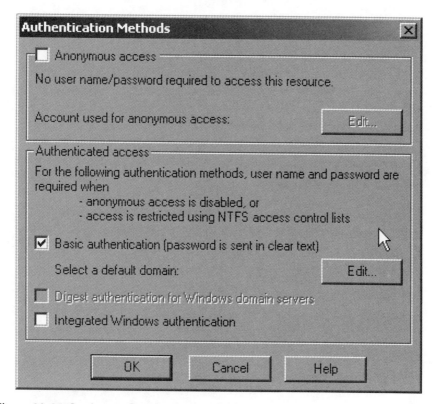

Figure 10-32. Setting authentication methods

Modifying the Consumer

In the Web service consumer, you need to add the following lines (in boldface):

```
   SoapClient.mssoapinit "http://win2000as/FlightsInfo.wsdl",
 "FlightsInfo", "FlightSchedulesSoapPort"
   SoapClient.ConnectorProperty("EndPointURL") =
 "http://lwm:secretpasswd@win2000as/FlightsInfo.wsdl"
```

The `ConnectorProperty("EndPointURL")` collection defines the end point that the SOAP client connects to. In this case we specify the path of the WSDL and credentials that can be used to authenticate the user. The syntax for sending the credentials is:

```
http://userID:password@Server/PathOfFile
```

To make the Web service accessible to people with the proper credentials, you could modify the consumer to prompt for the user name and password and insert them into the `ConnectorProperty` collection. We will leave it to you to implement this.

Useful Web Links

- Simple Object Access Protocol (SOAP) specification 1.1 at
  `http://www.w3.org/TR/SOAP/`

- Web Service Description Language (WSDL) 1.1 at
  `http://www.w3.org/TR/wsdl`

- IIS 4.0 and 5.0 Authentication Methods Chart at
  `http://www.microsoft.com/technet/iis/authmeth.asp`

- Microsoft SOAP Toolkit 2.0 at `http://msdn.microsoft.com/xml`

Summary

In this chapter, we introduced you to how XML can be used in a distributed environment such as the Web. The fact that XML messages are plain text makes them platform-agnostic and encourages the development of distributed systems using XML.

You have seen one use of XML for distributed computing—SOAP. On the basis of SOAP, you can create Web services that allow machines on different platforms to interoperate.

Installing Microsoft XML Tools

Microsoft makes available its Internet Explorer Tools for Validating XML and Viewing XSLT output.

Installing IE Tools for Validating XML Documents

You can download IE Tools from http://msdn.microsoft.com/downloads/ as shown in Figure A-1.

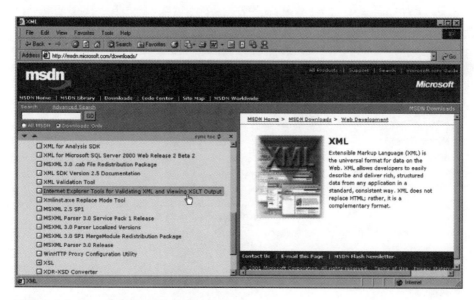

Figure A-1. Downloading the IE tools

The file to download is iexmltls.exe.

Upon running the iexmltls.exe file, the program will prompt you to install the files into a folder. The default folder is: c:\iexmltls.

You'll find the following files and folder in this folder:

- Msxmlval.htm

- Msxmlval.inf

- Msxmlvw.htm

- Msxmlvw.inf

- Readme.txt

- IE XML (folder)

To install the validating tools, right-click on the two .inf files and select Install, as shown in Figure A-2.

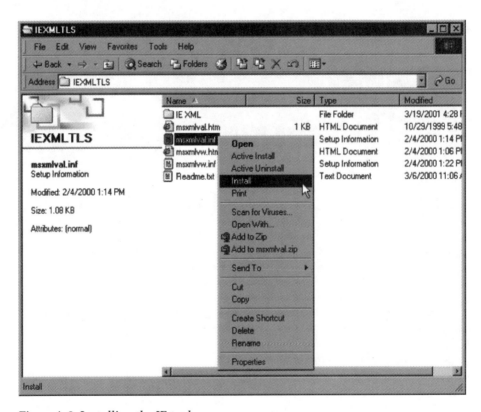

Figure A-2. Installing the IE tools

To use the tools, be sure to restart Internet Explorer.

Checking the Version of the Installed XML Parser

Before trying out the examples in this book, it is important to ensure that you have installed the Microsoft XML Parser (version 3 or above). As most computers running the Microsoft Windows Operating System come preinstalled with the older XML parser (version 2.X), most examples in this book will fail to work if the latest parser is not installed. The easiest way to ensure that you have the required parser is to download the latest parser from Microsoft's Web site (`http://msdn.microsoft.com/xml`) and install it on your machine.

Alternatively, if you want to check out the version number of the parsers that are installed on your system, Microsoft provides an XML version checker. The XML version checker can be downloaded from `http://support.microsoft.com/support/kb/articles/q278/6/74.asp?id=278674&SD=MSKB`.

Alternatively, look for the knowledge base article ID: Q278674. The file to download is Xmlversion.exe.

Installing the XML Version Checker

To install the XML version checker, simply double-click on the file that you downloaded and select a directory to which you want to extract the files. The extracted files are

- Register.bat

- Unregister.bat

- Xmlversion.htm

- Xmlversions.ocx

To use the XML version checker, launch the Xmlversion.htm document using Internet Explorer, as shown in Figure A-3.

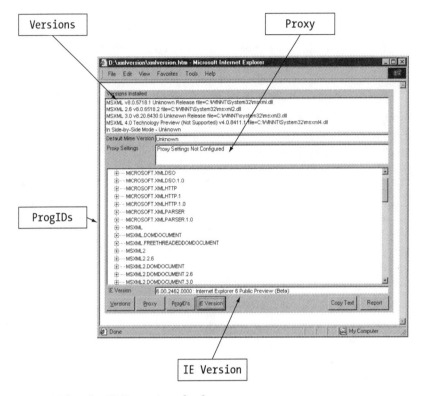

Figure A-3. Using the XML version checker

In Figure A-3, you can see that XML parser versions 2.6 through 4.0 are installed on my computer. You'll also notice the ProgIDs that are supported by the various versions of the XML parsers.

ProgIDs Modes

In the XML parser 3.0, you have the option to install the parser in two modes:

- Side-by-side

- Replace Mode

Installing the parser in side-by-side mode allows you to maintain your existing applications (using the older MSXML.dll or MSXML2.dll). To make use of the new XML parser, you need to use the *version dependent ProgID* as shown in Table A-1.

Table A-1. Version Dependent and Independent ProgIDs

VERSION DEPENDENT PROGID	VERSION INDEPENDENT PROGID
Msxml2.DOMDocument.3.0	Msxml2.DOMDocument
Msxml2.FreeThreadedDOMDocument.3.0	Msxml2.FreeThreadedDOMDocument
Msxml2.DSOControl.3.0	Msxml2.DSOControl
Msxml2.XMLHTTP.3.0	Msxml2.XMLHTTP
Msxml2.XMLSchemaCache.3.0	Msxml2.XMLSchemaCache
Msxml2.XSLTemplate.3.0	Msxml2.XSLTemplate
Msxml2.SAXAttributes.3.0	Msxml2.SAXAttributes
Msxml2.SAXXMLReader.3.0	Msxml2.SAXXMLReader
Msxml2.MXXMLWriter.3.0	Msxml2.MXXMLWriter
Msxml2.MXHTMLWriter.3.0	Msxml2.MXHTMLWriter

If you install the XML parser in replace mode, be sure to check that it does not break existing applications that are using the older ProgIDs. In this case, you can now use the *version independent ProgID.*

Document Object Model (DOM) Level 1 Core Interfaces

THIS APPENDIX SUMMARIZES the fundamental and extended interfaces of DOM Level 1 Core that are used in Chapter 4 of this book.

You can find more detailed documentation at http://www.w3.org/TR/REC-DOM-Level-1/.

Understanding Basic Terms in the DOM

Before we present the exception and various interfaces of the DOM Level 1 Core specifications, we want to clearly define the basic terms that are used in the specification and explanations. The basic terms are *interface*, *exception*, *object*, as well as the *DOMString* type.

Interface, Exception, Object

We will first define the three basic terms: interface, exception, and object. Since DOMString is of a different category, basically a data type used in the DOM terminology, we will define it in the next subsection.

The DOM Level 1 specifies the interfaces as well as one exception.

The purpose of an *interface* specification is to lay down the properties and methods that an interface contains and exposes. There is no dictation of how the properties' values should be obtained or how the methods should be implemented. There is only one special case, where an *exception* specification is used instead of an interface. An exception specification may be viewed as a special interface specification, that is, specifically used for exceptions.

An instance of an exception (e.g., DOMException) or an interface (e.g., Document) is called an *object*.

The DOMString Type

A DOMString is a sequence of 16-bit characters. Applications must encode DOMString using UTF-16. In some platforms, DOMString is bound to some native data type. For example, in Java, DOMString is bound to the String type as the latter also uses UTF-16 as its encoding.

In this appendix, the word "string" is used interchangeably with "DOMString."

Fundamental Interfaces

All implementations of DOM must fully support all the fundamental interfaces that are listed in this section.

DOMException

An exception is raised when a DOM operation encounters some abnormal or exceptional situation. Each exceptional situation is assigned a unique code (Table B-1).

Table B-1. DOMException Property

PROPERTY/ATTRIBUTE	DESCRIPTION
code	A number of the short integer data type. It is a unique code to indicate the type of error or exceptional case occurring.

The following constant code values in Table B-2 have been defined:

Table B-2. Constant Code Values for DOMException

CODE VALUE	DESCRIPTION OF ASSOCIATED ERROR
INDEX_SIZE_ERR (1)	Index or size is negative, or greater than the allowed value
DOMSTRING_SIZE_ERR (2)	Specified range of text does not fit into a DOMString
HIERARCHY_REQUEST_ERR (3)	A node is inserted somewhere it does not belong
WRONG_DOCUMENT_ERR (4)	A node is used in a different document than the one that created it and the document does not support it
INVALID_CHARACTER_ERR (5)	An invalid character is specified, such as in a name
NO_DATA_ALLOWED_ERR (6)	Data specified for a node that does not support data
NO_MODIFICATION_ALLOWED_ERR (7)	An attempt is made to modify an object where modification is not allowed
NOT_FOUND_ERR (8)	An attempt is made to reference a node in a context where it does not exist
NOT_SUPPORTED_ERR (9)	The implementation does not support the type of object requested
INUSE_ATTRIBUTE_ERR (10)	An attempt is made to add an attribute that is already in use elsewhere

DOMImplementation

The method (Table B-3) that is provided in this interface does not apply to specific document instances, but rather to all documents from the particular DOM implementation.

Table B-3. DOMImplementation Method

METHOD	FUNCTION
hasFeature(*feature, version*)	Tests if a DOMImplementation implements a specified feature, *feature* (e.g., HTML and XML), where *version* indicates the version of the feature to be tested. This method returns `true` if the specified feature is implemented and `false` otherwise.

DocumentFragment

A DocumentFragment object is a lightweight Document object that is commonly used to represent a portion of a containing document. It is used to extract a group of nodes from a document's tree or to create a group of nodes with the intent of joining them to the containing document (Document object) at a later point in time.

This interface extends the Node interface with no additional properties and methods.

Document

The Document interface represents an HTML or XML document. It is the root of a document tree that provides the top-most level access to the document's data.

The Document interface extends the Node interface. It contains additional properties and methods listed in Table B-4 and Table B-5. The term *this document* as used in Table B-4 and Table B-5 refers to the document in question, whose properties and methods are being discussed.

Table B-4. Extended Properties in Document Interface

PROPERTY/ATTRIBUTE	DESCRIPTION
doctype	The Document Type Declaration associated with this document. The value has an interface type of DocumentType. If the document does not have a Document Type Declaration, this property has the value NULL.
implementation	The DocumentImplementation object that handles this document in question.
documentElement	The root element for this document.

A Document will contain different types of nodes such as element and text nodes. As such, it also provides the factory methods to create the nodes or objects that a Document can contain. The names of the factory methods (shown in Table B-5) start with the word "create," which is indeed indicative of their functions.

Table B-5. Extended Methods in Document Interface

METHOD	FUNCTION
createElement(*tagname*)	Creates and returns an element with the specified tagname. This method can raise a DOMException with the code value INVALID_CHARACTER_ERR.
createDocumentFragment()	Creates and returns an initial empty DocumentFragment object.
createTextNode(*data*)	Creates and returns a Text node that contains text data specified as *data.*
createComment(*data*)	Creates and returns a Comment node that represents a comment containing text data specified as *data.*
createCDATASection(*data*)	Creates and returns a CDATA node that contains text data specified as *data.* The method can raise a DOMException with the code value, NOT_SUPPORTED_ERR.
createProcessingInstruction(*target, data*)	Creates and returns a ProcessingInstruction node containing target and text data specified as *target* and *data* respectively. The method can raise a DOMException with the code value, INVALID_CHARACTER_ERR or NOT_SUPPORTED_ERR.
createAttribute(*name*)	Creates and returns an Attribute node whose name is specified as *name.* This method can raise a DOMException with the code value, INVALID_CHARACTER_ERR.

(continued)

Table B-5. Extended Methods in Document Interface (continued)

METHOD	FUNCTION
createEntityReference(*name*)	Creates and returns an EntityReference node with the name specified as *name.* This method can raise a DOMException with the code value, INVALID_CHARACTER_ERR or NOT_SUPPORTED_ERR.
getElementsByTagName(*tagname*)	Returns a NodeList of elements in the document that have the specified tagname. The elements are arranged in the document order in the NodeList object.

Node

The Node interface is used to implement a single node in a document tree. It is the basic type from which the interfaces for other more specific node types extend. This section lists the basic properties and methods of all types of node that are exposed by a Node interface. In the description of properties (Table B-6) and methods (Table B-9), the term *this node* refers to the node in question whose properties and methods are being discussed.

Table B-6. Properties of Node Interface

PROPERTY/ATTRIBUTE	DESCRIPTION
nodeName	The name of this node, which depends on the type of the node.
nodeValue	The value of this node, which depends on the type of the node. If this node is read-only, the NO_MODIFICATION_ALLOWED_ERR exception will be raised when there is an attempt to set the value. A DOMSTRING_SIZE_ERR exception is raised if this value contains more characters than they can fit into a DOMString variable on the implementation platform.
nodeType	The type of this node.
parentNode	The node that is parent of this node.

(continued)

Table B-6. Properties of Node Interface (continued)

PROPERTY/ATTRIBUTE	DESCRIPTION
childNodes	A NodeList of all nodes that are children of this node. If this node does not have any child node, an empty NodeList is returned.
firstChild	The first child of this node. It is NULL if this node does not have a child node.
lastChild	The last child of this node. It is NULL if this node does not have a child node.
previousSibling	The node immediately preceding this node. It is NULL if this node has no preceding node.
nextSibling	The node immediately following this node. It is NULL if this node has no node following it.
attributes	A NamedNodeMap containing the attributes of this node. If this node is not an Element node, this property returns NULL.
ownerDocument	The Document object associated with this node.

The Node interface defines a list of constants for the type of node, i.e., nodeType. They are summarized in Table B-7.

Table B-7. Constant Values for nodeType

NODETYPE VALUE	DESCRIPTION
ELEMENT_NODE (1)	This node is an Element.
ATTRIBUTE_NODE (2)	This node is an Attribute.
TEXT_NODE (3)	This node is a Text node.
CDATA_SECTION_NODE (4)	This node is a CDATASection.
ENTITY_REFERENCE_NODE (5)	This node is an EntityReference.
ENTITY_NODE (6)	This node is an Entity.
PROCESSING_INSTRUCTION_NODE (7)	This node is a ProcessingInstruction.
COMMENT_NODE (8)	This node is a Comment.
DOCUMENT_NODE (9)	This node is a Document.
DOCUMENT_TYPE_NODE (10)	This node is a DocumentType.
DOCUMENT_FRAGMENT_NODE (11)	This node is a DocumentFragment.
NOTATION_NODE (12)	This node is a Notation.

The value of the nodeType property determines the values for the nodeName and nodeValue of a node. They are summarized in Table B-8.

Table B-8. Values for nodeName and nodeValue Determined by nodeType

INTERFACE NAME OF NODE	NODETYPE	NODENAME	NODEVALUE
Element	ELEMENT_NODE	Tagname of the element	NULL
Att	ATTRIBUTE_NODE	Name of attribute	Value of attribute
Text	TEXT_NODE	#text	Text content of the node
CDATASECTION	CDATA_SECTION_NODE	#cdata-section	Content of the CDATASection node
EntityReference	ENTITY_REFERENCE_NODE	Name of entity reference	NULL
Entity	ENTITY_NODE	Name of entity	NULL
ProcessingInstruction	PROCESSING_INSTRUCTION_NODE	Target of PI	Content of PI excluding the target
Comment	COMMENT_NODE	#comment	Content of the comment
Document	DOCUMENT_NODE	#document	NULL
DocumentType	DOCUMENT_TYPE_NODE	Document type name	NULL
DocumentFragment	DOCUMENT_FRAGMENT_NODE	#document-fragment	NULL
Notation	NOTATION_NODE	Name of notation	NULL

The following methods in Table B-9 are exposed by the Node interface.

Table B-9. Methods Exposed by Node Interface

METHOD	FUNCTION
insertBefore(*newChild, refChild*)	Inserts the *newChild* node before the existing child node specified as *refChild*. If *refChild* is NULL, *newChild* is inserted at the end of the list of children of this node. Possible exceptions that may be raised through a DOMException object are those that correspond to the values: HIERARCHY_REQUEST_ERR, WRONG_DOCUMENT_ERR, NO_MODIFICATION_ALLOWED_ERR, NOT_FOUND_ERR.
replaceChild(*newChild, oldChild*)	Replaces the child node specified as *oldChild* with the *newChild* node, and returns the *oldChild* node. If *newChild* is already in the document tree to which it is inserted, it is first removed from the tree. Possible exceptions of this method are HIERARCHY_REQUEST_ERR, WRONG_DOCUMENT_ERR, NO_MODIFICATION_ALLOWED_ERR, and NOT_FOUND_ERR.
removeChild(*oldChild*)	Removes the child node specified as *oldChild*, and returns the *oldChild* node. Possible exceptions of this method are NO_MODIFICATION_ALLOWED_ERR, and NOT_FOUND_ERR.
appendChild(*newChild*)	Inserts the *newChild* node at the end of the list of children of this node. Possible exceptions of this method are HIERARCHY_REQUEST_ERR, WRONG_DOCUMENT_ERR, and NO_MODIFICATION_ALLOWED_ERR.
hasChildNodes()	Determines whether this node has any children. It returns `true` if this node has any children, and `false` otherwise.
cloneNode(*deep*)	Creates and returns a duplicate of this node. If the *deep* parameter has the value `true`, the method recursively clones the subtree under this node.

NodeList

This interface provides the abstraction of an ordered collection of nodes, without defining how this collection is implemented. It exposes one property (Table B-10) and one method (Table B-11).

Table B-10. NodeList Property

PROPERTY/ATTRIBUTE	DESCRIPTION
length	A number of the long integer data type. It indicates the number of nodes in the ordered collection.

Table B-11. NodeList Method

METHOD	DESCRIPTION
item(i)	Returns the $(i+1)^{th}$ node in the ordered collection of nodes. The parameter is used as an index to the list of nodes. Indexing runs from 0 to size of list minus one. NULL is returned if i is an invalid index value.

NamedNodeMap

A NamedNodeMap object or *map* implements this interface for representing an unordered collection of nodes that can be accessed by name. The objects contained in a map may be accessed by an ordinal index. This indexing allows convenient enumeration of the contained objects and does not imply any DOM ordering specification to the object implemented using this interface. It has one property, listed in Table B-12.

Table B-12. NamedNodeMap Property

PROPERTY/ATTRIBUTE	DESCRIPTION
length	A number of the long integer data type. It indicates the number of nodes in the unordered collection.

The following methods in Table B-13 are exposed by the NamedNodeMap interface:

Table B-13. NamedNodeMap Methods

METHOD	DESCRIPTION
getNamedItem(*name*)	Returns a node in this map that has the specified name. The method returns NULL if no node with the specified name is found.
setNamedItem(*node*)	Adds the node specified as the parameter of the method into this map. The name of the node is derived using the nodeName property of the node to be added. If a node with the same name already exists in the map, it is replaced by the new one. The method returns the replaced node if indeed a replacement occurs. Otherwise the method returns NULL. Possible exceptions this method may raise are WRONG_DOCUMENT_ERR, NO_MODIFICATION_ALLOWED_ERR, and INUSE_ATTRIBUTE_ERR.
removeNamedItem(*name*)	Removes a node in this map that has the specified name, and returns the removed node. The method returns NULL and raises a NOT_FOUND_ERR exception if no node with the specified name is found.
item(*i*)	Returns the $(i+1)^{th}$ item in this map. NULL is returned if i is an invalid index value.

CharacterData

The purpose of this interface is to extend the Node interface with specific properties (Table B-14) and methods (Table B-15) to handle character data. No DOM objects correspond directly to CharacterData, but instead this interface is inherited by other interfaces, such as the Text interface that needs to handle character data.

Table B-14. CharacterData Properties

PROPERTY/ATTRIBUTE	DESCRIPTION
data	The character data of this node.
length	A number of the long integer data type. It indicates the number of characters that are available through the data property and the sustringData method.

The term *offset* used as a parameter of some of the following methods starts from 0.

Table B-15. CharacterData Methods

METHOD	DESCRIPTION
substringData(*offset, count*)	Returns a DOMString of character data from this node, starting at the specified offset. The number of characters in the returned string is specified as the parameter, *count*. If the sum of *offset* and *count* exceeds the length property of this node, then all characters starting from the specified offset to the end of the data are returned. Possible exceptions that this method may raise are INDEX_SIZE_ERR and DOMSTRING_SIZE_ERR.
appendData(*newdata*)	Appends the DOMString specified as *newdata* to the end of the character data of this node. This method returns nothing. One possible exception it may raise is NO_MODIFICATION_ALLOWED_ERR.
insertData(*offset, newdata*)	Inserts the DOMString specified as *newdata* at the specified offset. This method returns nothing. Possible exceptions this method may raise are INDEX_SIZE_ERR and NO_MODIFICATION_ALLOWED_ERR.
deleteData(*offset, count*)	Removes a string of characters, whose length is specified as *count*, starting from the location specified by *offset*. If the sum of *offset* and *count* exceeds the length property of this node, then all characters starting from the specified offset to the end of the data are deleted. This method returns nothing. Possible exceptions that this method may raise are INDEX_SIZE_ERR and NO_MODIFICATION_ALLOWED_ERR.
replaceData(*offset, count, newdata*)	Replaces the characters starting at the specified offset with the DOMString specified as *newdata*. The *count* parameter specifies the number of characters to replace. If the sum of *offset* and *count* exceeds the length property of this node, then all characters to the end of the data are replaced. This method returns nothing. Possible exceptions that this method may raise are INDEX_SIZE_ERR and NO_MODIFICATION_ALLOWED_ERR.

`Attr`

The Attr interface represents the attribute in an Element object. It extends the Node interface with three additional properties shown in Table B-16.

Table B-16. Extended Properties in Attr Interface

PROPERTY/ATTRIBUTE	DESCRIPTION
name	The name of this attribute.
specified	A flag that has the value `true` if the attribute has an assigned value in the document, or the value `false` if no value is assigned to the attribute and the default value specified in the DTD is used as the attribute value.
value	The value of this attribute.

`Element`

This interface represents an Element in a document tree. It extends the Node interface with the property shown in Table B-17.

Table B-17. Extended Property in Element Interface

PROPERTY/ATTRIBUTE	DESCRIPTION
tagname	The name of this element.

The Element interface provides methods (Table B-18) that are relevant specifically to element nodes.

Table B-18. Extended Methods in Element Interface (continued)

METHOD	DESCRIPTION
getAttribute(*name*)	Returns a DOMString, which is the value of the attribute with the specified name. If the attribute does not have a specified or default value, this method returns an empty string.
setAttribute(*name, value*)	Sets the value of the attribute with the specified name to the value specified as *value*. If the specified attribute does not exist, a new attribute with the specified name is created with the specified value. This method returns nothing. Possible exceptions that the method may raise are INVALID_CHARACTER_ERR and NO_MODIFICATION_ALLOWED_ERR.
removeAttribute(*name*)	Removes the attribute with the specified name. This method returns nothing. One possible exception that the method may raise is NO_MODIFICATION_ALLOWED_ERR.
getAttributeNode(*name*)	Returns an Attr node with the specified name. If no such attribute exists, this method returns NULL.
setAttributeNode(*newAttr*)	Adds an Attr node specified as *newAttr*. If an existing Attr node whose name is the same as that of *newAttr*, it is replaced by the *newAttr* node. If a replacement occurs, the replaced Attr node is returned, otherwise the method returns NULL. Possible exceptions that this method may raise are WRONG_DOCUMENT_ERR, NO_MODIFICATION_ALLOWED_ERR, and INUSE_ATTRIBUTE_ERR.
removeAttributeNode(*oldAttr*)	Removes the specified Attr node specified as *oldAttr*, and returns the removed node. Possible exceptions that this method may raise are NO_MODIFICATION_ALLOWED_ERR and NOT_FOUND_ERR.
getElementsByTagName(*name*)	Returns a NodeList of all the descendant elements with the specified name, where the elements are arranged according to the document order. If the value of the parameter is the wildcard character *, then all descendant elements will be returned.

(continued)

Table B-18. Extended Methods in Element Interface (continued)

METHOD	DESCRIPTION
normalize()	Normalizes all the Text nodes in the full depth of the sub-tree under this Element node, where only markups such as tags, comments, PIs, CDATA sections, and entity references separate Text nodes. The effect is that there are not adjacent Text nodes. This method returns nothing and raises no exceptions.

Text

The Text interface extends the CharacterData interface with one method (Table B-19) to handle text data.

Table B-19. Extended Method in Text Interface

METHOD	DESCRIPTION
splitText(*offset*)	Splits this Text node into two sibling Text nodes at the specified offset. This node then contains data up to the offset point. A new Text node is inserted as the sibling following this Text node. This method returns the new Text node. Possible exceptions that the method may raise are INDEX_SIZE_ERR and NO_MODIFICATION_ALLOWED_ERR.

Comment

This interface represents the contents of a comment. It extends the CharacterData interface, but with no additional properties or methods.

Extended Interfaces

Not all implementations of DOM are required to have objects that implement the extended interfaces. For example, an HTML-only DOM implementation will not need to deal with objects implemented by interfaces listed in this section.

CDATASection

This interface represents a CDATA section. It extends the Text interface and thus also extends the CharacterData interface. However, unlike Text nodes, adjacent CDATASection nodes are not merged by the normalize() method of their containing Element node.

DocumentType

Each Document object has a doctype attribute whose value is either NULL or a DocumentType object. The DocumentType interface extends the Node interface with provision of access to the entities and notations declared in the DTD of a document. The properties are shown in Table B-20.

Table B-20. DocumentType Properties

PROPERTY/ATTRIBUTE	DESCRIPTION
name	The name of this DTD.
entities	A NamedNodeMap containing the general entities (both external and internal) declared in the DTD.
notations	A NamedNodeMap containing the notations declared in the DTD.

Notation

This interface represents a notation declared in the DTD. It extends the Node interface with two additional properties (Table B-21). A Notation node does not have any parent and it is read-only since DOM Level 1 does not support editing of a Notation node.

Table B-21. Notation Properties

PROPERTY/ATTRIBUTE	DESCRIPTION
publicID	The public identifier of this notation. The value is NULL if the public identifier was not specified.
systemID	The system identifier of this notation. The value is NULL if the system identifier was not specified.

Entity

The Entity interface represents a parsed or unparsed entity. It extends the Node interface with three additional properties (Table B-22). An Entity node and all its descendants are read-only since DOM Level 1 does not support editing of an Entity node.

Table B-22. Extended Properties in Entity Interface

PROPERTY/ATTRIBUTE	DESCRIPTION
publicID	The public identifier of this entity. The value is NULL if the public identifier was not specified.
systemID	The system identifier of this entity. The value is NULL if the system identifier was not specified.
notationName	The name of the notation for this entity if it is unparsed. For a parsed entity, the value is NULL.

EntityReference

This interface represents entity reference. It extends the Node interface, but with no additional properties or methods.

ProcessingInstruction

This interface represents a processing instruction. It extends the Node interface with two additional properties shown in Table B-23.

Table B-23. Extended Properties in ProcessingInstruction Interface

PROPERTY/ATTRIBUTE	DESCRIPTION
target	The target of this processing instruction.
data	The content of this processing instruction returned as a DOMString. The content starts as the first non-whitespace character after the target and ends just before the ?> substring in the specification of a processing instruction. If this ProcessingInstruction node is read-only, the NO_MODIFICATION_ALLOWED_ERR exception will be raised if there is an attempt to set the value of this property.

APPENDIX C

XML-Data Reduced (XDR) Schema

THIS APPENDIX LISTS the basic elements in the XDR Schema language and the attributes that are used to specify the structure and constraints on the contents of an XML document. It also presents the data types that are supported by the XDR Schema as well as the annotations that can be used to specify XML-to-relational mapping.

You can find more detailed documentation on the Web at Microsoft's library site at `http://msdn.microsoft.com/`.

Basic Elements in XDR Schema

Table C-1 shows the basic elements that are used in the XDR Schema.

Table C-1. Basic Elements Used in the XDR Schema

ELEMENT	DESCRIPTION
<Schema>	This is the document root element of a schema. It can be assigned a name through the name attribute. Namespace declarations for the schema are specified within the <Schema> start-tag.
<ElementType>	Defines an element. For example: `<ElementType name="BOOK" />`
<element>	Declares an instance of a specified element type. For example: `<element name="BOOK" />`
<AttributeType>	Defines an attribute. For example: `<AttributeType name="ISBN" />`
<attribute>	Declares an instance of a specified attribute type. For example: `<attribute name="ISBN" />`

(continued)

Table C-1. Basic Elements Used in the XDR Schema (continued)

ELEMENT	DESCRIPTION
<group>	Groups together a subset of child elements so that constraints can be specified that apply on this subset of elements. For example:

```
<group name="ISBN" order="seq">
    <element name="TITLE" />
    <element name="AUTHOR" />
</group>
```

General Layout

An XDR schema uses the XML syntax. A schema begins with the XML declaration, and is followed by the <Schema> document root element in which at least the namespace for Microsoft XDR is specified.

The following code shows a simple XDR schema:

```
<?xml version="1.0"?>
<Schema name="mySchema"
        xmlns="urn:schemas-microsoft-com:xml-data">
    <ElementType name="TITLE" content="textOnly" />
    <ElementType name="AUTHOR" content="textOnly" />
    <ElementType name="PRICE" />
    <AttributeType name="ISBN" />
    <AttributeType name="Pages" />

    <ElementType name="BOOK">
        <element type="TITLE" />
        <element type="AUTHOR" />
        <element type="PRICE" />
        <attribute type="ISBN" />
        <attribute type="Pages" />
    </ElementType>

    <ElementType name="BOOKS">
        <element type="BOOK" maxOccurs="*" />
    </ElementType>
</Schema>
```

The schema specifies that a <BOOKS> element in an XML document can contain any number of <BOOK> elements. The schema also specifies that the <BOOK> element in turn contains the <TITLE>, <AUTHOR>, and <PRICE> elements as well as the ISBN and Pages attributes. Also, the <TITLE> and <AUTHOR> elements contain only text contents.

Specification of the Content Model

The content model describes the content structure of elements and attributes in an XML document. In this section, we present the attributes that enable us to define the content model for an XML document.

The model Attribute

This attribute specifies if a model is open or closed.

Containing Elements

<ElementType>

Possible Values

Table C-2 provides possible values of the model attribute.

Table C-2. Values of the model Attribute

VALUE	DESCRIPTION
"open"	Specifies that an element can contain additional child elements and attributes that are not declared in the XDR schema that an XML document references.
"closed"	Specifies that an element cannot contain additional information that is not specified in the XDR schema.

Default Value

"open"

The content Attribute

This attribute specifies the content type of an element.

Containing Elements

<ElementType> and <AttributeType>

Possible Values

Table C-3 lists possible values of the content attribute.

Table C-3. Values of the content Attribute

VALUE	DESCRIPTION
"eltOnly"	Specifies that an element can contain only elements.
"textOnly"	Specifies that an element can contain only text.
"mixed"	Specifies that an element can contain a mixture of elements and text.
"empty"	Specifies that an element contains nothing.

Default Value

"mixed"

The minOccurs and maxOccurs Attributes

The minOccurs attribute specifies the minimum number of times an element can occur within its parent element. The maxOccurs attribute specifies the maximum number of times an element can occur within its parent element.

Containing Elements

<element> and <group>

Possible Values

Table C-4 lists possible values of the `minOccurs` and `maxOccurs` attributes.

Table C-4. Values of the `minOccurs` and `maxOccurs` Attributes

ATTRIBUTE	VALUE	DESCRIPTION
minOccurs	"0"	Specifies that this child element can be absent. That is, the element is optional.
minOccurs	"1"	Specifies that this element must occur at least once within its parent element.
maxOccurs	"1"	Specifies that an element can occur at most once only within its parent element.
maxOccurs	"*"	Specifies that an element can occur any number of times within its parent element.

Default Value

"1" for `minOccurs`
"1" for `maxOccurs` if the `content` attribute of the element is not "mixed"
"*" for `maxOccurs` if the `content` attribute of the element is "mixed"

The minLength and maxLength Attributes

For element or attribute, the value can be associated with a data type using the namespace, urn:schemas-microsoft-com:datatypes. The `minLength` and `maxLength` attributes defined in this namespace can be used to set constraint on the length of data.

For string and number data types, the `minLength` attribute specifies the minimum number of characters while the `maxLength` attribute specifies the maximum number of characters allowed.

For bin.hex and bin.base64 data types, the `minLength` attribute specifies the minimum number of bytes while the `maxLength` attribute specifies the maximum number of bytes allowed for the binary object.

NOTE *The available data types using the urn:schemas-microsoft-com:datatypes namespace are listed in a later section in this appendix.*

Containing Elements

<ElementType> and <AttributeType>

Possible Values

Any non-negative integer value specified within quotes.

The order Attribute

The attribute specifies how sequences of enclosed child elements can appear in the document instance.

Containing Elements

<ElementType> and <group>

Possible Values

Table C-5 lists possible values of the order attribute.

Table C-5. Values of the order *Attribute*

VALUE	DESCRIPTION
"seq"	Specifies that the enclosed child elements must appear in the same order as they appear in the schema.
"one"	Specifies that only one of the child elements defined in an <ElementType> can appear.
"many"	Specifies that the child elements can occur in any order and in any quantity.

Default Value

"seq"—if the content attribute is set to "eltOnly"
"many"—if the content attribute is set to "mixed"

The default Attribute

The default attribute specifies the default value of an attribute.

Containing Elements

<AttributeType> and <attribute>

Possible Values

Any value specified within quotes.

The required Attribute

This attribute specifies whether an attribute is required.

Containing Elements

<AttributeType> and <attribute>

Possible Values

Table C-6 provides possible values of the required attribute.

Table C-6. Values of the required *Attribute*

VALUE	DESCRIPTION
"yes"	Specifies that the attribute is required for its parent element in the XML document that references the schema. If the same <AttributeType> or <attribute> containing the required attribute also specifies a default attribute value for the named attribute, then not only must the parent element contain the named attribute in the XML document, the attribute must also have the value specified by the default attribute in the schema.
"no"	Specifies that the attribute is not required.

Default Value

"no"

Data Types

The XDR Schema supports the attribute types used in a document type definition (DTD). In addition, it also provides support for a range of data types that may be used if the following namespace declaration is included in the <Schema> start-tag:

```
xmlns:dt="urn:schemas-microsoft-com:datatypes"
```

Note that dt is a user-given name for the prefix that is associated with the specified data types namespace.

To specify the data type of an attribute, we use the type attribute with the prefix associated with the data types namespace within the <AttributeType> or <ElementType> tags.

Alternatively, we can include a child <datatype> element within the <AttributeType> or <ElementType> element. The data type value is then specified through the type attribute with the prefix associated with the data types namespace within the <datatype> tag.

Table C-7 lists the XDR data types that correspond to the existing DTD attribute types, and Table C-8 lists the additional data types that are supported.

Table C-7. DTD Types Supported by the XDR Schema

XDR DATA TYPE	CORRESPONDING DTD TYPE	DESCRIPTION
id	ID	This attribute contains a value that is unique throughout the document.
		`<AttributeType name="EmployeeID" dt:type="id" />`
idref	IDREF	This attribute contains a value that corresponds to the value of some attribute of the id data type.
		`<AttributeType name="SupervisorID">` `<datatype dt:type="idref" />` `</AttributeType>`
idrefs	IDREFS	Similar to idref except the attribute here contains multiple id values separated by white space.
nmtoken	NMTOKEN	This attribute contains a value that conforms to the rules of the name token.
nmtokens	NMTOKENS	Similar to nmtoken except the attribute here can have a list of nmtoken values separated by white space.
enumeration	Enumeration	Similar to nmtoken, but with an explicit list of allowed values specified through the values attribute.
		`<AttributeType name="Cover" dt:type="enumeration" dt:values="Soft Hard" />`
string	CDATA	This attribute has a string value.

Table C-8. Additional XDR Data Types

DATA TYPE	DESCRIPTION
bin.base64	MIME-style Base64 encoded binary data
bin.hex	Hexadecimal-encoded binary data
boolean	Boolean value, true (1) or false (0)
char	A number corresponding to the Unicode representation of a character
date	Date specified in a subset of the ISO 8601 format (e.g., 1994-11-05) without time information
dateTime	Date specified in a subset of the ISO 8601 format, with optional time but no optional zone. Fractional seconds can be as precise as nanoseconds.
dateTime.tz	Date specified in a subset of the ISO 8601 format, with optional time and optional zone. Fractional seconds can be as precise as nanoseconds.
fixed.14.4	A number with no more than 14 digits to the left of the decimal point and no more than 4 to the right
float	Floating point number with optional sign, minimum value 2.2250738585072014E-308, and maximum value 1.7976931348623157E+308
int	Signed integer
i1	One-byte integer with optional sign (-128 to 127)
i2	Two-byte integer with optional sign (-32768 to 32767)
i4	Four-byte integer with optional sign (-2147483648 to 2147483647)
i8	Eight-byte integer with optional sign (-9223372036854775808 to 9223372036854775807)
number	A number with no limits on the digits
r4	Same as float but with 4-byte encoding. The minimum value is 1.17549435E-38F and the maximum is 3.40282347E+38F
r8	Same as float
ui1	One-byte unsigned integer (0 to 255)
ui2	Two-byte unsigned integer (0 to 65535)

(continued)

Table C-8. Additional XDR Data Types (continued)

DATA TYPE	DESCRIPTION
ui4	Four-byte unsigned integer (0 to 4294967295)
ui8	Eight-byte unsigned integer (0 to 18446744073709551615)
uri	Uniform Resource Identifier (URI)
uuid	Hexadecimal digits representing octets, with optional embedded hyphens ignored.

Annotations

Annotations are used within an XDR schema to specify XML-to-relational mapping, which includes mapping between elements and attributes in the XDR schema to tables (or views) and columns in the databases. An annotated schema is also called a mapping schema.

By default, an element name in an annotated schema maps to a table or view name in the specified database and the attribute name maps to the column name.

Query to a database against a mapping schema extracts data from the database table or view in the form of an XML document.

The schema should contain the following namespace declaration:

```
xmlns:sql="urn:schemas-microsoft-com:xml-sql"
```

Table C-9 lists annotations to the XDR schema.

Table C-9. Annotations to the XDR Schema

ANNOTATION	DESCRIPTION
sql:relation	Maps an XML element or attribute to a database table.
sql:field	Maps an XML element or attribute to a database column.
sql:is-constant	Creates an XML element to appear in the query output. However, the element does not map to any database table or column.
sql:map-field	Allows schema items to be excluded from the result.
<sql:relationship>	Specifies relationships between XML elements. The key, key-relation, foreign-key and foreign-relation attributes are used to establish the relationship.

(continued)

Table C-9. Annotations to the XDR Schema (continued)

ANNOTATION	DESCRIPTION
sql:limit-field, sql:limit-value	Allows limiting the values of an underlying database column or field to be returned based on a limiting value.
sql:key-fields	Allows specification of database column(s) that uniquely identifies the rows in a table.
sql:target-namespace	Allows placing the elements and attributes from the default namespace into a different namespace for query results.
sql:id-prefix	Creates valid XML ID, IDREF, and IDREFS. Prepends the values of ID, IDREF, and IDREFS with a string.
sql:use-cdata	Allows specifying CDATA sections to be used for certain elements in the XML document.
sql:url-encode	When an XML element/attribute is mapped to an SQL Server BLOB column, allows a reference (URI) to be returned that can be used later for BLOB data.
sql:overflow-field	Identifies the database column that contains the overflow data.

Index

SYMBOLS

// (recursive descent operation), 82
{ }(braces), 94

A

Active Server Pages. *See* Microsoft Active
    Server Pages
ActiveX DLL project, creating and nam-
    ing, 364–365
ADO (ActiveX Data Objects), 151–195
    Command object, 154, 170–174
    Connection object, 154, 155–161
        about, 155
        connecting to data source with
            Open method, 155–157
    ConnectionString arguments, 156
    error handling, 179–182
    Record object, 155, 175
    Recordset object, 155, 161–170
    Stream object, 155, 175–179
        about, 175
        closing, 179
        creating, 176
        loading content into, 178
        opening, 176–177
        reading content from, 178–179
        saving content from, 179
    top-level objects of, 154–155
    Universal Data Access strategy, 151
        Microsoft Data Access
            Components and, 151–152
        objective of ADO in, 153, 154
        OLE DB, 152–154
        Open Database Connectivity, 152
    updating book prices, 183–194
    Web links, 194–195
adovbs.inc file, 160
alias names with FOR XML AUTO ex
    tension, 213
Allow URL queries option (New Virtual
    Directory Properties), 239, 241
<annotation> element (XML Schema),
    313–314
annotations to XDR schema, 427–428

APIs for processing DOM tree, 119–131
    Attr node, 130–131
    element node, 127–130
    NodeList interface, 125–127
    nodes, 120–125
    reference to document root element,
        119–120
    reference to DOM tree, 119
architecture
    of OLE DB, 152–153
    WAP, 319–322
        illustrated, 320
        roles of WAP gateway, 320
        WAP Protocol stack, 321–322
arguments in ConnectionString, 156
arithmetic operators, XPath, 42
ASP. *See* Microsoft Active Server Pages
ASP listener file, 376–377
asynchronization flag for DOM tree,
    116–117
Attr interface, 411
Attr node, 130–131
attribute node, 48
attributes
    choosing between elements or, 19–21
    creating with <xsl:attribute>, 92–94
    defining and declaring XML, 309
    directives in SQL queries specifying
        type of, 223
    grouping in schema, 310–311
    illustrated, 6
    placing values in quotes, 8
    retrieving information from node ref-
        erenced by element node,
        129–130
    retrieving value of, 78
    XDR, 419–424
        content, 420
        default, 423
        minLength and maxLength,
            421–422
        minOccurs and maxOccurs,
            420–422
        model, 419
        order, 422–423
        required, 423–424
    for <xsl:output> element, 97

Authentication Methods dialog box (IIS), 389–390
authors table of BooksCatalog database, 198, 199
axes in XPath, 54–58

B

Basic Authentication method, 388–390
before-after pair for multiple transactions, 262–263
Binaries folder (SOAP Toolkit)
    trace utility in, 385
    wsdlgen utility, 369
BINARY BASE64 specification for FOR XML clause, 204
binary data
    retrieving with FOR XML AUTO extension, 217–218
    retrieving with FOR XML RAW extension, 207–210
binding element, 356–357
BizTalk protocol, 3
Books.asp sample listing, 103
books table of BooksCatalog database, 198, 199
Books.xml
    adding codes to form_load event of, 272
    converted to HTML, 332–333
    document for XSLT transformation, 73
    example document for XSLT transformation, 73
    how stylesheet transforms document, 76–78
    modifying document, 342
    sample listings, 271, 331–332
BooksCatalog database
    column fields of books and authors tables of, 198
    examples in, 198–199
    See also Microsoft SQL Server 2000
BookServer.asp script, 192–194
    batch updating book prices, 194
    retrieving books, 194
BooksISBN.xml, 284
booksSchema.xml, 265
Boolean expressions in XPath, 42
Boolean functions in XPath, 59–60
braces (), 94
browscap.ini file
    about, 344
    adding information to, 341–342
    dissecting, 343
    Web link for, 344

C

C/C++, printing content in both, 286
cards
    <card> element, 325
    defined, 324
    structure of decks and, 323–326
case studies
    updating book prices, 183–194
        batch updating prices, 194
        BookServer.asp script on Web server, 192–194
        data store for, 185
        illustrated, 184
        listing books, 187–188
        overview, 183–184
        reducing prices of books, 189–190
        retrieving books, 194
        submitting updated prices to Web server, 190–192
        user interface, 185–187
        Web page for client, 185
    Web service using SOAP toolkit, 359–388
        compiling COM object, 367–368
        consuming Web service, 381–382
        creating COM object, 364–367
        creating instance of SOAPClient, 380
        creating Web service consumer-SOAP client, 378–379
        database structure, 363–364
        existing solutions, 361–362
        generating WSDL, WSML, and Listener files, 368–378
        how SOAP Toolkit works, 384–385
        initializing SOAPClient object, 380–381
        proposed Web service, 362–363
        referencing SOAP type library, 379
        scenario for, 359–361
        stylesheet for XSL transformation, 382–383
        testing Web service, 383–384
        tracing SOAP messages, 385–388
CDATA in XML, 18–19
CDATASection extended interface, 413
CharacterData interface, 409–410
checking out client-side DOM shopping cart, 139–142
    displaying server's response, 141
    overview, 139
    passing DOM object to HTTP server, 140–141
    prompting for user ID, 139–141
    re-initializing shopping cart, 141–142

child node, accessing DOM, 123–124
cHTML (Compact HTML), 330
clients
    creating instance of SOAPClient, 380
    generating response to shopping cart
        from server, 147
    initializing SOAPClient object,
        380–381
    receiving Stream object from server,
        183, 184
    retrieving contents of shopping cart
        from, 146–147
    sending Stream object to Web server
        from, 184
    setting content type for server-side
        shopping cart, 145–146
    shopping cart receives DOM object
        from, 146
    Web page for updating book prices,
        185
client-side applications
    DOM shopping cart, 131–144
        application requirements for, 132
        checking out, 139–142
        complete listing of script, 142–144
        creating DOM tree for shopping
            cart, 133–134
        creating order form, 134–136
        initialization tasks for, 132–133
        invoking loading of order form, 134
        loading XML document into DOM
            tree, 133
        updating, 136–139
    XSLT transformation, 102–105
closing Stream object, 179
columns
    associating with universal table col-
        umn name, 219–220
    directive in name of universal table,
        222–224
    example of partial universal table, 221
    mapping to elements, 214
    returning computed, 214–215
    unconsumed, 234–235
COM (Component Object Model) object
    compiling, 367–368
    creating, 364–367
    mapping services in WSDL file to, 375
Command object, 170–174
    collection objects in ADO, 154
    CommandText property, 173
    overview, 170–171
    persisting SQL statement, 173–174
    querying database with Execute
        method of, 171–172
CommandText property, 173

CommandTypeEnum values of Execute
        method, 158
Comment interface, 413
comment node, 50
comments, XSLT, 101–102
complex types for XML Schema, 303–309
    defining mixed content in XML docu-
        ment, 307–309
    empty elements, 309
    listings for storing shipping and
        ordering information, 304–307
config.xml, 343
Connection object, 155–161
    about, 155
    accessing data source with, 159–161
    accessing records in data source with
        Execute method, 157–159
    collection objects in, 154
    connecting to data source with Open
        method, 155–157
    Error object of, 179, 180
    Errors collection of, 179, 180
ConnectionString arguments, 156
ConnectModeEnum values for Open
        method, 177
constant code values to DOMException,
        401
constants for nodeType of Node inter-
        face, 405
consumer. *See* Web service consumer
consuming Web services, 358, 381–382
content attribute, 420
contentHandler Visual Basic project, 272
    adding codes to selected methods of
        IVBSAXContentHandler,
        274–275
    implementing
        IVBSAXContentHandler inter-
        face, 272–273
    methods available in, 275–276
context node, 46, 50
copying XML elements, 91–92
cross-platform compatibility
    ensuring Web services, 351
    SOAP, 350, 351, 391
custom entities, 10–11

D

data consumers, 152
data model for XPath, 44–50
    attribute node, 48
    comment node, 50
    context, 50
    element node, 47–48
    namespace node, 49

data model for Xpath (*continued*)
    PI node, 49–50
    properties of nodes, 46
    representing XML document as tree,
        44–46
    root node, 47
    text node, 48–49
data providers, 152
data source
    accessing records with Execute
        method of Connection object,
        157–159
    connecting with ADO Connection
        object, 155–157
    example of accessing with Connection
        object, 159–161
    queries held in Recordset object, 161
Data Source tab (New Virtual Directory
    Properties dialog box), 238
data store for updating book prices, 185
data types
    DTD lack of support for, 291–292
    list of ADO, 174
    XDR, 424–427
    XML Schema, 300–309
        complex types, 303–309
        derived, 300–301
        deriving new simple types, 303
        enumeration, 302
        primitive, 300
        restricting range with, 301–302
        simple types, 301
databases
    BooksCatalog, 198–199
    column fields of books and authors
        tables in BooksCatalog,
        198–199
    creating virtual directory, 235–241
    deleting record from, 170
    inserting record in, 168–169
    modifying number of characters in
        row, 203
    querying
        with Execute method of Command
            object, 171–172
        records with Recordset object,
            166–168
        structure of Web service using SOAP
            toolkit, 363–364
    See also ADO
dbobject, 217
DCD (Document Content Description),
    22, 292
DDML (Document Description Markup
    Language), 22–23

decks, 323–326
    <card> element, 325
    defined, 323
    DTD for, 325
    paragraph and anchor elements, 326
    processing, 328
    structure of cards and, 323–326
    WAP gateway and, 324
    WML root element, 325
    XML PI, 325
default attribute, 423
Default Web Site Properties dialog box
    (IIS), 340
deleting data in Updategram, 258–259
derived data types, 300–301
directives
    defining mapping between columns
        and XML data, 224
    examples using, 225–228
    in SQL queries specifying type of attri-
        butes, 223
    in universal table column name,
        222–224
DLL
    compiling, 367–368
    creating and naming ActiveX DLL
        project, 364–365
    registering for XSL ISAPI, 339
Document Content Description (DCD),
    22, 292
Document Description Markup
    Language (DDML), 22–23
Document instance
    creating in DOM level 1, 115
    loading XML data in DOM instance,
        117–118
Document interface, 402–404
Document Object Model. *See* DOM
document order, 46
Document Type Definition. *See* DTD
document-decks. *See* decks
DocumentFragment interface, 402
documenting XML Schema, 313–314
documents
    adding XSLT to, 73–78
        adding stylesheet to document, 75
        example document, 73
        example stylesheet, 73–74
        how stylesheet transforms docu-
            ment, 76–78
        transformation by Internet
            Explorer, 75–76
    addressing XML part with XPath, 41
    advantages
        of DOM and XSLT with XML, 269

of SAX with XML, 269, 288–289
of XML, 31
creating DOM tree of, 114–118
creating instance of DOM, 115
loading XML data in DOM
instance, 117–118
specifying asynchronization flag,
116–117
creating in XMLSpy, 315–316
defining
mixed content in XML, 307–309
structure with DTD, 11–15
in XML Schema for XML, 296–297
generating XML Schema with XML,
316–317
with internal DTD, 15–16, 291
loading
for processing in Visual Basic,
271–272
XML document for use with
OPENXML provider, 229
manipulating data and structure with
DOM, 107
processing with SAX, 276–277
reducing size of for WAP devices,
328–329
representing in DOM tree, 111–113
rewriting with XSL ISAPI, 342–344
rules of well-formed, 6–11
SAX processing and structure of XML,
286–287
selecting stylesheet XSL ISAPI,
337–338
SOAP messages as XML, 348
transforming structure with XSLT, 70,
90–102
controlling output, 95–97
copying XML elements, 91–92
creating attributes, 92–94
creating elements, 94–95
generating comments, 101–102
inserting text, 98–99
transforming namespaces, 99–101
transforming universal table into
XML, 218
valid XML, 18
validating
against XML Schema with Visual
Basic, 295–296
XML document in XMLSpy, 316
WSDL as XML-based, 352
XDR attributes defining content
model for XML, 419–424
XML Schema files as XML, 294
XPath data model of XML, 44–46
XSLT stylesheet as, 71

DocumentType extended interface,
413–414
DOM (Document Object Model),
107–149
about, 107–108
APIs for processing DOM tree,
119–131
Attr node, 130–131
element node, 127–130
NodeList interface, 125–127
nodes, 120–125
reference to document root element, 119–120
reference to DOM tree, 119
basic terms, 399–400
DOMString type, 400
interface, exception, and object,
399
creating DOM tree of document,
114–118
creating instance of DOM, 115
loading XML data in DOM
instance, 117–118
specifying asynchronization flag,
116–117
interfaces, 111, 400–415
Attr, 411
CDATASection, 413
CharacterData, 409–410
Comment, 413
Document, 402–404
DocumentFragment, 402
DocumentType, 413–414
DOMException, 400–401
DOMImplementation, 401–402
Element, 411–412
Entity, 414–415
EntityReference, 415
NamedNodeMap, 408–409
Node, 404–407
NodeList, 408
Notation, 414
ProcessingInstruction, 415
Text, 413
manipulating XML documents with,
107
representing XML document in DOM
tree, 111–113
retrieving information from XML doc-
ument, 269
saving DOM tree, 118
SAX as alternative to, 108, 269–277,
289
shopping cart
client-side programming of,
131–144

DOM (*continued*)
    server-side programming of,
      145–148
    support of in MSXML3, 108–111
      DOM Level 1 extended interfaces,
        111
      DOM Level 1 interfaces and ex
        ceptions, 109–110
    Web links for, 148–149
    XML DOM parsers, 108
    See also DOM Level 1 Core interfaces;
      DOM tree
DOM Level 1 Core interfaces, 109–110,
    399–415
    basic terms in DOM, 399–400
      DOMString type, 400
      interface, exception, and object,
        399
    extended interfaces, 111, 413–415
      CDATASection, 413
      DocumentType, 413–414
      Entity, 414–415
      EntityReference, 415
      Notation, 414
      ProcessingInstruction, 415
    fundamental interfaces, 400–413
      Attr, 411
      CharacterData, 409–410
      Comment, 413
      Document, 402–404
      DocumentFragment, 402
      DOMException, 400–401
      DOMImplementation, 401–402
      Element, 411–412
      NamedNodeMap, 408–409
      Node, 404–407
      NodeList, 408
      Text, 413
DOM tree
    creating
      for client-side shopping cart,
        133–134
      for XML document, 114–118
    loading XML document into, 133
    processing, 119–131
      Attr node, 130–131
      element node, 127–130
      NodeList interface, 125–127
      nodes, 120–125
      reference to document root ele-
        ment, 119–120
      reference to DOM tree, 119
    representing XML document in,
      111–113
    retrieving individual nodes in
      NodeList interface, 126–127

saving, 118
traversing all nodes creating order
    form, 135–136
XML document reference to, 119
DOMException interface, 400–401
DOMImplementation interface, 401–402
downloading
    documentation and Help files for XML
      Parser, 38
    and installing
      IE tools, 393–394
      XML version checker, 395–396
    Microsoft XML Parser, 36–37
    SQL Server support for Updategrams,
      198
    XML support features for SQL Server,
      197–198
DTD (Document Type Definition), 11–18
    data types support by XDR schema,
      424, 425
    for decks, 325
    defined, 13
    document structure defined with,
      11–15
    as external file, 16–18
    internal, 15–16, 291
    shortcomings of schemas, 291–292
    valid XML documents, 18
    validating document against in
      Internet Explorer, 34
    XML Schema and limitations of, 22–23
    as XML standard, 3

E

ebXML protocol, 3
editors for XML, 39
Element interface, 411–412
element node
    DOM, 127–130
      illustrated, 127
      names of, 127–128
      relating to other, 128–129
      retrieving information from refer-
        enced attributes, 129–130
    XML, 47–48
elements
    adding to order form, 136
    binding element, 356–357
    <card>, 325
    choosing between attributes and,
      19–21
    closing, 9
    copying XML, 91–92
    creating with <xsl:element>, 94–95
    defining and declaring XML, 309

empty, 6
illustrated, 6
mapping columns to, 214
message, 355
nesting, 9, 211–213
paragraph and anchor, 326
prefixes used in XML source and XSLT
    template, 101
service, 357
<soap:address>, 386–387
<sql:header>, 246
<sql:param>, 246
<sql:query>, 244
types, 355
<updg:sync>, 263–264
WML, 325
XDR, 417–418
XML attributes vs., 19–21
<xsd:include>, 312
<xsd:sequence>, 299
XSLT, 74, 79–87
    recursive descent operation (//), 82
    <xsl:apply-templates>, 82–84
    <xsl:attribute>, 92–94
    <xsl:comment>, 101–102
    <xsl:copy> and <xsl:copy-of>,
       91–92
    <xsl:element>, 94–95
    <xsl:for-each>, 80
    <xsl:if>, 84–86
    <xsl:output>, 95–97
    <xsl:stylesheet> root, 71
    <xsl:template>, 80
    <xsl:text>, 98–99
    <xsl:value-of>, 80
    <xsl:variable>, 87
    See also root element
ELEMENTS specification for FOR XML
    clause, 204
empty elements, 6
emulators
    displaying WML deck on, 324
    for testing WML applications, 329–330
end tag, 6
entities
    defining custom, 10–11
    special characters represented by,
       9–10
Entity extended interface, 414–415
EntityReference extended interface, 415
error handling, 179–182
    ADO Error object and Errors
       collection, 180
    browser displays with and without,
       182
    error checking in ASP script, 180–182

errors overwriting COM object in use,
    368
Internet Explorer messages for failed
    DTD validation, 35
SAX, 281–283
Updategram and possible errors,
    260–261
Error object, 179, 180
errorCheck.html, 182
Errors collection, 179, 180
event driven programming of SAX, 269
exception specification for DOM Level 1
    Core, 399
Execute method
    of Command object, querying data-
       base with, 171–172
    of Connection object
       CommandTypeEnum values of,
          158
       ExecuteOptionEnum values, 159
ExecuteOptionEnum values of Execute
    method, 159
expressions
    XPath, 42–43
       Boolean, 42
       node-set, 43
       numeric, 42–43
       string, 43
Extensible Data Reduced (XDR)
    Schema Language, 293
Extensible HTML (XHTML), 4
Extensible Stylesheet Language
    Transformation. *See* XSLT
external DTD, 16–18

F

file format for SQL statement results, 200,
    202
File Types dialog box (IIS 5.0), 327
files
    adding additional information to
       browscap.ini, 341–342
    DTD as external, 16–18
    generating WSDL, WSML, and
       Listener, 368–378
    Help, 38
    loading encoded characters, 23–27
    saving
       DOM object as text, 118
       in NotePad, 39
       template as XML, 243
       See also sample listings
Flags parameter, 230–231
flight information system form, 378
flight scheduler, 360, 361

Flights.xsl, 382
FlightsInfo.asp, 376–377
FlightsInfo Web service
    components needed for, 363
    database structure of, 363
    function to search for flights, 365–366
    illustrated, 362
    XML result string with matching flight
        information, 366–367
FlightsInfo.wsdl, 374–375
FlightsInfo.wsml, 375–376
FlightsInfoSystem Web service, 378
FOR XML AUTO extension, 210–218
    about queries with, 210–211
    alias names with, 213
    computed columns with, 214–215
    GROUP BY and aggregate functions
        with, 215–217
    hierarchy of nested XML elements
        with, 211–213
    mapping columns to elements, 214
    retrieving binary data with, 217–218
FOR XML clause
    FOR XML AUTO extension, 210–218
        about queries with, 210–211
        alias names with, 213
        computed columns with, 214–215
        GROUP BY and aggregate
            functions with, 215–217
        hierarchy of nested XML elements
            with, 211–213
        mapping columns to elements, 214
        retrieving binary data with,
            217–218
    FOR XML EXPLICIT extension,
        218–228
        formulating query with, 218–221
        processing of universal table,
            221–222
        using directives, 225–228
    FOR XML RAW extension, 204–210
        changing default attribute names,
            205–206
        requesting XML-Data schema, 210
        retrieving binary data, 207–210
        row retrieval with, 204–205
        using GROUP BY and aggregate
            functions, 206–207
    specifications for, 204
    syntax of SELECT statement with,
        203–204
    XML modes for, 203
FOR XML EXPLICIT extension, 218–228
    formulating query with, 218–221
    processing of universal table, 221–222
    using directives, 225–228

FOR XML RAW extension, 204–210
    changing default attribute names,
        205–206
    requesting XML-Data schema, 210
    retrieving binary data, 207–210
    row retrieval with, 204–205
    using GROUP BY and aggregate
        functions, 206–207
functions
    XPath, 58–65
        Boolean, 59–60
        node-set type, 60
        number, 60–62
        overview, 58
        string, 63–65
    XSLT, 87–90
        format pattern string controlling
            output, 90
        sample listing using XPath
            functions, 88–89
        table of, 68

G

general layout of XDR, 418–419
General tab (New Virtual Directory
        Properties dialog box), 237
grammars for XML, 2, 4
graphics retrieval with XML data,
        207–209
grid format, 200, 201
GROUP BY clause
    with FOR XML RAW, 206–207
    nested queries with FOR XML AUTO,
        215–217
grouping attributes in XML Schema,
        310–311

H

hdoc parameter, 230
Help files, 38
HTML (Hypertext Markup Language)
    code generated by XSLT transformation
        in Internet Explorer, 76–78
    generated by Book.asp sample listing,
        104–105
    posting templates through HTML
        form, 253–256
    roots of XML and, 1
    XML vs., 4–5
HTML.xsl stylesheet
    how document transformed by, 76–78
    listing of, 73–74
HTTP (HyperText Transport Protocol)
    access to SQL Server, 235–257

creating virtual root to expose database, 235
direct URL queries, 241–243
IIS Virtual Directory Management for SQL Server Utility, 235–241
posting templates, 252–257
specifying XPath query in template, 251–252
template queries, 243–248
XPath queries, 248–251
cross-platform compatibility and, 351–352
SOAP messages and, 348, 349
HTTP_USER_AGENT variable, 336, 337
Hypertext Markup Language. *See* HTML
HyperText Transport Protocol. *See* HTTP

I

IIS. *See* Microsoft Internet Information Server
IIS Virtual Directory Management for SQL Server Utility, 235–241
Allow URL queries option, 239, 241
creating virtual directory in, 237–241
invoking, 235–236
See also Microsoft Internet Information Server
insertAuthor.html, 266–267
inserting data in Updategram, 258–259
installing
IE tools, 393–394
Microsoft XSL ISAPI, 338–339
XML Parser in side-by-side or replace mode, 396–397
XML version checker, 395–396
interfaces
DOM Level 1 Core, 109–110, 399–415
for SAX supported in MSXML3, 278
specification for DOM Level 1 Core, 399
See also specific interfaces
internal DTD, 15–16, 291
Internet Explorer. *See* Microsoft Internet Explorer
Internet Web services, 350–352
ISAPI. *See* Microsoft XSL ISAPI
IVBSAXErrorHandler interface, 283

J

JAXP parser, 30

L

languages
DOM's platform- and language-neutral qualities, 107
subset of XPath implemented in SQL Server, 249
See also specific languages
linking schemas, 312–313
loading
content into Stream object, 178
XML data in DOM instance, 117–118
XML document
to be processed by Visual Basic, 271–272
into DOM tree, 133
into memory with OPENXML provider, 229
location path, 50–58
arithmetic operators, 54
axes, 54–58
comparative operators, 53
examples of, 51
location steps, 52
logical operators, 54
node-test function, 52
operators in complex predicate expressions, 54
predicates used with, 53
using predicates, 52–53
location steps, 52

M

Magazine.xml, 293–294
Magazine.xsd, 294
mapping columns to elements, 214
MDAC (Microsoft Data Access Components), 151–152
message element, 355
methods
CharacterData, 410
for contentHandler Visual Basic project, 275–276
Document interface, 403–404
DOMImplementation, 402
Element, 411–412
exposed by Node interface, 407
NamedNodeMap, 409
for Node Interface (XML Parser), 124
NodeList, 408
of Recordset object, 164–166

methods (*continued*)
 supported by IVBSAXContentHandler interface in MSXML3, 280
 supported by IVBSAXErrorHandler interface, 283
microbrowsers, 320, 335–337
Microsoft
 data sources and names of OLE DB providers, 153
 implementing SAX2 as COM object, 278
 Universal Data Access strategy, 151–154
 XDR Schema Language, 293
 See also specific applications
Microsoft Active Server Pages (ASP)
 ASP listener file, 376–377
 complete listing of shopping cart script, 148
 defined, 102
 server-side programming of shopping cart, 145–148
 server-side transformation in, 102–105
  of XML document to WML, 334–335
Microsoft Data Access Components (MDAC), 151–152
Microsoft Internet Explorer
 ensuring use of MSXML3 by, 37
 error checking in ASP script, 182
 formatting XML information into HTML format, 256
 HTTP input form, 254
 performing XSL Transformation in, 102
 retrieving book information with template sent via HTTP form, 254
 transforming XML document with XSLT in, 75–76
 using XSLT-compliant stylesheets in version 5.0, 72
 validation tools, 34–35, 393–394
 viewing XML documents in, 32–33
 XML DOM parser in, 108
 XPath queries in URL, 250, 251
Microsoft Internet Information Server (IIS) 5.0
 installing XSL ISAPI filter in, 339–340
 securing Web server, 389–390
 setting MIME types in, 326–327
Microsoft Mobile Explorer (MME), 337
Microsoft Personal Web Server, 327
Microsoft SOAP Toolkit 2.0
 developing Web services with, 358–359

generating WSDL, WSML, and Listener files, 368–378
 ASP listener file, 376–377
 selecting services to expose, 371
 setting path to store WSDL and WSML files, 373
 setting up listener and XSD type, 371–372
 WSDL file, 373–375
 wsdlgen utility, 358, 369
 WSML file, 375–376
 using wizard, 370–373
Microsoft SQL Server 2000, 197–268
 accessing with HTTP, 235–257
  creating virtual root to expose database, 235
  direct URL queries, 241–243
  IIS Virtual Directory Management for SQL Server Utility, 235–241
  posting templates, 252–257
  specifying XPath query in template, 251–252
  template queries, 243–248
  XPath queries, 248–251
 creating prepared SQL statement, 173–174
 downloading XML support features for, 197–198
 examples in BooksCatalog database, 198–199
 persisting changes using Updategram, 257–268
  annotated XDR schema in, 264–266
  before-after pair for multiple transactions, 262–263
  inserting, deleting, and updating, 258–259
  multiple <updg:sync> blocks, 263–264
  overview, 257–258
  possible errors, 260–261
  posting Updategram, 266–268
  reviewing code of Updategram, 259–260
 providing rowset data with OPENXML provider, 228–235
  example of using OPENXML, 232–234
  loading XML document into memory, 229
  overview, 228–229
  removing in-memory XML representation, 232
  unconsumed columns, 234–235
  writing Transact-SQL statements with OPENXML, 230–232

retrieving and transforming rowset data into XML data, 203–228
  FOR XML AUTO extension, 210–218
  FOR XML EXPLICIT extension, 218–228
  FOR XML RAW extension, 204–210
  requesting query results in XML-Data schema, 210
  syntax and modes for FOR XML clause, 203–204
schema for Schedules table, 363, 364
SQL Query Analyzer
  executing SQL statement and specifying results format, 200–203
  invoking, 199–200
subset of XPath implemented in, 249
support for XML in, 197
Web links for, 268
Microsoft VBScript, displaying DOM object in message box, 115
Microsoft Visual Basic
  creating
    COM object to expose as Web service, 364–367
    Web service consumer-SOAP client, 378–379
  using SAX in, 270–276
    adding error-handling class module for SAX, 281
    adding reference to MSXML3, 270
    creating new project, 270
    error message display, 283
    implementing method in abstract classes, 272–275
    loading XML document to be processed, 271–272
    methods in IVBSAXContentHandler, 275–276
    running program, 276
  validating XML document against XML Schema with, 295–296
Microsoft Windows 2000 ODBC drivers, 152
Microsoft XDR (XML-Data Reduced), 22, 417–428
  annotated schema in Updategram, 264–266
  annotations, 427–428
  basic elements in, 417–418
  data types, 424–427
  general layout, 418–419
  overview, 417
  as solution to DTD limitations, 292

specification of content model, 419–424
  content attribute, 420
  default attribute, 423
  minLength and maxLength attributes, 421–422
  minOccurs and maxOccurs attributes, 420–422
  model attribute, 419
  order attribute, 422–423
  required attribute, 423–424
Microsoft XML Parser 3.0
  about, 31
  adding reference to Visual Basic project, 270
  checking installed versions of, 394–395
  DOM support in, 108–111
    DOM Level 1 extended interfaces, 111
    DOM Level 1 interfaces and exceptions, 109–110
  downloading and installing XML version checker, 395–396
  Help files for, 38
  lacks support for W3C XML Schema, 295
  methods for Node Interface, 124
  obtaining and installing, 36–37
  ProgID modes and, 396–397
  saving files in NotePad, 39
  SAX, 278–281
    interfaces supported in MSXML3, 278
    methods supported by IVBSAXContentHandler interface, 280
    properties supported by IVBSAXContentHandler interface, 280
  using, 36–38
  XSLT processor, 70
  XSLT support in, 72
  See also Microsoft XML Parser 4.0; XML parsers
Microsoft XML Parser 4.0, 295–299
  rearranging schema, 298–299
  sequencing, 299
  XML document definition in XML Schema, 296–297
  XML Schema validation in, 295–299
  See also Microsoft XML Parser 3.0
Microsoft XSL ISAPI, 337–345
  adding additional browser information, 341–342

Microsoft XSL ISAPI (*continued*)
  installing ISAPI filter in IIS, 339–340
  obtaining and installing, 338–339
  registering DLL for, 339
  rewriting XML document with,
      342–344
  selecting stylesheet for XML docu-
      ments with, 337–338
  testing installation, 340–341
MIME types
  list of, 326
  setting, 326–327
    under IIS 5.0, 326–327
    under Microsoft Personal Web
      Server, 327
minLength and maxLength attributes,
    421–422
minOccurs and maxOccurs attributes,
    297, 420–422
MME (Microsoft Mobile Explorer), 337
model attribute, 419
MSXML3. *See* Microsoft XML Parser 3.0
MSXML4. *See* Microsoft XML Parser 4.0

N

NamedNodeMap interface, 408–409
names
  alias names with FOR XML AUTO
      clause, 213
  changing default attribute names with
      FOR XML RAW extension,
      205–206
  of DOM element node, 127–128
  of DOM node, 120–121
namespace node, 49
namespaces, 27–29
  differences in template and XML
      source prefixes, 101
  transforming with XSL, 99–101
  in XSL(T), 72
nesting elements, 9, 211–213
Netscape Navigator, 35–36
New file dialog box (XMLSpy), 315
New Virtual Directory Properties dialog
    box, 237, 238, 239
Node interface, 124, 404–407
NodeList interface, 125–127, 408
  APIs for processing DOM tree,
      125–127
  retrieving individual nodes in,
      126–127
  size of, 126
nodeproperties.html, 122–123

nodes
  attribute, 48
  comment, 50
  DOM, 120–125
    features and functions of, 123–125
    name, types, and values of,
        120–122
    properties of, 121–123
    retrieving individual nodes in
        NodeList interface, 126–127
  element, 47–48
  namespace, 49
  PI, 49–50
  properties of XPath, 46
  root, 47
  text, 48–49
node-set expressions (XPath), 43
node-set type function (XPath), 60
node-test function, 52
nodeType of Node interface
  constants for, 405
  nodeName and nodeValue deter-
      mined by, 406
Notation extended interface, 414
NotePad, 39
number function (XPath), 60–62
numeric expressions, in XPath, 42–43

O

ODBC (Open Database Connectivity),
    152
OLE DB, 152–154
  architecture of, 152–153
  data sources and providers for, 153
  function of, 152
Open Database Connectivity (ODBC),
    152
opening Stream object, 176–177
OPENXML provider, 228–235
  loading XML document into memory,
      229
  overview, 228–229
  parameters for
    Flags, 230–231
    hdoc, 230
    SchemaDeclaration expression,
        231–232
    TableName, 232
    WITH clause, 231
    XPathPattern expression, 230
  removing in-memory XML represen-
      tation, 232
  syntax for, 230

unconsumed columns, 234–235
Updategrams vs., 258
using, 232–234
writing Transact-SQL statements with
OPENXML, 230–232
operators
arithmetic, 54
comparative, 53
in complex predicate expressions, 54
logical, 54
Options dialog box (SQL Query
Analyzer), 203
Oracle XML Parser for Java, 30, 108
order attribute, 422–423
order form
adding elements to, 136
for client-side shopping cart, 134–136
traversing all node of DOM tree in creating, 135–136
origin server, 320
output
controlling XSLT stylesheet, 95–97
format pattern string controlling, 90

P

Pages attribute, 131
paragraph and anchor elements for
decks, 326
parameter placeholders, 173
parameters
ADO parameter direction indicators,
174
of direct URL queries, 242
OPENXML provider
Flags, 230–231
hdoc, 230
SchemaDeclaration expression,
231–232
TableName, 232
WITH clause, 231
XPathPattern expression, 230
template, 243–244
PCDATA (Parsed Character Data), 19
PDAs. *See* WML
persisting changes using Updategram,
257–268
annotated XDR schema in, 264–266
before-after pair for multiple trans
actions, 262–263
inserting, deleting, and updating,
258–259
multiple <updg:sync> blocks, 263–264
overview, 257–258
possible errors, 260–261
posting Updategram, 266–268
reviewing code of Updategram,
259–260
persisting SQL statements, 173–174
Personal Web Server, 327
PI node, 49–50
PI (processing instruction)
defined, 7
XML PI for WML deck, 325
for XSLT denotes XML document, 71
portType element, 356
posting
templates, 252–257
invoking templates through URL
specification, 252–253
through HTML form, 253–256
through XMLHTTP object, 256–257
Updategrams, 266–268
predicates, 52–53
defined, 52
location paths using, 53
prefixes
for XML and XSLT, 101
for XML Schema, 294
prepared SQL statements, creating,
173–174
primitive data types, 300
processing instruction. *See* PI
ProcessingInstruction extended interface, 415
properties
Attr, 411
CharacterData, 409
Command Text, 173
Document interface, 402
DocumentType, 413–414
DOM node, 121–123
Element, 411
Entity, 415
NamedNodeMap, 408
Node interface, 404–405
NodeList, 408
Notation, 414
ProcessingInstruction, 415
Recordset object, 162–164
supported by IVBSAXContentHandler
interface, 280
protocols
ensuring Web service cross-platform
compatibility, 350, 351–352,
391
SOAP, 347
types of XML, 2, 3
WAP Protocol stack, 321–322
See also SOAP

Q

queries
    computed columns with FOR XML AUTO clause, 214–215
    direct URL, 241–243
    with Execute method of Command object, 171–172
    formulating with FOR XML EXPLICIT, 218–221
    ordering XML elements with FOR XML AUTO clause, 211–213
    records in database with Recordset object, 166–168
    requesting XML-Data schema, 210
    retrieving binary data with FOR XML RAW extension, 207–210
    tabulating results of with GROUP BY function, 206–207
    template, 243–248
        about, 243–244
        containing execution of stored procedure, 246–248
        containing SQL query, 244–246
        posting templates, 252–257
    XPath, 248–252
        about, 248–250
        specifying in template, 251–252
        specifying in URL, 248, 249–251
        subset of language implemented in SQL Server 2000, 249

R

reading content from Stream object, 178–179
readyState property, 116
rearranging schema, 298–299
Record object
    about, 175
    collection object of, 155
records
    accessing in data source with Execute method, 157–159
    deleting from database, 170
    inserting in database, 168–169
    querying with Recordset object, 166–168
Recordset object, 161–170
    about, 161–162
    collection objects of, 155
    deleting record from database with, 170
    inserting record in database, 168–169
    properties and methods of, 162–166
    querying records in database with, 166–168

recursive descent operation (//), 82
redefining definitions, 312–313
referencing SOAP type library, 379
re-initializing shopping cart, 141–142
repeating patterns, locating, 80–81
required attribute, 423–424
root element
    DOM reference to document, 119–120
    well-formed documents and, 8
    WML, 325
    of XLST stylesheet, 71
root node, 47
rows
    modifying number of characters in, 202–203
    retrieving with FOR XML RAW extension, 204–205
rowset data
    providing from XML using OPENXML provider, 228–235
        example of using OPENXML, 232–234
        loading XML document into memory, 229
        overview, 228–229
        removing in-memory XML representation, 232
        unconsumed columns, 234–235
        writing Transact-SQL statements with OPENXML, 230–232
    retrieving and transforming into XML data, 203–228
        FOR XML AUTO extension, 210–218
        FOR XML EXPLICIT extension, 218–228
        FOR XML RAW extension, 204–210
        syntax and modes for FOR XML clause, 203–204

S

sample listings
    adding codes
        to form_load event of Books.xml, 272
        to selected methods of IVBSAXContentHandler, 274–275
    ASP shopping cart script, 148
    Bestpicks.xml document and tree representation, 112–113
    Books1.asp, 336–337
    Books.asp, 103, 334–335
    Books.xml, 271, 331–332
        converted to HTML, 332–333

document for XSLT
transformation, 73
BooksISBN.xml, 284
booksSchema.xml, 265
config.xml, 343
displaying book title based on ISBN,
285–286
DOM client-side shopping cart,
142–144
DTD lacks support for data types,
291–292
external DTD file, 16
Flights.xsl, 382
FlightsInfo.asp, 376–377
FlightsInfo.wsdl, 374–375
FlightsInfo.wsml, 375–376
function to search for flights, 365–366
grouping attributes in schema,
310–311
HTML generated by Book.asp,
104–105
HTML.xsl stylesheet, 73–74
insertAuthor.html, 266–267
Magazine1.xsd, 298
Magazine.xml, 293–294
Magazine.xsd, 294
modifying Books.xml document, 342
multipleSyncGram.xml, 263–264
NamespaceApressBooks.xml, 28
nodeproperties.html, 122–123
poster.html, 256–257
schemaGram.xml, 264
simpleGram.xml, 258–259
of SOAP, 348–349
SOAP message transported by HTTP
request, 348
response, 349
storing information in XML and XML
Schema, 304–307
Template.xml, 15
with external DTD file, 17
TourGuides.xml, 79
Unicode.xml, 26
using XPath functions, 88–89
of well-formed document, 7
WML.xsl, 334
WMLDeck.wml, 323
WSDL file, 353–354
XML document
(1), 12
(2), 12
with GB2312 encoding, 23
with internal DTD, 291
and schema for mixed content,
307–308
XML result string with matching flight
information, 366–367

<xsl:apply-templates> element to
match other templates, 82–84
<xsl:for-each> to locate repeating pat-
terns, 80–81
<xsl:if> for decision making, 84–86
<xsl:output>, 95–96
XSLT stylesheet, 71, 73–74
SaveOptionsEnum values for SaveToFile
method, 179
saving
content of Stream object, 179
DOM tree, 118
XML documents containing special
characters, 27
XML files in NotePad, 39
SAX (Simple API for XML), 31
alternative to DOM, 108, 269–270, 277,
289
error handling, 281–283
methods supported by
IVBSAXErrorHandler interface,
283
event driven programming of, 269
examples using, 284–286
limitations of, 286–287
in MSXML3, 278–281
interfaces supported in MSXML3,
278
methods supported by
IVBSAXContentHandler interface, 280
properties supported by
IVBSAXContentHandler interface, 280
processing XML document with,
276–277
using with Visual Basic, 270–276
adding reference to MSXML3, 270
creating new project, 270
implementing method in abstract
classes, 272–275
loading XML document to be
processed, 271–272
methods in
IVBSAXContentHandler,
275–276
running program, 276
Web links, 290
when to use, 288–289
SAX processing model, 277
SAXON XSLT processor, 70
Schedules table, 363, 364
Schema for Object Oriented XML (SOX),
22
SchemaDeclaration expression, 231–232
schemaGram.xml, 264
schemas. *See* XML Schema

security
    setting for virtual directory, 237–238
    with template queries, 245
    Web services, 388–390
        about, 388
        modifying consumer, 390
        securing Web server for case study
            example, 389–390
SELECT statements
    executing and displaying results
        in grid format, 201
        in text format, 202
    retrieving XML data using, 203–204
    transformation of universal table into
        XML document, 218
sequencing, 299
servers
    displaying response of, 141
    origin, 320
    passing DOM object to HTTP, 140–141
    server-side transformation of XML
        document to WML in ASP,
        334–335
    Web services on, 352
    writing ASP Stream object to client
        from, 183, 184
server-side applications
    DOM shopping cart, 145–148
        receiving DOM object from client,
        146
    shopping cart
        complete listing of ASP script, 148
        generating response to client, 147
        retrieving contents of, 146–147
    XSL transformation in ASP, 102–105
service element, 357
Settings tab (New Virtual Directory
    Properties dialog box), 239
SGML (Standard Generalized Markup
    Language), 1
shopping cart
    client-side application, 131–144
        application requirements for, 132
        checking out, 139–142
        complete script for, 142–144
        creating DOM tree for shopping
            cart, 133–134
        creating order form, 134–136
        initialization tasks for, 132–133
        invoking loading of order form, 134
        loading XML document into DOM
            tree, 133
        updating, 136–139
    server-side application, 145–148
        complete listing of ASP script, 148
        generating response to client, 147

overview, 145
    receiving DOM object from client,
        146
    retrieving shopping cart contents,
        146–147
    setting content type for client,
        145–146
Simple API for XML. *See* SAX
Simple Object Access Protocol. *See* SOAP
simple types
    deriving new, 303
    enumeration and, 302
    restricting range with, 301–302
    in XML Schema, 301
<soap:address> element, 386–387
SOAP (Simple Object Access Protocol),
    347–391
    about, 347–348
    case study for Web service, 359–388
        compiling COM object, 367–368
        consuming Web service, 381–382
        creating COM object, 364–367
        creating instance of SOAPClient,
        380
        creating Web service consumer-
        SOAP client, 378–379
        database structure, 363–364
        existing solutions, 361–362
        generating WSDL, WSML, and
        Listener files, 368–378
        how SOAP Toolkit works, 384–385
        initializing SOAPClient object,
        380–381
        proposed Web service, 362–363
        referencing SOAP type library, 379
        scenario for, 359–361
        stylesheet for XSL transformation,
        382–383
        testing Web service, 383–384
        tracing SOAP messages, 385–388
    changing technologies and, 347
    components of messages, 349–350
    defined, 3
    intercommunication and interoper-
        ability of, 350, 391
    sample listings of, 348–349
    Web links, 390
    Web services, 350–357
        about, 350–352
        binding element, 356–357
        consuming, 358, 381–382
        creating, 357
        developing with SOAP Toolkit 2.0,
        358–359
        message element, 355
        portType element, 356

service element, 357
types element, 355
WSDL, 352–354
Web services security, 388–390
about, 388
modifying consumer, 390
securing Web server for case study
example, 389–390
SOAP Toolkit 2.0 wizard
how it works, 384–385
selecting services to expose, 371
setting path to store WSDL and WSML
files, 373
setting up listener and XSD type,
371–372
using, 370
SOAPClient
creating instance of, 380
initializing, 380–381
SOX (Schema for Object Oriented XML),
22
special characters
represented by entities, 9–10
saving XML documents containing, 27
sp_xml_prepareddocument system
stored procedure, 229
sp_xml_removedocument system stored
procedure, 229, 232
<sql:header> element, 246
<sql:param> element, 246
<sql:query> element, 244
SQL Query Analyzer
executing SQL statement and specifying results format, 200–203
illustrated, 200
invoking, 199–200
modifying number of characters in
row, 202–203
using OPENXML provider, 232–234
See also Microsoft SQL Server 2000
Standard Generalized Markup Language
(SGML), 1
start tag, 6
Stored Procedure Properties dialog box
(SQL Server Enterprise
Manager), 247
stored procedures
sp_xml_prepareddocument system,
229
sp_xml_removedocument system,
229, 232
template queries containing, 246–248
stream
forming ADO objects into XML, 195
saving DOM object as text file, 118

Stream object, 155, 175–179
about, 175
closing, 179
creating, 176
loading content into, 178
opening, 176–177
reading content from, 178–179
saving content of, 179
sending from client to Web server, 184
writing from server to client, 183, 184
StreamOpenOptionsEnum values for
Open method, 177
string expressions (XPath), 43
string function (XPath), 63–65
strings
braces convert name() result to, 94
searching for returning flights,
365–366
using as namespace, 29
syntax
abbreviated XPath, 65–66
components of SOAP messages,
349–350
general layout of XDR, 418–419
of location steps, 52
for removing XML representation
from memory, 232
rules of well-formed documents, 6–11
attribute values in quotes, 8
case sensitivity, 9
defining custom entities, 10–11
elements closed and nested properly, 9
PI (processing instruction), 7
root element, 8
sample listing, 7
special characters represented by
entities, 9–10
of SELECT statement with FOR XML
clause, 203–204
for XML, 6

T

TableName parameter, 232
tags
start and end, 6
XSLT stylesheet, 74
template parameter, 243–244
template queries, 243–248
about templates and, 243–244
containing execution of stored
procedure, 246–248
posting templates, 252–257

template queries (*continued*)
    invoking templates through URL
        specification, 252–253
        through HTML form, 253–256
        through XMLHTTP object, 256–257
    template containing SQL query,
        244–246
    XPath queries, 248
        specifying in template, 251–252
    See also templates
Template.xml sample listing, 15, 17
templates
    defined, 243
    posting, 252–257
        invoking through URL specific
        ation, 252–253
        through HTML form, 253–256
        through XMLHTTP object, 256–257
    for XML document, 316
    See also template queries
terminology for XML, 6
testing
    Web service, 383–384
    WML applications, 329–330
    XSL ISAPI installation, 340–341
text
    inserting with XSLT, 98–99
    saving DOM object as, 118
    specifying SQL statement results as
        formatted, 200, 201–202
Text interface, 413
text node, 48–49
tokenization, 328–329
tools
    in SOAP Toolkit, 359
    validation
        for DTD in Internet Explorer, 34–35
        for XML Schema, 314–317
TourGuides.xml sample listing, 79
Trace Setup dialog box (SOAP Toolkit),
    386
tracing SOAP messages, 385–388
transforming document structure with
    XSLT, 90–102
    controlling output, 95–97
    copying XML elements, 91–92
    creating
        attributes, 92–94
        elements, 94–95
    generating comments, 101–102
    inserting text, 98–99
    transforming namespaces, 99–101
tree model
    DOM tree
        creating from XML document in
        memory, 117–118
        processing, 119–131

representing XML document in,
        111–113
    saving, 118
    XML document reference to, 119
  for XML documents
    tracing XSLT transformations with,
        79
    with XPath data model, 44–46
types element, 355
types of DOM node, 120–121

U

unconsumed columns, 234–235
Unicode
    Unicode.xml sample listing, 26
    XML encoding and, 23–27
Uniform Resource Locators. *See* URLs
UNION operator in SQL query, 219
Universal Data Access strategy, 151
    Microsoft Data Access Components
        and, 151–152
    objective of ADO in, 153, 154
    OLE DB, 152–154
    Open Database Connectivity, 152
universal table, 218
    associating data columns with univer-
        sal table column name,
        219–220
    directives
        in column name of, 222–224
        examples of, 225–228
        mapping columns and XML final
        data with, 224
        specifying attributes in, 223
    examples of, 221, 222
    processing, 221–222
Update.html
    listing books, 187–188
    reducing prices of books, 189–190
    submitting updated prices to Web
        server, 190–192
    user interface for, 185–187
    Web page for updating client book
        prices, 185
Updategram, 257–268
    annotated XDR schema in, 264–266
    before-after pair for multiple trans
        actions, 262–263
    downloading SQL Server support for,
        198
    inserting, deleting, and updating,
        258–259
    multiple <updg:sync> blocks in,
        263–264
    overview, 257–258
    possible errors, 260–261

posting, 266–268
reviewing code of, 259–260
updating
    book prices, 183–194
        BookServer.asp script on Web
            server, 192–194
        data store for, 185
        illustration of events in, 183
        listing books, 187–188
        overview, 183–184
        reducing prices of books, 189–190
        submitting updated prices to Web
            server, 190–192
        user interface, 185–187
        Web page for client, 185
    data in Updategram, 258–259
    DOM client-side shopping cart,
        136–139
<updg:sync> element, 263–264
URLs (Uniform Resource Locators)
    direct queries via, 241–243
    displaying data source for DOM
        object in VBScript message
        box, 117
    invoking template queries through,
        252–253
    in namespaces, 29
    specifying XPath queries in, 248,
        249–251
user interface
    for updating book prices, 185–187
    of Web service, 351
user requirements for client-side shop-
    ping cart, 132
userID attribute, 140
UTF-8/UTF-16 character-encoding, 23

V

valid XML documents, 18
validation tools
    for DTD in Internet Explorer, 34–35
    for XML Schema, 314–317
variables in XSLT, 87
vendor development of WML, 322
version dependent ProgID modes,
    396–397
versions
    checking installed XML Parser,
        394–395
    downloading and installing XML
        version checker, 395–396
    namespaces for XSL(T), 72

of SAX, 269
SOAP, 348–349
WAP, 323
XML Parser 3.0 documented in book,
    30
XSLT, 70
virtual directory
    creating in IIS Virtual Directory
        Management, 237–241
    security for, 237–238
Virtual Name Configuration dialog box,
    240
virtual root
    creating to expose database, 235
    direct URL queries, 241–243
Visual Basic. *See* Microsoft Visual Basic
VoiceXML (Voice Extensible Markup
    Language), 4

W

W3C (World Wide Web Consortium)
    adopts XML, 2
    DOM specifications, 107–108
    XML Schema vs. XML schemas, 292
WAP architecture, 319–322
    illustrated, 320
    roles of WAP gateway, 320
    WAP Protocol stack, 321–322
WAP browsers, 320, 335–337
WAP gateway, 320, 324
WAP Protocol stack, 321–322
WAP (Wireless Application Protocol)
    Forum, 319
.WBMP MIME string, 326
WBXML (WAP Binary XML format),
    328–329
Web browsers, 32–36
    differentiating WAP and, 335–337
    Internet Explorer, 32–35
    Netscape Navigator, 35–36
    performing XSL Transformation in,
        102
    testing XSL ISAPI installation, 340–341
    transforming XML document into
        HTML, 333
Web links
    ADO, 194–195
    for browscap.ini file, 344
    data types and parameter direction
        indicators, 174
    DOM, 148–149
    for DOM Level 1 Core interfaces, 399

Web links (*continued*)
  downloading
    and installing IE tools, 393–394
    and installing XML version
      checker, 395–396
    SQL Server support for
      Updategrams, 198
    XML Parser, 36–37, 38
    XML support for SQL Server,
      197–198
  for glossary of wireless network tech-
    nologies, 321
  links for XPath, 67
  Microsoft Data Access Components,
    152
  namespaces for XSL(T), 72
  for obtaining Microsoft XSL ISAPI, 338
  SAX, 290
  SOAP, 390
  for SQL Server 2000, 268
  useful links for XML, 39–40
  for WinHex editor, 329
  for WML, 345
  XML Schema, 318
  XSLT, 105
Web pages
  for updating client book prices, 185
  WAP devices and HTML, 323
Web server
  acknowledgment message to client
    browser for updated Recordset
    contents, 192
  BookServer.asp script, 192–194
    batch updating book prices, 194
    retrieving books, 194
  submitting updated prices to, 190–192
  updating book prices on, 184, 185
Web service consumer
  creating Web service consumer-SOAP
    client, 378–379
  defined, 353
  modifying Web services for security,
    390
  WSDL contract between Web service
    provider and, 352
  See also Web services
Web services, 350–357
  about, 350–352
  binding element, 356–357
  case study, 359–388
    scenario for, 359–361
  consuming, 358, 381–382
  creating, 357
    Web service consumer-SOAP
      client, 378–379
  developing with SOAP Toolkit 2.0,
    358–359
  message element, 355

portType element, 356
proposed, 362–363
security, 388–390
  about, 388
  modifying consumer, 390
  securing Web server for case study
    example, 389–390
service element, 357
testing, 383–384
types element, 355
WSDL, 352–354
Web Services Description Language. *See*
  WSDL
well-formed documents, 6–11
  attribute values in quotes, 8
  case sensitivity, 9
  defining custom entities, 10–11
  elements closed and nested properly, 9
  PI (processing instruction), 7
  root element, 8
  sample listing, 7
  special characters represented by
    entities, 9–10
WinHex editor, 329
Wireless Markup Language. *See* WML
wireless terminal, 320
WITH clause
  in OPENXML declarations, 231
  specifying SchemaDeclaration
    expression, 231–232
WML (Wireless Markup Language),
  319–345
  defined, 4
  emulators for testing applications,
    329–330
  Microsoft XSL ISAPI, 337–345
    adding additional browser infor-
      mation, 341–342
    installing ISAPI filter in IIS,
      339–340
    obtaining and installing, 338–339
    registering DLL for, 339
    rewriting XML document with,
      342–344
    selecting stylesheet for XML docu-
      ments with, 337–338
    testing installation, 340–341
  tailoring content with XML and XSLT,
    330–337
    differentiating Web and WAP
      browsers, 335–337
    displaying XML document on WAP
      device, 335
    illustrated, 31
    server-side transformation in ASP,
      334–335
    transforming XML into HTML and
      WML, 332–334

using XML for content, 330–332
understanding, 322–329
    history of vendor development, 322
    processing WML decks, 328
    rationale for WML, 323
    setting MIME type, 326–327
    structure of document-decks and
        cards, 323–326
    WBXML and tokenization, 328–329
WAP architecture, 319–322
    illustrated, 320
    roles of WAP gateway, 320
    WAP Protocol stack, 321–322
WAP Forum, 319
Web links, 345
See also decks
WML deck. *See* decks
WML root element, 325
.WML MIME string, 326
WMLDeck.wml, 323
.WMLS MIME string, 326
World Wide Web Consortium. *See* W3C
WSDL (Web Services Description
       Language), 352–354
    defining contract between Web ser-
       vice provider and consumer,
       352
    sample files in, 373–375
    setting path to store WSDL and WSML
       files, 373
    as XML-based document, 352
WSDL contract
    accessing, 381
    defining between Web service
       provider and consumer, 352
WSDL file, 373–375
wsdlgen utility
    about, 358
    generating WSDL, WSML, and
       Listener files, 368–378
    illustrated, 369
WSML (Web Service Meta Language) file,
       375–376

X

XALAN XSLT processor, 70
XDR (Extensible Data Reduced)
       Schema Language, 293
XDR (XML-Data Reduced). *See* Microsoft
       XDR
Xerces-C++ parser, 30, 108
XHTML (Extensible HTML), 4

XML (Extensible Markup Language),
       1–40
    about, 1
    adoption by W3C, 2
    CDATA and PCDATA, 18–19
    choosing between elements or attri-
       butes, 19–21
    document type definition, 11–18
        defining document structure with,
            11–15
        as external file, 16–18
        including within document, 15–16
        valid XML documents, 18
    downloading for SQL Server, 197–198
    editors, 39
    grammars for, 2, 4
    HTML vs., 4–5
    Microsoft XML Parser, 31, 36–38
    namespaces, 27–29
    protocols for, 2, 3
    requesting SQL query results in XML-
       Data schema, 210
    roots of HTML and, 1
    SOAP as XML-based protocol,
       347–348
    SOAP messages coded in, 349
    standards for, 2, 3
    syntactical rules of well-formed docu-
       ments, 6–11
        attribute values in quotes, 8
        case sensitivity, 9
        defining custom entities, 10–11
        elements closed and nested prop-
            erly, 9
        PI (processing instruction), 7
        root element, 8
        sample listing, 7
        special characters represented by
            entities, 9–10
    tailoring WML content with, 330–337
        differentiating Web and WAP
            browsers, 335–337
        displaying XML document on WAP
            device, 335
        illustrated, 31
        server-side transformation in ASP,
            334–335
        transforming XML into HTML and
            WML, 332–334
        using XML for content, 330–332
    terminology and syntax of, 6
    transforming with XSLT, 70
    uses and benefits of, 31
    Web browser support, 32–36

XML (*continued*)
    Internet Explorer, 32–35
    Netscape Navigator, 35–36
  Web links for, 39–40
  XML encoding and Unicode, 23–27
  XML parsers, 29–30
  XML schemas, 22–23
XML applications. *See* SOAP; WML
XML documents. *See* documents
XML DOM parsers, 108
XML editors, types of, 39
XML grammars, 2, 4
XML Parser. *See* Microsoft XML Parser 3.0
XML parsers
  about, 29–30
  listing of available, 30
  types of, 30
  See also Microsoft XML Parser 3.0
XML Path Language. *See* XPath
XML PI for decks, 325
XML RPC (Remote Procedure Calling)
    protocol, 3
XML Schema, 22–23
  data types, 300–309
    complex types, 303–309
    defining and declaring elements
      and attributes, 309
    derived, 300–301
    deriving new simple types, 303
    enumeration, 302
    primitive, 300
    restricting range with, 301–302
    simple types, 301
  documenting with <annotation>,
    313–314
  examples of, 293–294
  features ideally supported by XML
    schemas, 292
  groupings in, 310–311
  linking schemas and redefining
    definitions, 312–313
  specifications for, 293
  validating in MSXML4, 295–299
    rearranging schema, 298–299
    sequencing, 299
    XML document definition in XML
      Schema, 296–297
  validating with XMLSpy, 314–317
  Web links, 318
  XDR Schema, 293
  XML schema vs. W3C's, 292
XML schemas, 291–318
  examples of XML Schema, 293–294
  features ideally supported by, 292
  shortcomings of DTD schemas,
    291–292

W3C's XML Schema vs., 292
Web links, 318
XDR Schema, 293
See also XML Schema
XML-Data Reduced. *See* Microsoft XDR
XML-Data schema, 210
XMLDATA specification for FOR XML
    clause, 204
xmlinst.exe utility, 37
XMLSpy, 314–317
  creating
    XML document based on XML
      Schema, 315–316
    XML Schema in, 314–315
  template for XML document, 316
  using XML document to generate
    XML Schema, 316–317
  validating XML document, 316
  Web link for, 318
  window, 315
XPath (XML Path Language), 41–67
  abbreviated syntax, 65–66
  about, 41
  data model, 44–50
    attribute node, 48
    comment node, 50
    context, 50
    element node, 47–48
    namespace node, 49
    PI node, 49–50
    properties of nodes, 46
    representing XML document as
      tree, 44–46
    root node, 47
    text node, 48–49
  expressions, 42–43
    Boolean, 42
    node-set, 43
    numeric, 42–43
    string, 43
  functions, 58–65
    Boolean, 59–60
    node-set type, 60
    number, 60–62
    overview, 58
    string, 63–65
  location path, 50–58
    arithmetic operators, 54
    axes, 54–58
    comparative operators, 53
    examples of, 51
    location steps, 52
    logical operators, 54
    node-test function, 52
    operators in complex predicate
      expressions, 54

using predicates, 52–53
queries, 248–252
    about, 248–250
    specifying in template, 251–252
    specifying in URL, 248, 249–251
    subset of language implemented in
        SQL Server 2000, 249
Web links for, 67
XSLT and, 41, 69
XPathPattern expression, 230
<xsd:include> element, 312
<xsd:sequence> element, 299
XSD (XML Schema Definition Language),
    292
<xsl:apply-templates> element, 82–84
<xsl:attribute> element, 92–94
<xsl:comment> element, 101–102
<xsl:copy> and <xsl:copy-of> elements,
    91–92
<xsl:element>, 94–95
<xsl:for-each> element, 80
<xsl:if> element, 84–86
<xsl:output> element, 95–97
    to control stylesheet output, 95–96
    to suppress XML PI, 96
<xsl:stylesheet> root element, 71
<xsl:template> element, 80
<xsl:text> element, 98–99
<xsl:value-of> element, 80
<xsl:variable> element, 87
XSL ISAPI. *See* Microsoft XSL ISAPI
XSL-FO (XSL Formatting Objects), XSLT
    and, 69
XSLT (Extensible Stylesheet Language
    Transformation), 69–105
    about, 31, 70–72
    adding to XML document, 73–78
        adding stylesheet to document, 75
        example document, 73
        example stylesheet, 71, 73–74
        how stylesheet transforms docu-
            ment, 76–78
        transformation by Internet
            Explorer, 75–76
    advantages of format transformation
        with XML document, 269

client-side versus server-side transfor-
    mation, 102–105
elements of, 79–87
    recursive descent operation (//),
        82
    <xsl:apply-templates>, 82–84
    <xsl:for-each>, 80
    <xsl:if>, 84–86
    <xsl:template> and <xsl:value-of>,
        80
    <xsl:variable>, 87
functions, 87–90
    format pattern string controlling
        output, 90
    sample listing using XPath
        functions, 88–89
    table of, 68
processing instructions for, 71
stylesheet for Web service, 382–383
support for in XML Parser 4, 72
tailoring WML content with XML and,
    330–337
    differentiating Web and WAP
        browsers, 335–337
    displaying XML document on WAP
        device, 335
    illustrated, 31
    server-side transformation in ASP,
        334–335
    transforming XML into HTML and
        WML, 332–334
    using XML for content, 330–332
transforming XML document struc-
    ture, 90–102
    controlling output, 95–97
    copying XML elements, 91–92
    creating attributes, 92–94
    creating elements, 94–95
    generating comments, 101–102
    inserting text, 98–99
    transforming namespaces, 99–101
Web links for, 105
XPath and, 41, 69
<xsl:stylesheet> root element, 71
<xsl:template>, 72
XSL-FO and, 69

Apress Titles

ISBN	PRICE	AUTHOR	TITLE
1-893115-73-9	$34.95	Abbott	Voice Enabling Web Applications: VoiceXML and Beyond
1-893115-01-1	$39.95	Appleman	Appleman's Win32 API Puzzle Book and Tutorial for Visual Basic Programmers
1-893115-23-2	$29.95	Appleman	How Computer Programming Works
1-893115-97-6	$39.95	Appleman	Moving to VB. NET: Strategies, Concepts, and Code
1-893115-09-7	$29.95	Baum	Dave Baum's Definitive Guide to LEGO MINDSTORMS
1-893115-84-4	$29.95	Baum, Gasperi, Hempel, and Villa	Extreme MINDSTORMS: An Advanced Guide to LEGO MINDSTORMS
1-893115-82-8	$59.95	Ben-Gan/Moreau	Advanced Transact-SQL for SQL Server 2000
1-893115-48-8	$29.95	Bischof	The .NET Languages: A Quick Translation Guide
1-893115-67-4	$49.95	Borge	Managing Enterprise Systems with the Windows Script Host
1-893115-28-3	$44.95	Challa/Laksberg	Essential Guide to Managed Extensions for C++
1-893115-44-5	$29.95	Cook	Robot Building for Beginners
1-893115-99-2	$39.95	Cornell/Morrison	Programming VB .NET: A Guide for Experienced Programmers
1-893115-72-0	$39.95	Curtin	Developing Trust: Online Privacy and Security
1-59059-008-2	$29.95	Duncan	The Career Programmer: Guerilla Tactics for an Imperfect World
1-893115-71-2	$39.95	Ferguson	Mobile .NET
1-893115-90-9	$44.95	Finsel	The Handbook for Reluctant Database Administrators
1-893115-42-9	$44.95	Foo/Lee	XML Programming Using the Microsoft XML Parser
1-893115-55-0	$39.95	Frenz	Visual Basic and Visual Basic .NET for Scientists and Engineers
1-893115-85-2	$34.95	Gilmore	A Programmer's Introduction to PHP 4.0
1-893115-36-4	$34.95	Goodwill	Apache Jakarta-Tomcat
1-893115-17-8	$59.95	Gross	A Programmer's Introduction to Windows DNA
1-893115-62-3	$39.95	Gunnerson	A Programmer's Introduction to C#, Second Edition
1-893115-30-5	$49.95	Harkins/Reid	SQL: Access to SQL Server
1-893115-10-0	$34.95	Holub	Taming Java Threads
1-893115-04-6	$34.95	Hyman/Vaddadi	Mike and Phani's Essential C++ Techniques
1-893115-96-8	$59.95	Jorelid	J2EE FrontEnd Technologies: A Programmer's Guide to Servlets, JavaServer Pages, and Enterprise JavaBeans
1-893115-49-6	$39.95	Kilburn	Palm Programming in Basic
1-893115-50-X	$34.95	Knudsen	Wireless Java: Developing with Java 2, Micro Edition
1-893115-79-8	$49.95	Kofler	Definitive Guide to Excel VBA

ISBN	PRICE	AUTHOR	TITLE
1-893115-57-7	$39.95	Kofler	MySQL
1-893115-87-9	$39.95	Kurata	Doing Web Development: Client-Side Techniques
1-893115-75-5	$44.95	Kurniawan	Internet Programming with VB
1-893115-46-1	$36.95	Lathrop	Linux in Small Business: A Practical User's Guide
1-893115-19-4	$49.95	Macdonald	Serious ADO: Universal Data Access with Visual Basic
1-893115-06-2	$39.95	Marquis/Smith	A Visual Basic 6.0 Programmer's Toolkit
1-893115-22-4	$27.95	McCarter	David McCarter's VB Tips and Techniques
1-893115-76-3	$49.95	Morrison	C++ For VB Programmers
1-893115-80-1	$39.95	Newmarch	A Programmer's Guide to Jini Technology
1-893115-58-5	$49.95	Oellermann	Architecting Web Services
1-893115-81-X	$39.95	Pike	SQL Server: Common Problems, Tested Solutions
1-893115-20-8	$34.95	Rischpater	Wireless Web Development
1-893115-93-3	$34.95	Rischpater	Wireless Web Development with PHP and WAP
1-893115-89-5	$59.95	Shemitz	Kylix: The Professional Developer's Guide and Reference
1-893115-40-2	$39.95	Sill	The qmail Handbook
1-893115-24-0	$49.95	Sinclair	From Access to SQL Server
1-893115-94-1	$29.95	Spolsky	User Interface Design for Programmers
1-893115-53-4	$39.95	Sweeney	Visual Basic for Testers
1-59059-002-3	$44.95	Symmonds	Internationalization and Localization Using Microsoft .NET
1-893115-29-1	$44.95	Thomsen	Database Programming with Visual Basic .NET
1-893115-65-8	$39.95	Tiffany	Pocket PC Database Development with eMbedded Visual Basic
1-893115-59-3	$59.95	Troelsen	C# and the .NET Platform
1-893115-26-7	$59.95	Troelsen	Visual Basic .NET and the .NET Platform
1-893115-54-2	$49.95	Trueblood/Lovett	Data Mining and Statistical Analysis Using SQL
1-893115-16-X	$49.95	Vaughn	ADO Examples and Best Practices
1-893115-68-2	$49.95	Vaughn	ADO.NET and ADO Examples and Best Practices for VB Programmers, Second Edition
1-59059-012-0	$34.95	Vaughn/Blackburn	ADO.NET Examples and Best Practices for C# Programmers
1-893115-83-6	$44.95	Wells	Code Centric: T-SQL Programming with Stored Procedures and Triggers
1-893115-95-X	$49.95	Welschenbach	Cryptography in C and C++
1-893115-05-4	$39.95	Williamson	Writing Cross-Browser Dynamic HTML
1-893115-78-X	$49.95	Zukowski	Definitive Guide to Swing for Java 2, Second Edition
1-893115-92-5	$49.95	Zukowski	Java Collections

Available at bookstores nationwide or from Springer Verlag New York, Inc. at 1-800-777-4643; fax 1-212-533-3503. Contact us for more information at sales@apress.com.

Apress Titles Publishing SOON!

ISBN	AUTHOR	TITLE
1-893115-91-7	Birmingham/Perry	Software Development on a Leash
1-893115-39-9	Chand	A Programmer's Guide to ADO.NET in C#
1-59059-009-0	Harris/Macdonald	Moving to ASP.NET
1-59059-016-3	Hubbard	Windows Forms in C#
1-893115-38-0	Lafler	Power AOL: A Survival Guide
1-59059-003-1	Nakhimovsky/Meyers	XML Programming: Web Applications and Web Services with JSP and ASP
1-893115-27-5	Morrill	Intermediate Linux
1-893115-43-7	Stephenson	Standard VB: An Enterprise Developer's Reference for VB 6 and VB .NET
1-59059-007-4	Thomsen	Building Web Services with VB .NET
1-59059-010-4	Thomsen	Database Programming with C#
1-59059-011-2	Troelsen	COM and .NET Interoperability
1-59059-004-X	Valiaveedu	SQL Server 2000 and Business Intelligence in an XML/.NET World
1-893115-98-4	Zukowski	Learn Java with JBuilder 6

Available at bookstores nationwide or from Springer Verlag New York, Inc. at 1-800-777-4643; fax 1-212-533-3503. Contact us for more information at sales@apress.com.

books for professionals by professionals™

About Apress

Apress, located in Berkeley, CA, is an innovative publishing company devoted to meeting the needs of existing and potential programming professionals. Simply put, the "A" in Apress stands for the "Author's Press™." Apress' unique author-centric approach to publishing grew from conversations between Dan Appleman and Gary Cornell, authors of best-selling, highly regarded computer books. In 1998, they set out to create a publishing company that emphasized quality above all else, a company with books that would be considered the best in their market. Dan and Gary's vision has resulted in over 30 widely acclaimed titles by some of the industry's leading software professionals.

Do You Have What It Takes to Write for Apress?

Apress is rapidly expanding its publishing program. If you can write and refuse to compromise on the quality of your work, if you believe in doing more than rehashing existing documentation, and if you're looking for opportunities and rewards that go far beyond those offered by traditional publishing houses, we want to hear from you!

Consider these innovations that we offer all of our authors:

- **Top royalties with *no* hidden switch statements**
  Authors typically only receive half of their normal royalty rate on foreign sales. In contrast, Apress' royalty rate remains the same for both foreign and domestic sales.

- **A mechanism for authors to obtain equity in Apress**
  Unlike the software industry, where stock options are essential to motivate and retain software professionals, the publishing industry has adhered to an outdated compensation model based on royalties alone. In the spirit of most software companies, Apress reserves a significant portion of its equity for authors.

- **Serious treatment of the technical review process**
  Each Apress book has a technical reviewing team whose remuneration depends in part on the success of the book since they too receive royalties.

Moreover, through a partnership with Springer-Verlag, one of the world's major publishing houses, Apress has significant venture capital behind it. Thus, we have the resources to produce the highest quality books *and* market them aggressively.

If you fit the model of the Apress author who can write a book that gives the "professional what he or she needs to know™," then please contact one of our Editorial Directors, Gary Cornell (gary_cornell@apress.com), Dan Appleman (dan_appleman@apress.com), Karen Watterson (karen_watterson@apress.com) or Jason Gilmore (jason_gilmore@apress.com) for more information.